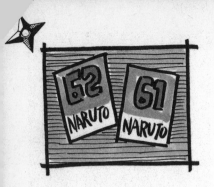

62
NARUTO
61
NARUTO

Sasuke and Itachi's tale concludes in this volume. I actually wanted to put it all in volume 61 so that you could read it all at once, but it just wasn't possible. (D'oh!) Please read volume 61 before 62! Please!

岸本斉史

—Masashi Kishimoto, 2012

Author/artist Masashi Kishimoto was born in 1974 in rural Okayama Prefecture, Japan. After spending time in art college, he won the Hop Step Award for new manga artists with his manga **Karakuri** (Mechanism). Kishimoto decided to base his next story on traditional Japanese culture. His first version of **Naruto**, drawn in 1997, was a one-shot story about fox spirits; his final version, which debuted in **Weekly Shonen Jump** in 1999, quickly became the most popular ninja manga in Japan.

一楽
ラーメン
一楽

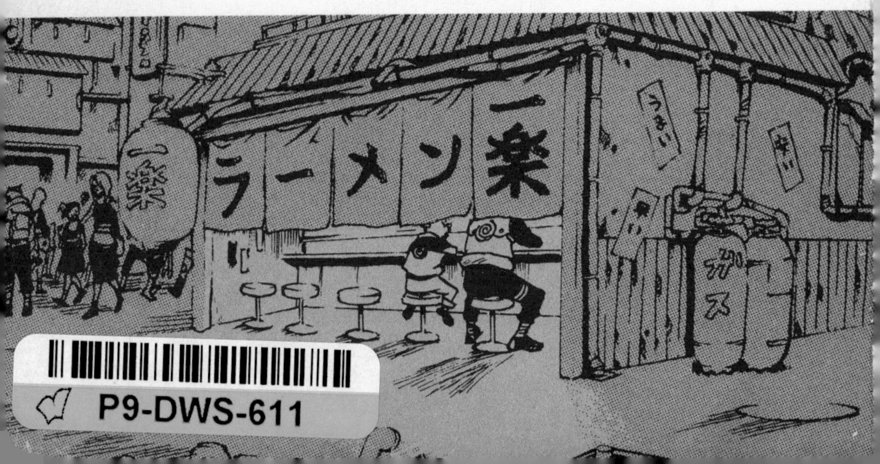

NARUTO VOL. 62
SHONEN JUMP Manga Edition

STORY AND ART BY MASASHI KISHIMOTO

Translation/Mari Morimoto
Touch-up Art & Lettering/John Hunt
Design/Sam Elzway
Editor/Alexis Kirsch

Printed in the U.S.A.

Published by VIZ Media, LLC
P.O. Box 77010
San Francisco, CA 94107

10 9 8 7 6 5 4 3 2 1
First printing, August 2013

www.viz.com

THE WORLD'S MOST POPULAR MANGA
www.shonenjump.com

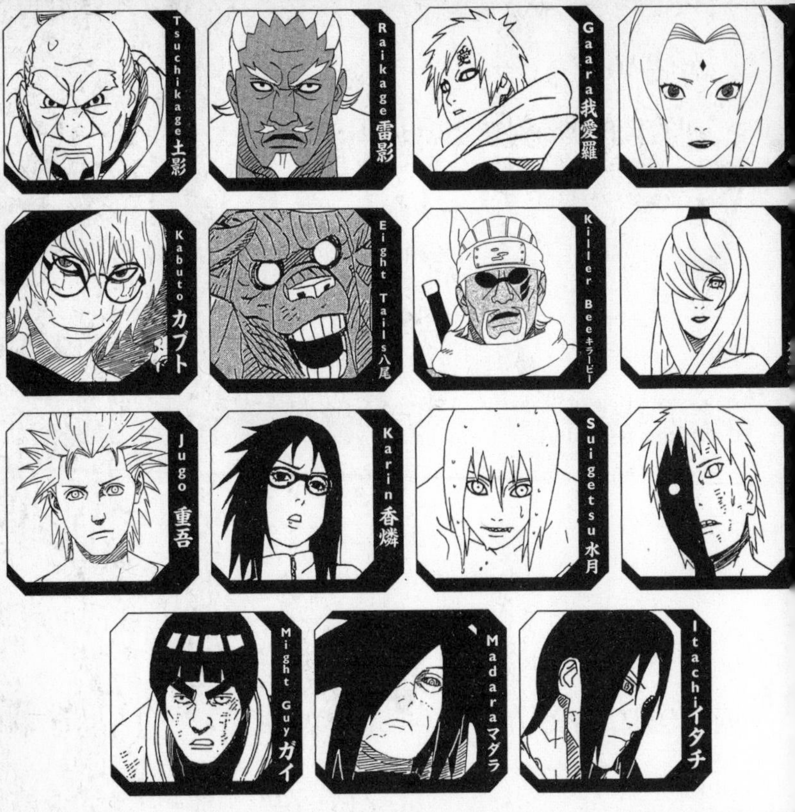
Gaara 我愛羅
Raikage 雷影
Tsuchikage 土影
Killer Bee キラービー
Eight Tails 八尾
Kabuto カブト
Suigetsu 水月
Karin 香燐
Jugo 重吾
Itachi イタチ
Madara マダラ
Might Guy ガイ

THE STORY SO FAR...

Naruto, the biggest troublemaker at the Ninja Academy in the Village of Konohagakure, finally becomes a ninja along with his classmates Sasuke and Sakura. They grow and mature through countless trials and battles. However, Sasuke, unable to give up his quest for vengeance, leaves Konohagakure to seek Orochimaru and his power…

Two years pass. Naruto grows up and engages in fierce battles against the Tailed Beast-targeting Akatsuki. Elsewhere, after winning the heroic battle against Itachi and learning his older brother's true intentions, Sasuke allies with Akatsuki and sets out to destroy Konoha.

The Fourth Great Ninja War against the Akatsuki begins. The Five Shadows seem powerless against the revived Madara's power. Meanwhile, Sasuke and Itachi confront Kabuto, who is dragging the battlefield into a vortex of chaos. Having surmounted their past differences, will the brothers' united front finally succeed in stopping Kabuto?!

NARUTO

VOL. 62
THE CRACK

CONTENTS

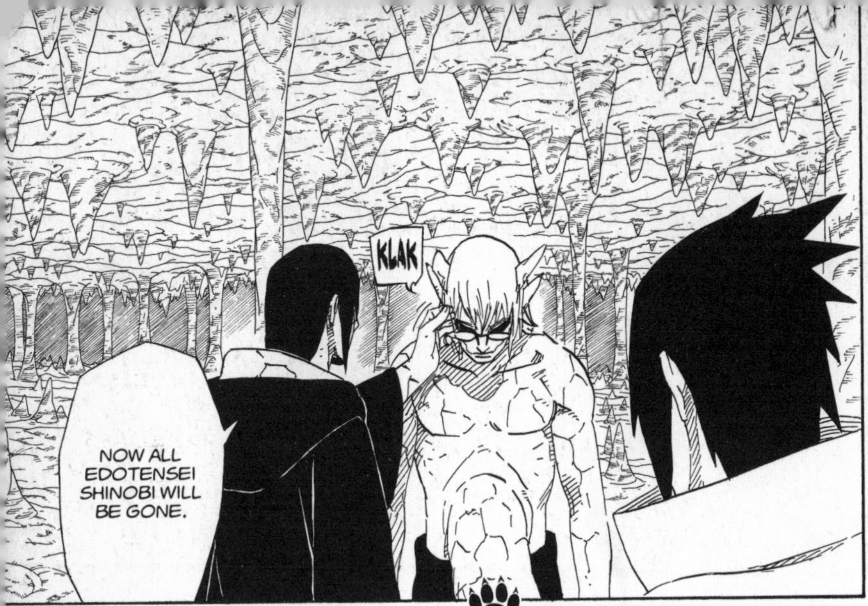
KLAK
NOW ALL EDOTENSEI SHINOBI WILL BE GONE.

Number 588: Burden of a Kage

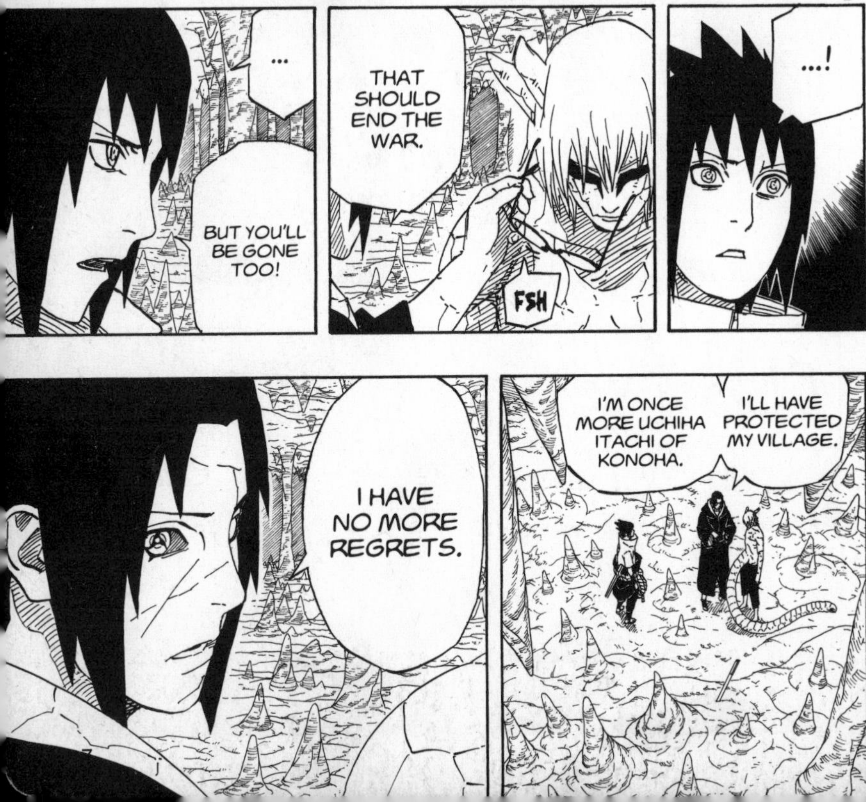
...!
THAT SHOULD END THE WAR.
FSH
...
BUT YOU'LL BE GONE TOO!
I'LL HAVE PROTECTED MY VILLAGE.
I'M ONCE MORE UCHIHA ITACHI OF KONOHA.
I HAVE NO MORE REGRETS.

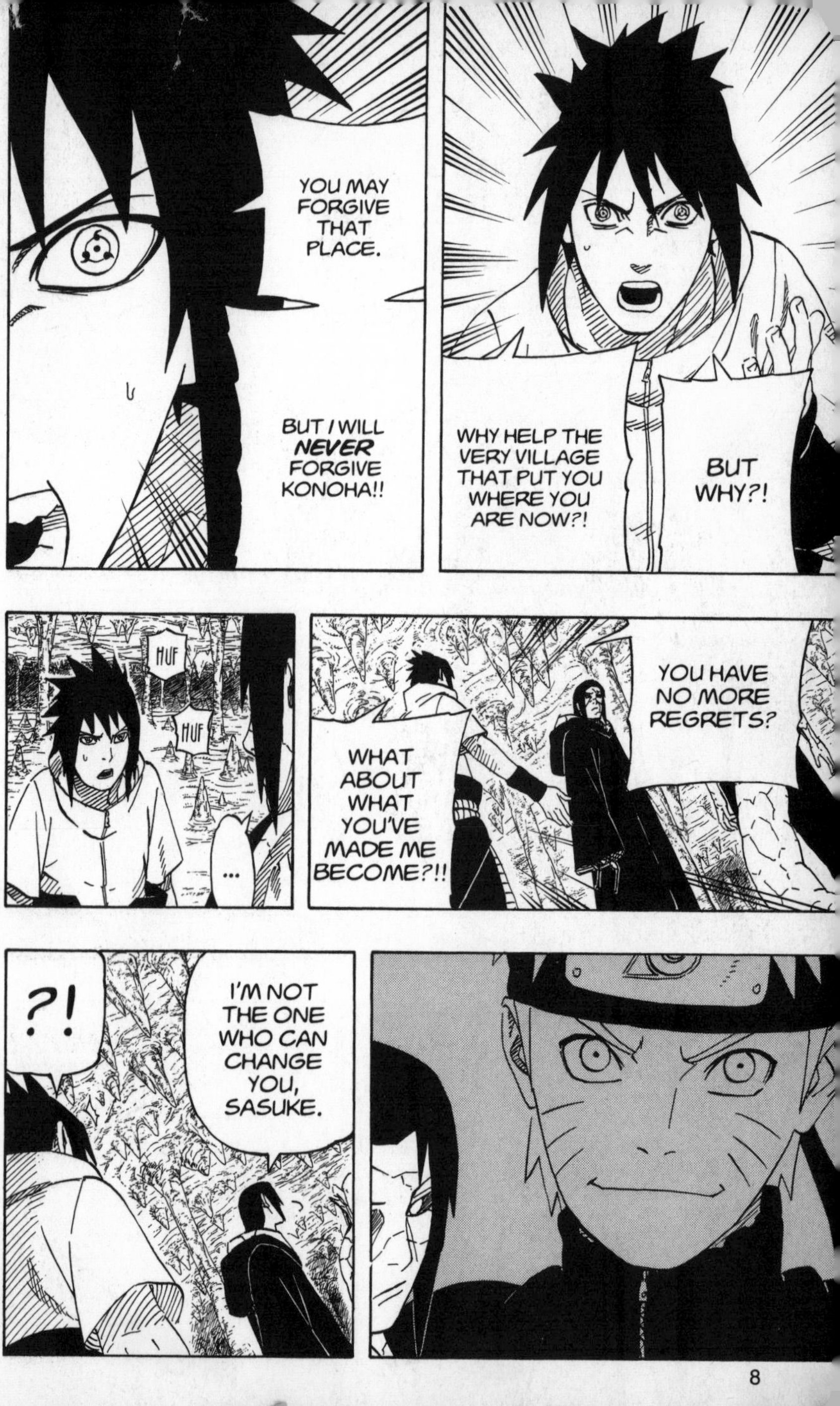
BUT WHY?!
WHY HELP THE VERY VILLAGE THAT PUT YOU WHERE YOU ARE NOW?!
YOU MAY FORGIVE THAT PLACE.
BUT I WILL ***NEVER*** FORGIVE KONOHA!!
YOU HAVE NO MORE REGRETS?
WHAT ABOUT WHAT YOU'VE MADE ME BECOME?!!
HUF
HUF
...
I'M NOT THE ONE WHO CAN CHANGE YOU, SASUKE.
?!

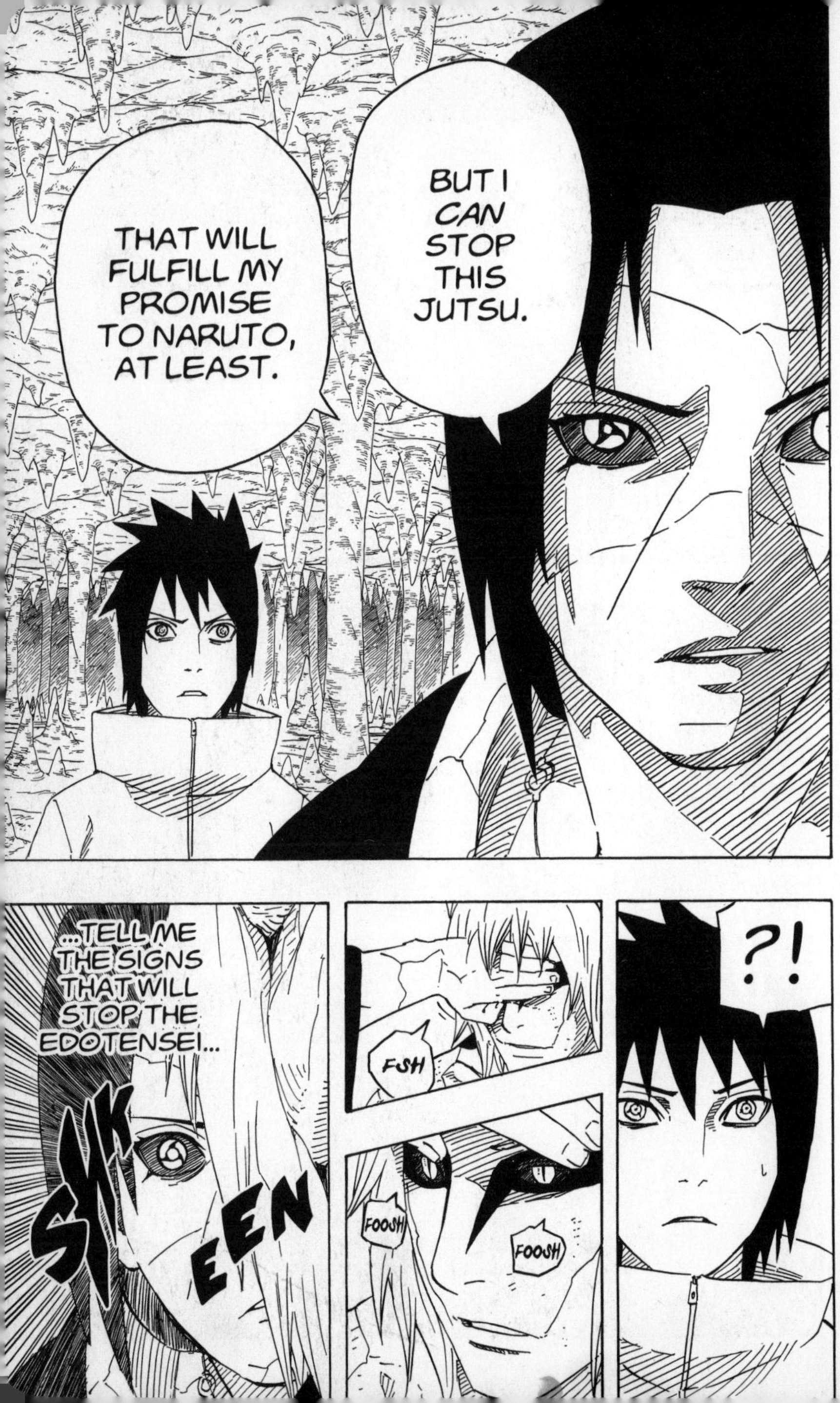
BUT I CAN STOP THIS JUTSU.
THAT WILL FULFILL MY PROMISE TO NARUTO, AT LEAST.
?!
FSH
FOOSH
FOOSH
...TELL ME THE SIGNS THAT WILL STOP THE EDOTENSEI...
SHKEEN

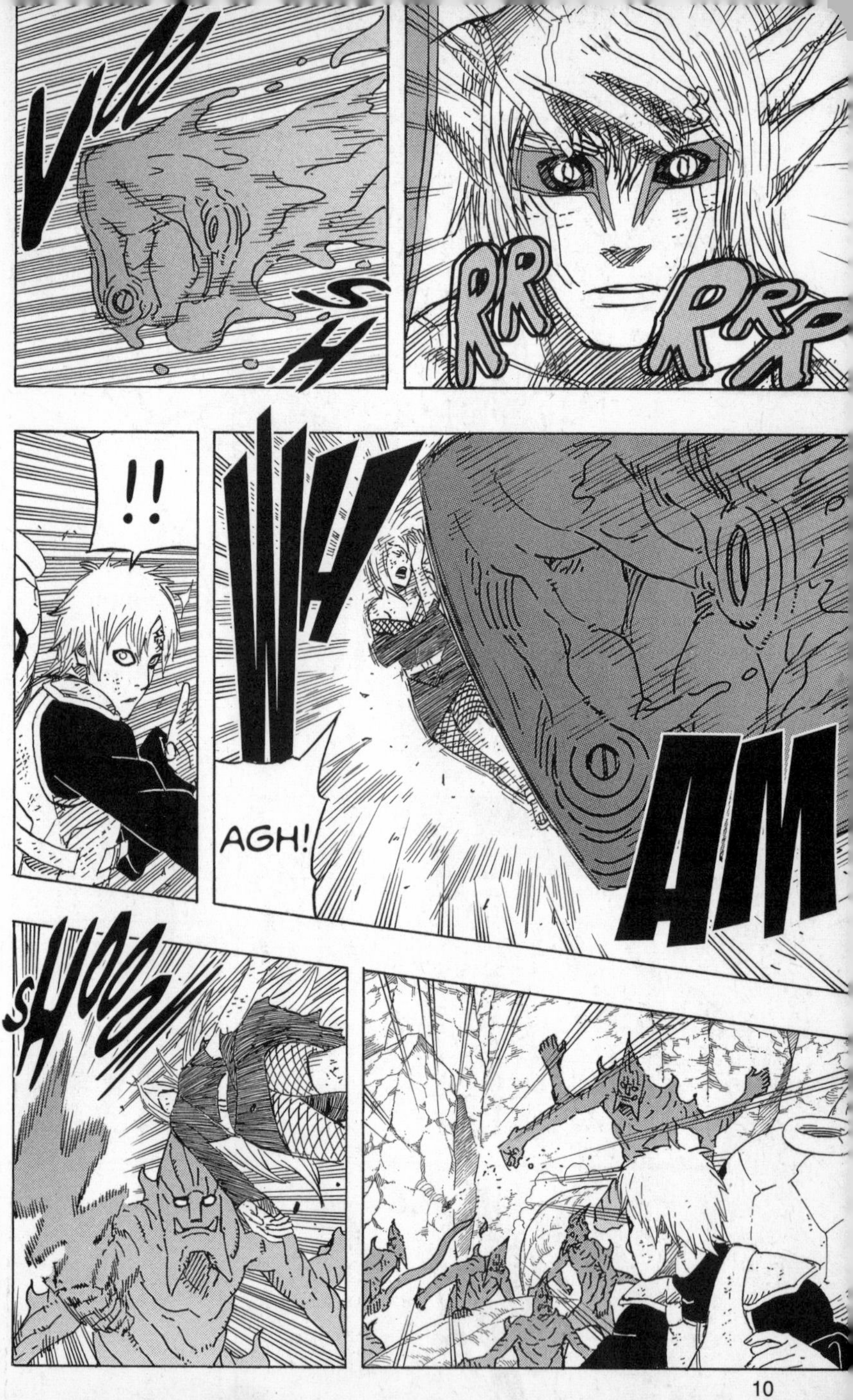
RR
RRR
VOOSH
WHAM
AGH!
!!
SHOOOM

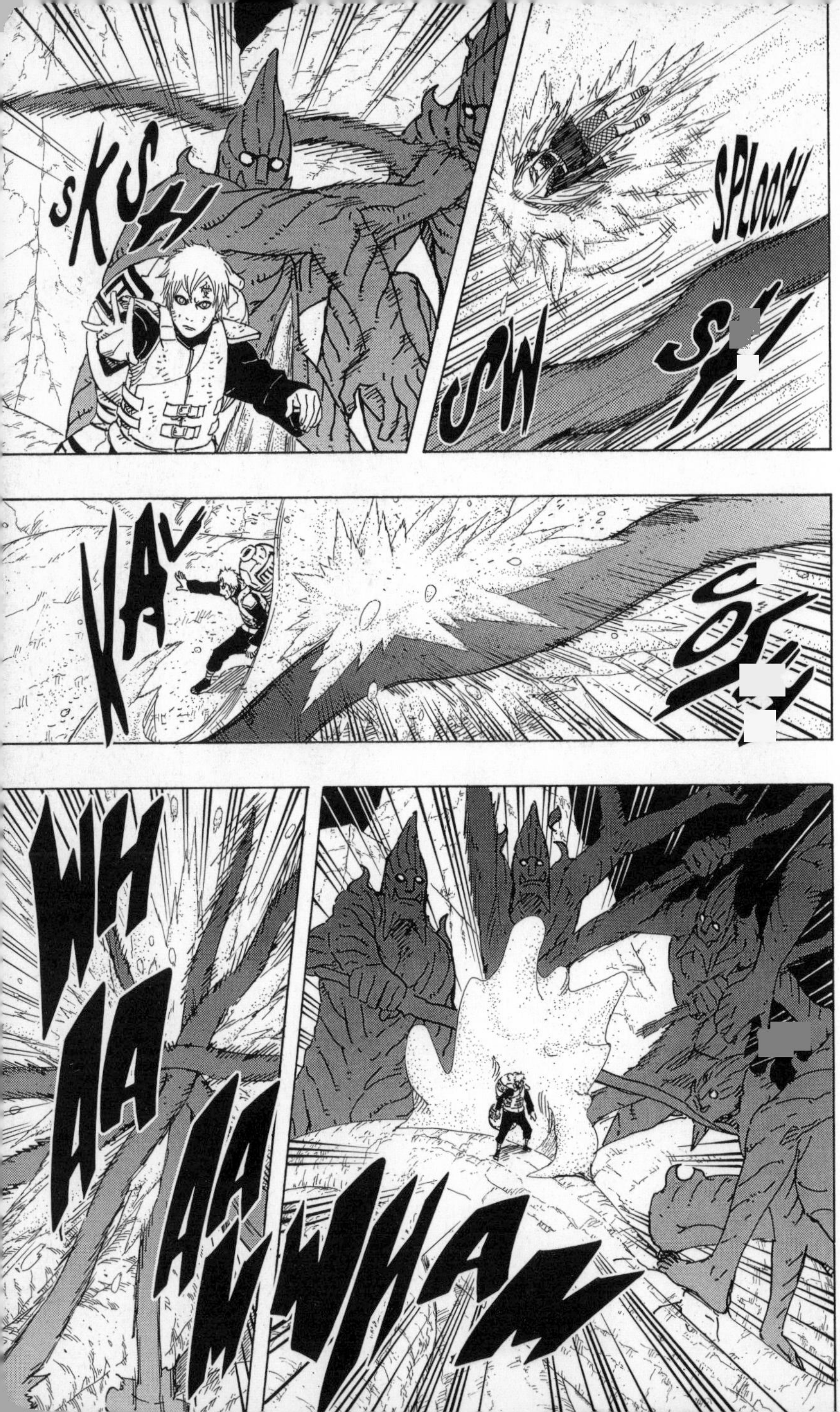
SPLOOSH
SPW
SKSH
KAV

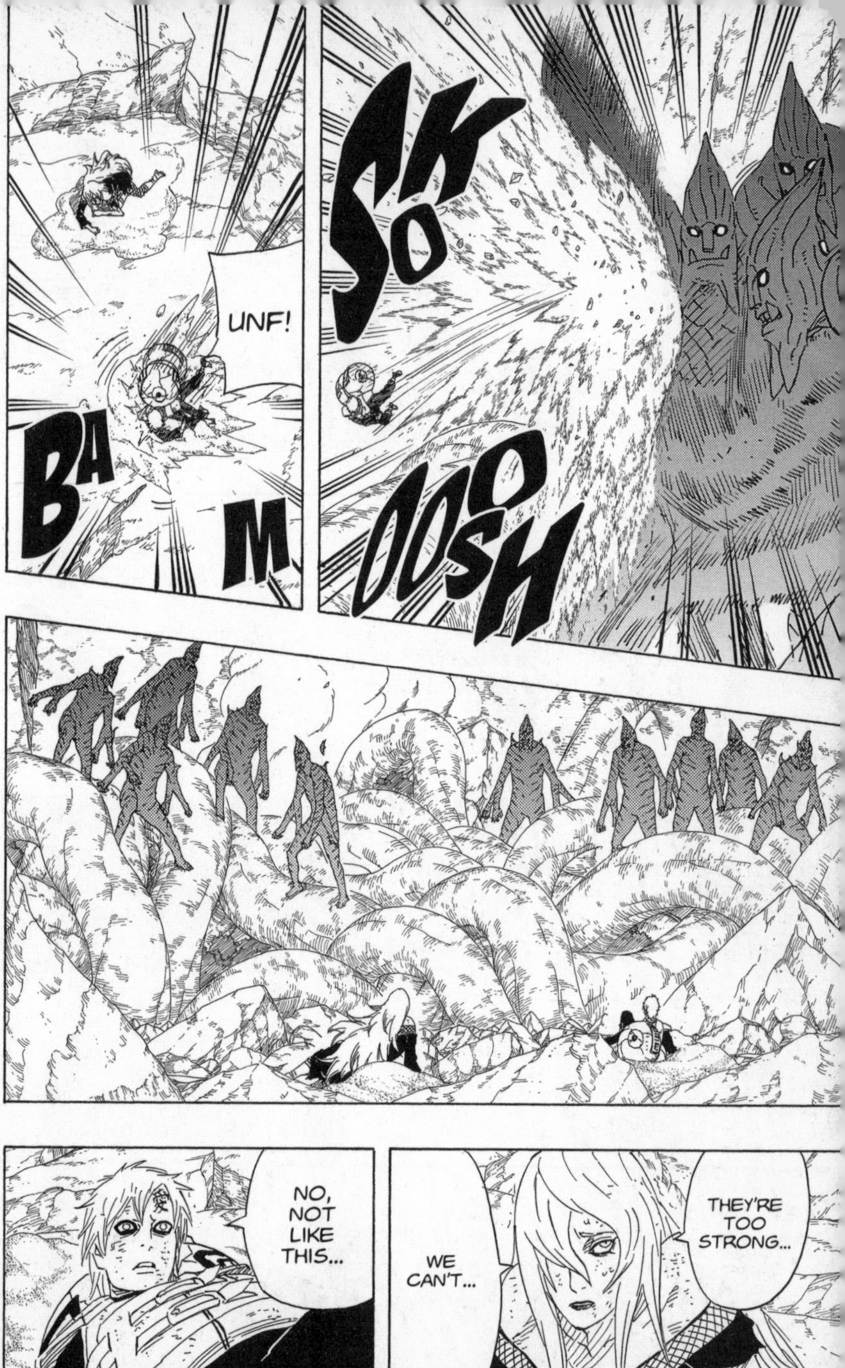
SWOOOOSH
UNF!
BAM
THEY'RE TOO STRONG...
WE CAN'T...
NO, NOT LIKE THIS...

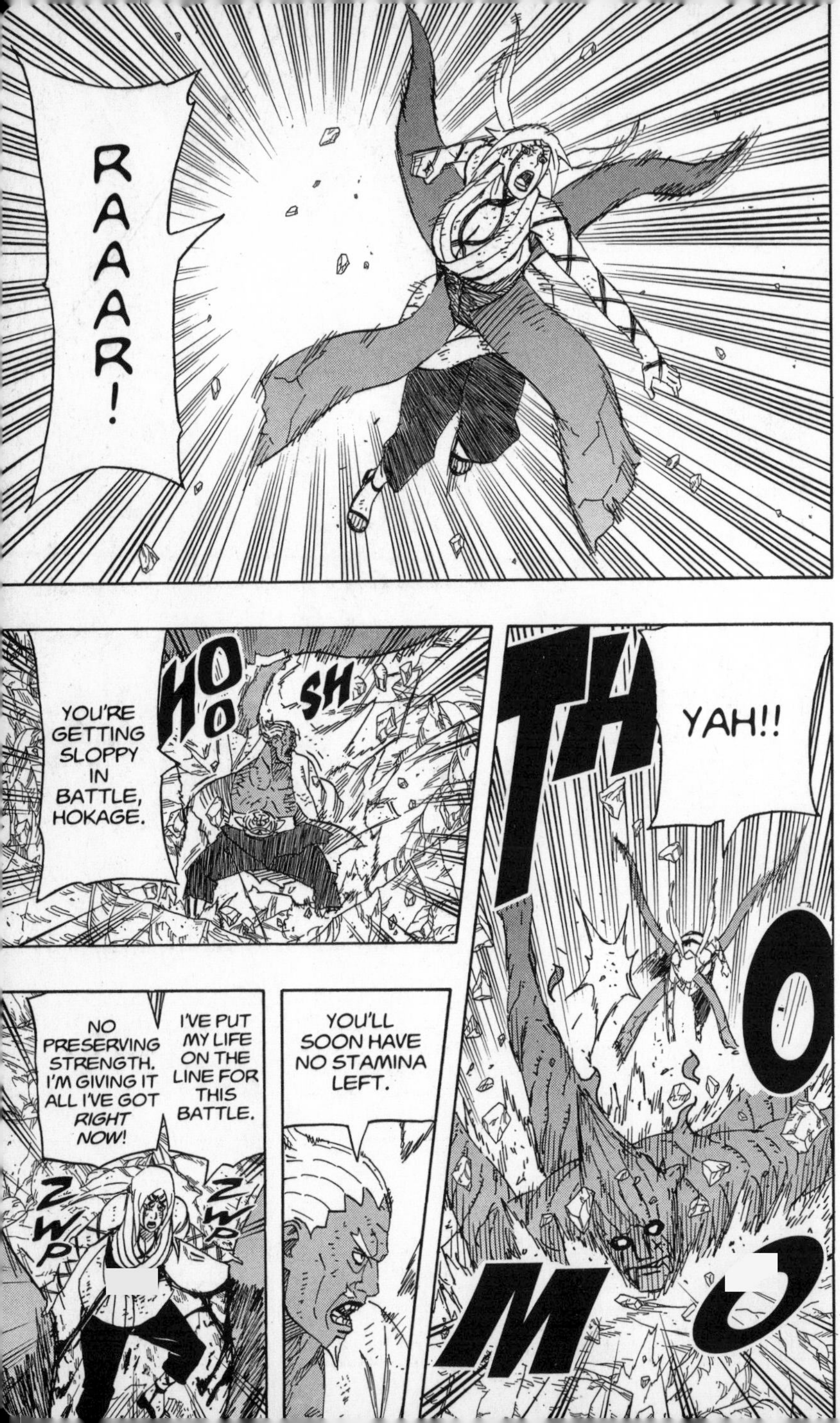
RAAAR!
YAH!!
THOOM
WHOOSH
YOU'RE GETTING SLOPPY IN BATTLE, HOKAGE.
YOU'LL SOON HAVE NO STAMINA LEFT.
I'VE PUT MY LIFE ON THE LINE FOR THIS BATTLE.
NO PRESERVING STRENGTH. I'M GIVING IT ALL I'VE GOT RIGHT NOW!
ZWP
ZWP

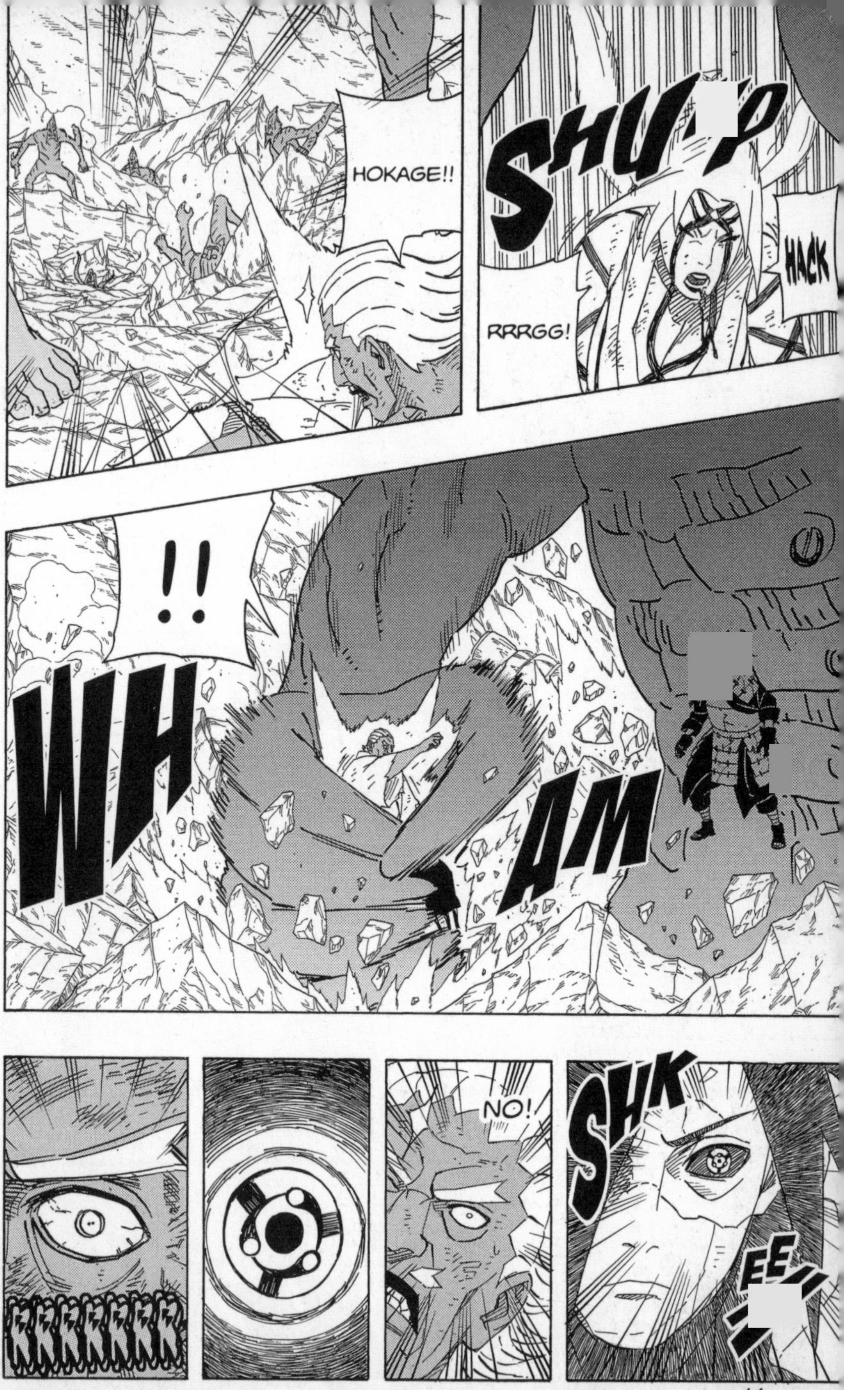
SHU P
HACK
RRRGG!
HOKAGE!!
!!
WH
AM
SHK
EE
NO!

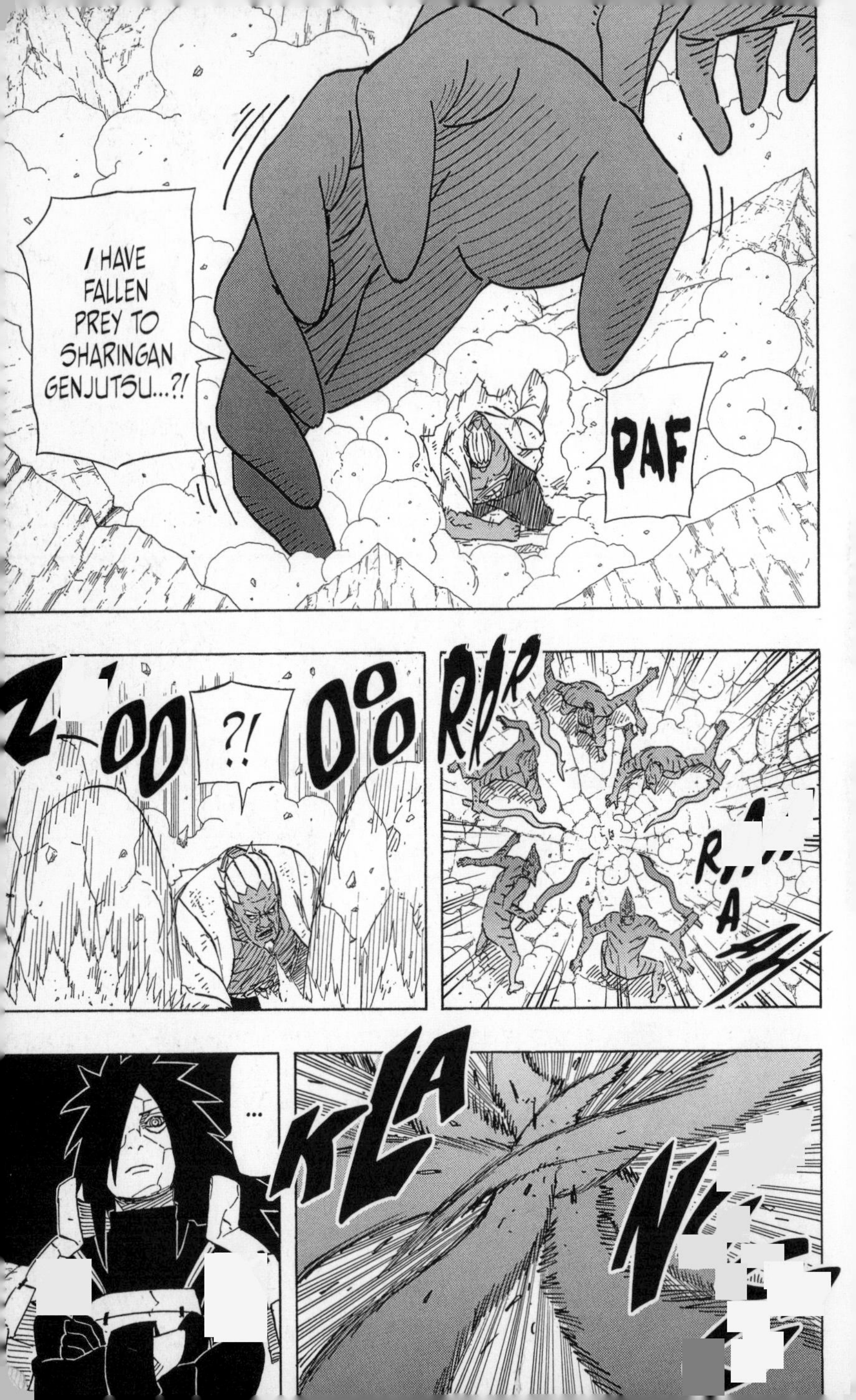
I HAVE FALLEN PREY TO SHARINGAN GENJUTSU...?!
PAF
?!
KLA
...

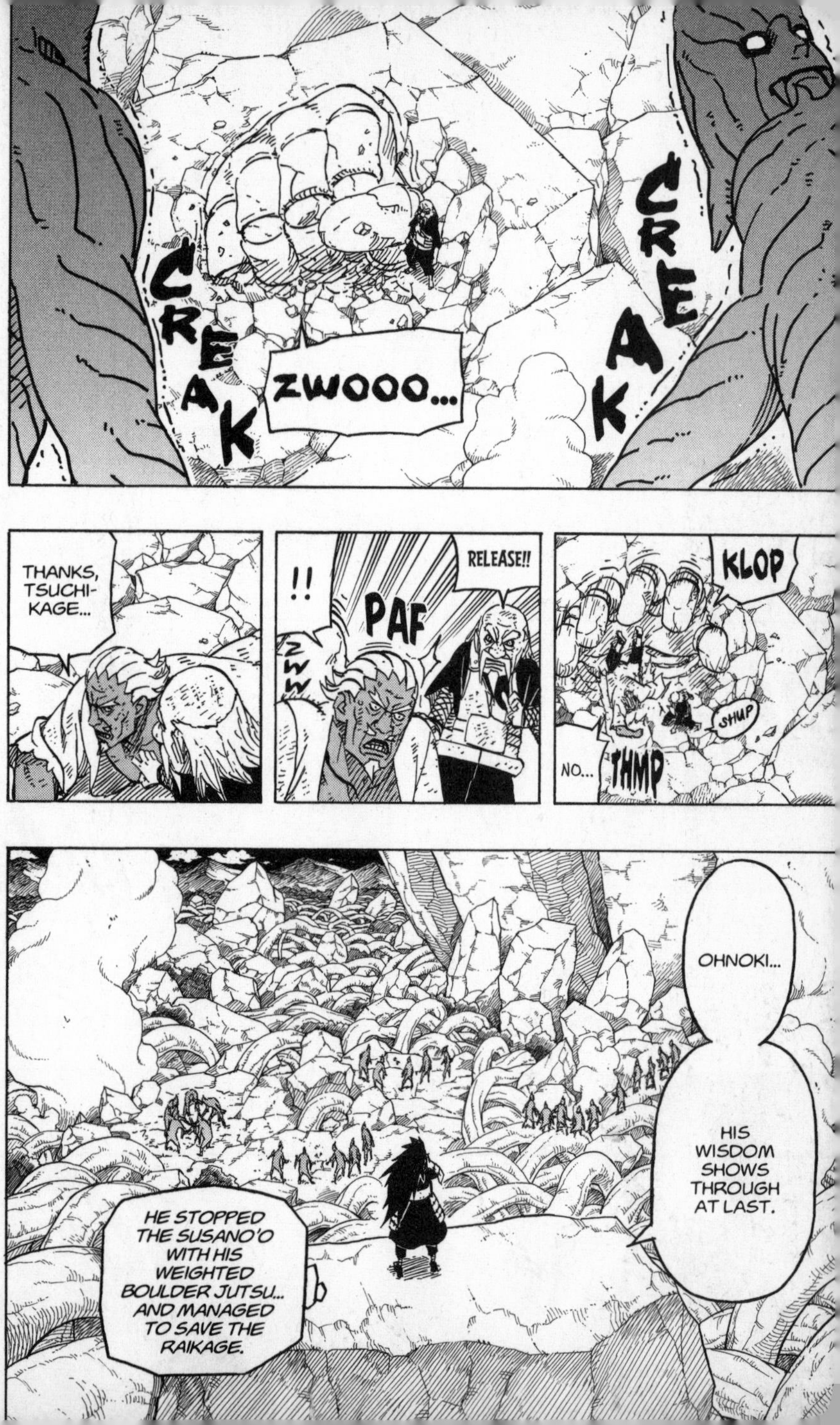
CREAK
ZWOOO...
CREAK
KLOP
SHUP
THMP
NO...
RELEASE!!
PAF
!!
ZWW
THANKS, TSUCHIKAGE...
OHNOKI...
HIS WISDOM SHOWS THROUGH AT LAST.
HE STOPPED THE SUSANO'O WITH HIS WEIGHTED BOULDER JUTSU... AND MANAGED TO SAVE THE RAIKAGE.

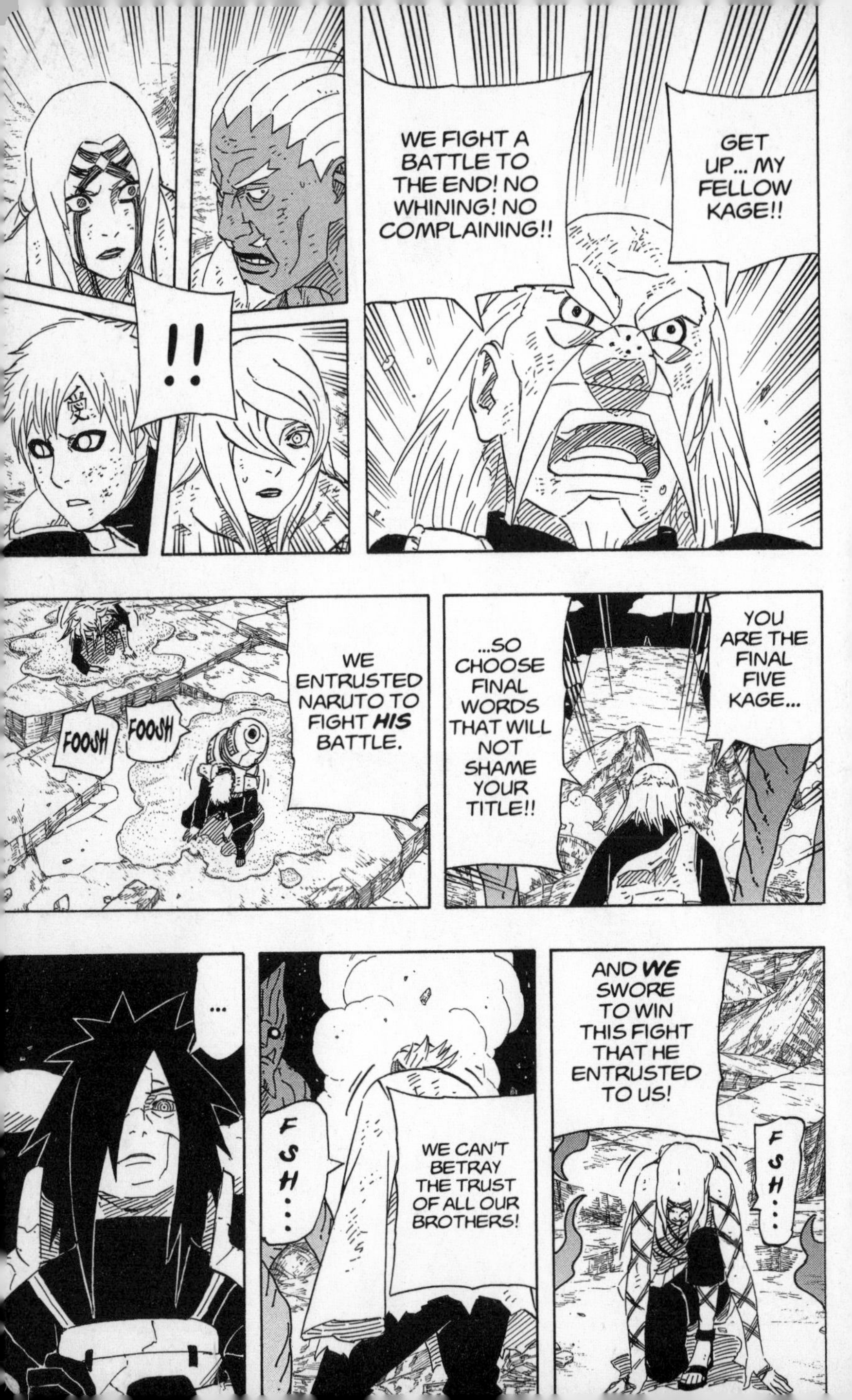
GET UP... MY FELLOW KAGE!!
WE FIGHT A BATTLE TO THE END! NO WHINING! NO COMPLAINING!!
!!
YOU ARE THE FINAL FIVE KAGE...
...SO CHOOSE FINAL WORDS THAT WILL NOT SHAME YOUR TITLE!!
WE ENTRUSTED NARUTO TO FIGHT HIS BATTLE.
FOOSH
FOOSH
AND WE SWORE TO WIN THIS FIGHT THAT HE ENTRUSTED TO US!
FSH...
WE CAN'T BETRAY THE TRUST OF ALL OUR BROTHERS!
FSH...
...

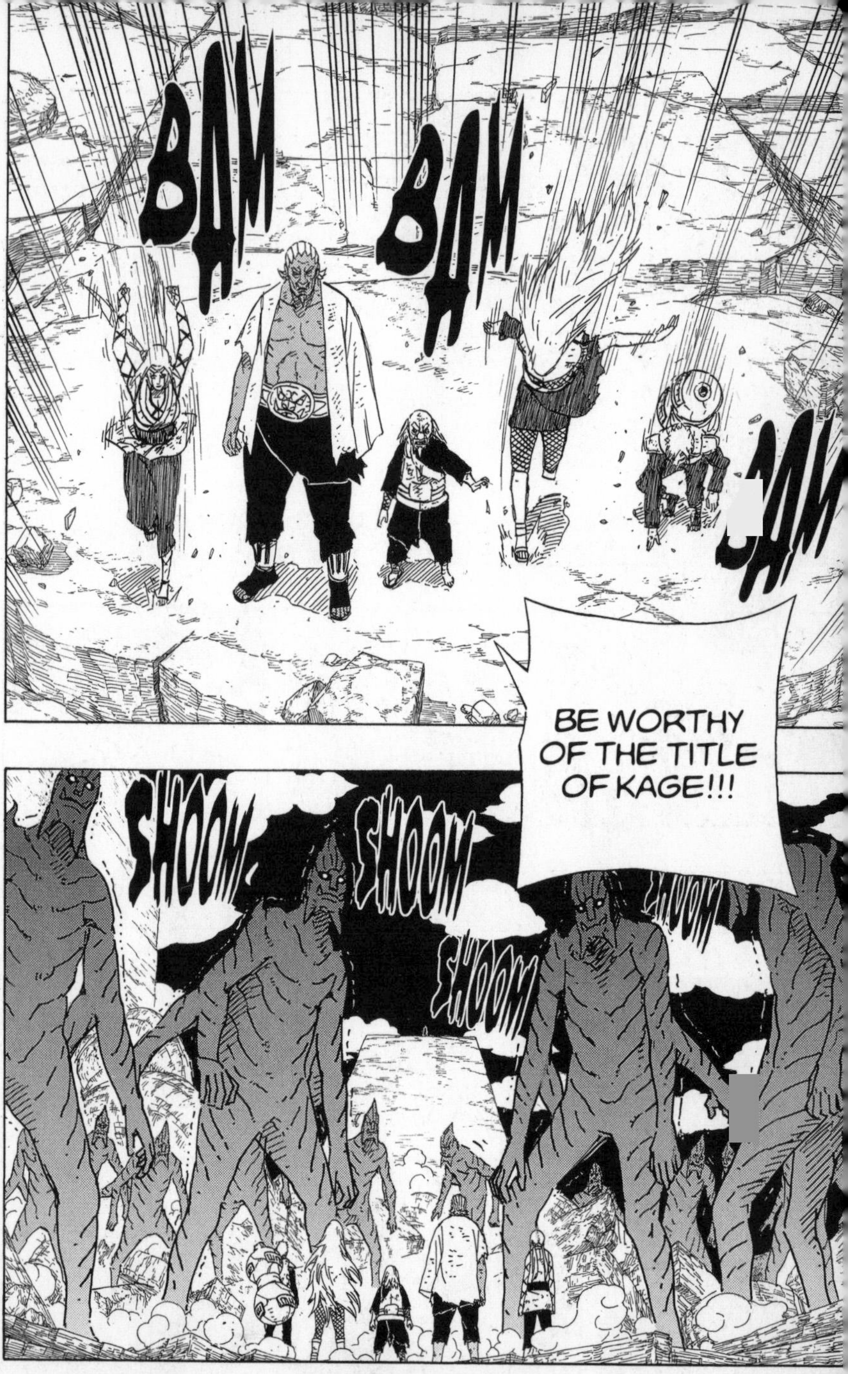
BAM
BAM
BE WORTHY OF THE TITLE OF KAGE!!!
SHOOM
SHOOM
SHOOM
SHOOM

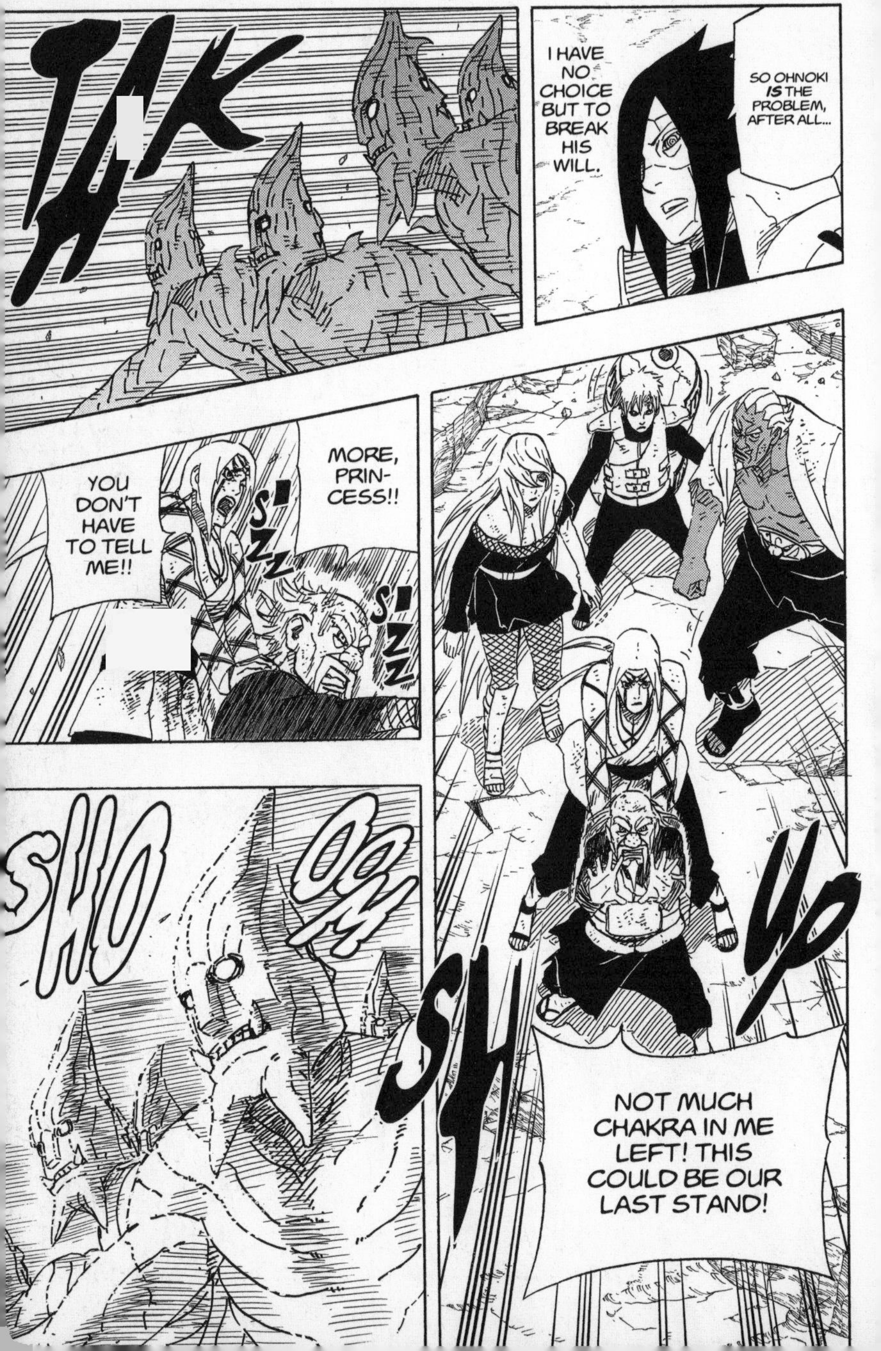
SO OHNOKI IS THE PROBLEM, AFTER ALL...
I HAVE NO CHOICE BUT TO BREAK HIS WILL.
TAK
NOT MUCH CHAKRA IN ME LEFT! THIS COULD BE OUR LAST STAND!
SHUP
MORE, PRINCESS!!
YOU DON'T HAVE TO TELL ME!!
S'ZZ
S'ZZ
SHOOOM

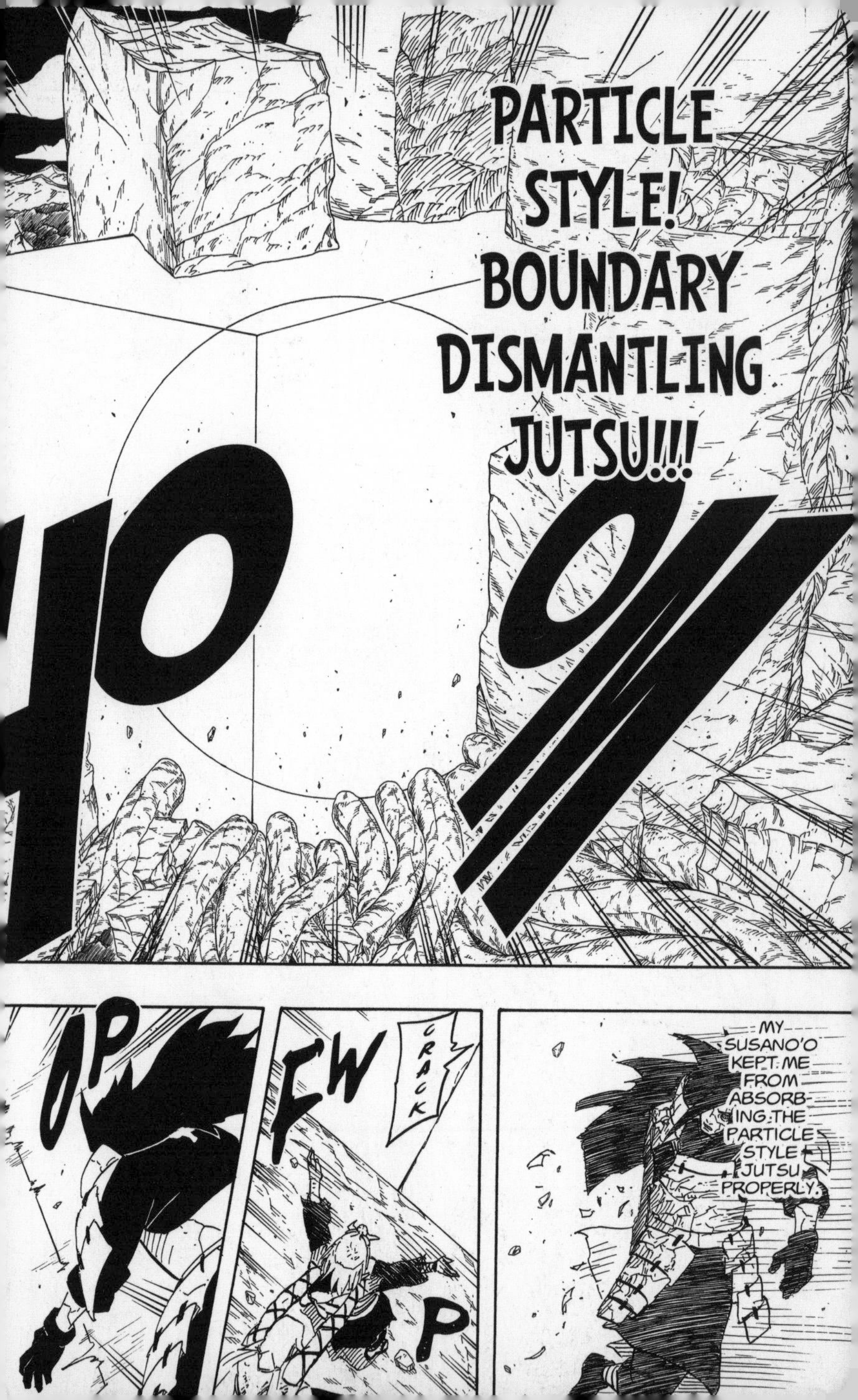
PARTICLE STYLE! BOUNDARY DISMANTLING JUTSU!!!
MY SUSANO'O KEPT ME FROM ABSORB-ING THE PARTICLE STYLE JUTSU PROPERLY.
CRACK

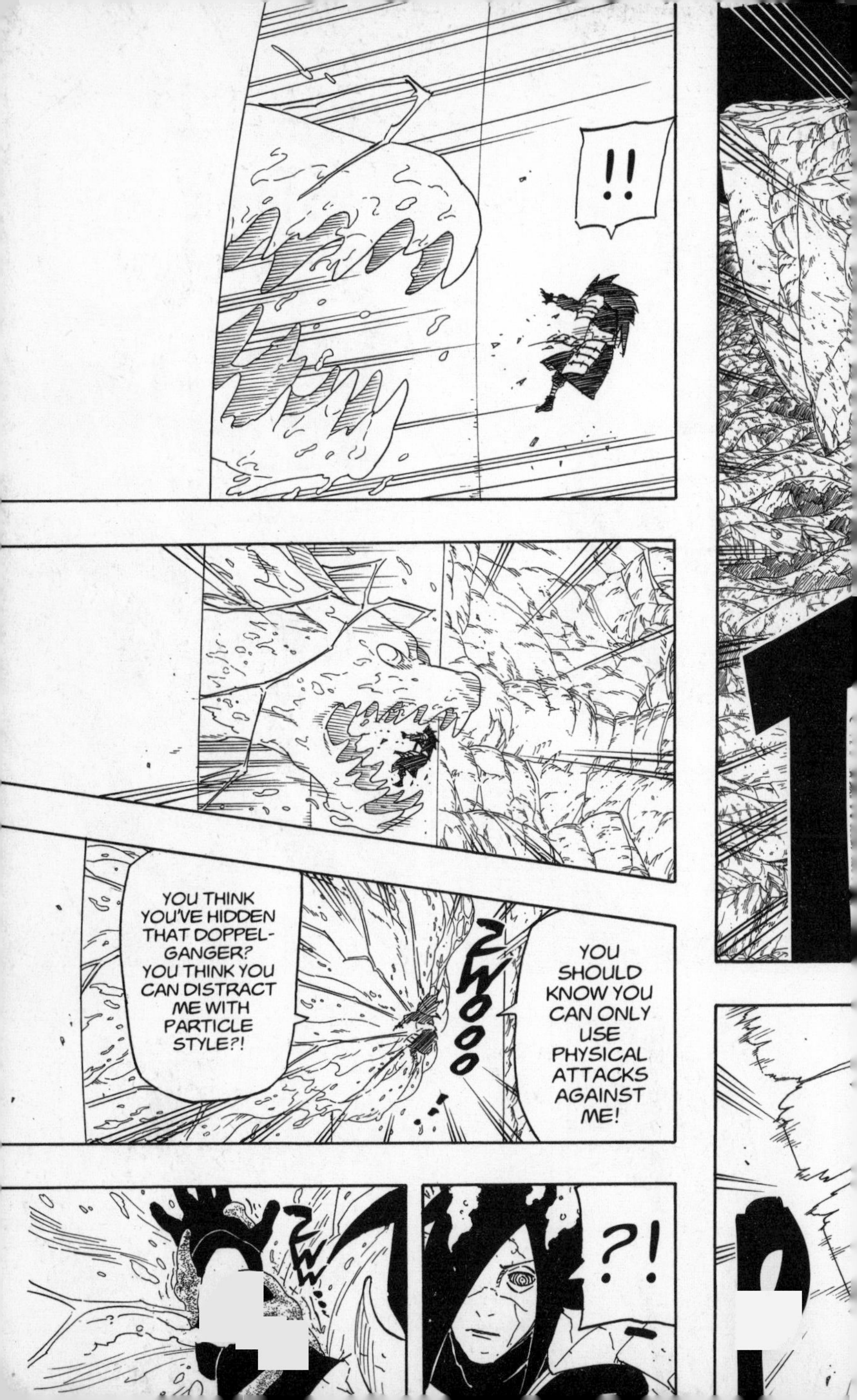
!!
YOU SHOULD KNOW YOU CAN ONLY USE PHYSICAL ATTACKS AGAINST ME!
ZWOOO
YOU THINK YOU'VE HIDDEN THAT DOPPEL-GANGER? YOU THINK YOU CAN DISTRACT ME WITH PARTICLE STYLE?!
?!
ZWW...

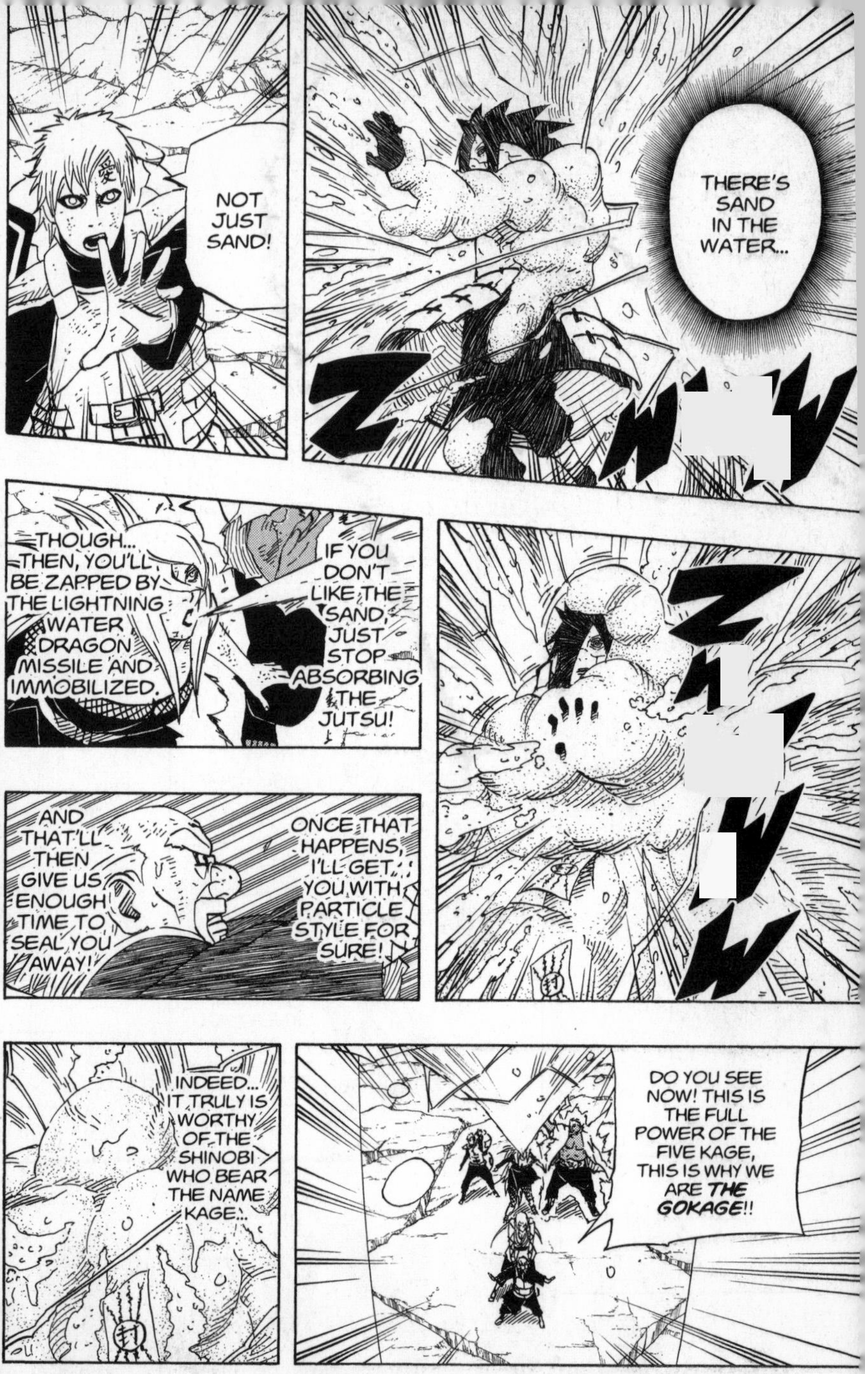

THERE'S SAND IN THE WATER...
NOT JUST SAND!
IF YOU DON'T LIKE THE SAND, JUST STOP ABSORBING THE JUTSU!
THOUGH... THEN, YOU'LL BE ZAPPED BY THE LIGHTNING WATER DRAGON MISSILE AND IMMOBILIZED.
ONCE THAT HAPPENS, I'LL GET YOU WITH PARTICLE STYLE FOR SURE!
AND THAT'LL THEN GIVE US ENOUGH TIME TO SEAL YOU AWAY!
DO YOU SEE NOW! THIS IS THE FULL POWER OF THE FIVE KAGE, THIS IS WHY WE ARE ***THE GOKAGE***!!
INDEED... IT TRULY IS WORTHY OF THE SHINOBI WHO BEAR THE NAME KAGE...

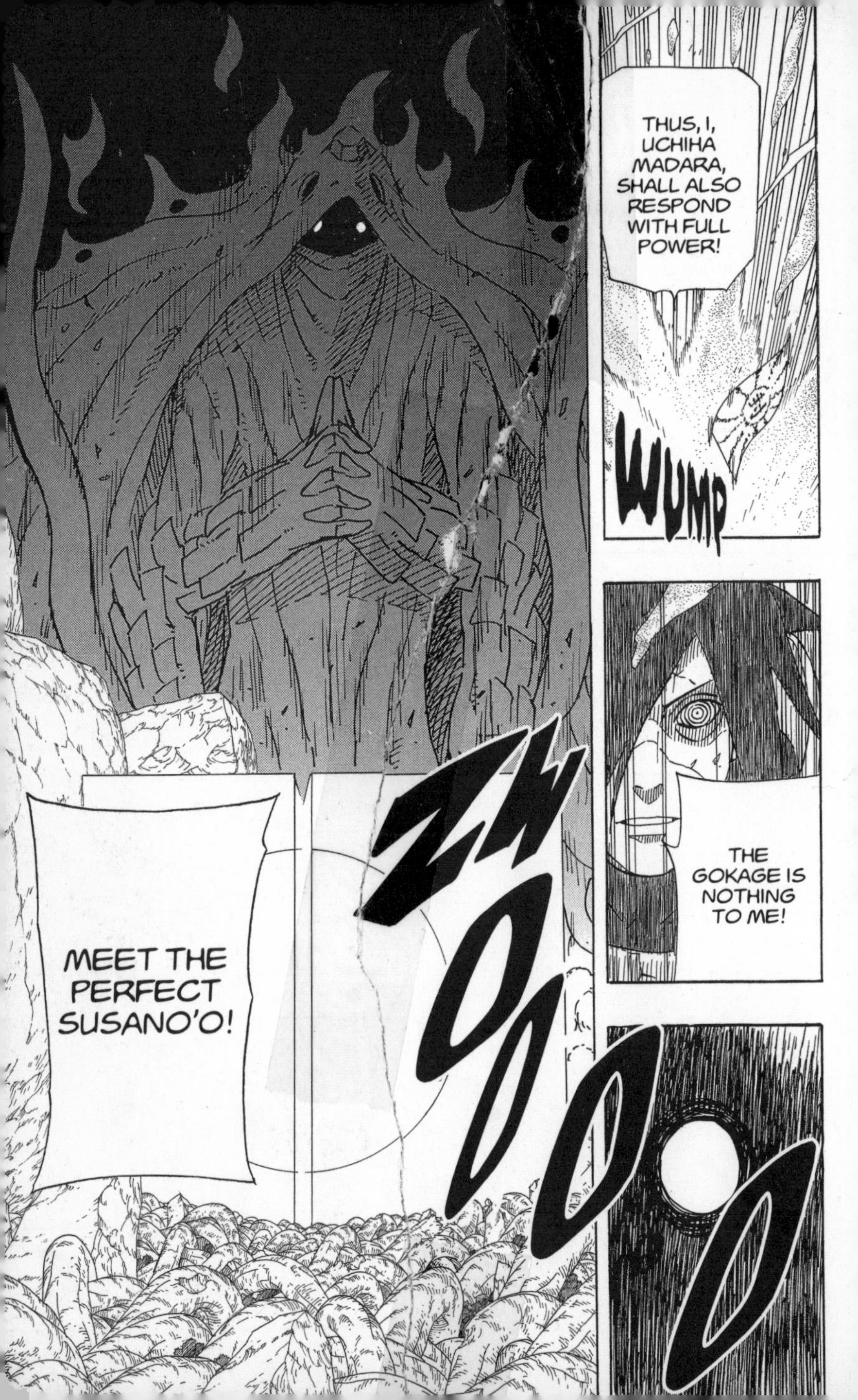
THUS, I, UCHIHA MADARA, SHALL ALSO RESPOND WITH FULL POWER!
WUMP
THE GOKAGE IS NOTHING TO ME!
ZOOOOO
MEET THE PERFECT SUSANO'O!

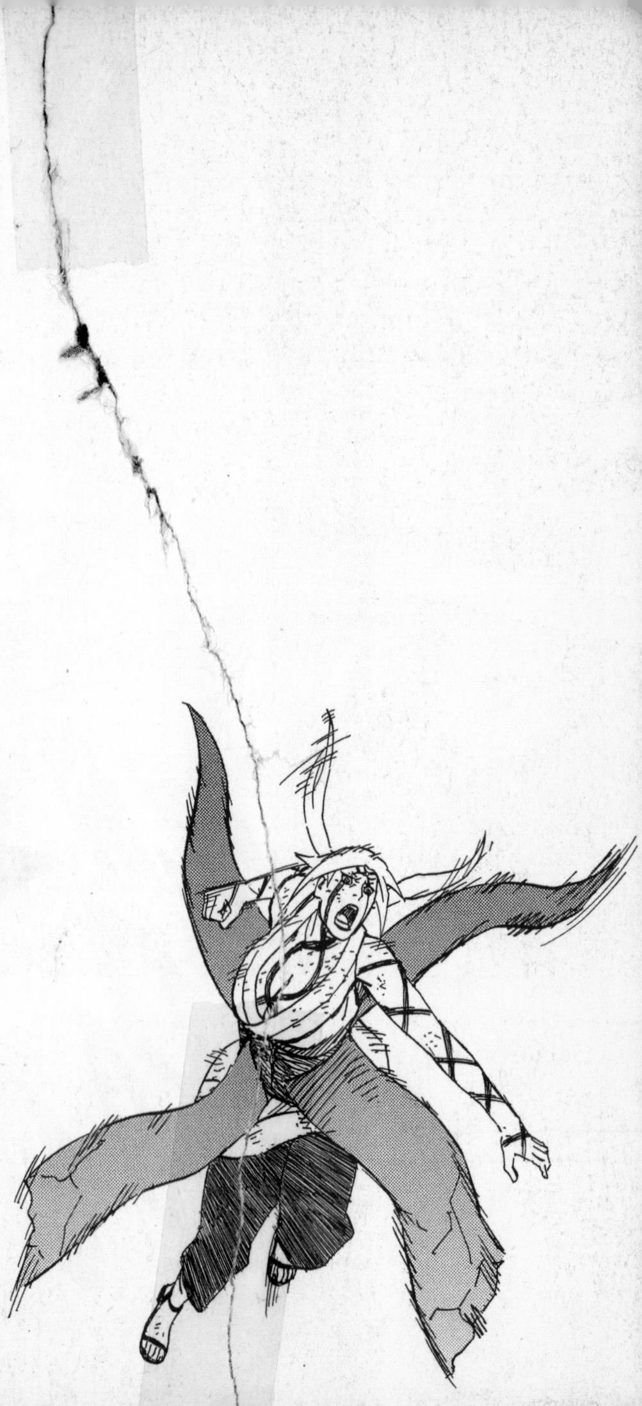

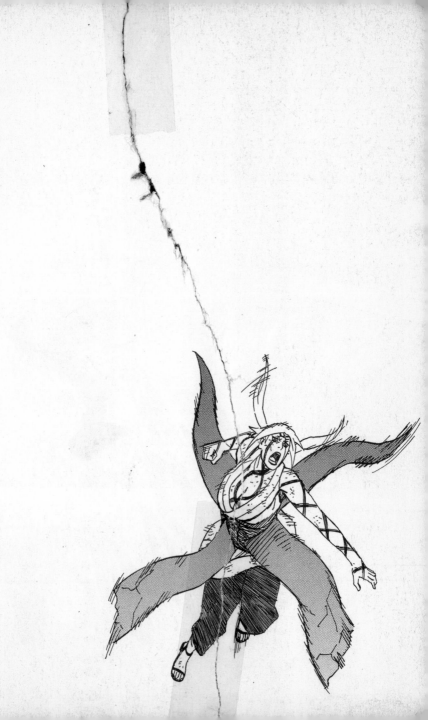

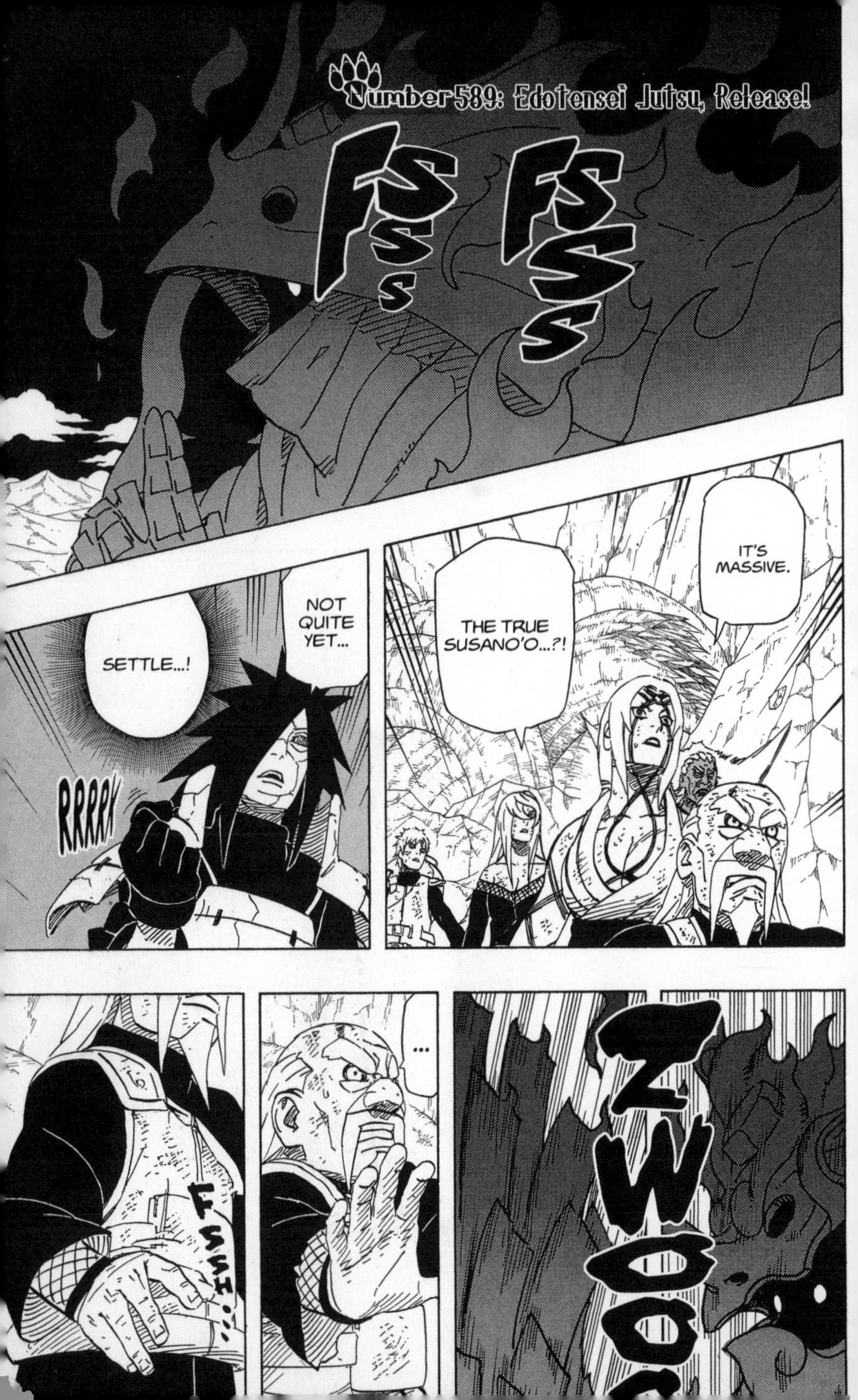
Number 589: Edotensei Jutsu, Release!
FSS FSSS
IT'S MASSIVE.
THE TRUE SUSANO'O...?!
NOT QUITE YET...
SETTLE...!
RRRRK
ZWOO
...
FSSH...

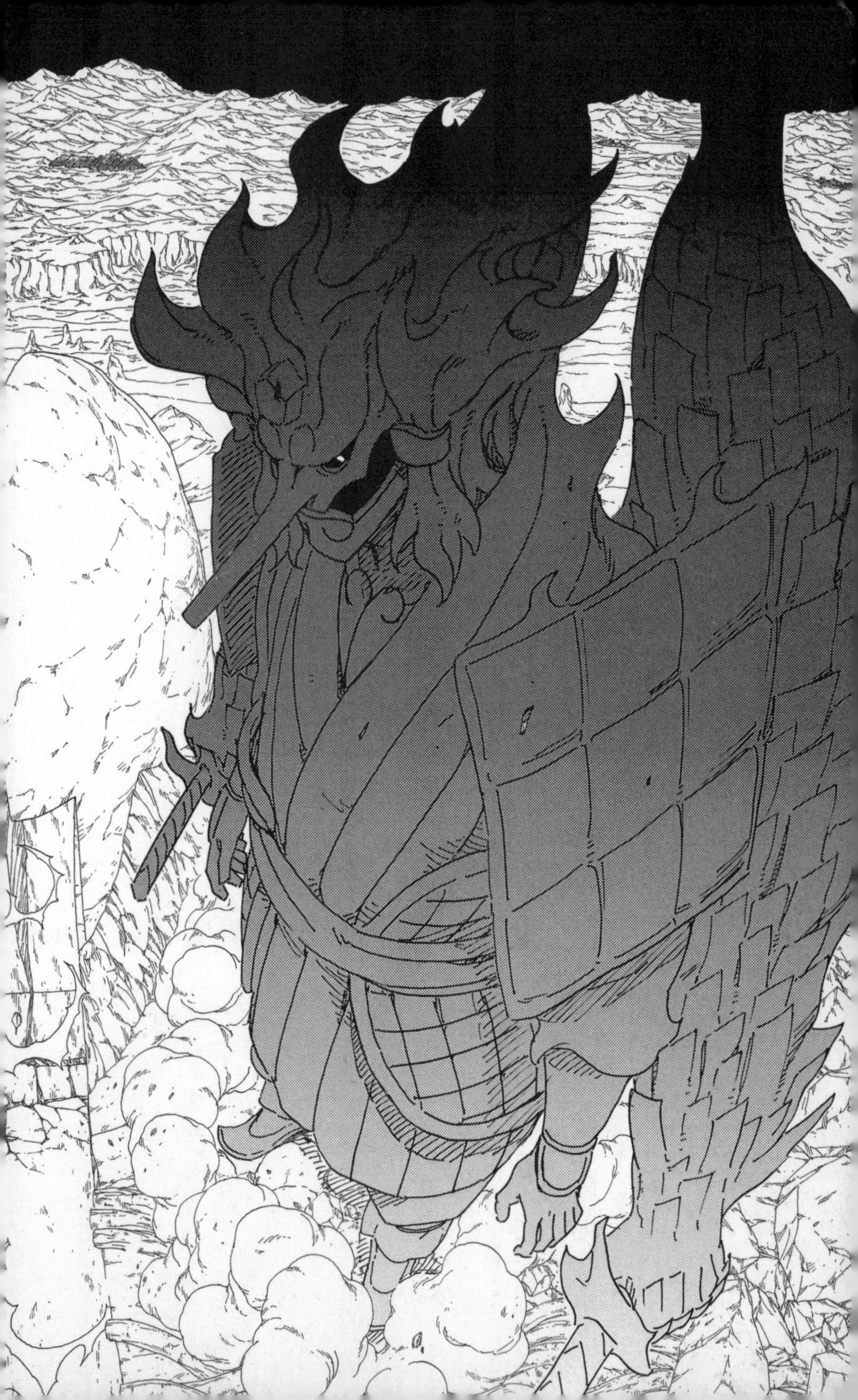

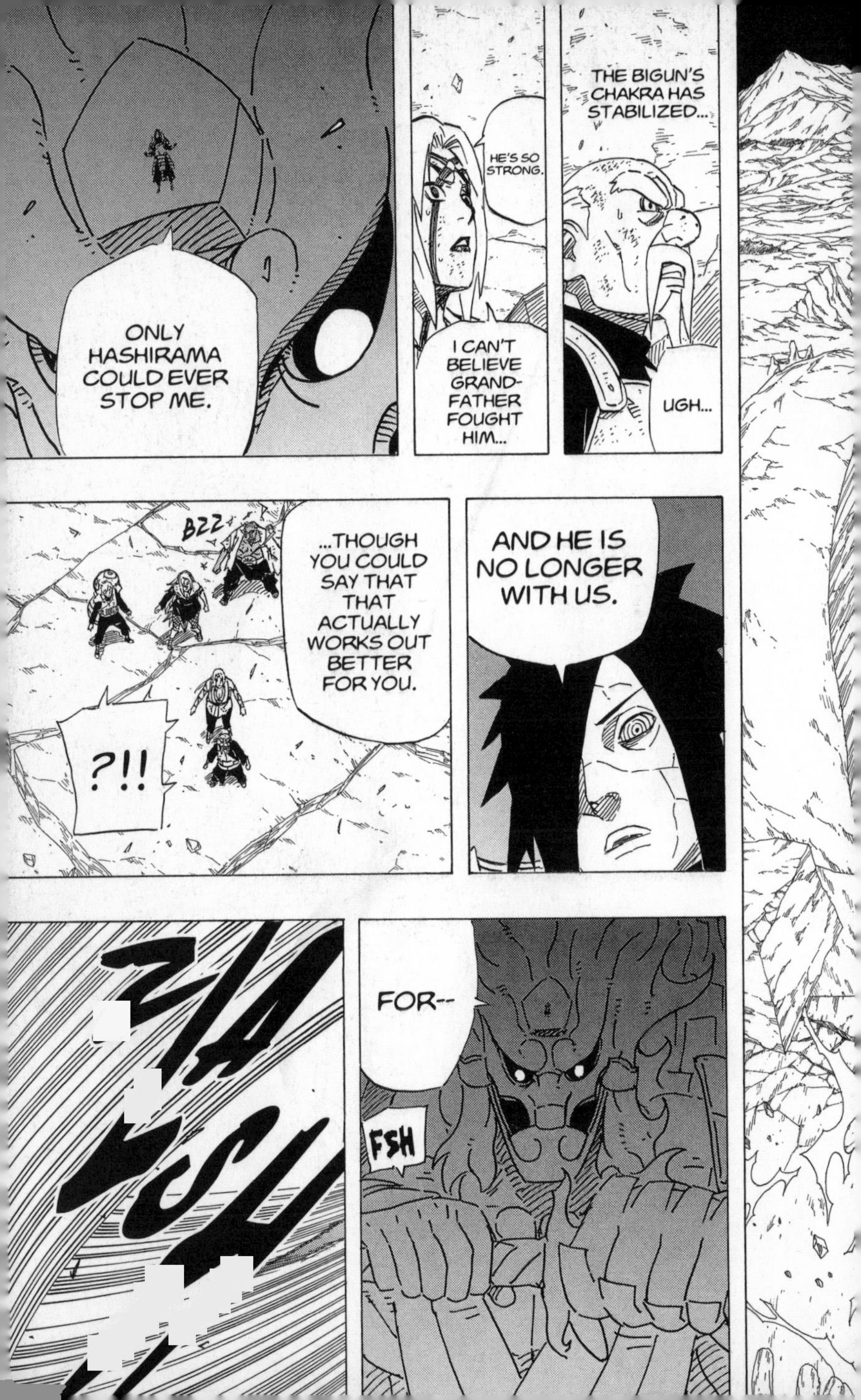
THE BIGUN'S CHAKRA HAS STABILIZED...
UGH...
HE'S SO STRONG.
I CAN'T BELIEVE GRANDFATHER FOUGHT HIM...
ONLY HASHIRAMA COULD EVER STOP ME.
AND HE IS NO LONGER WITH US.
...THOUGH YOU COULD SAY THAT THAT ACTUALLY WORKS OUT BETTER FOR YOU.
BZZ
?!!
FOR--
FSH

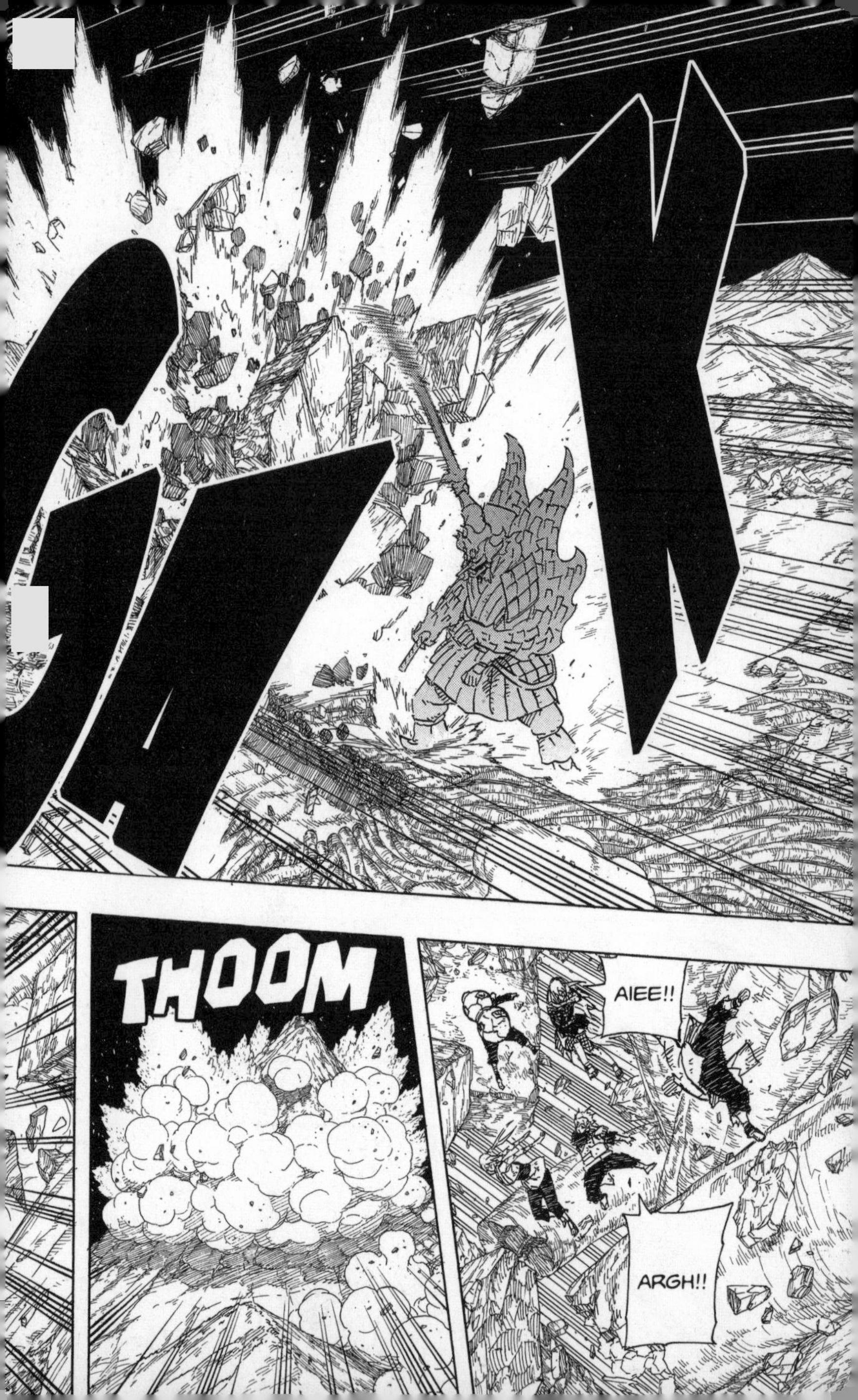
GAK
AIEE!!
ARGH!!
THOOM

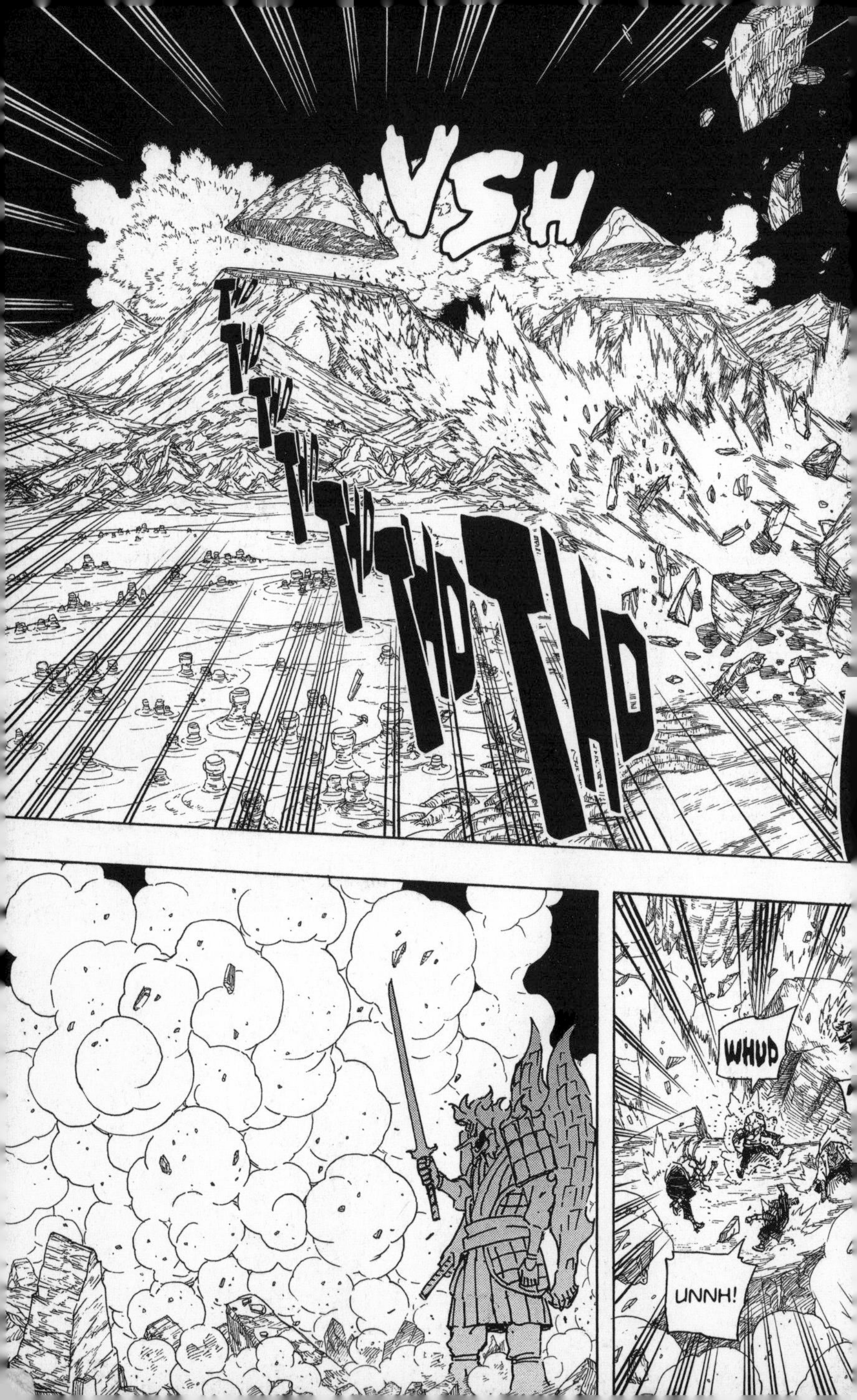
VSH
THD THD THD THD THD THD THD THD
WHUD
UNNH!

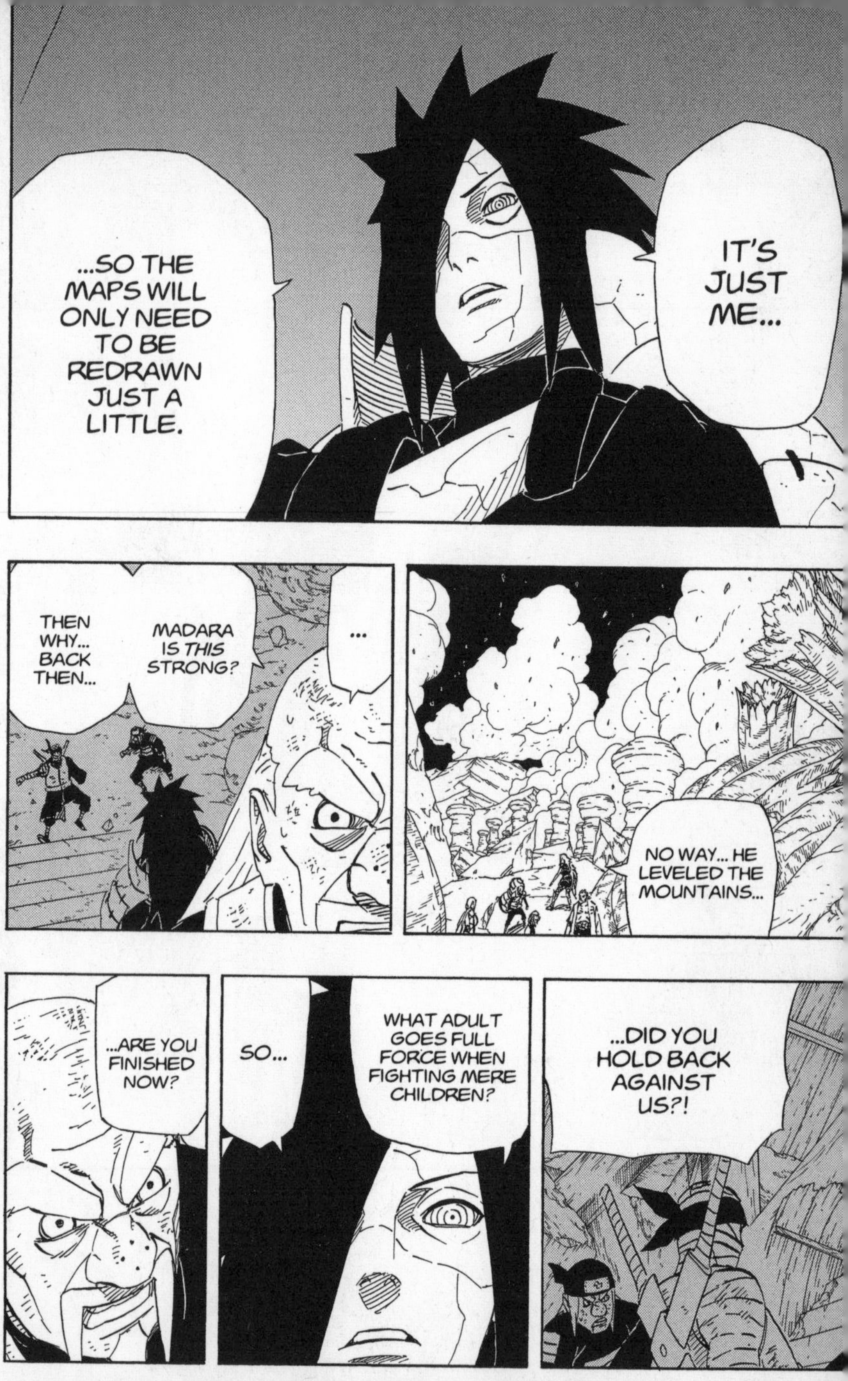
IT'S JUST ME...
...SO THE MAPS WILL ONLY NEED TO BE REDRAWN JUST A LITTLE.
NO WAY... HE LEVELED THE MOUNTAINS...
...
MADARA IS *THIS* STRONG?
THEN WHY... BACK THEN...
...DID YOU HOLD BACK AGAINST US?!
WHAT ADULT GOES FULL FORCE WHEN FIGHTING MERE CHILDREN?
SO...
...ARE YOU FINISHED NOW?

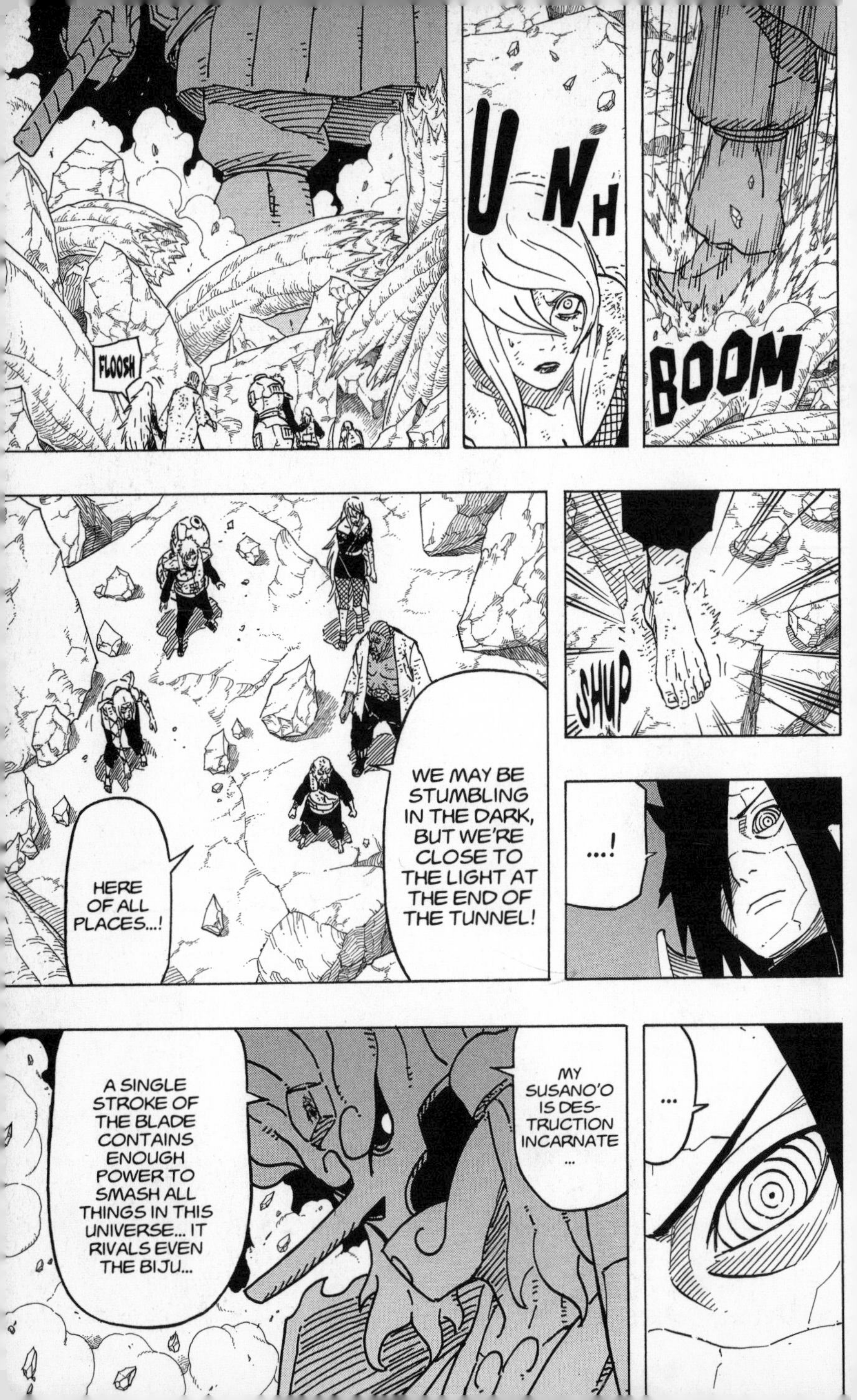
BOOM
UNH
FLOOSH
SHUP
...!
WE MAY BE STUMBLING IN THE DARK, BUT WE'RE CLOSE TO THE LIGHT AT THE END OF THE TUNNEL!
HERE OF ALL PLACES...!
...
MY SUSANO'O IS DESTRUCTION INCARNATE...
A SINGLE STROKE OF THE BLADE CONTAINS ENOUGH POWER TO SMASH ALL THINGS IN THIS UNIVERSE... IT RIVALS EVEN THE BIJU...

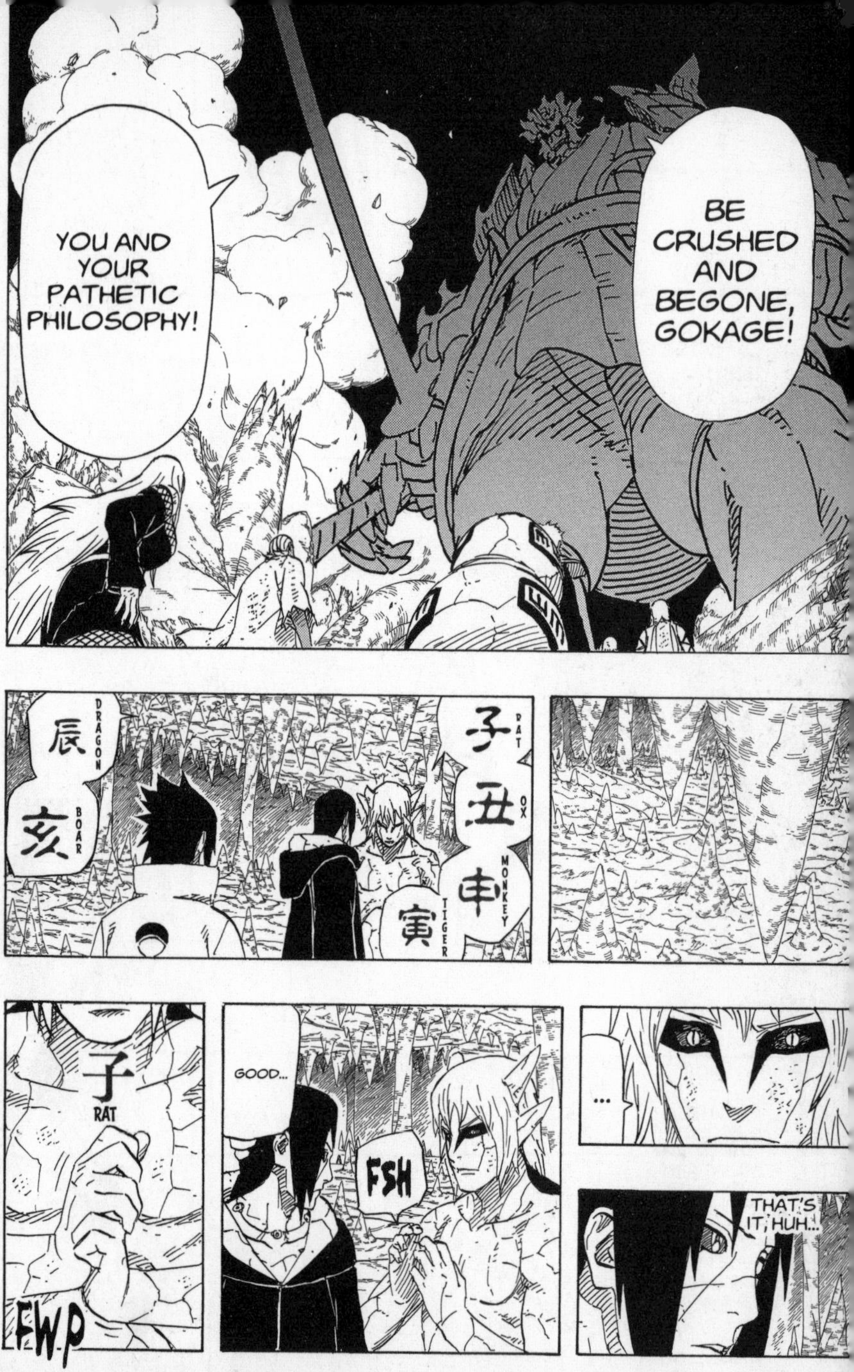
BE CRUSHED AND BEGONE, GOKAGE!
YOU AND YOUR PATHETIC PHILOSOPHY!
子 RAT
丑 OX
申 MONKEY
寅 TIGER
辰 DRAGON
亥 BOAR
...
THAT'S IT, HUH...
GOOD...
FSH
子 RAT
F.W.P

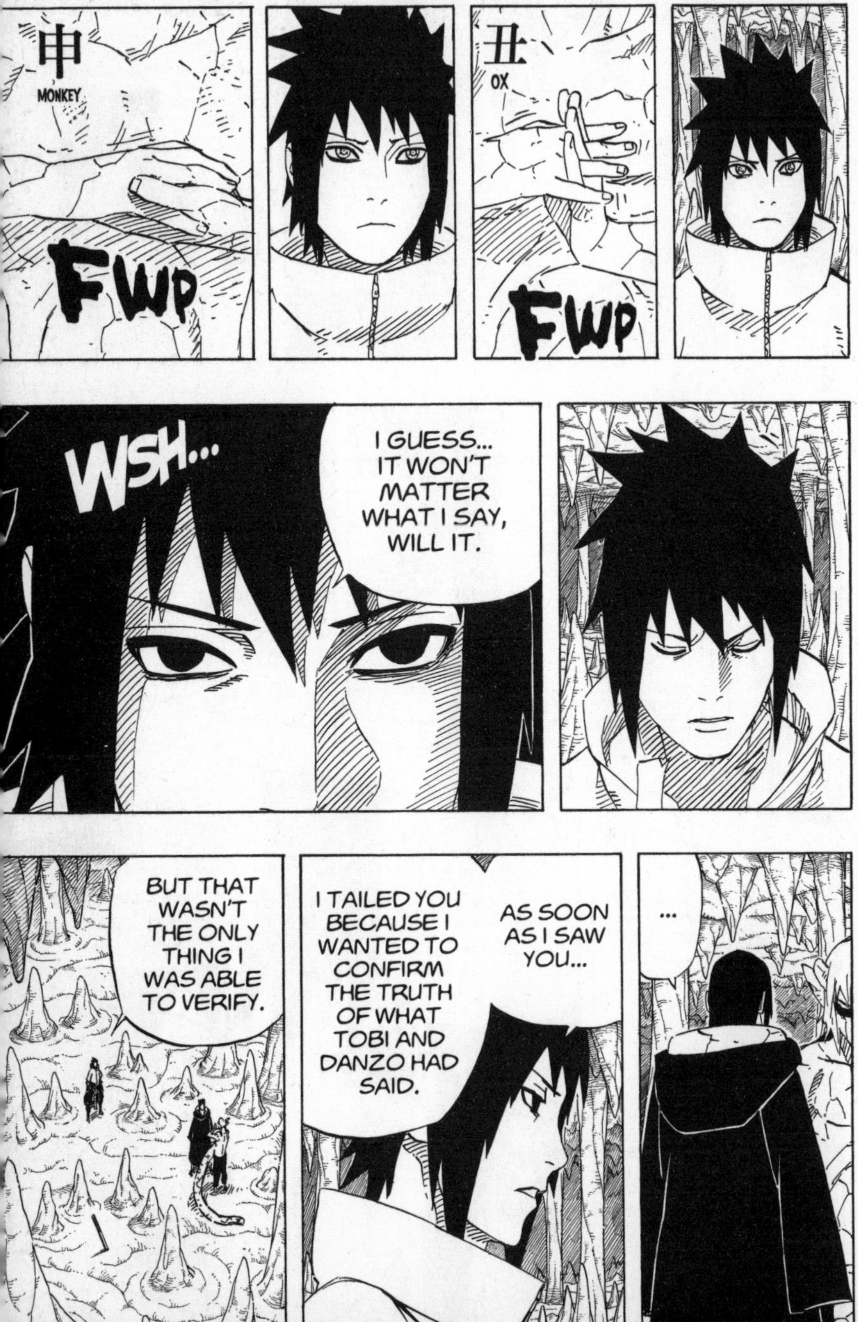
丑
OX
FWP
申
MONKEY
FWP
I GUESS... IT WON'T MATTER WHAT I SAY, WILL IT.
WSH...
...
AS SOON AS I SAW YOU...
I TAILED YOU BECAUSE I WANTED TO CONFIRM THE TRUTH OF WHAT TOBI AND DANZO HAD SAID.
BUT THAT WASN'T THE ONLY THING I WAS ABLE TO VERIFY.

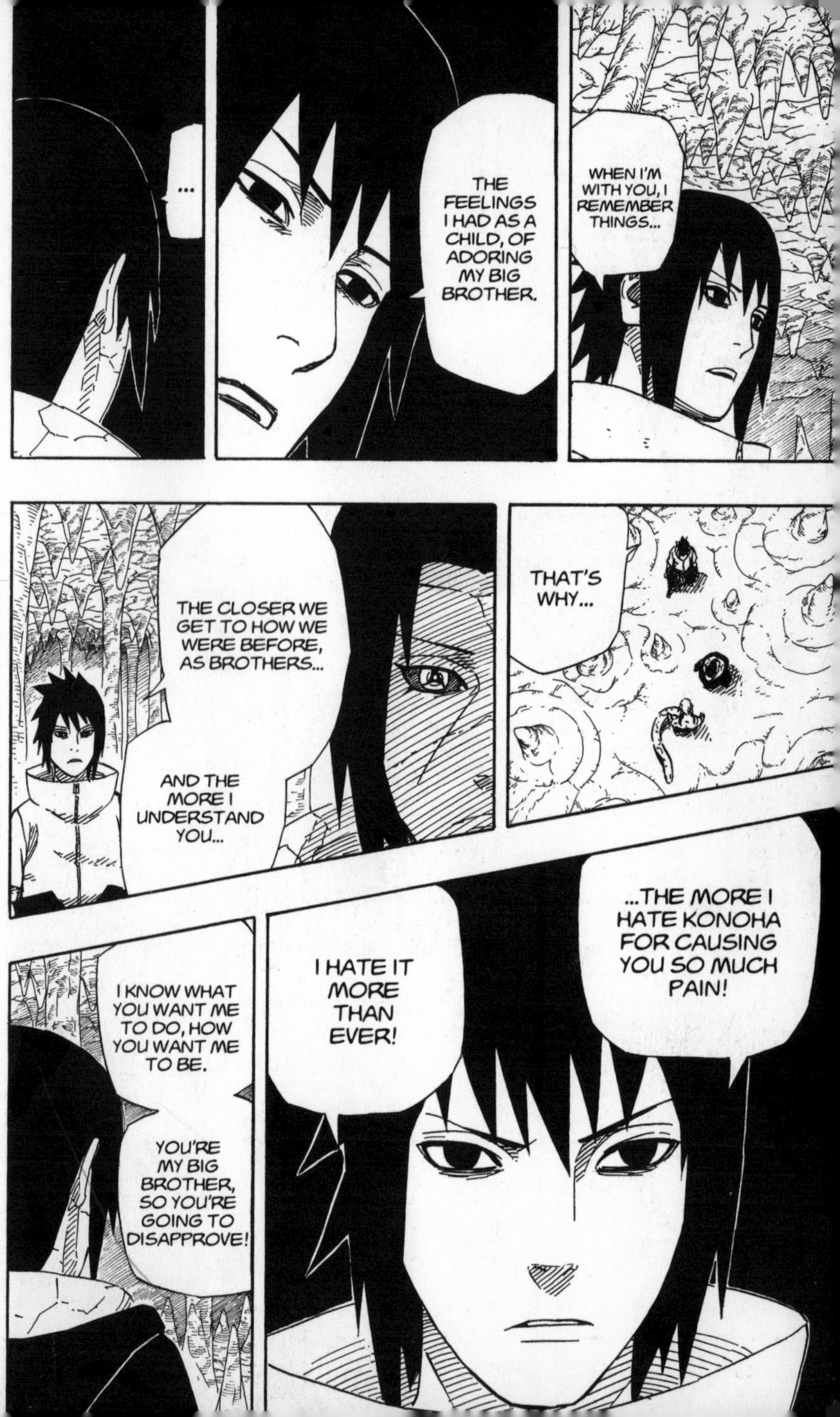
WHEN I'M WITH YOU, I REMEMBER THINGS...
THE FEELINGS I HAD AS A CHILD, OF ADORING MY BIG BROTHER.
...
THAT'S WHY...
THE CLOSER WE GET TO HOW WE WERE BEFORE, AS BROTHERS...
AND THE MORE I UNDERSTAND YOU...
...THE MORE I HATE KONOHA FOR CAUSING YOU SO MUCH PAIN!
I HATE IT MORE THAN EVER!
I KNOW WHAT YOU WANT ME TO DO, HOW YOU WANT ME TO BE.
YOU'RE MY BIG BROTHER, SO YOU'RE GOING TO DISAPPROVE!

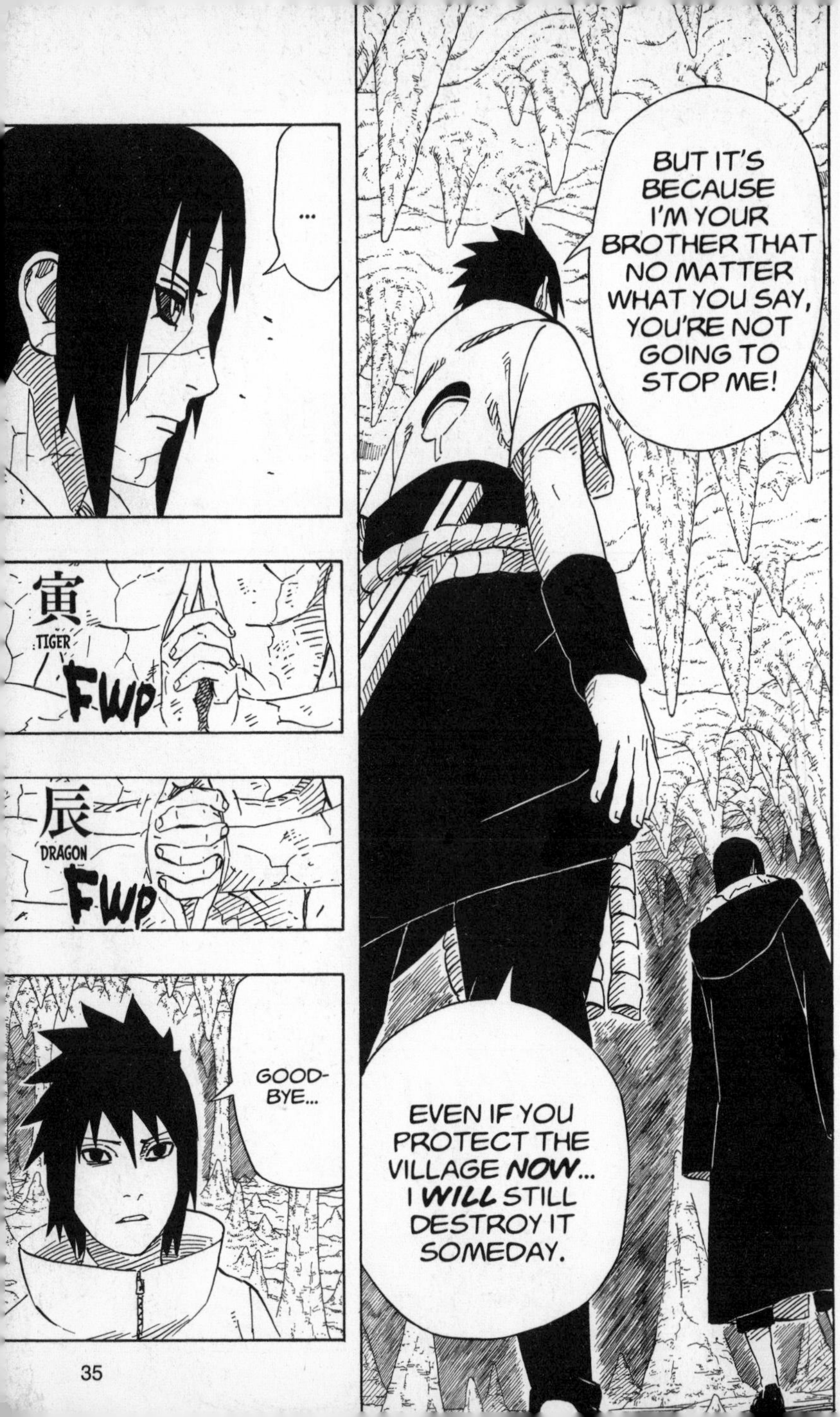
BUT IT'S BECAUSE I'M YOUR BROTHER THAT NO MATTER WHAT YOU SAY, YOU'RE NOT GOING TO STOP ME!
EVEN IF YOU PROTECT THE VILLAGE NOW... I WILL STILL DESTROY IT SOMEDAY.
...
寅
TIGER
FWP
辰
DRAGON
FWP
GOOD-BYE...

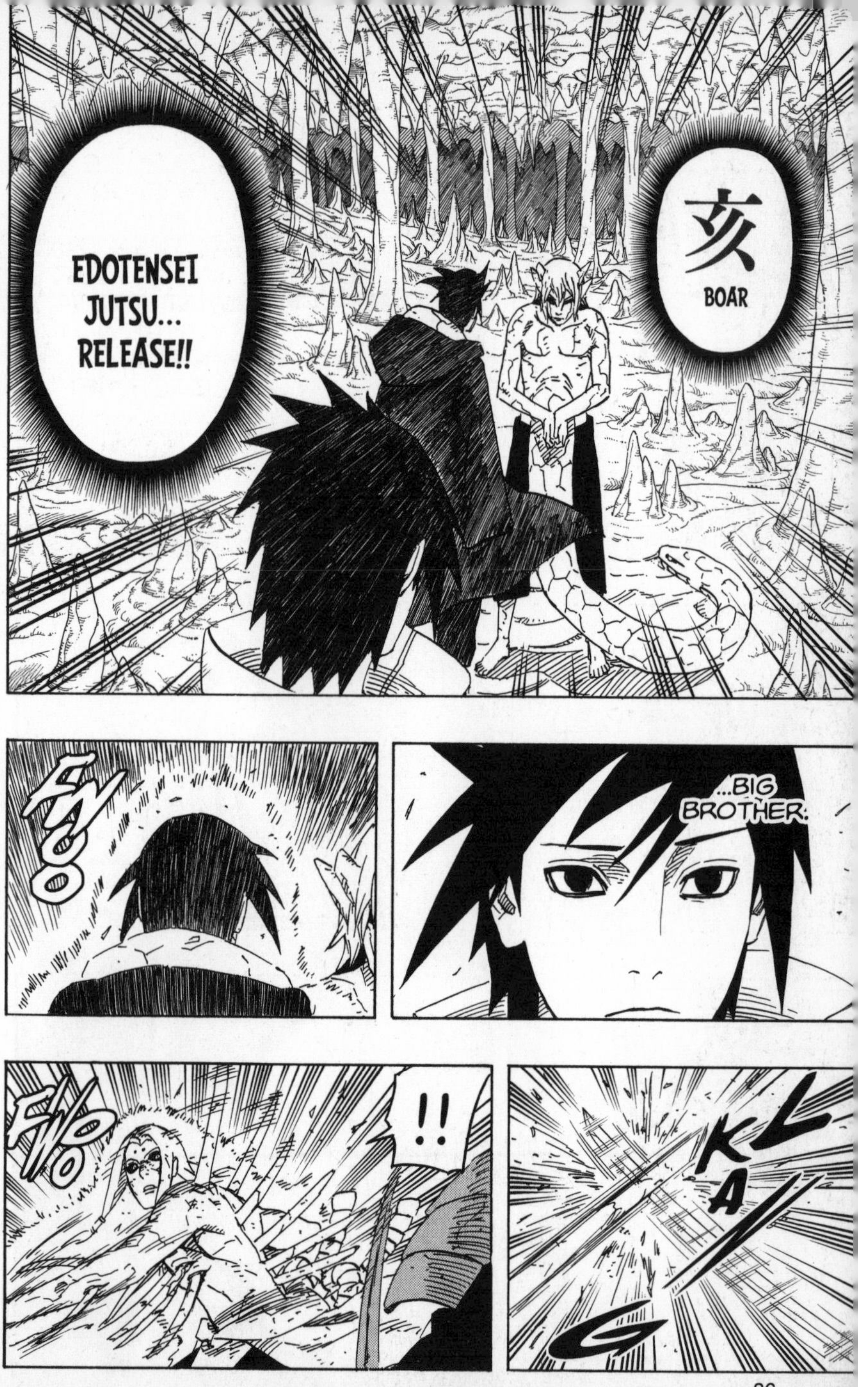
亥
BOAR
EDOTENSEI JUTSU... RELEASE!!
...BIG BROTHER.
FWOO
KLANG
!!
FWOO

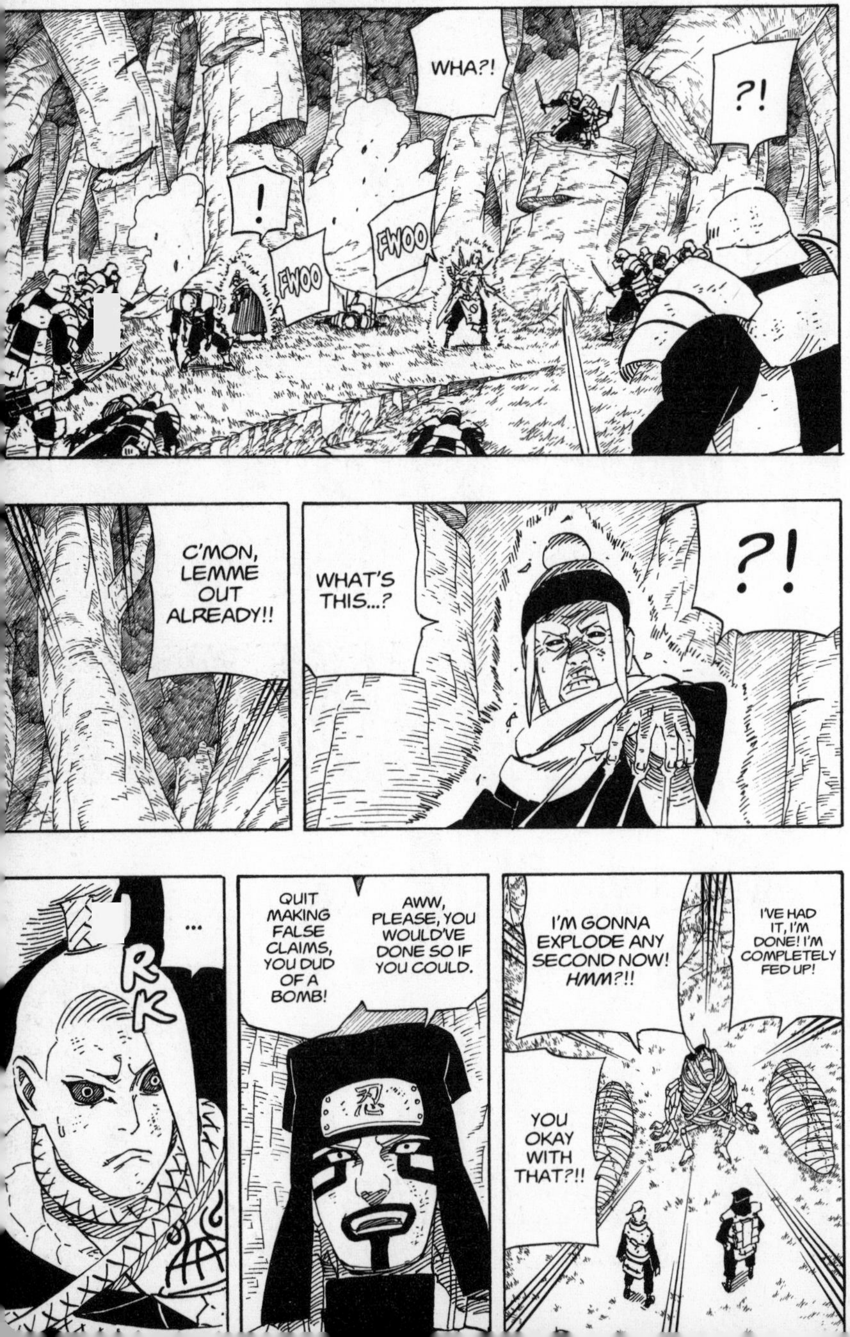
?!
WHA?!
!
FWOO
FWOO
?!
WHAT'S THIS...?
C'MON, LEMME OUT ALREADY!!
I'VE HAD IT, I'M DONE! I'M COMPLETELY FED UP!
I'M GONNA EXPLODE ANY SECOND NOW! HMM?!!
YOU OKAY WITH THAT?!!
AWW, PLEASE, YOU WOULD'VE DONE SO IF YOU COULD.
QUIT MAKING FALSE CLAIMS, YOU DUD OF A BOMB!
...
RK

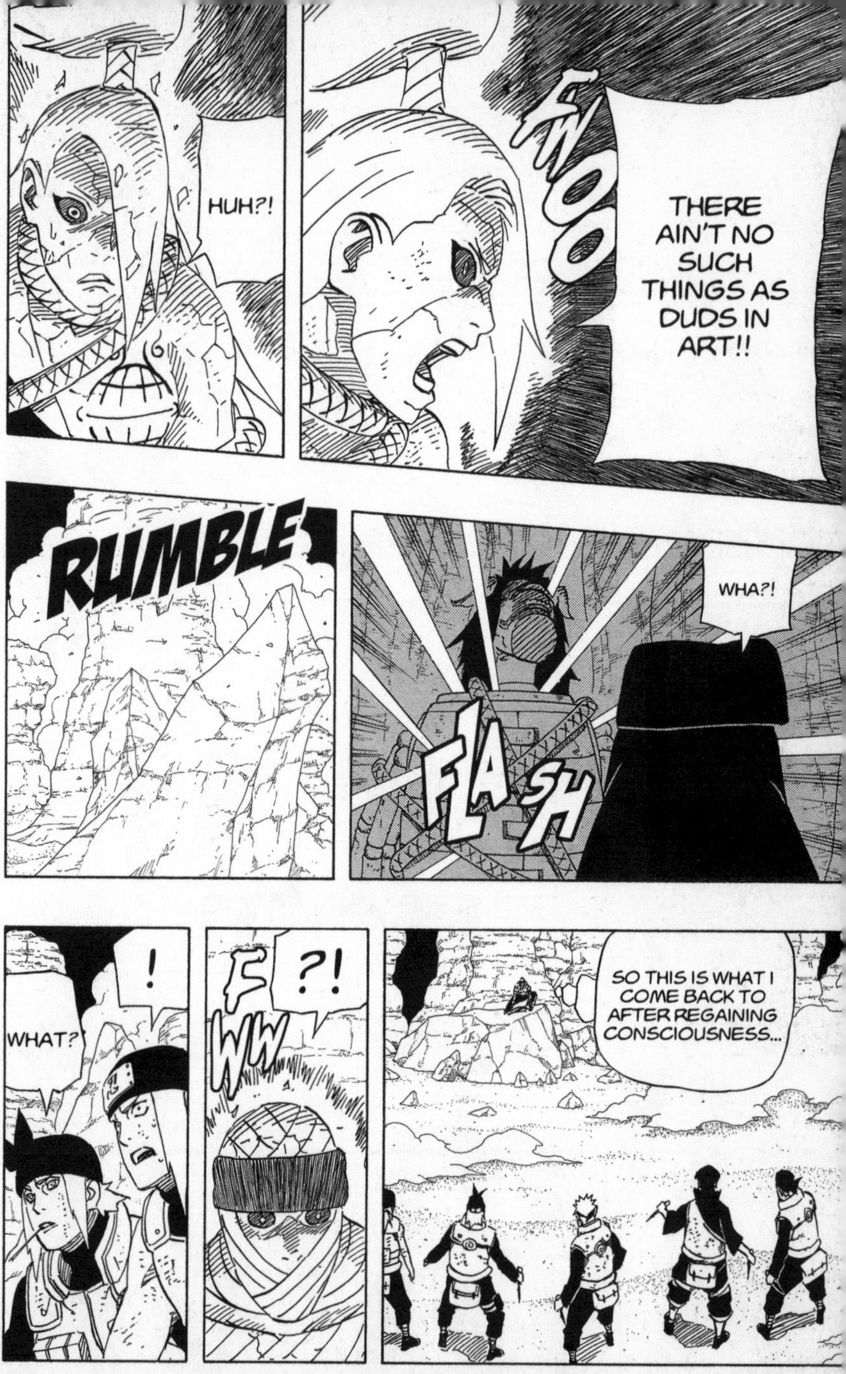
FWOOO
THERE AIN'T NO SUCH THINGS AS DUDS IN ART!!
HUH?!
WHA?!
FLASH
RUMBLE
SO THIS IS WHAT I COME BACK TO AFTER REGAINING CONSCIOUSNESS...
?!
FWW
!
WHAT?

LOOKS LIKE SOMEONE SUCCEEDED.

YEAH...

...

DAN...!

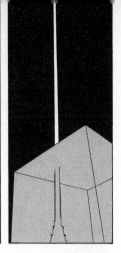

VWWWW ?! WW

VWW ?

!!

!!

NARUTO! THE JINCHURIKI ARE GONNA QUIT IT

LOOKS LIKE ITACHI DID IT

VWWWWWW

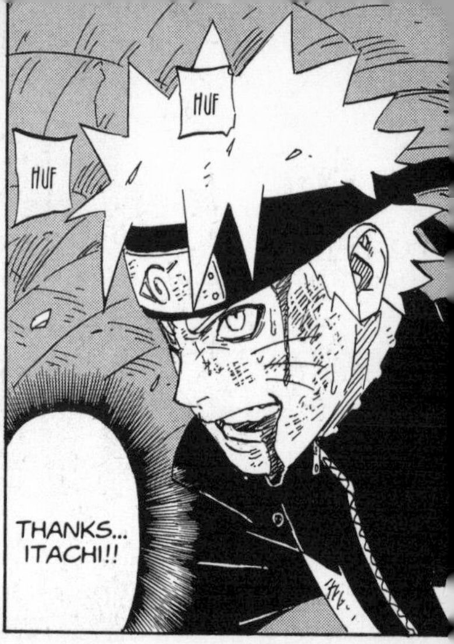
HUF
HUF
THANKS... ITACHI!!
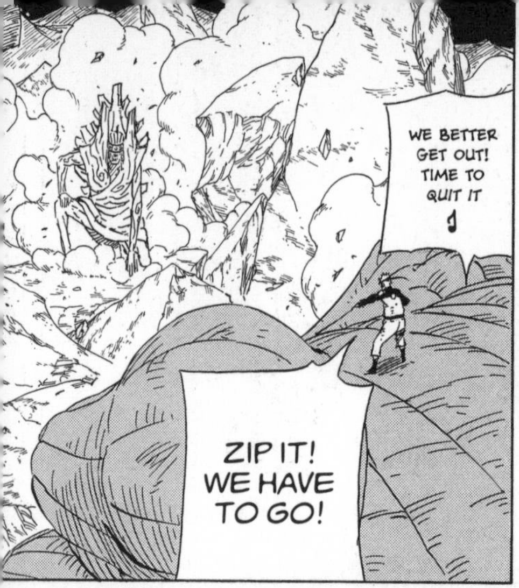
WE BETTER GET OUT! TIME TO QUIT IT ♪
ZIP IT! WE HAVE TO GO!
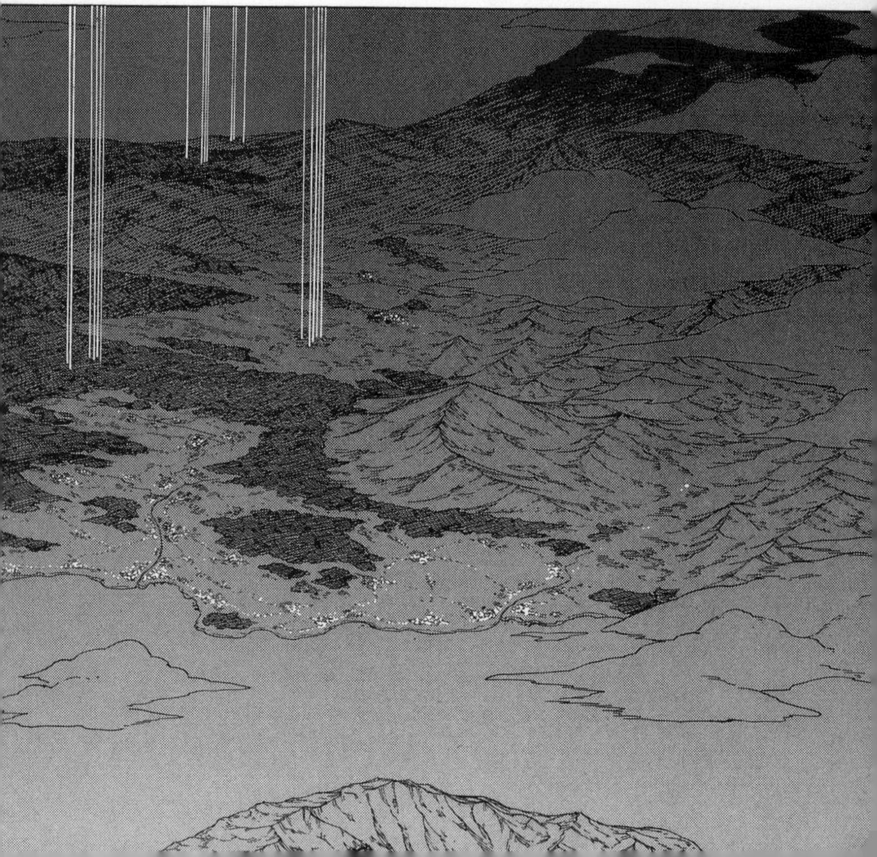

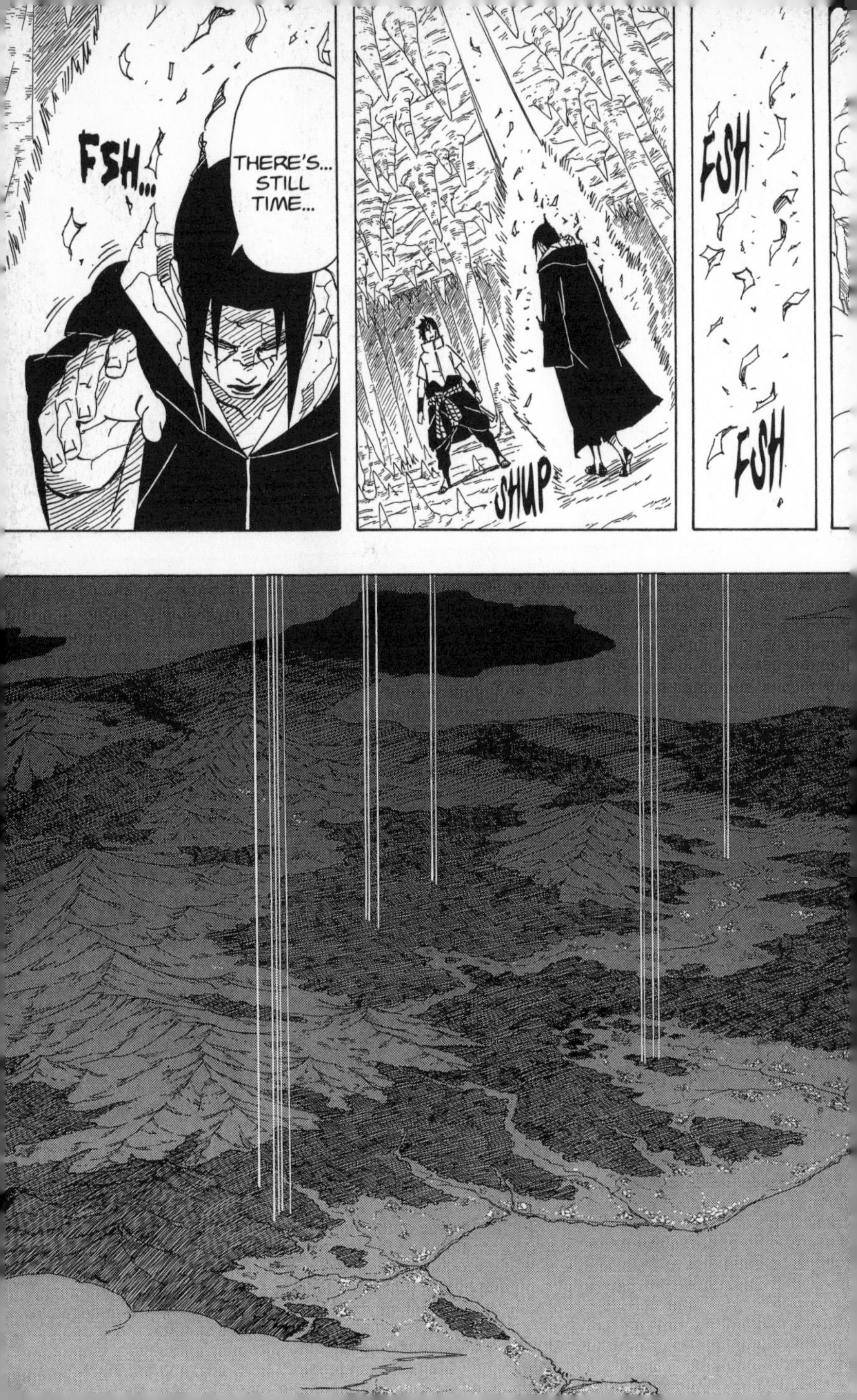
FSH
FSH
SHUP
THERE'S... STILL TIME...
FSH...

NARUTO

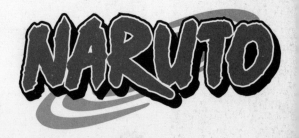

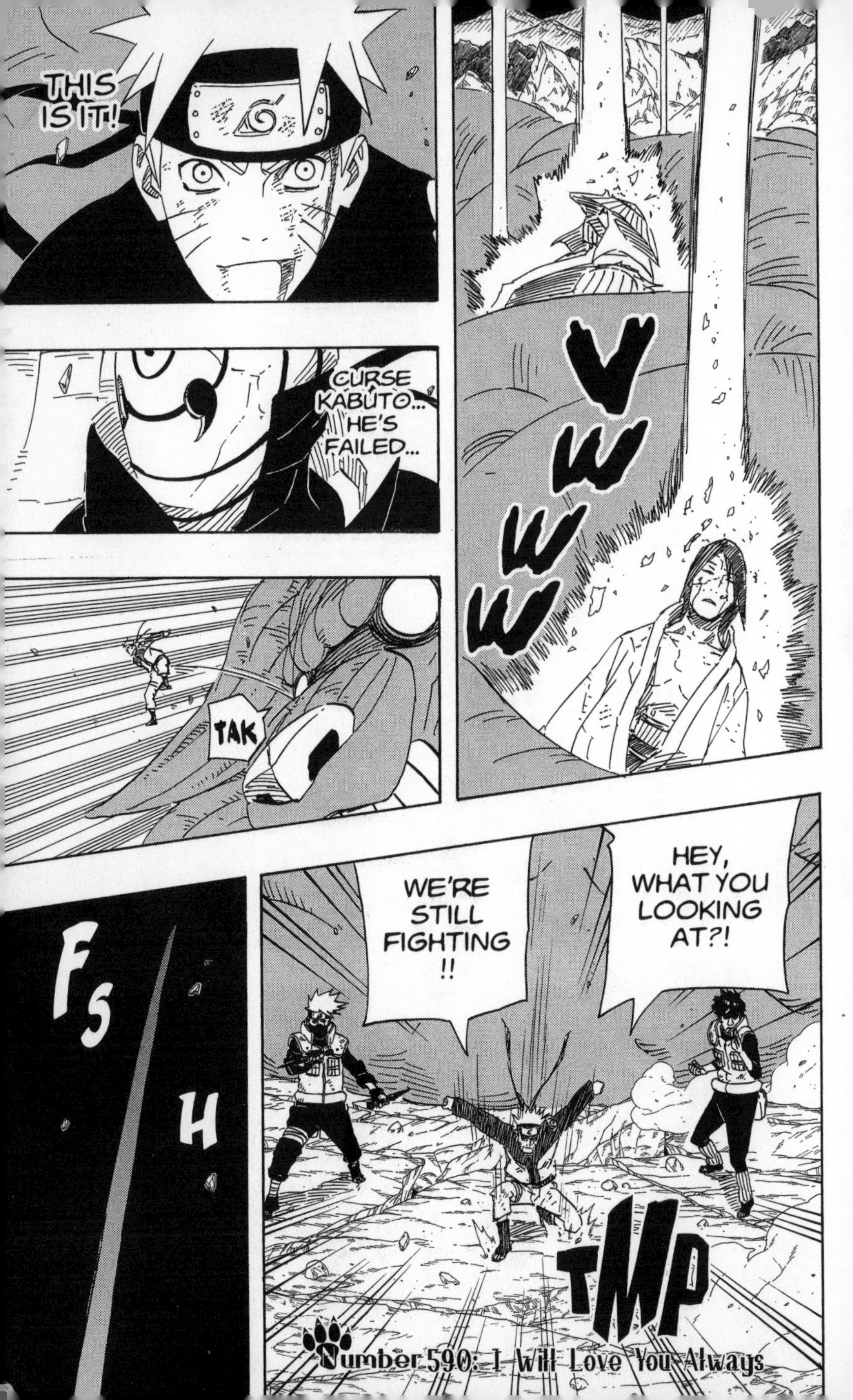
VWWW
THIS IS IT!
CURSE KABUTO... HE'S FAILED...
TAK
HEY, WHAT YOU LOOKING AT?!
WE'RE STILL FIGHTING!!
TMP
FSH

Number 590: I Will Love You Always

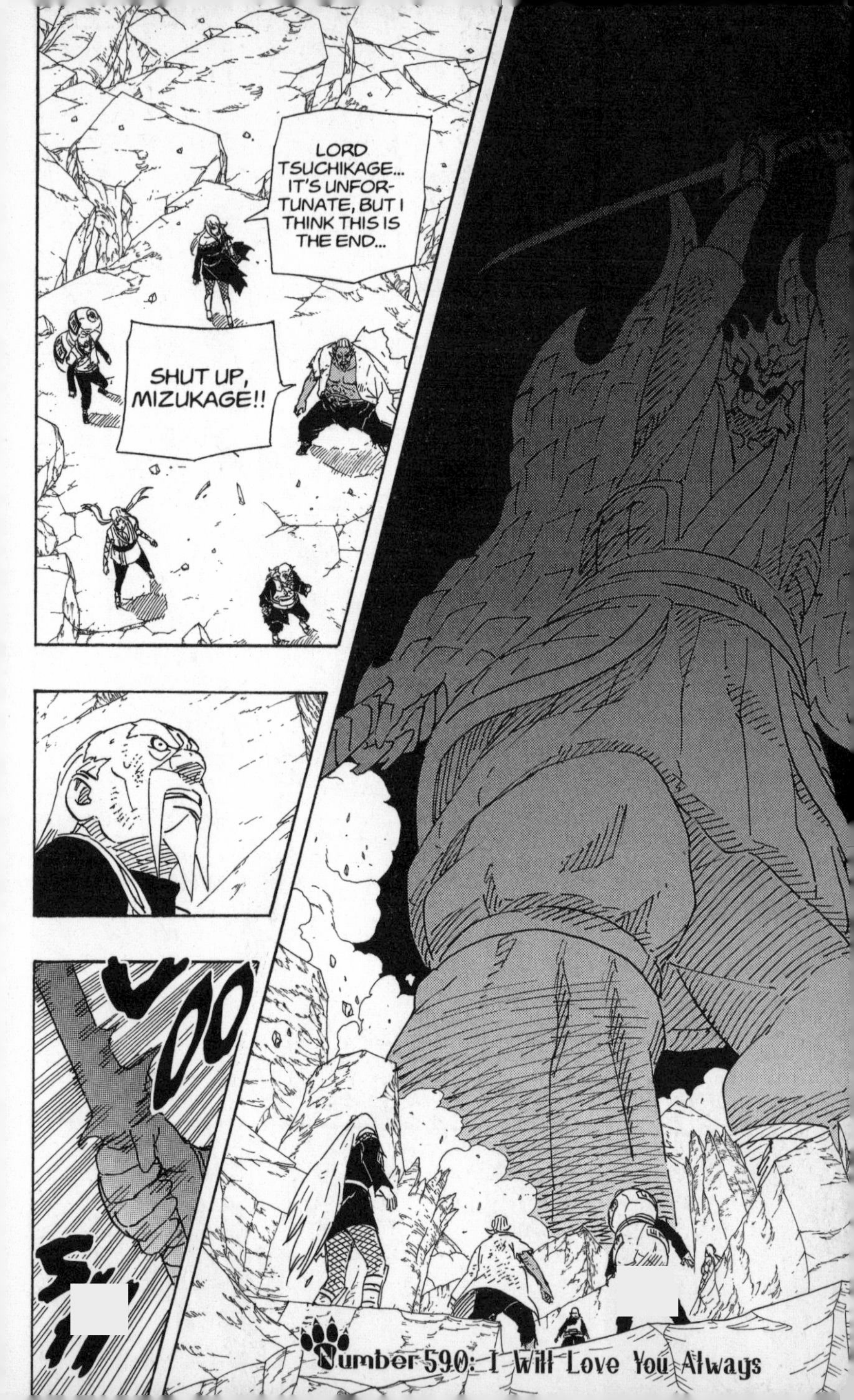
Number 590: I Will Love You Always
LORD TSUCHIKAGE... IT'S UNFOR-TUNATE, BUT I THINK THIS IS THE END...
SHUT UP, MIZUKAGE!!

SHUP

FWP

I'M NOT GIVING UP YET!!

!

TMP

WHAT'S THIS?

HM?

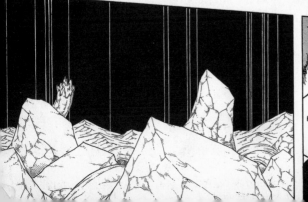

SOMETHING'S HAPPENED TO THE JUTSU CASTER.

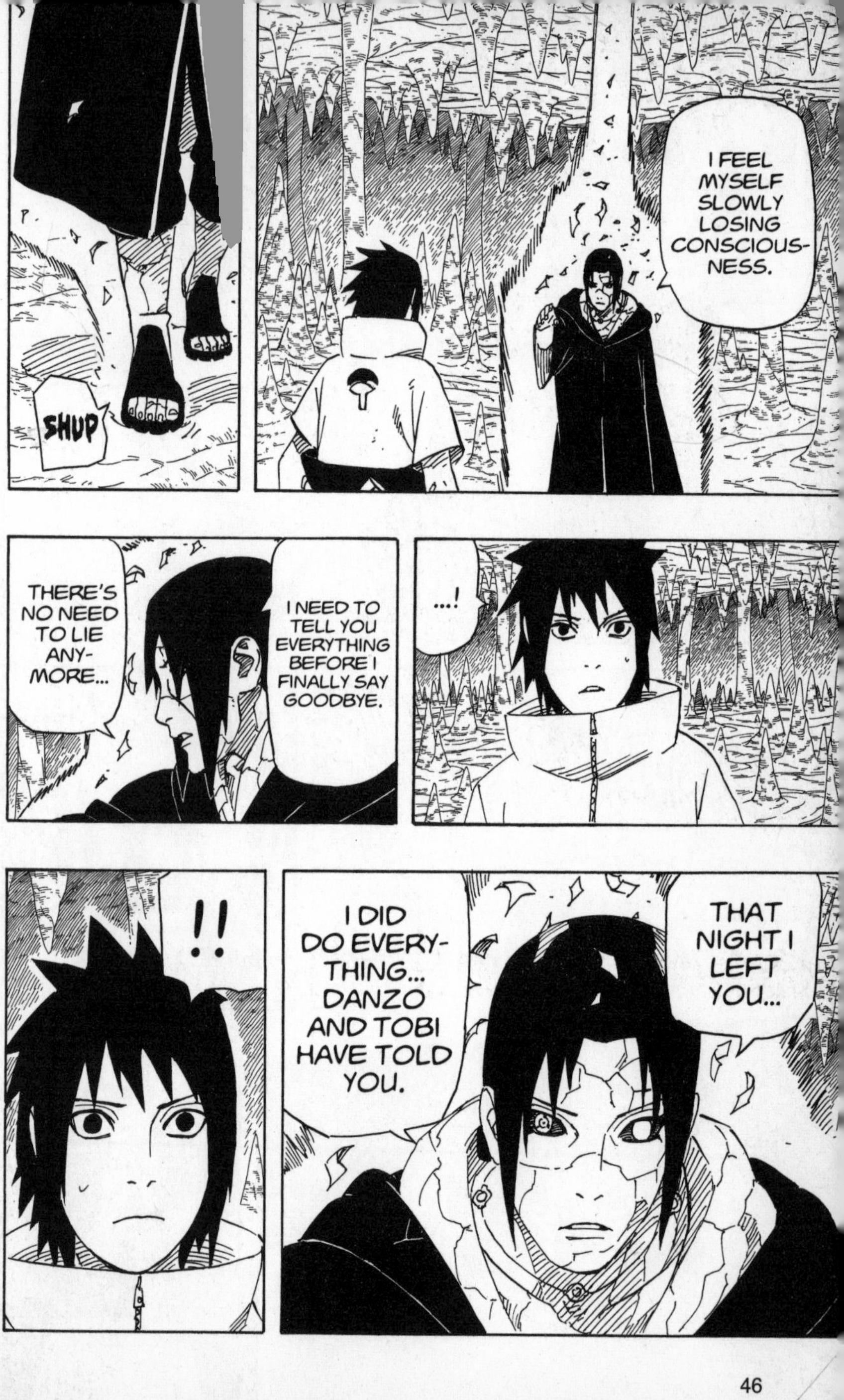
I FEEL MYSELF SLOWLY LOSING CONSCIOUS-NESS.
SHUP
...!
I NEED TO TELL YOU EVERYTHING BEFORE I FINALLY SAY GOODBYE.
THERE'S NO NEED TO LIE ANY-MORE...
THAT NIGHT I LEFT YOU...
I DID DO EVERY-THING... DANZO AND TOBI HAVE TOLD YOU.
!!

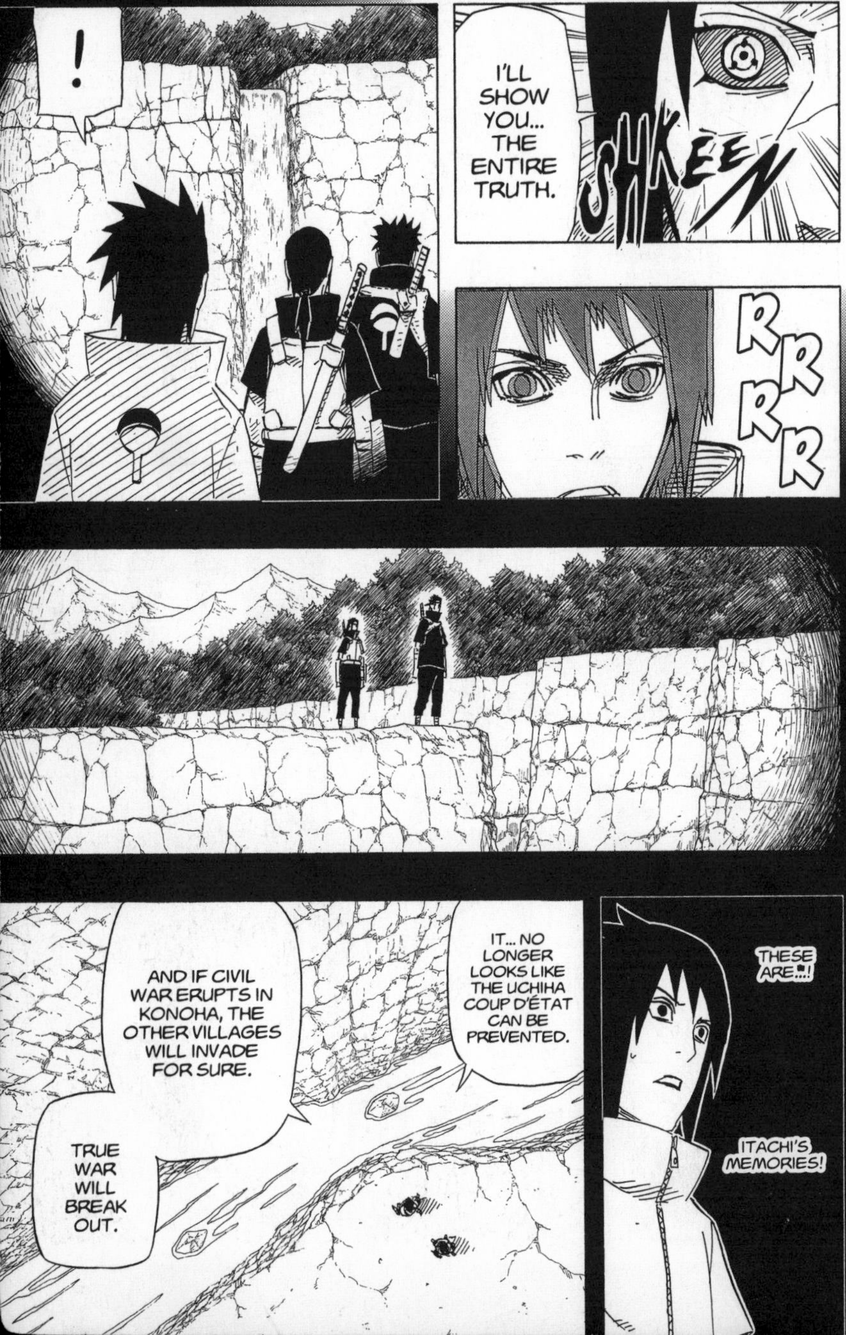
I'LL SHOW YOU... THE ENTIRE TRUTH.
SHKEEN
RRRR
!
THESE ARE...!
ITACHI'S MEMORIES!
IT... NO LONGER LOOKS LIKE THE UCHIHA COUP D'ÉTAT CAN BE PREVENTED.
AND IF CIVIL WAR ERUPTS IN KONOHA, THE OTHER VILLAGES WILL INVADE FOR SURE.
TRUE WAR WILL BREAK OUT.

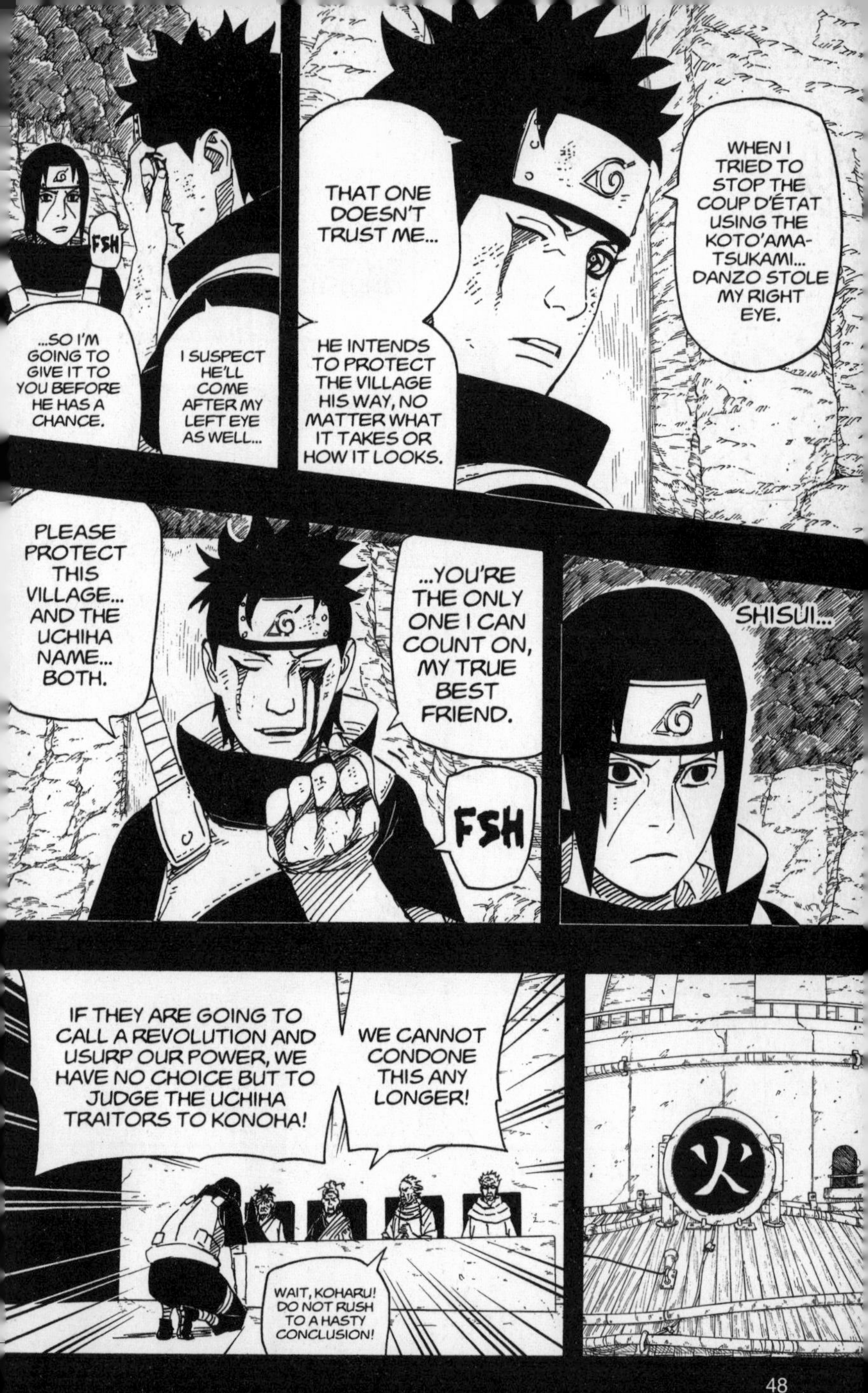
WHEN I TRIED TO STOP THE COUP D'ÉTAT USING THE KOTO'AMA-TSUKAMI... DANZO STOLE MY RIGHT EYE.
THAT ONE DOESN'T TRUST ME...
HE INTENDS TO PROTECT THE VILLAGE HIS WAY, NO MATTER WHAT IT TAKES OR HOW IT LOOKS.
I SUSPECT HE'LL COME AFTER MY LEFT EYE AS WELL...
...SO I'M GOING TO GIVE IT TO YOU BEFORE HE HAS A CHANCE.
FSH
SHISUI...
...YOU'RE THE ONLY ONE I CAN COUNT ON, MY TRUE BEST FRIEND.
PLEASE PROTECT THIS VILLAGE... AND THE UCHIHA NAME... BOTH.
FSH
WE CANNOT CONDONE THIS ANY LONGER!
IF THEY ARE GOING TO CALL A REVOLUTION AND USURP OUR POWER, WE HAVE NO CHOICE BUT TO JUDGE THE UCHIHA TRAITORS TO KONOHA!
WAIT, KOHARU! DO NOT RUSH TO A HASTY CONCLUSION!

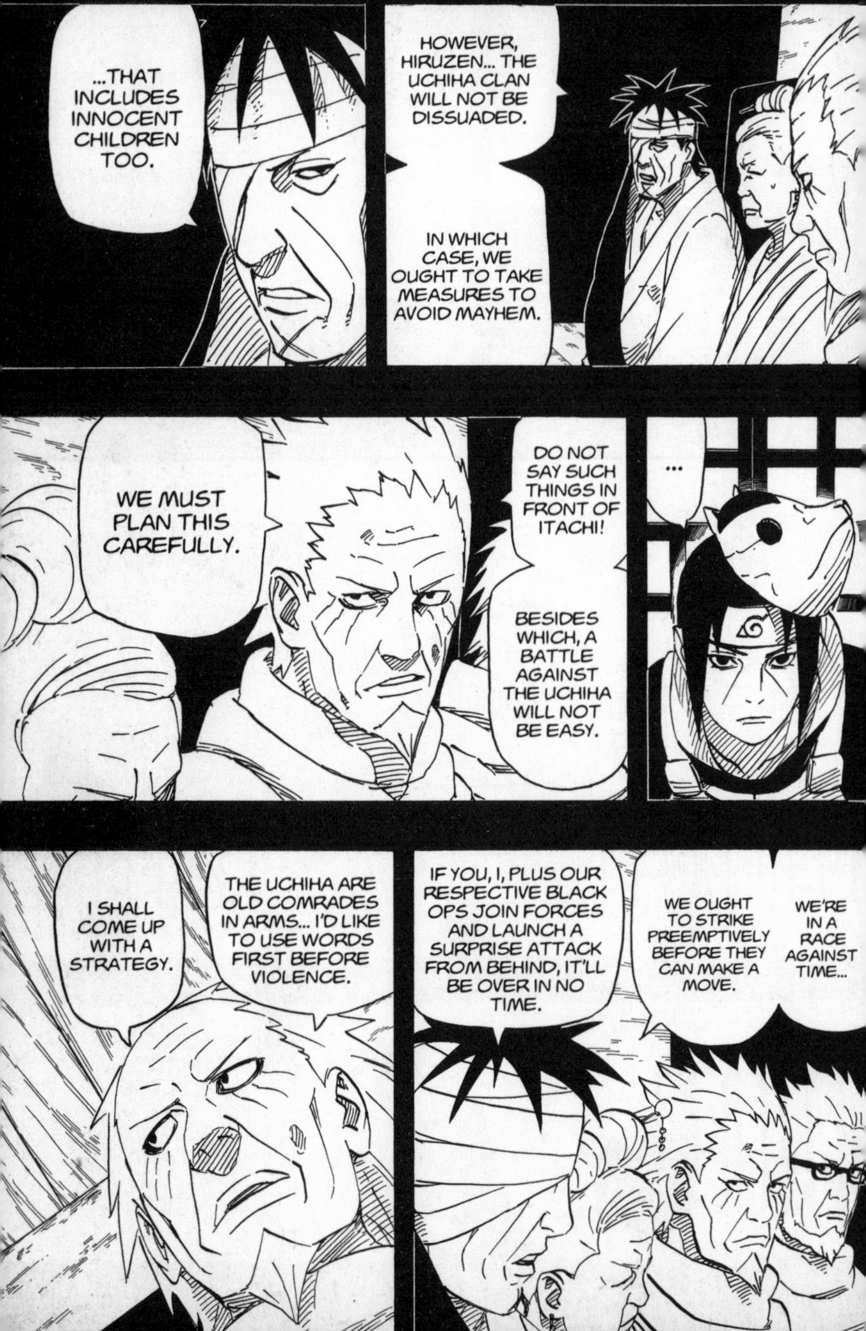
HOWEVER, HIRUZEN... THE UCHIHA CLAN WILL NOT BE DISSUADED.
IN WHICH CASE, WE OUGHT TO TAKE MEASURES TO AVOID MAYHEM.
...THAT INCLUDES INNOCENT CHILDREN TOO.
...
DO NOT SAY SUCH THINGS IN FRONT OF ITACHI!
BESIDES WHICH, A BATTLE AGAINST THE UCHIHA WILL NOT BE EASY.
WE MUST PLAN THIS CAREFULLY.
WE'RE IN A RACE AGAINST TIME...
WE OUGHT TO STRIKE PREEMPTIVELY BEFORE THEY CAN MAKE A MOVE.
IF YOU, I, PLUS OUR RESPECTIVE BLACK OPS JOIN FORCES AND LAUNCH A SURPRISE ATTACK FROM BEHIND, IT'LL BE OVER IN NO TIME.
THE UCHIHA ARE OLD COMRADES IN ARMS... I'D LIKE TO USE WORDS FIRST BEFORE VIOLENCE.
I SHALL COME UP WITH A STRATEGY.

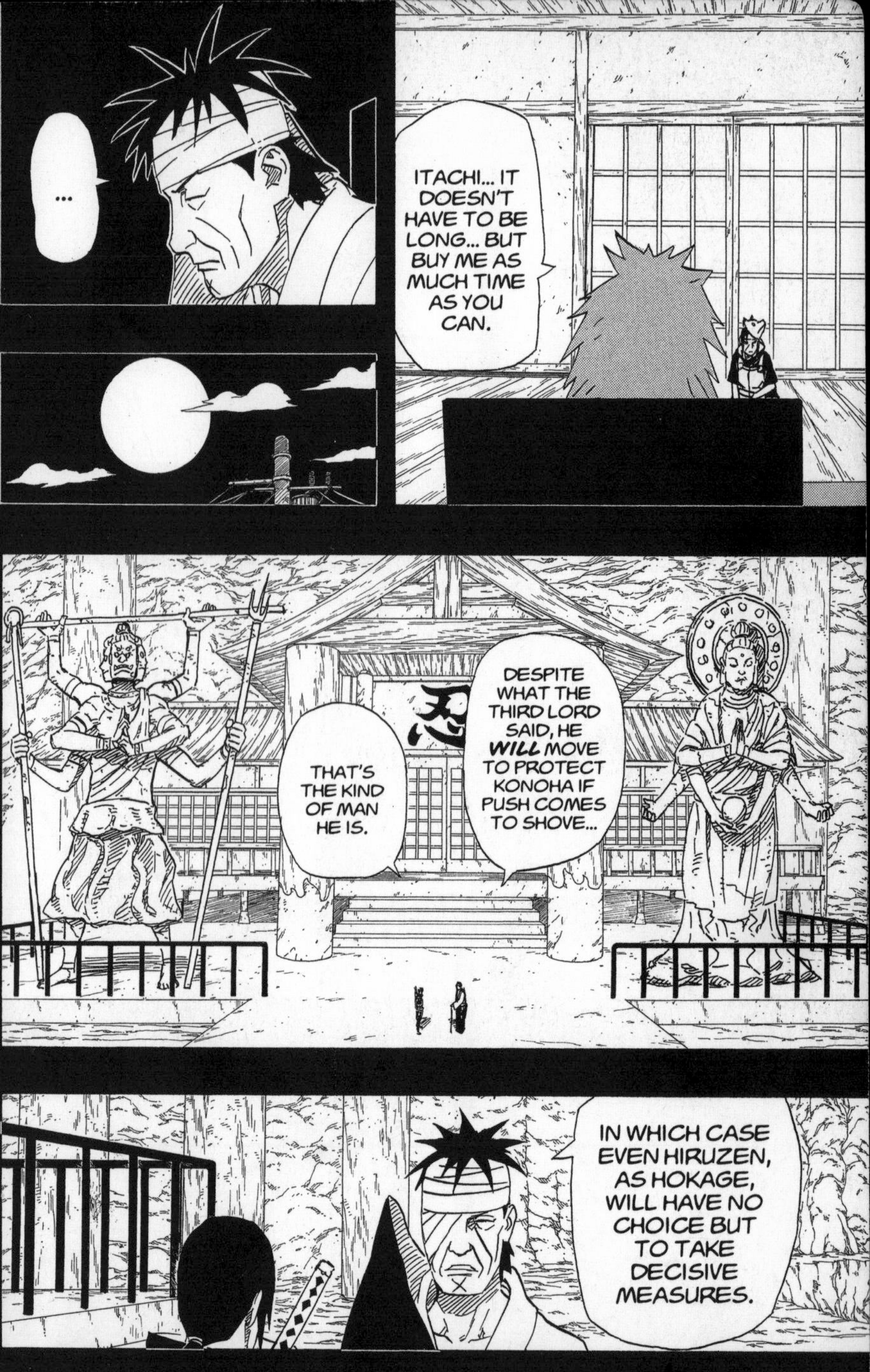
ITACHI... IT DOESN'T HAVE TO BE LONG... BUT BUY ME AS MUCH TIME AS YOU CAN.
...
DESPITE WHAT THE THIRD LORD SAID, HE ***WILL*** MOVE TO PROTECT KONOHA IF PUSH COMES TO SHOVE...
THAT'S THE KIND OF MAN HE IS.
IN WHICH CASE EVEN HIRUZEN, AS HOKAGE, WILL HAVE NO CHOICE BUT TO TAKE DECISIVE MEASURES.

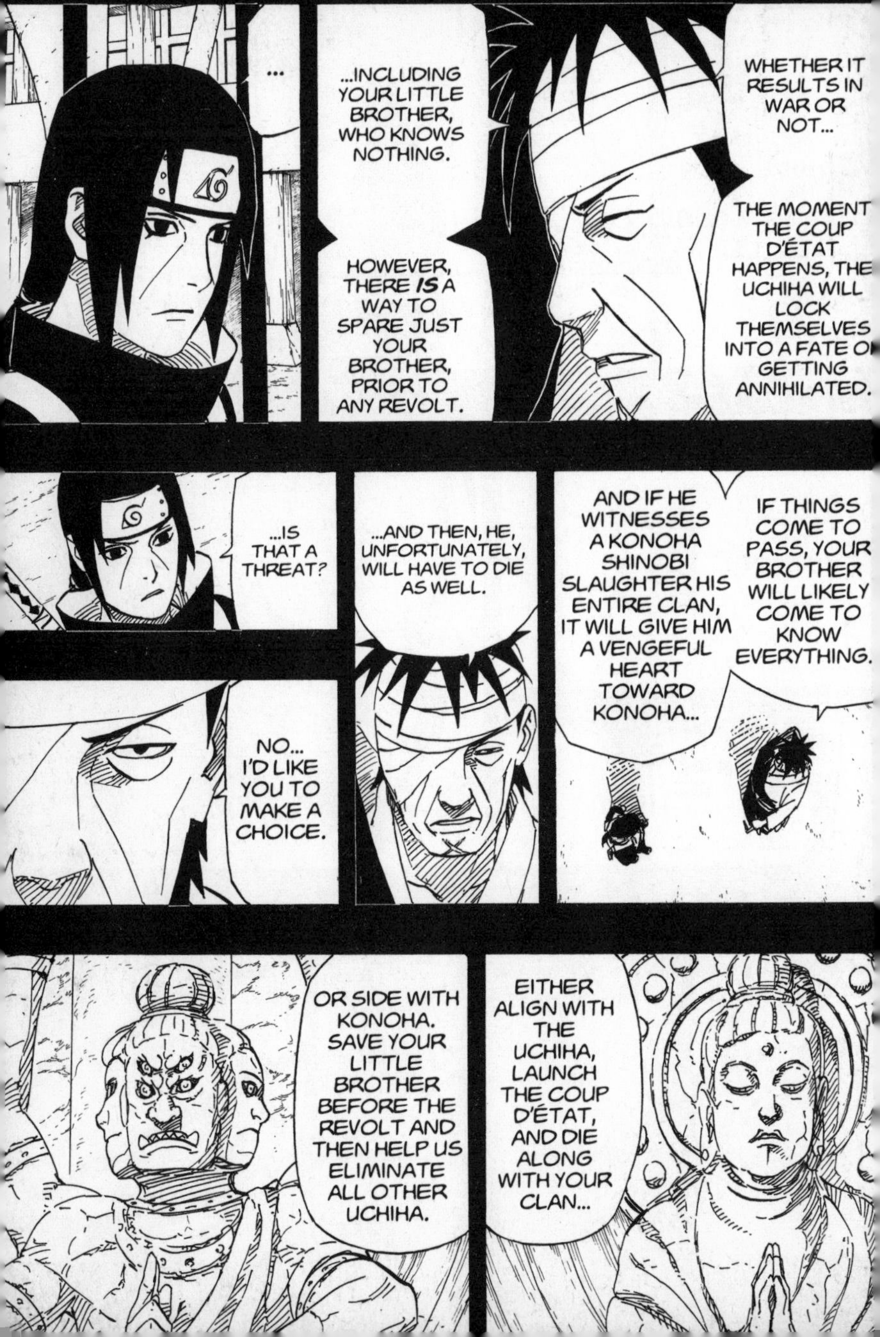
WHETHER IT RESULTS IN WAR OR NOT...
THE MOMENT THE COUP D'ÉTAT HAPPENS, THE UCHIHA WILL LOCK THEMSELVES INTO A FATE O GETTING ANNIHILATED.
...INCLUDING YOUR LITTLE BROTHER, WHO KNOWS NOTHING.
HOWEVER, THERE *IS* A WAY TO SPARE JUST YOUR BROTHER, PRIOR TO ANY REVOLT.
...
IF THINGS COME TO PASS, YOUR BROTHER WILL LIKELY COME TO KNOW EVERYTHING.
AND IF HE WITNESSES A KONOHA SHINOBI SLAUGHTER HIS ENTIRE CLAN, IT WILL GIVE HIM A VENGEFUL HEART TOWARD KONOHA...
...AND THEN, HE, UNFORTUNATELY, WILL HAVE TO DIE AS WELL.
...IS THAT A THREAT?
NO... I'D LIKE YOU TO MAKE A CHOICE.
EITHER ALIGN WITH THE UCHIHA, LAUNCH THE COUP D'ÉTAT, AND DIE ALONG WITH YOUR CLAN...
OR SIDE WITH KONOHA. SAVE YOUR LITTLE BROTHER BEFORE THE REVOLT AND THEN HELP US ELIMINATE ALL OTHER UCHIHA.

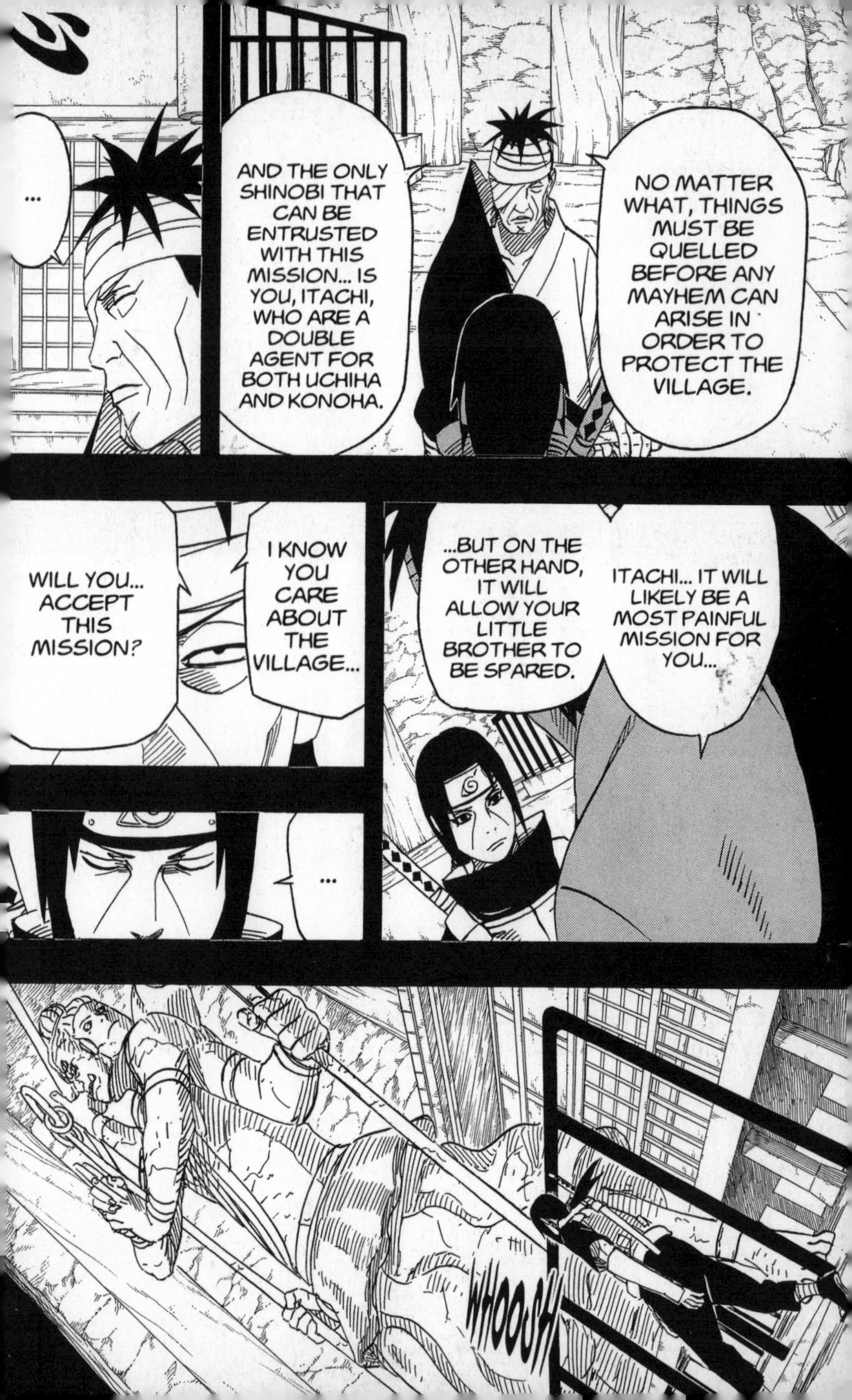
NO MATTER WHAT, THINGS MUST BE QUELLED BEFORE ANY MAYHEM CAN ARISE IN ORDER TO PROTECT THE VILLAGE.
AND THE ONLY SHINOBI THAT CAN BE ENTRUSTED WITH THIS MISSION... IS YOU, ITACHI, WHO ARE A DOUBLE AGENT FOR BOTH UCHIHA AND KONOHA.
...
ITACHI... IT WILL LIKELY BE A MOST PAINFUL MISSION FOR YOU...
...BUT ON THE OTHER HAND, IT WILL ALLOW YOUR LITTLE BROTHER TO BE SPARED.
I KNOW YOU CARE ABOUT THE VILLAGE...
WILL YOU... ACCEPT THIS MISSION?
...
WHOOSH

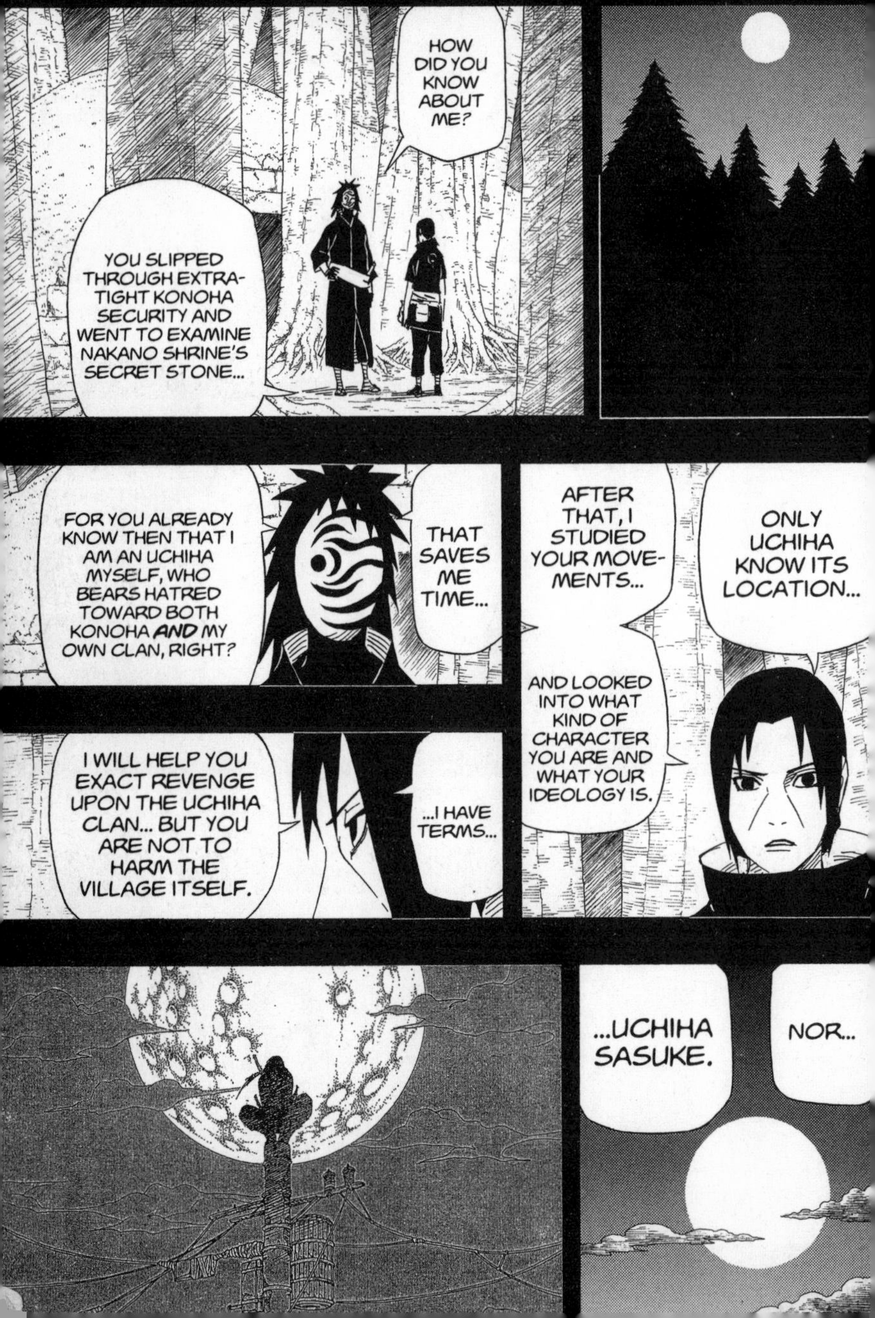
HOW DID YOU KNOW ABOUT ME?
YOU SLIPPED THROUGH EXTRA-TIGHT KONOHA SECURITY AND WENT TO EXAMINE NAKANO SHRINE'S SECRET STONE...
ONLY UCHIHA KNOW ITS LOCATION...
AFTER THAT, I STUDIED YOUR MOVEMENTS...
AND LOOKED INTO WHAT KIND OF CHARACTER YOU ARE AND WHAT YOUR IDEOLOGY IS.
THAT SAVES ME TIME...
FOR YOU ALREADY KNOW THEN THAT I AM AN UCHIHA MYSELF, WHO BEARS HATRED TOWARD BOTH KONOHA ***AND*** MY OWN CLAN, RIGHT?
...I HAVE TERMS...
I WILL HELP YOU EXACT REVENGE UPON THE UCHIHA CLAN... BUT YOU ARE NOT TO HARM THE VILLAGE ITSELF.
NOR...
...UCHIHA SASUKE.

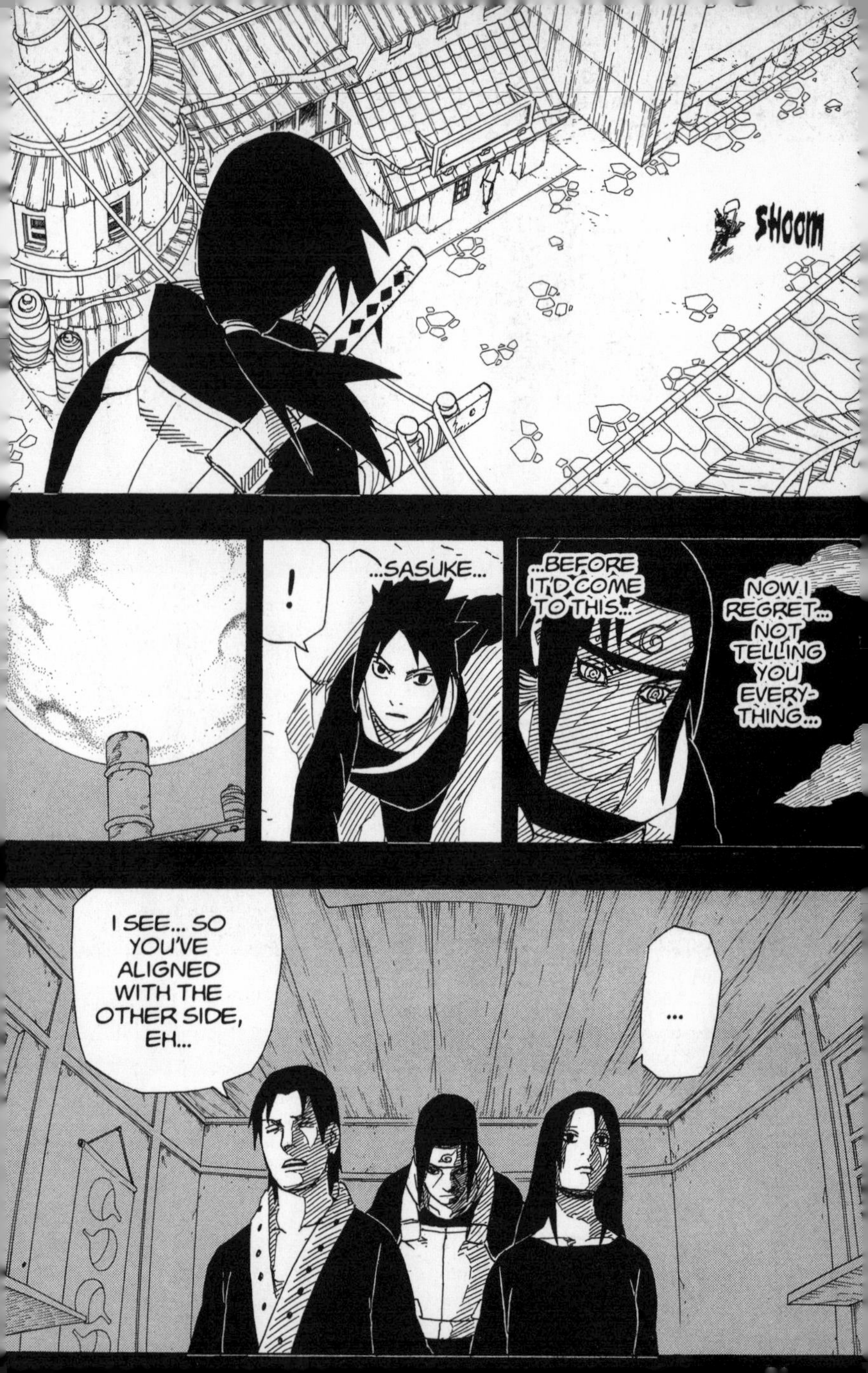

SHOOM
NOW I REGRET... NOT TELLING YOU EVERYTHING...
...BEFORE IT'D COME TO THIS...
...SASUKE...
!
...
I SEE... SO YOU'VE ALIGNED WITH THE OTHER SIDE, EH...

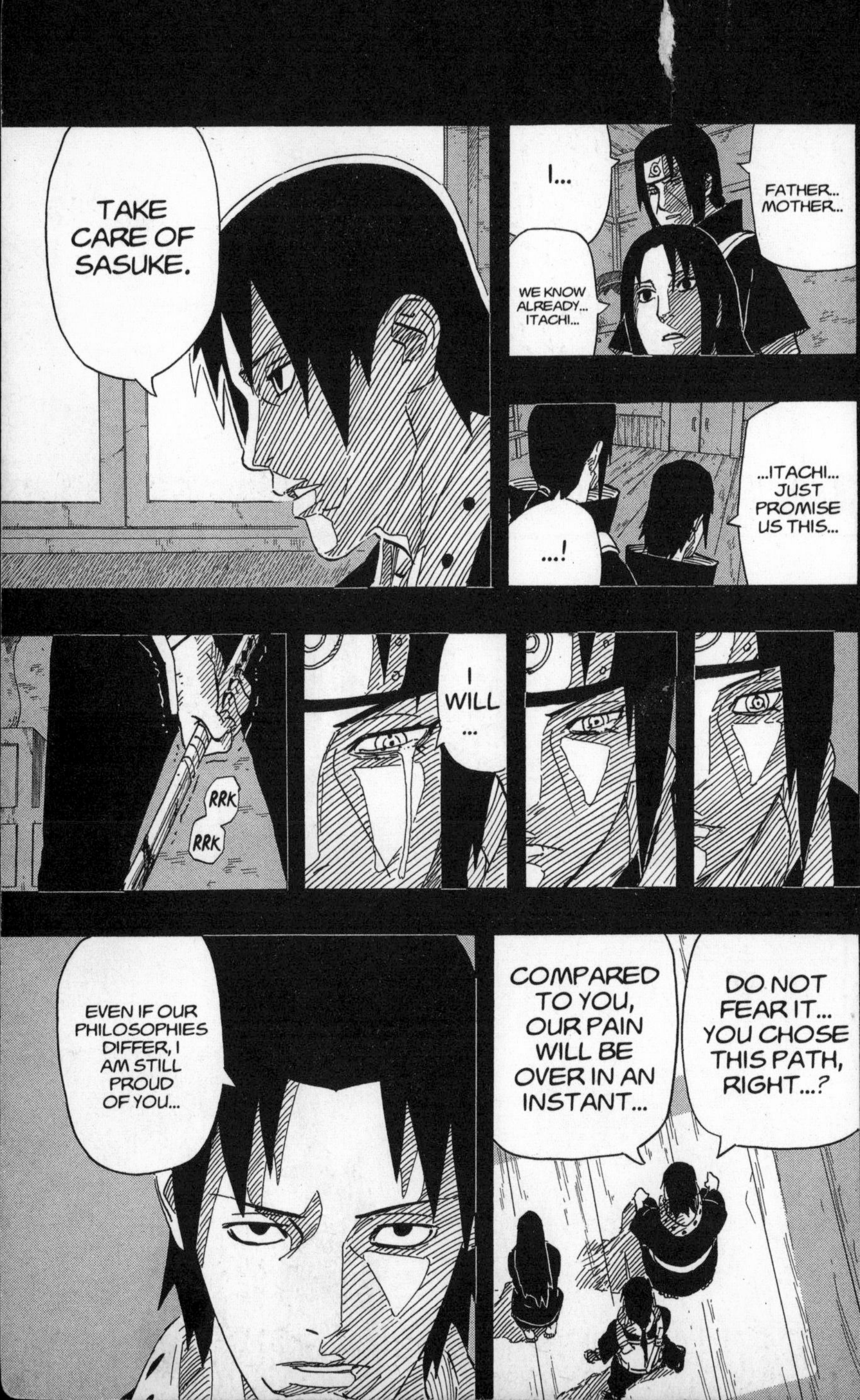
FATHER.. MOTHER..
I...
WE KNOW ALREADY... ITACHI...
...ITACHI... JUST PROMISE US THIS...
...!
TAKE CARE OF SASUKE.
I WILL ...
RRK
RRK
DO NOT FEAR IT... YOU CHOSE THIS PATH, RIGHT...?
COMPARED TO YOU, OUR PAIN WILL BE OVER IN AN INSTANT...
EVEN IF OUR PHILOSOPHIES DIFFER, I AM STILL PROUD OF YOU...

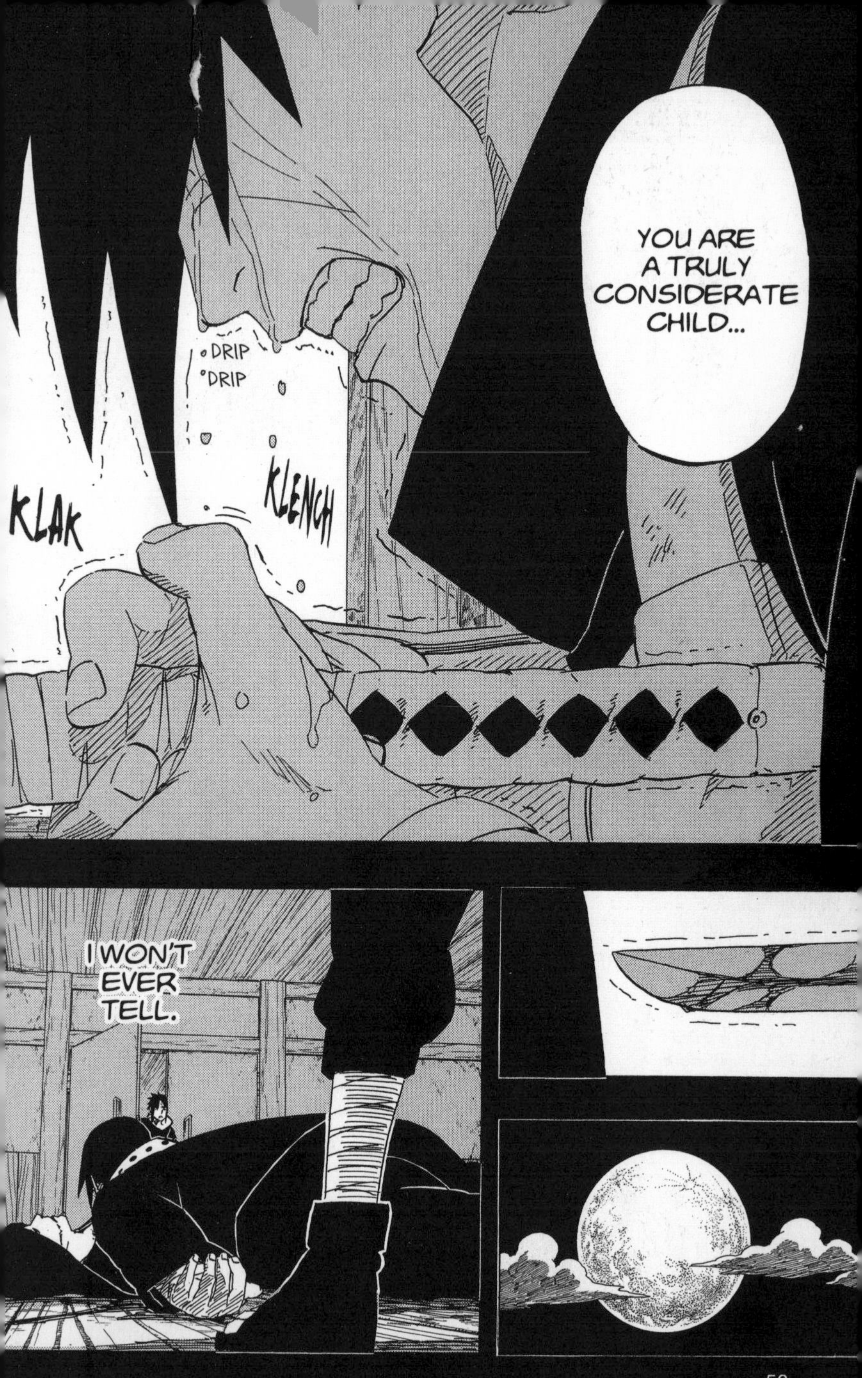
YOU ARE A TRULY CONSIDERATE CHILD...
DRIP
DRIP
KLENCH
KLAK
I WON'T EVER TELL.

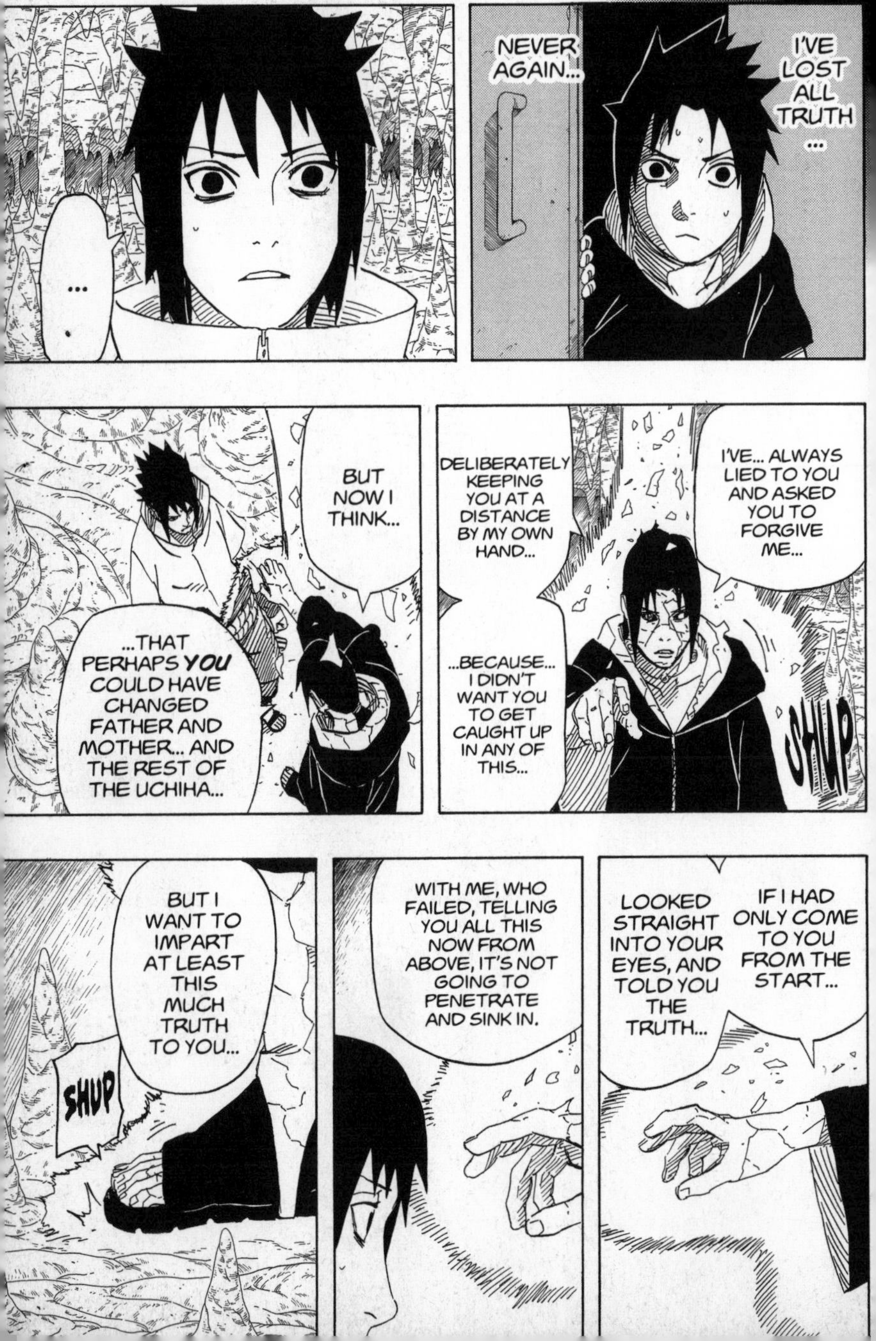
I'VE LOST ALL TRUTH ...
NEVER AGAIN...
...
I'VE... ALWAYS LIED TO YOU AND ASKED YOU TO FORGIVE ME...
DELIBERATELY KEEPING YOU AT A DISTANCE BY MY OWN HAND...
...BECAUSE... I DIDN'T WANT YOU TO GET CAUGHT UP IN ANY OF THIS...
SHUP
BUT NOW I THINK...
...THAT PERHAPS **YOU** COULD HAVE CHANGED FATHER AND MOTHER... AND THE REST OF THE UCHIHA...
IF I HAD ONLY COME TO YOU FROM THE START...
LOOKED STRAIGHT INTO YOUR EYES, AND TOLD YOU THE TRUTH...
WITH ME, WHO FAILED, TELLING YOU ALL THIS NOW FROM ABOVE, IT'S NOT GOING TO PENETRATE AND SINK IN.
BUT I WANT TO IMPART AT LEAST THIS MUCH TRUTH TO YOU...
SHUP

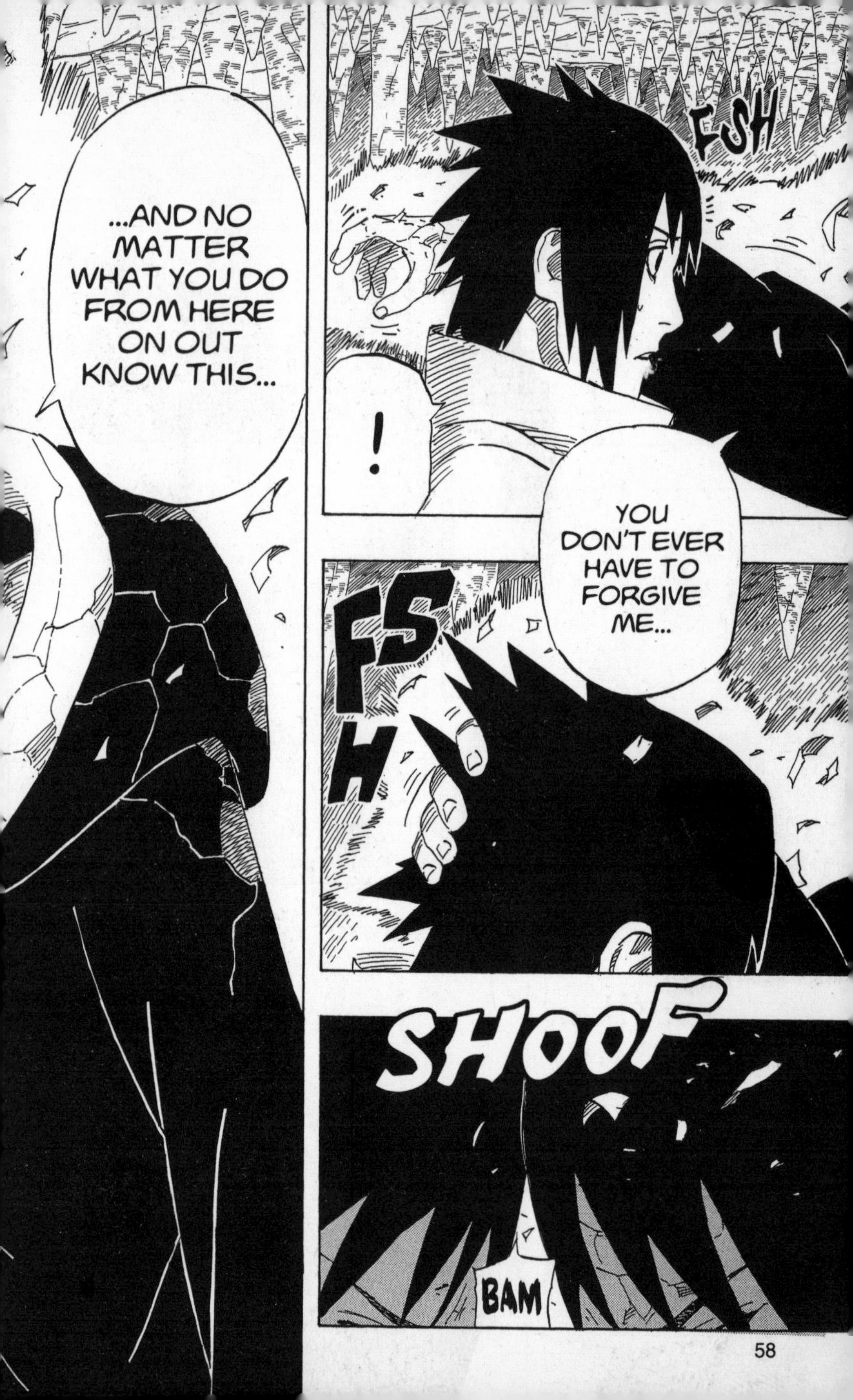
FSH
!
YOU DON'T EVER HAVE TO FORGIVE ME...
FSH
SHOOF
BAM
...AND NO MATTER WHAT YOU DO FROM HERE ON OUT KNOW THIS...

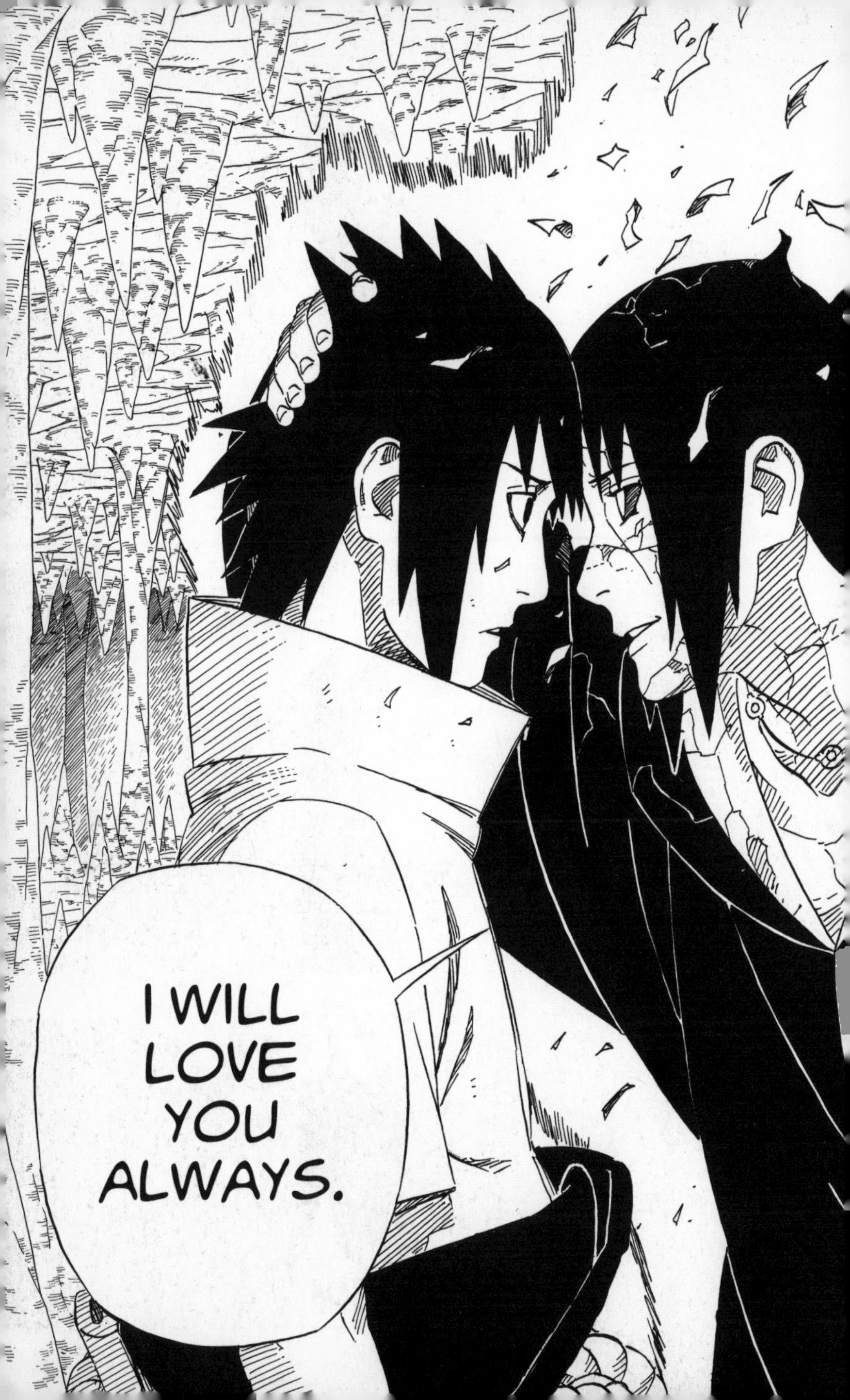
I WILL LOVE YOU ALWAYS.

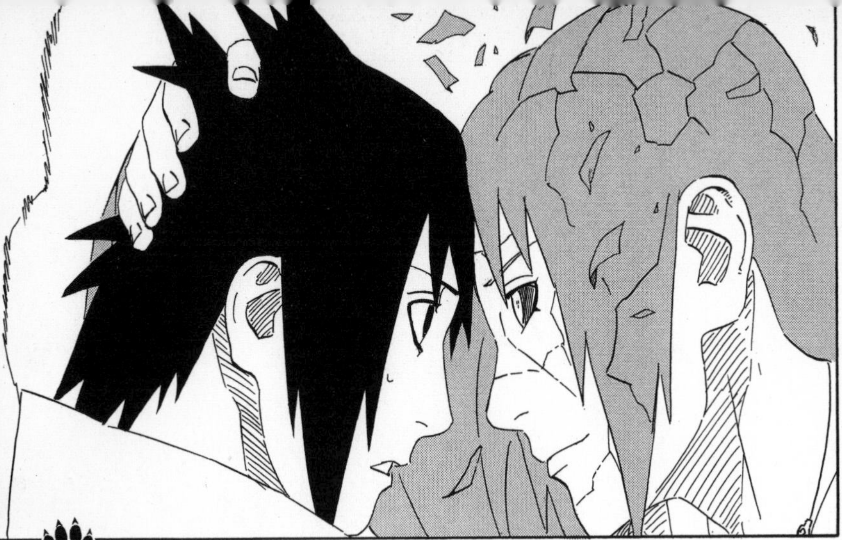

Number 591: Risk

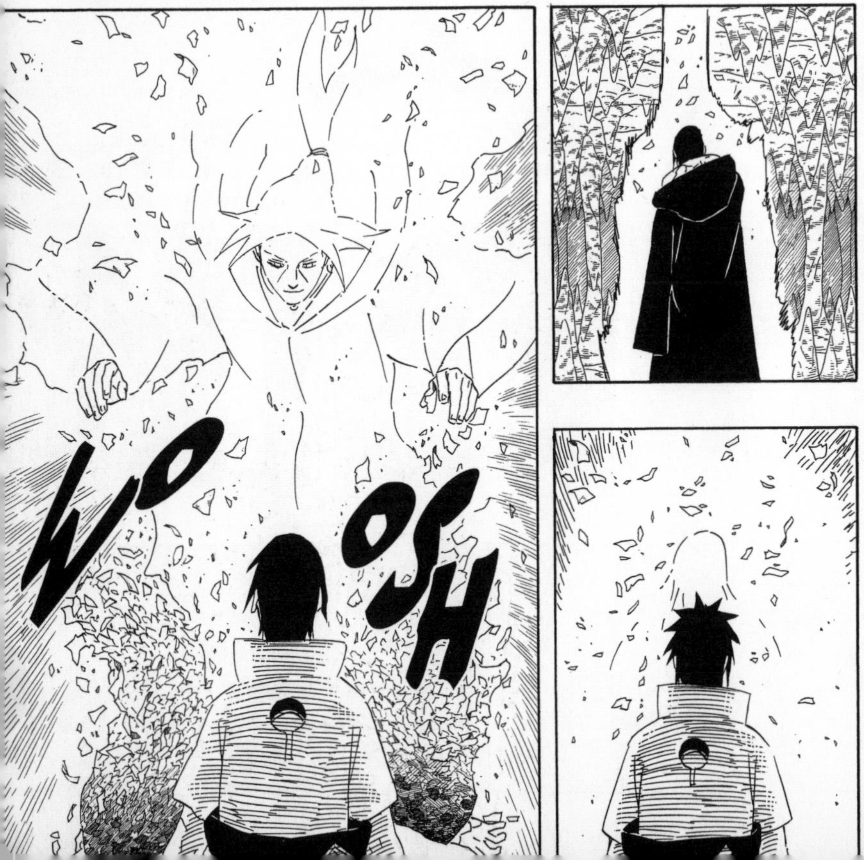
WOOSH

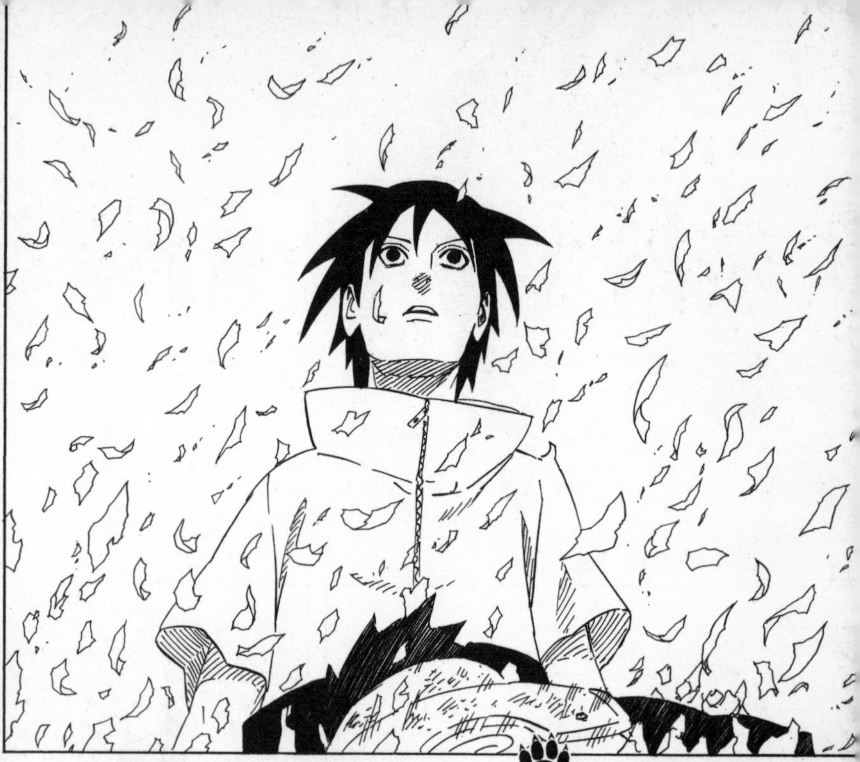

Number 591: Risk

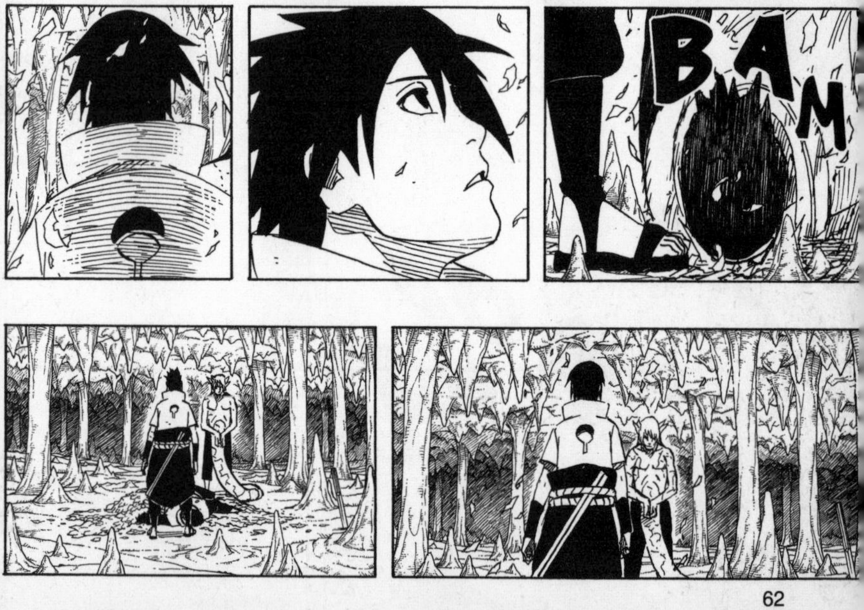
BAM

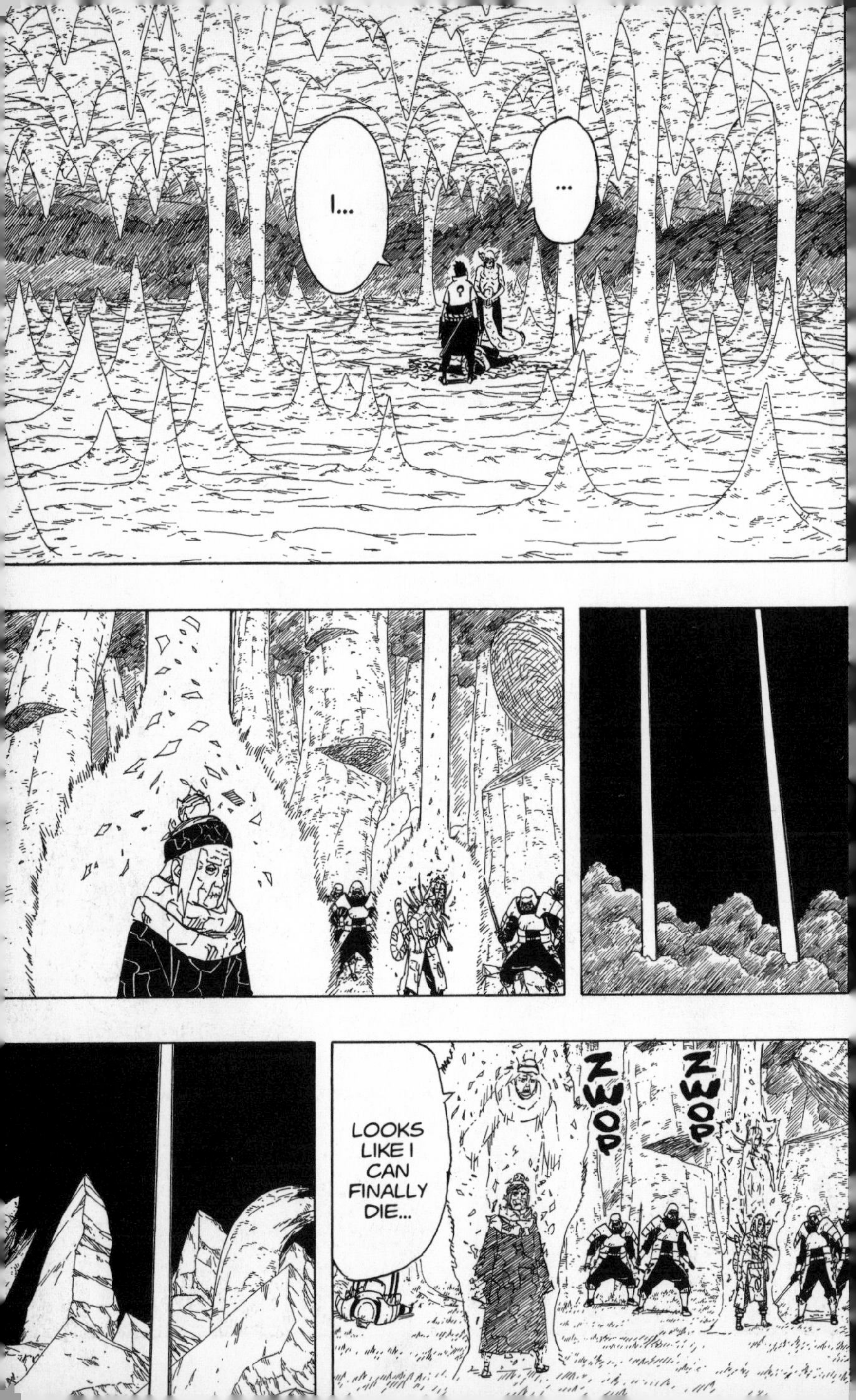
...
I...
ZWOP
ZWOP
LOOKS LIKE I CAN FINALLY DIE...

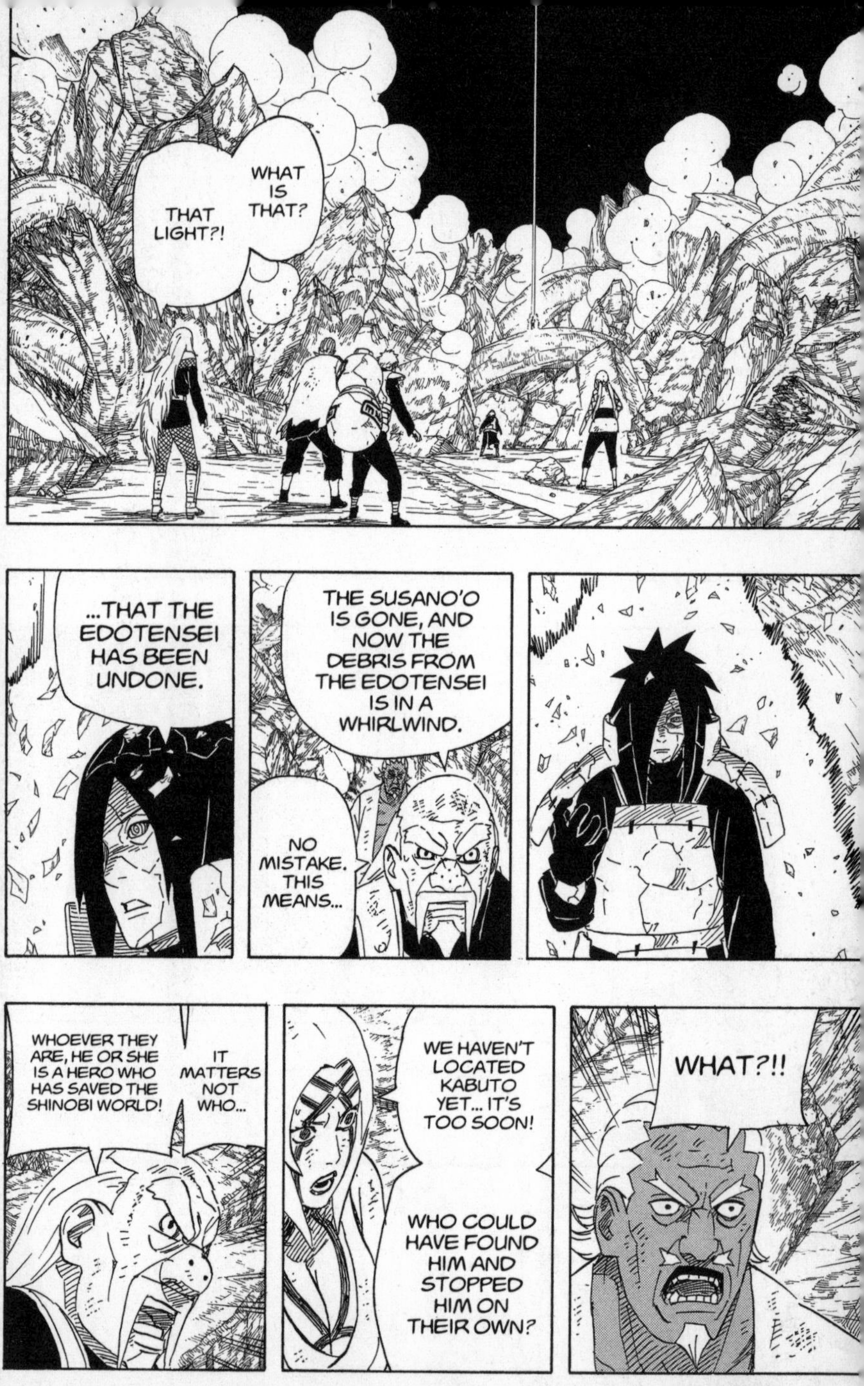
WHAT IS THAT? THAT LIGHT?!
THE SUSANO'O IS GONE, AND NOW THE DEBRIS FROM THE EDOTENSEI IS IN A WHIRLWIND.
NO MISTAKE. THIS MEANS...
...THAT THE EDOTENSEI HAS BEEN UNDONE.
WHAT?!!
WE HAVEN'T LOCATED KABUTO YET... IT'S TOO SOON!
WHO COULD HAVE FOUND HIM AND STOPPED HIM ON THEIR OWN?
IT MATTERS NOT WHO...
WHOEVER THEY ARE, HE OR SHE IS A HERO WHO HAS SAVED THE SHINOBI WORLD!

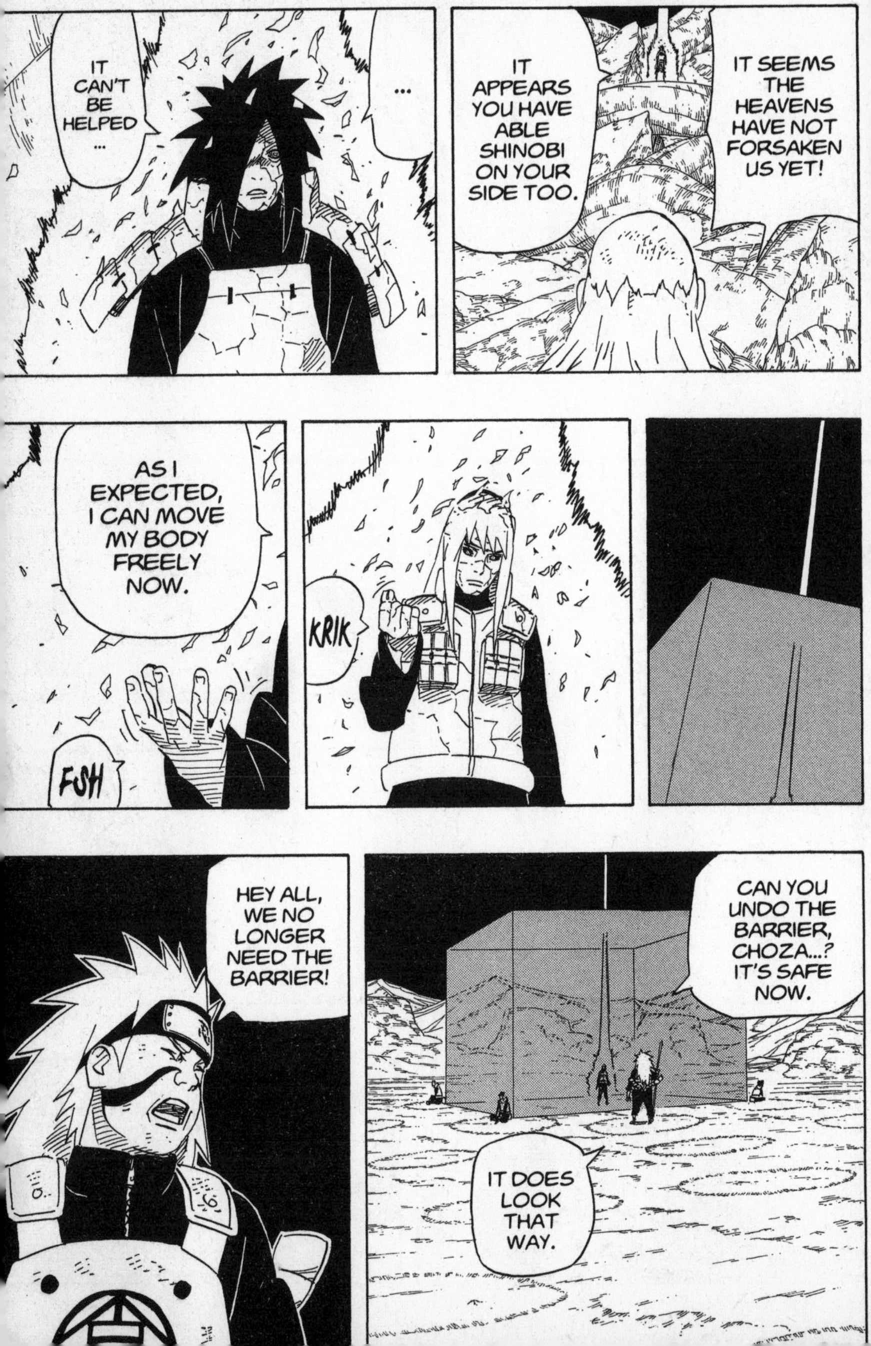
IT SEEMS THE HEAVENS HAVE NOT FORSAKEN US YET!
IT APPEARS YOU HAVE ABLE SHINOBI ON YOUR SIDE TOO.
...
IT CAN'T BE HELPED...
KRIK
AS I EXPECTED, I CAN MOVE MY BODY FREELY NOW.
FSH
CAN YOU UNDO THE BARRIER, CHOZA...? IT'S SAFE NOW.
IT DOES LOOK THAT WAY.
HEY ALL, WE NO LONGER NEED THE BARRIER!

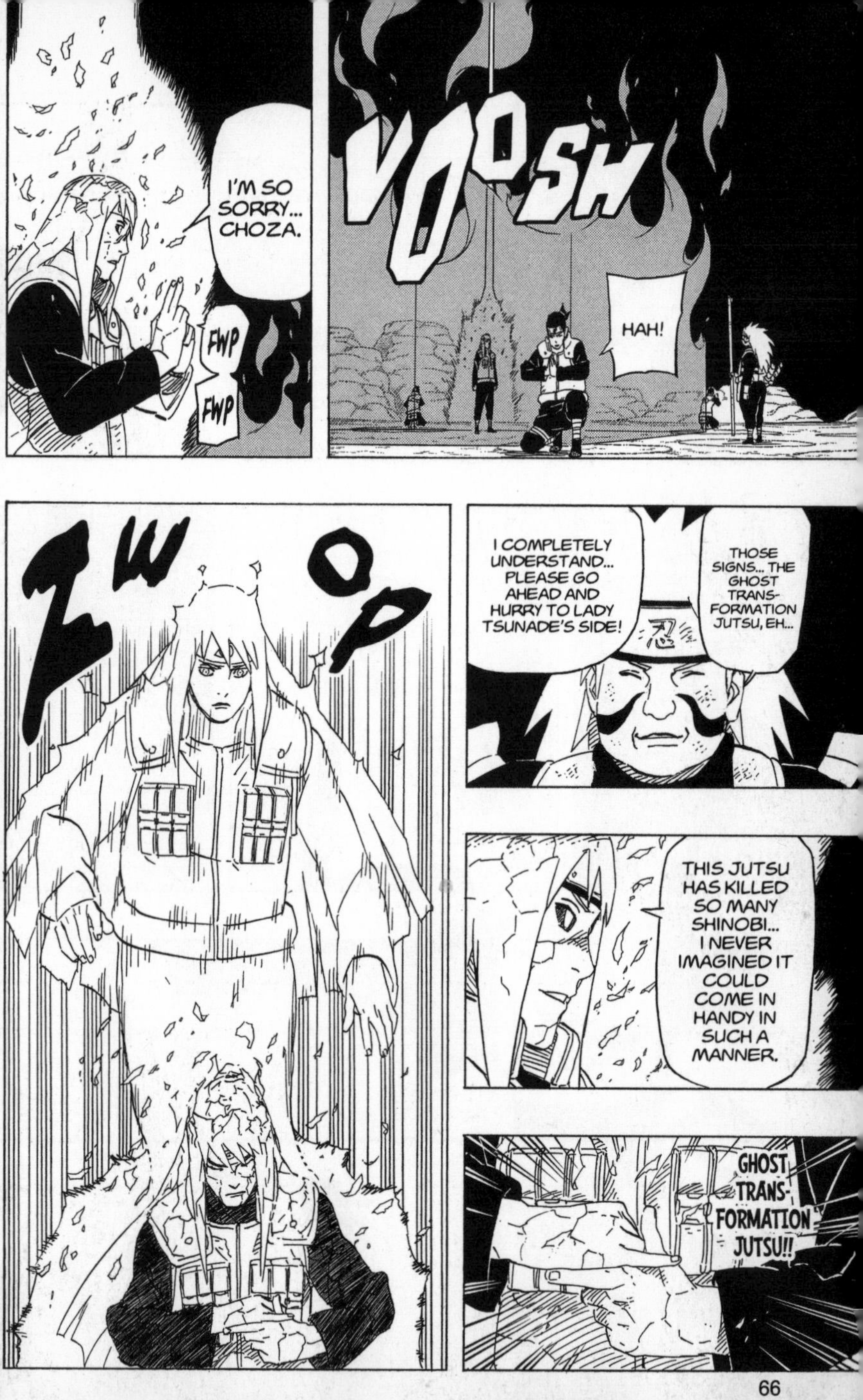
VOOSH
HAH!
I'M SO SORRY... CHOZA.
FWP
FWP
THOSE SIGNS... THE GHOST TRANS-FORMATION JUTSU, EH...
I COMPLETELY UNDERSTAND... PLEASE GO AHEAD AND HURRY TO LADY TSUNADE'S SIDE!
THIS JUTSU HAS KILLED SO MANY SHINOBI... I NEVER IMAGINED IT COULD COME IN HANDY IN SUCH A MANNER.
GHOST TRANS-FORMATION JUTSU!!
ZWOP

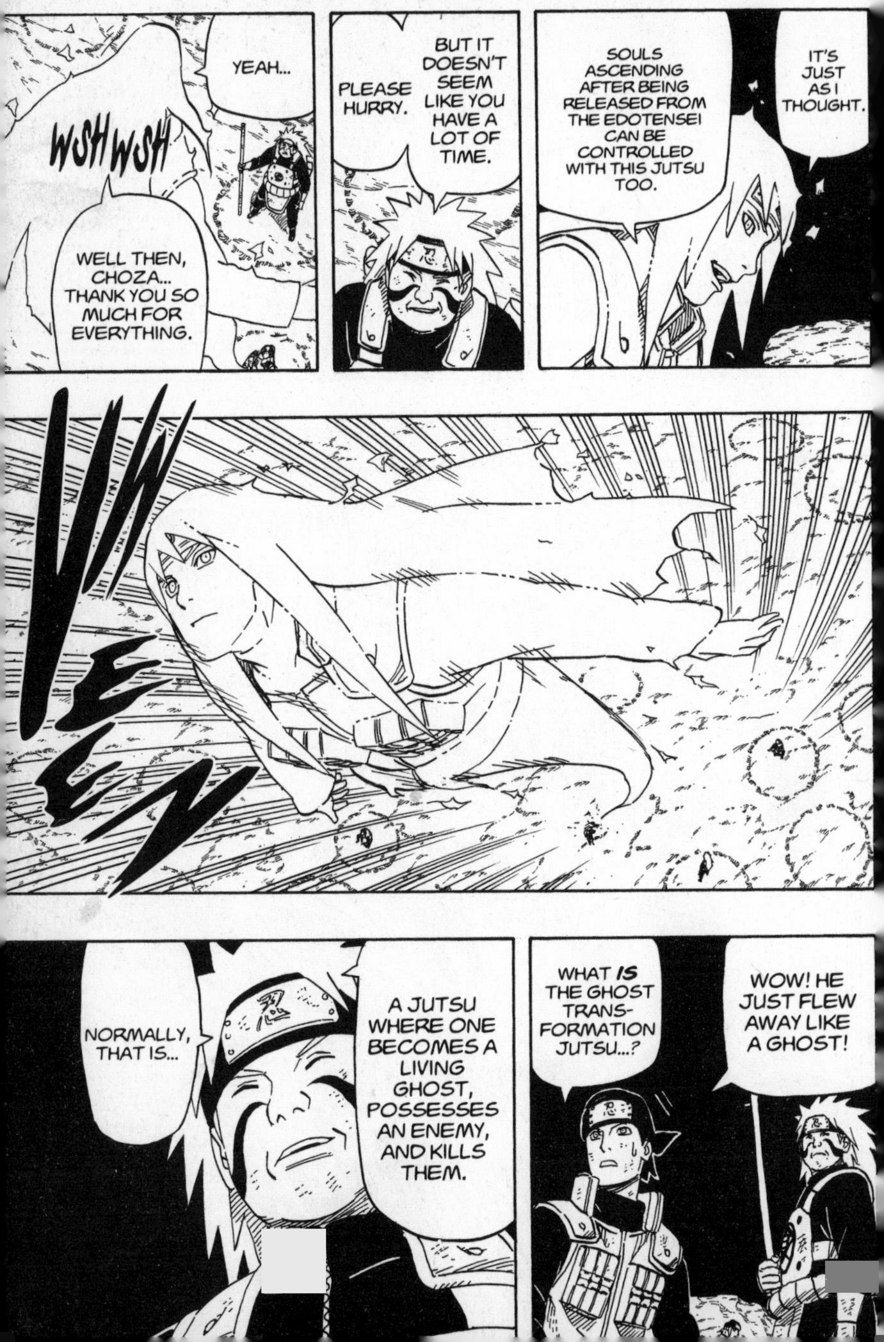
IT'S JUST AS I THOUGHT.
SOULS ASCENDING AFTER BEING RELEASED FROM THE EDOTENSEI CAN BE CONTROLLED WITH THIS JUTSU TOO.
BUT IT DOESN'T SEEM LIKE YOU HAVE A LOT OF TIME.
PLEASE HURRY.
YEAH...
WSH WSH
WELL THEN, CHOZA... THANK YOU SO MUCH FOR EVERYTHING.
VWEEN
WOW! HE JUST FLEW AWAY LIKE A GHOST!
WHAT *IS* THE GHOST TRANSFORMATION JUTSU...?
A JUTSU WHERE ONE BECOMES A LIVING GHOST, POSSESSES AN ENEMY, AND KILLS THEM.
NORMALLY, THAT IS...

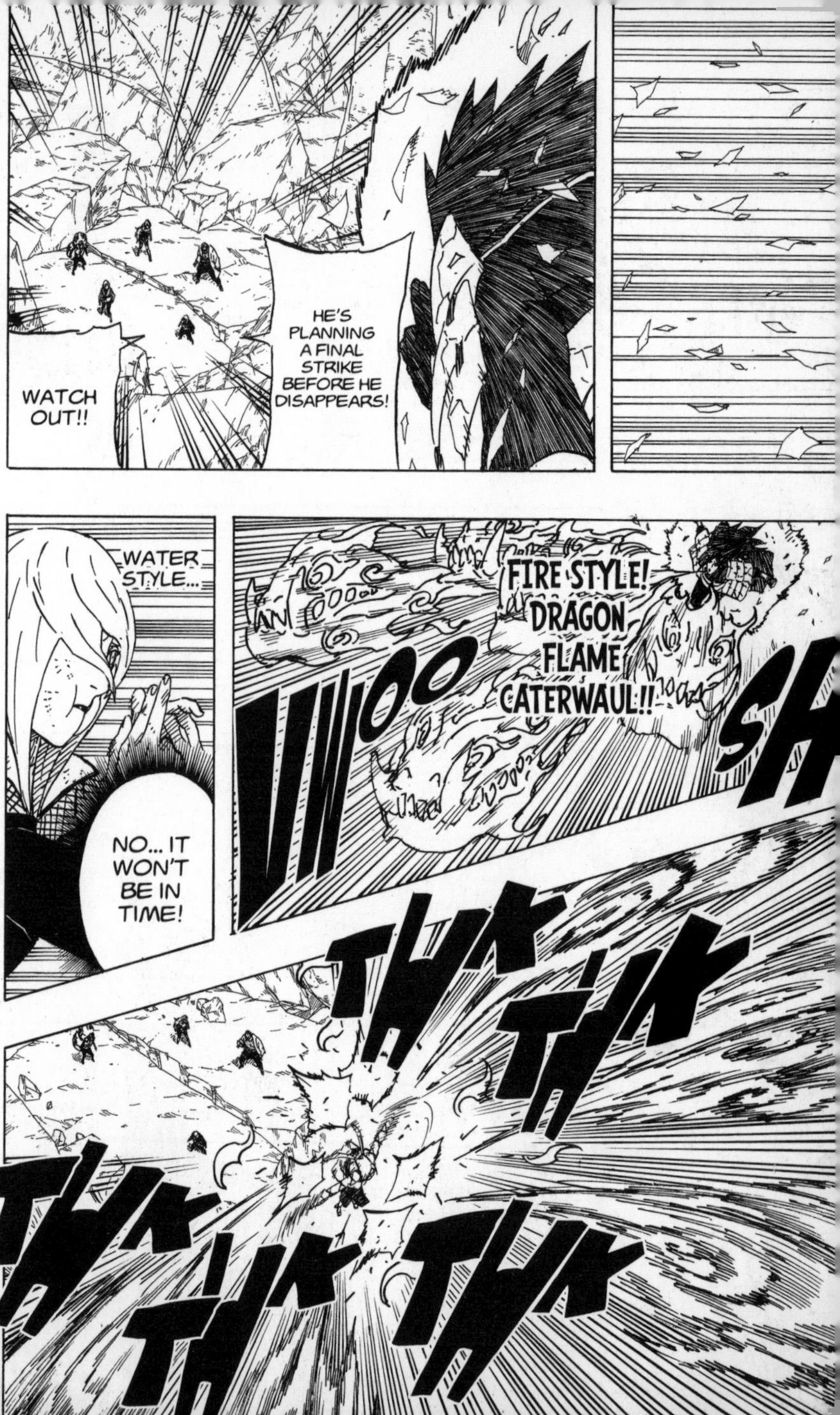
HE'S PLANNING A FINAL STRIKE BEFORE HE DISAPPEARS!
WATCH OUT!!
FIRE STYLE! DRAGON FLAME CATERWAUL!!
WATER STYLE...
NO... IT WON'T BE IN TIME!

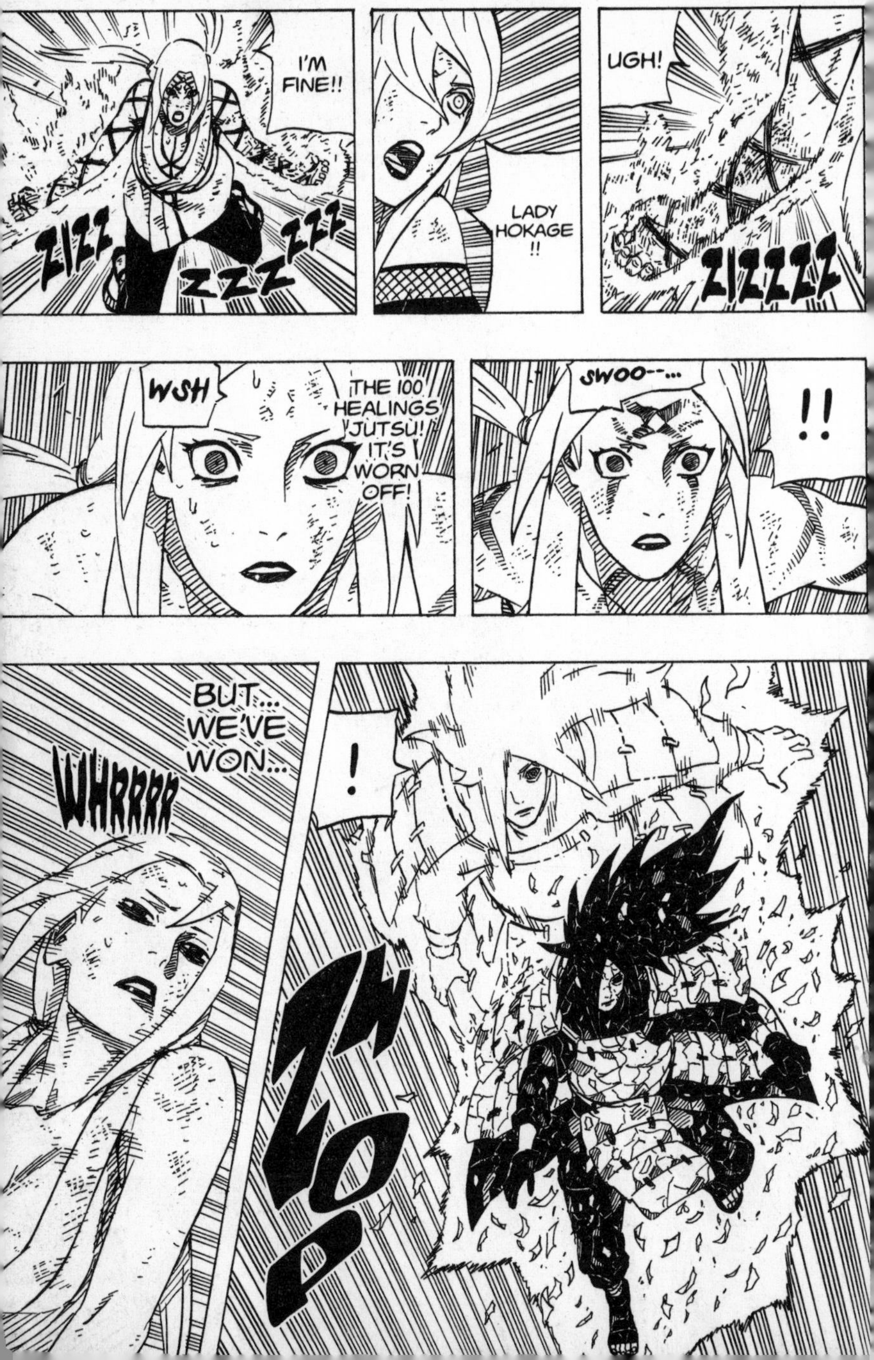
UGH!
ZIZZZZ
LADY HOKAGE!!
I'M FINE!!
ZIZZ
ZZZ
ZZZ
SWOO--...
!!
WSH
THE 100 HEALINGS JUTSU! IT'S WORN OFF!
!
BUT... WE'VE WON...
WHRRRR

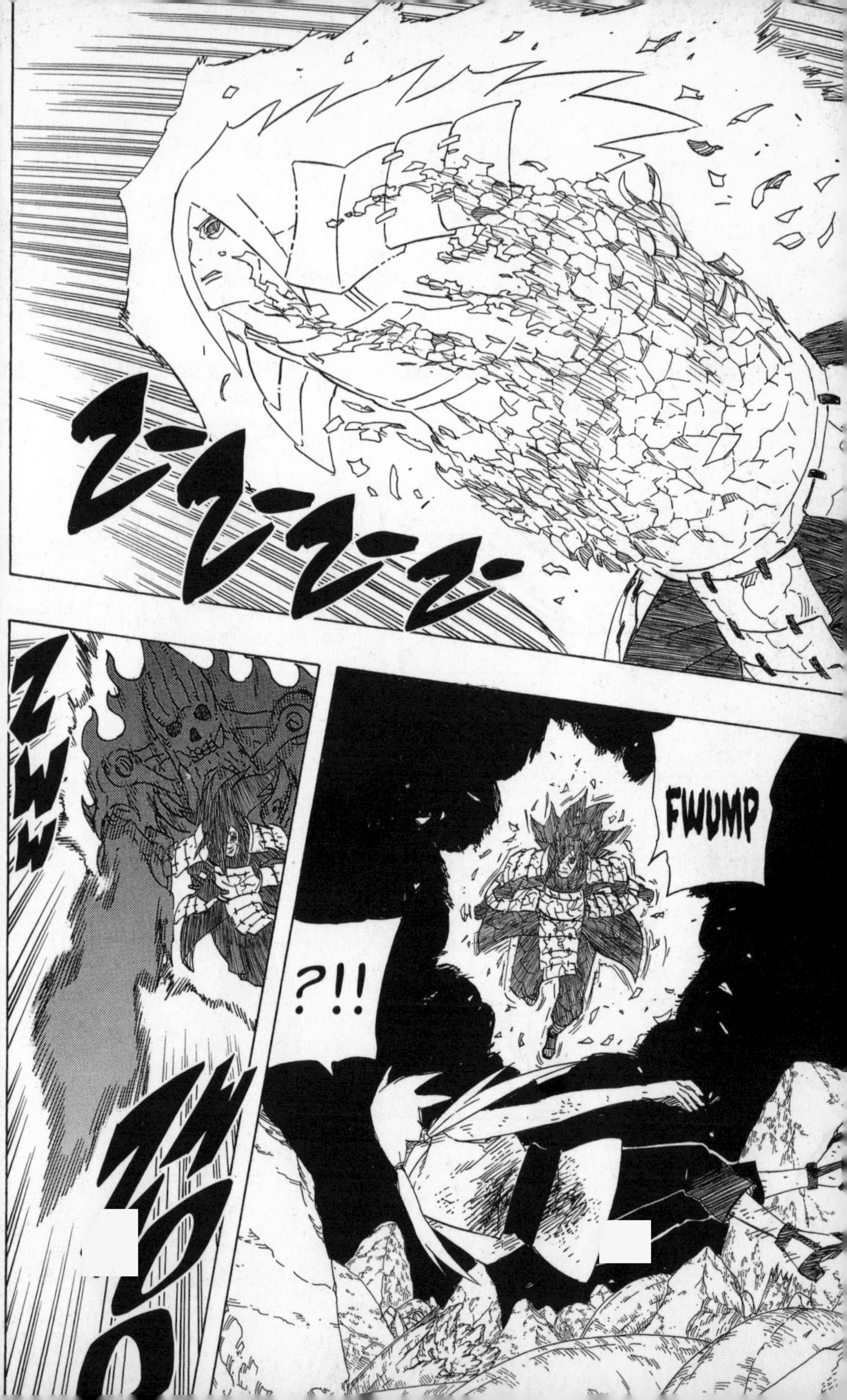
FWUMP
?!!

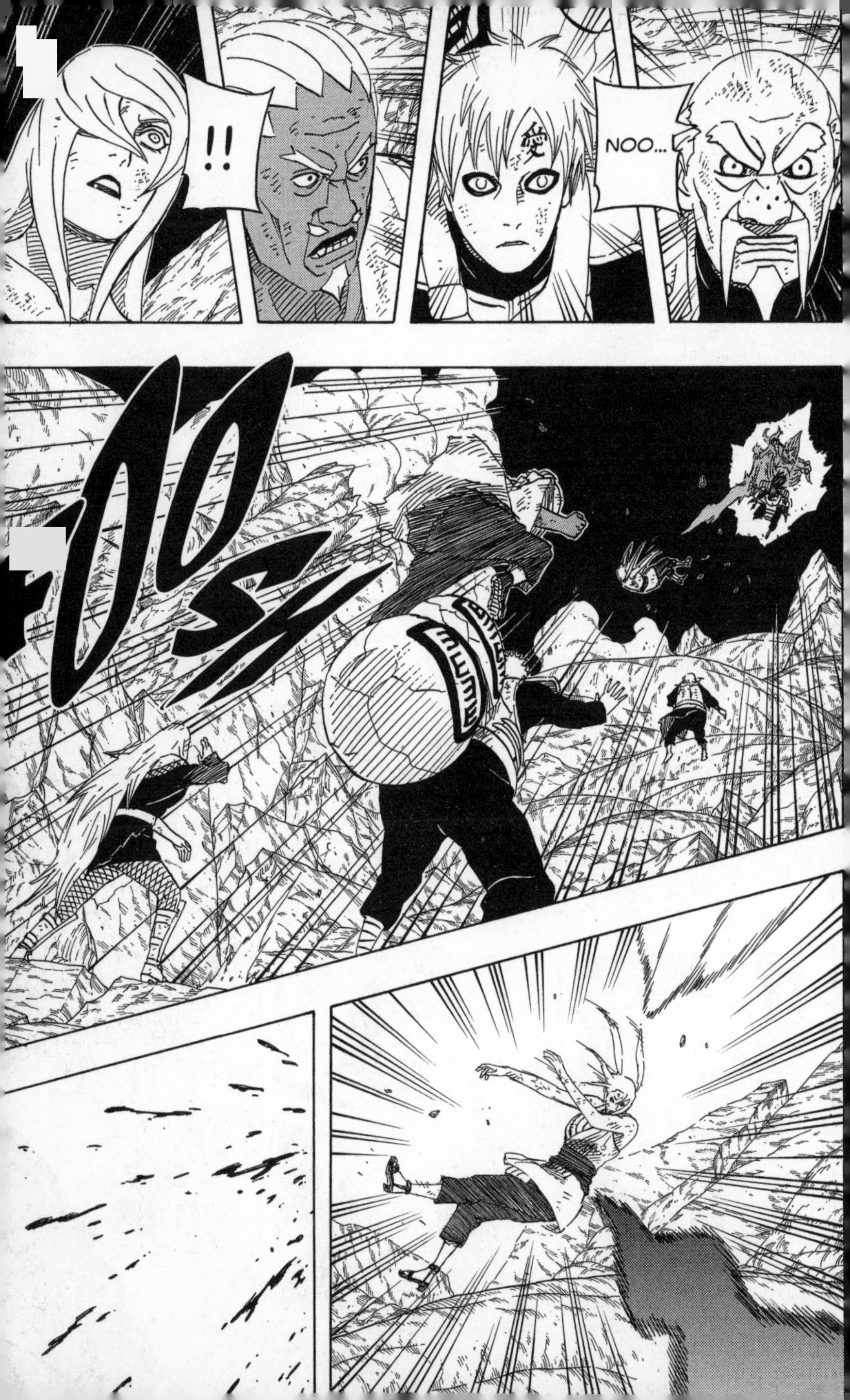
NOO...
!!

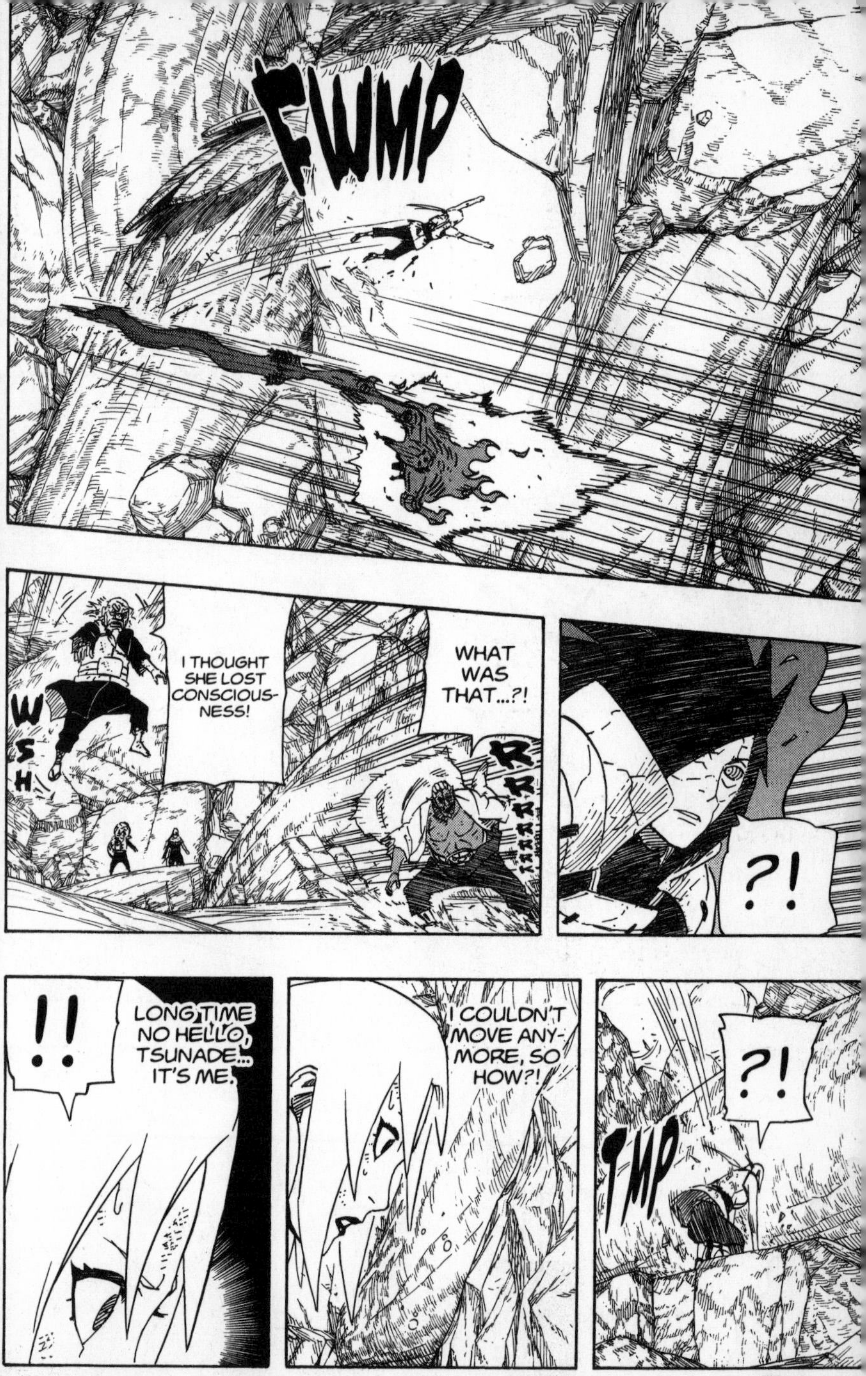
FWUMP
?!
WHAT WAS THAT...?!
RRRRRRR
I THOUGHT SHE LOST CONSCIOUS-NESS!
WSH
?!
TMP
I COULDN'T MOVE ANY-MORE, SO HOW?!
LONG TIME NO HELLO, TSUNADE... IT'S ME.
!!

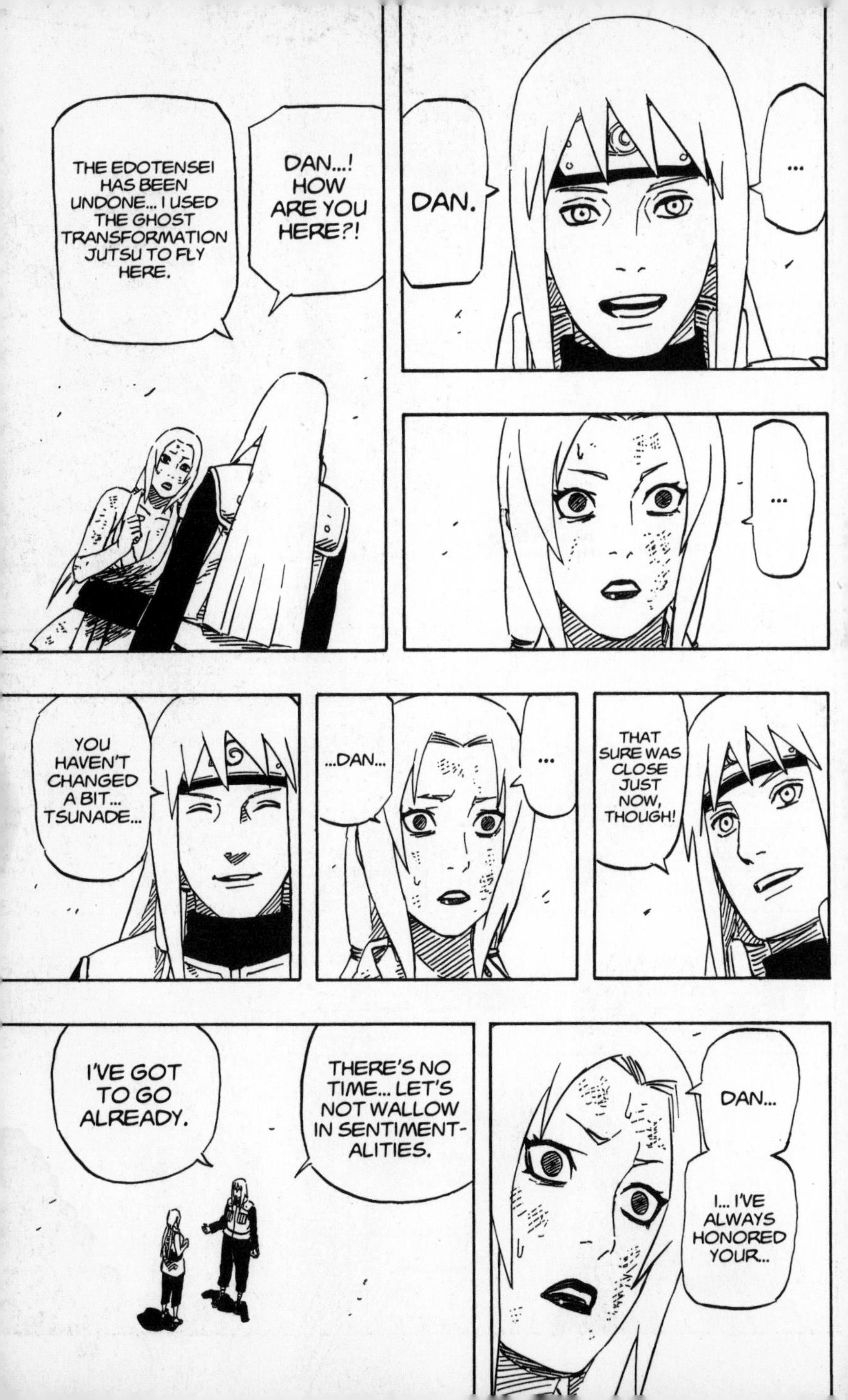
...
DAN.
...
DAN...! HOW ARE YOU HERE?!
THE EDOTENSEI HAS BEEN UNDONE... I USED THE GHOST TRANSFORMATION JUTSU TO FLY HERE.
THAT SURE WAS CLOSE JUST NOW, THOUGH!
...
...DAN...
YOU HAVEN'T CHANGED A BIT... TSUNADE...
DAN...
I... I'VE ALWAYS HONORED YOUR...
THERE'S NO TIME... LET'S NOT WALLOW IN SENTIMENT-ALITIES.
I'VE GOT TO GO ALREADY.

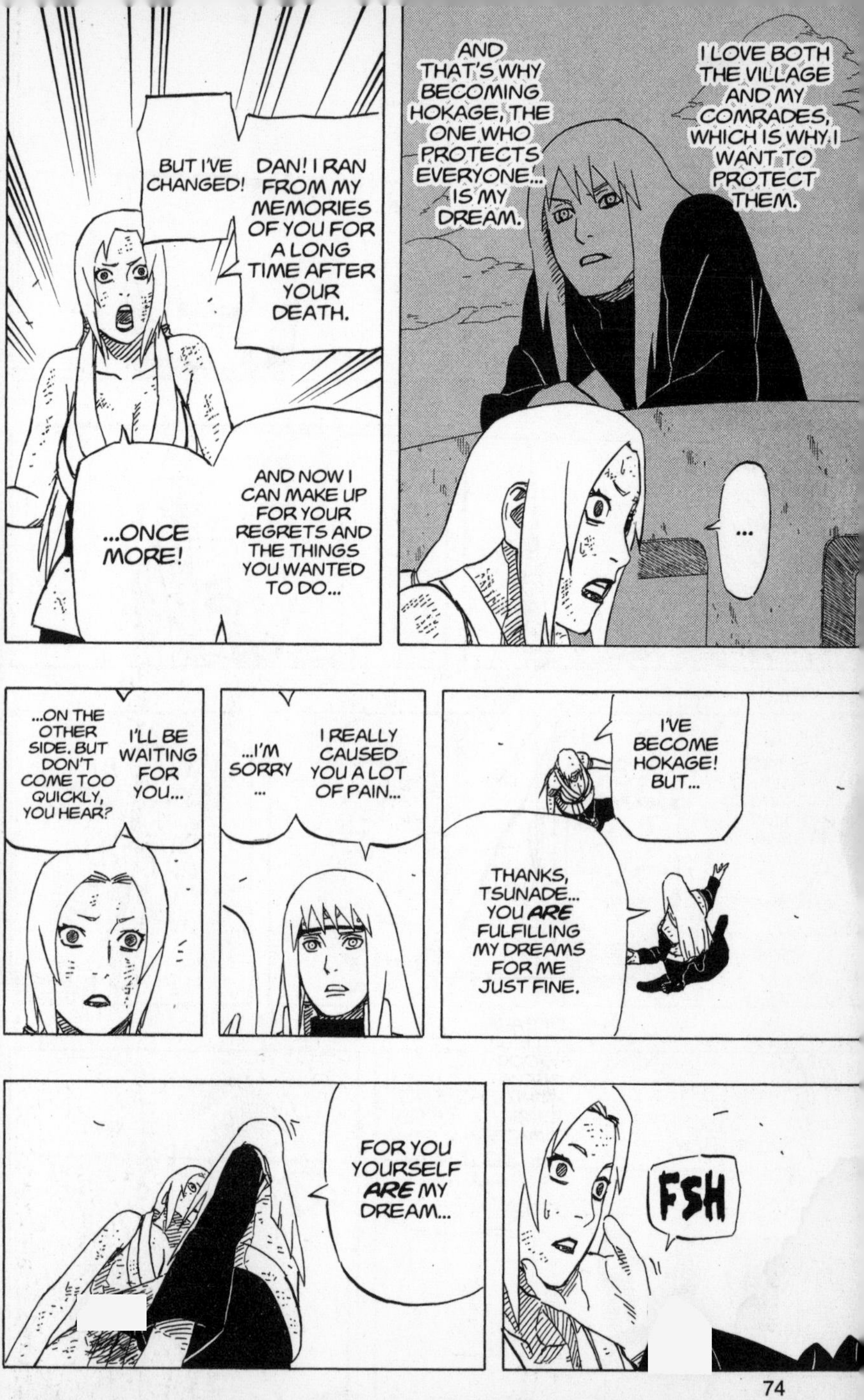
I LOVE BOTH THE VILLAGE AND MY COMRADES, WHICH IS WHY I WANT TO PROTECT THEM.
AND THAT'S WHY BECOMING HOKAGE, THE ONE WHO PROTECTS EVERYONE... IS MY DREAM.
...
DAN! I RAN FROM MY MEMORIES OF YOU FOR A LONG TIME AFTER YOUR DEATH.
BUT I'VE CHANGED!
AND NOW I CAN MAKE UP FOR YOUR REGRETS AND THE THINGS YOU WANTED TO DO...
...ONCE MORE!
I'VE BECOME HOKAGE! BUT...
THANKS, TSUNADE... YOU ***ARE*** FULFILLING MY DREAMS FOR ME JUST FINE.
I REALLY CAUSED YOU A LOT OF PAIN...
...I'M SORRY...
I'LL BE WAITING FOR YOU...
...ON THE OTHER SIDE. BUT DON'T COME TOO QUICKLY, YOU HEAR?
FSH
FOR YOU YOURSELF ***ARE*** MY DREAM...

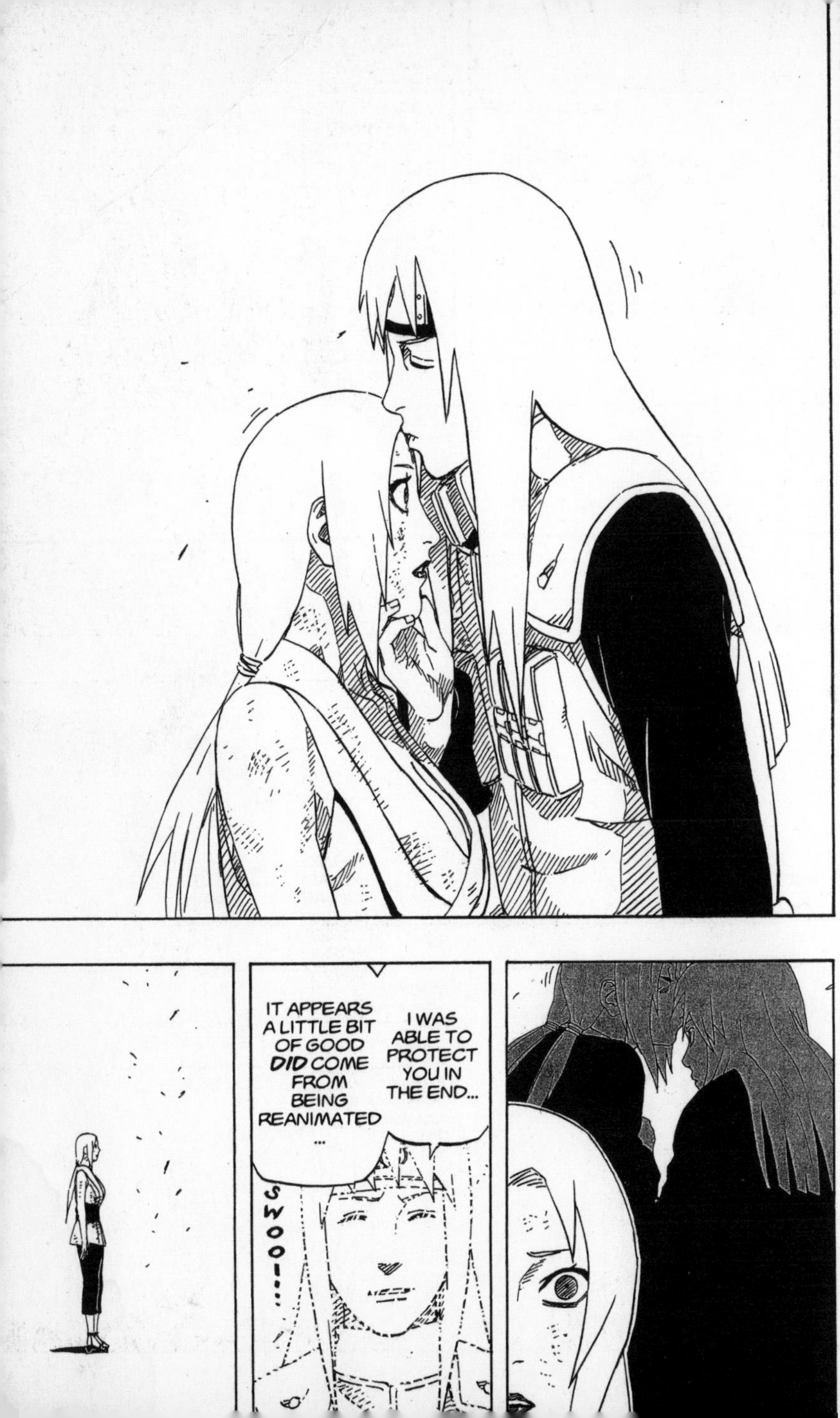
I WAS ABLE TO PROTECT YOU IN THE END...
IT APPEARS A LITTLE BIT OF GOOD DID COME FROM BEING REANIMATED ...
SWOO!...

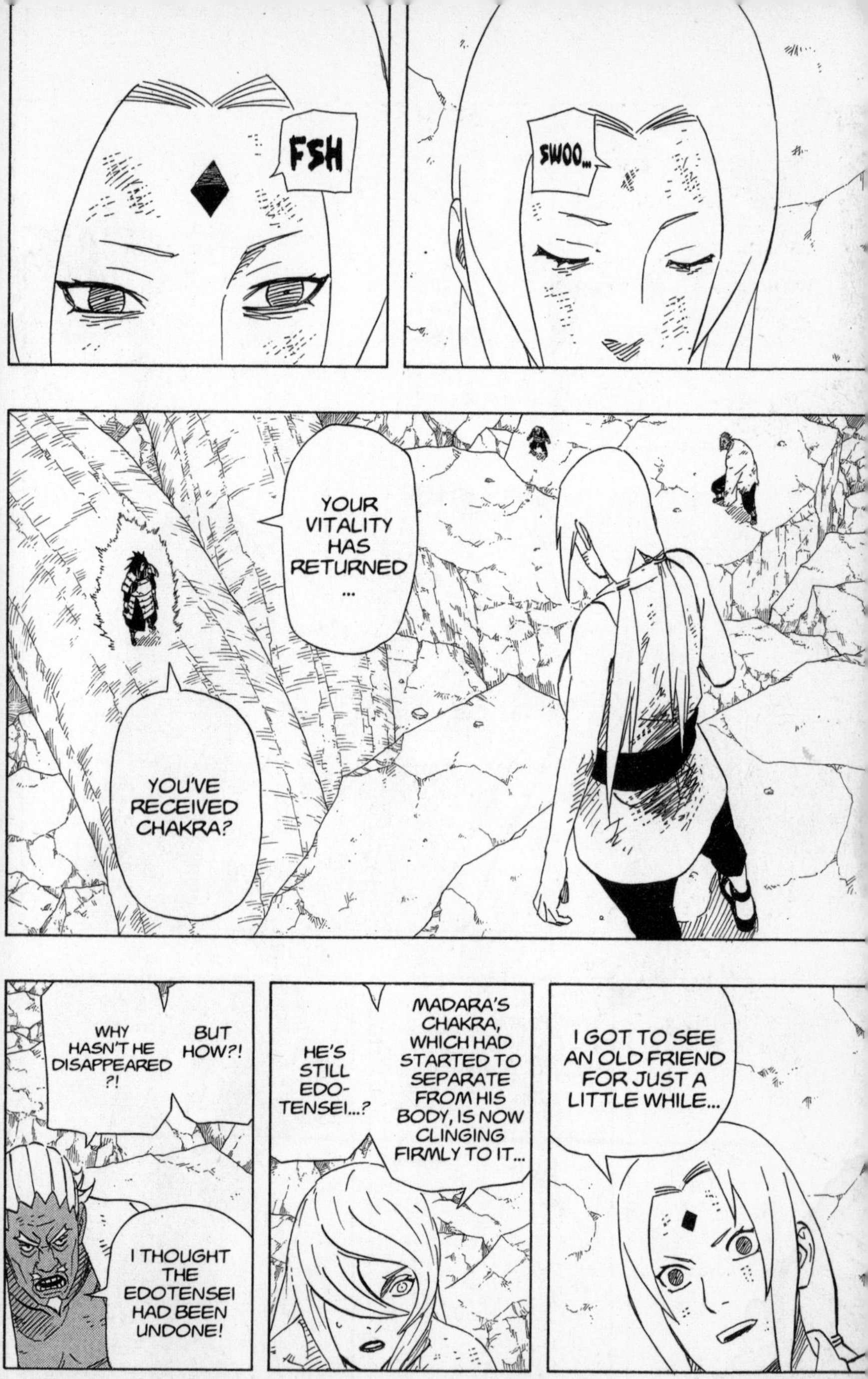
SWOO...
FSH
YOUR VITALITY HAS RETURNED...
YOU'VE RECEIVED CHAKRA?
I GOT TO SEE AN OLD FRIEND FOR JUST A LITTLE WHILE...
MADARA'S CHAKRA, WHICH HAD STARTED TO SEPARATE FROM HIS BODY, IS NOW CLINGING FIRMLY TO IT...
HE'S STILL EDO-TENSEI...?
BUT HOW?!
WHY HASN'T HE DISAPPEARED?!
I THOUGHT THE EDOTENSEI HAD BEEN UNDONE!

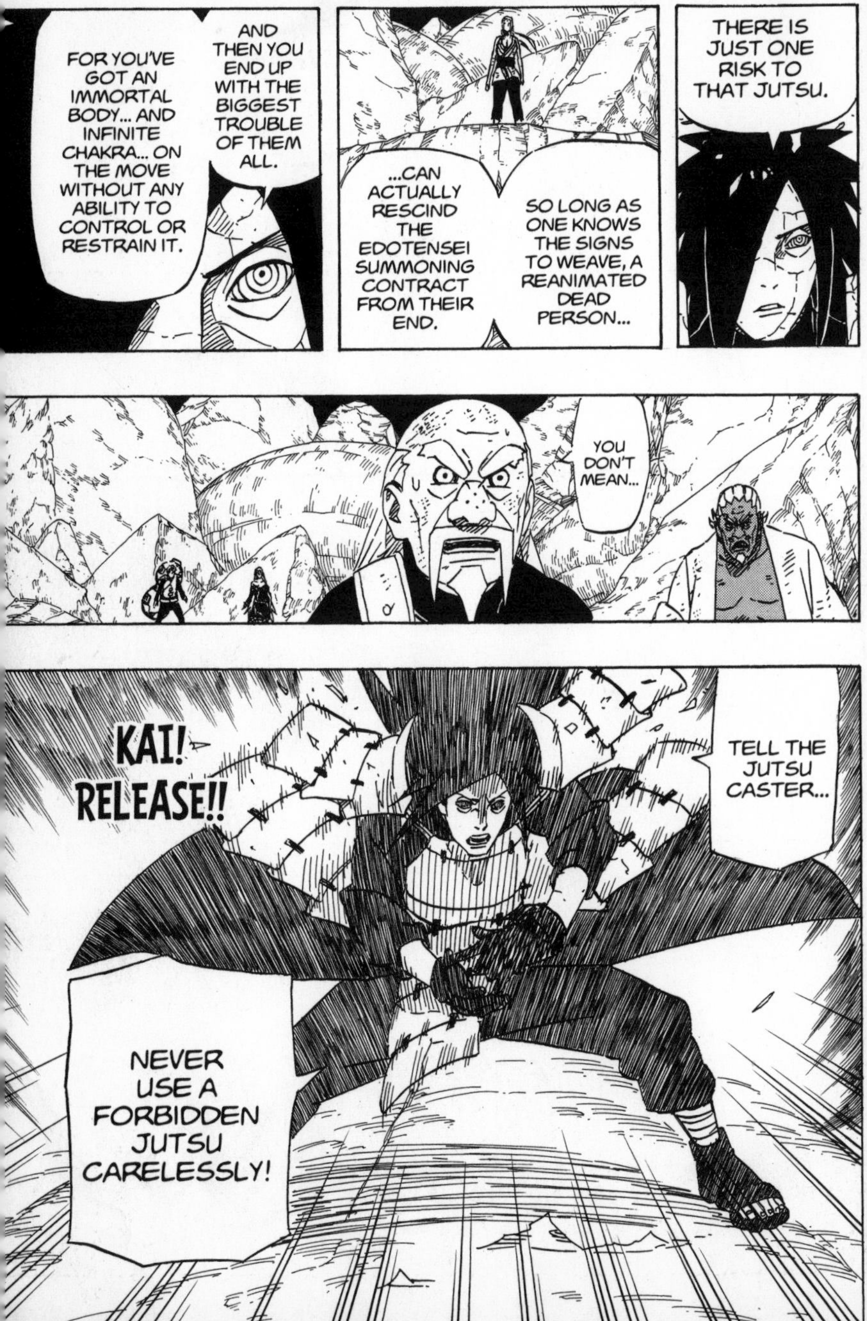

THERE IS JUST ONE RISK TO THAT JUTSU.
SO LONG AS ONE KNOWS THE SIGNS TO WEAVE, A REANIMATED DEAD PERSON...
...CAN ACTUALLY RESCIND THE EDOTENSEI SUMMONING CONTRACT FROM THEIR END.
AND THEN YOU END UP WITH THE BIGGEST TROUBLE OF THEM ALL.
FOR YOU'VE GOT AN IMMORTAL BODY... AND INFINITE CHAKRA... ON THE MOVE WITHOUT ANY ABILITY TO CONTROL OR RESTRAIN IT.
YOU DON'T MEAN...
TELL THE JUTSU CASTER...
KAI! RELEASE!!
NEVER USE A FORBIDDEN JUTSU CARELESSLY!

NARUTO

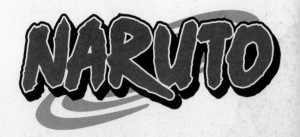

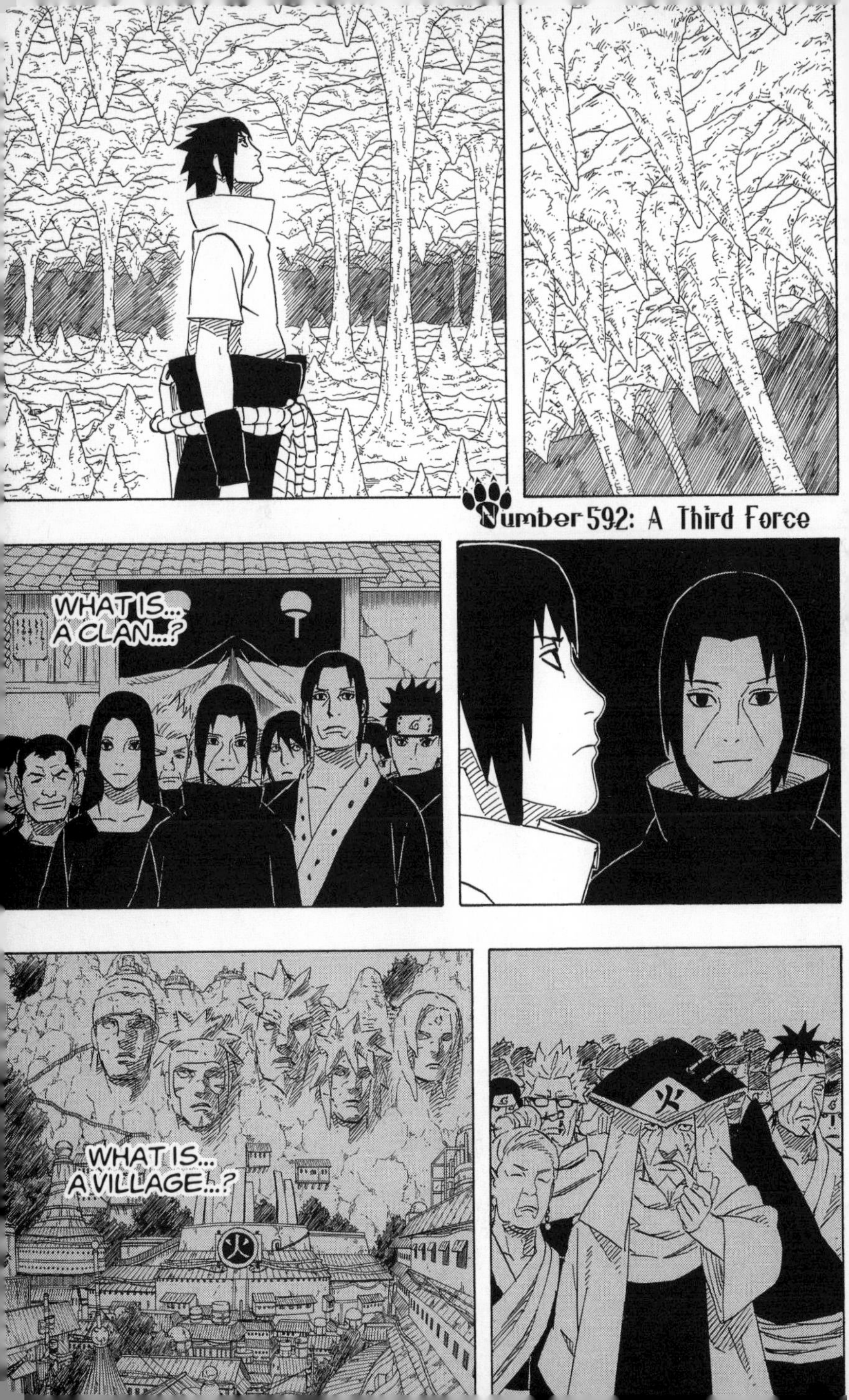
Number 592: A Third Force
WHAT IS... A CLAN...?
WHAT IS... A VILLAGE...?

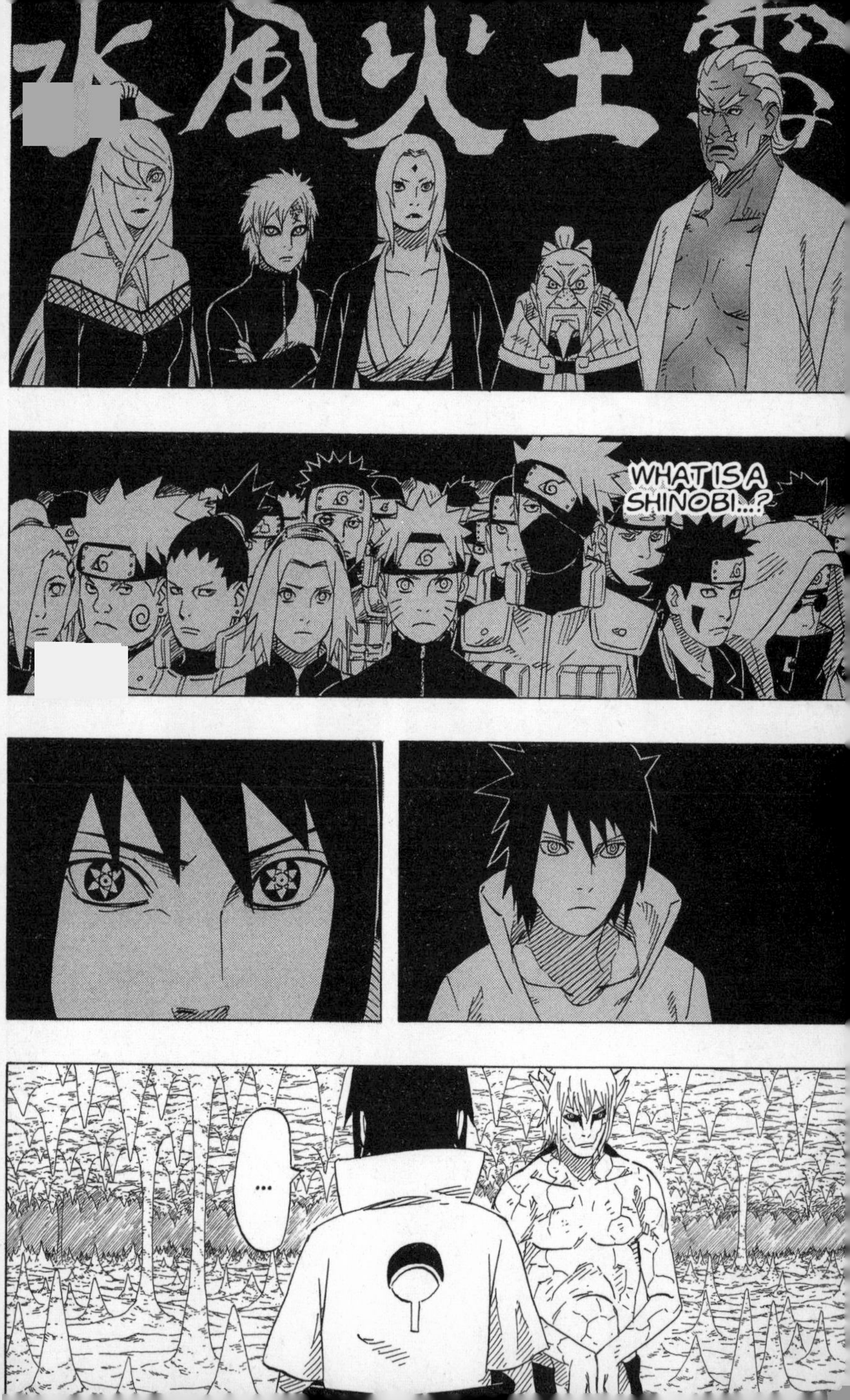
WHAT IS A SHINOBI...?
...

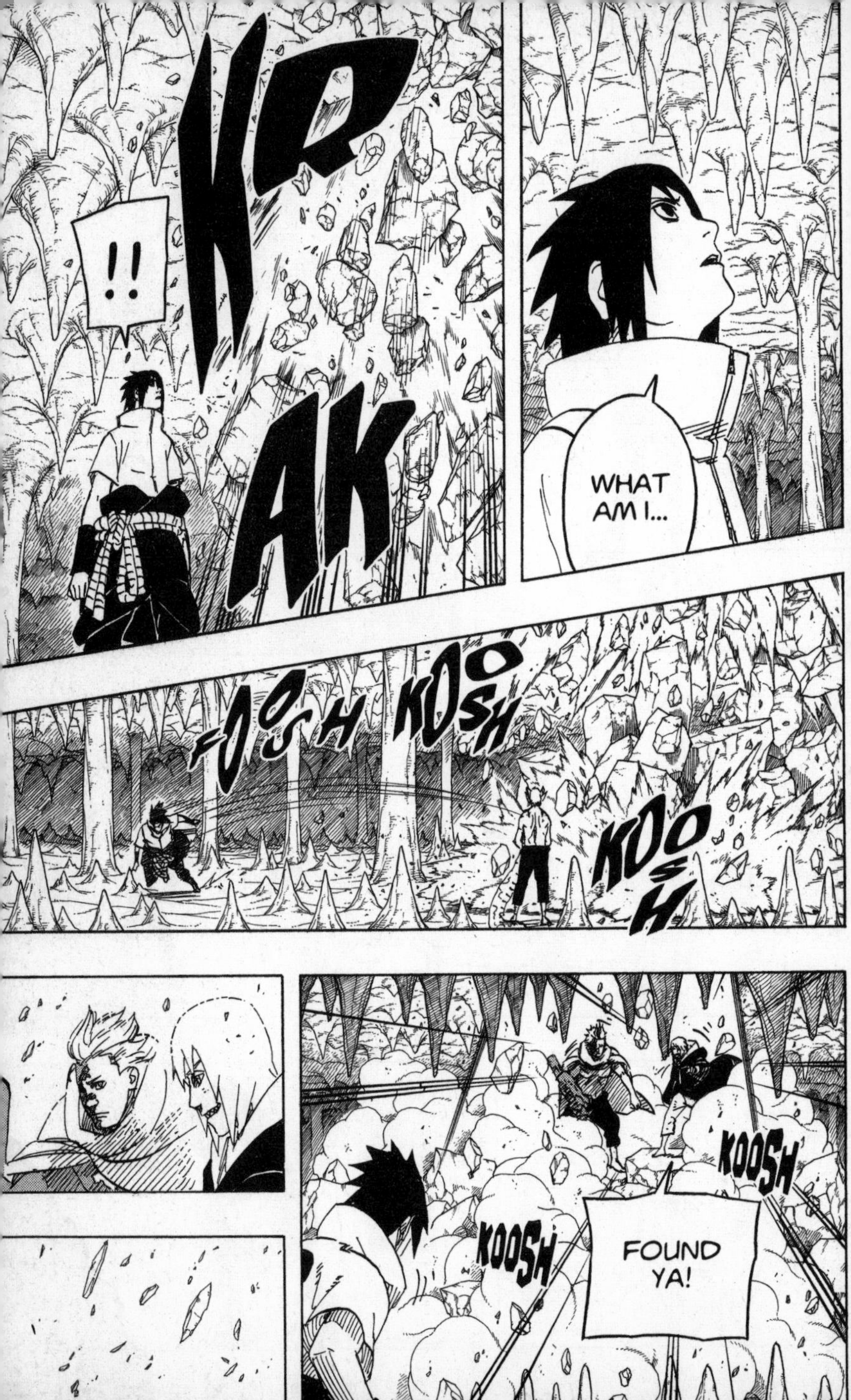
WHAT AM I...
KRAKAK
!!
KOOSH
KOOSH
FOOSH
KOOSH
FOUND YA!
KOOSH

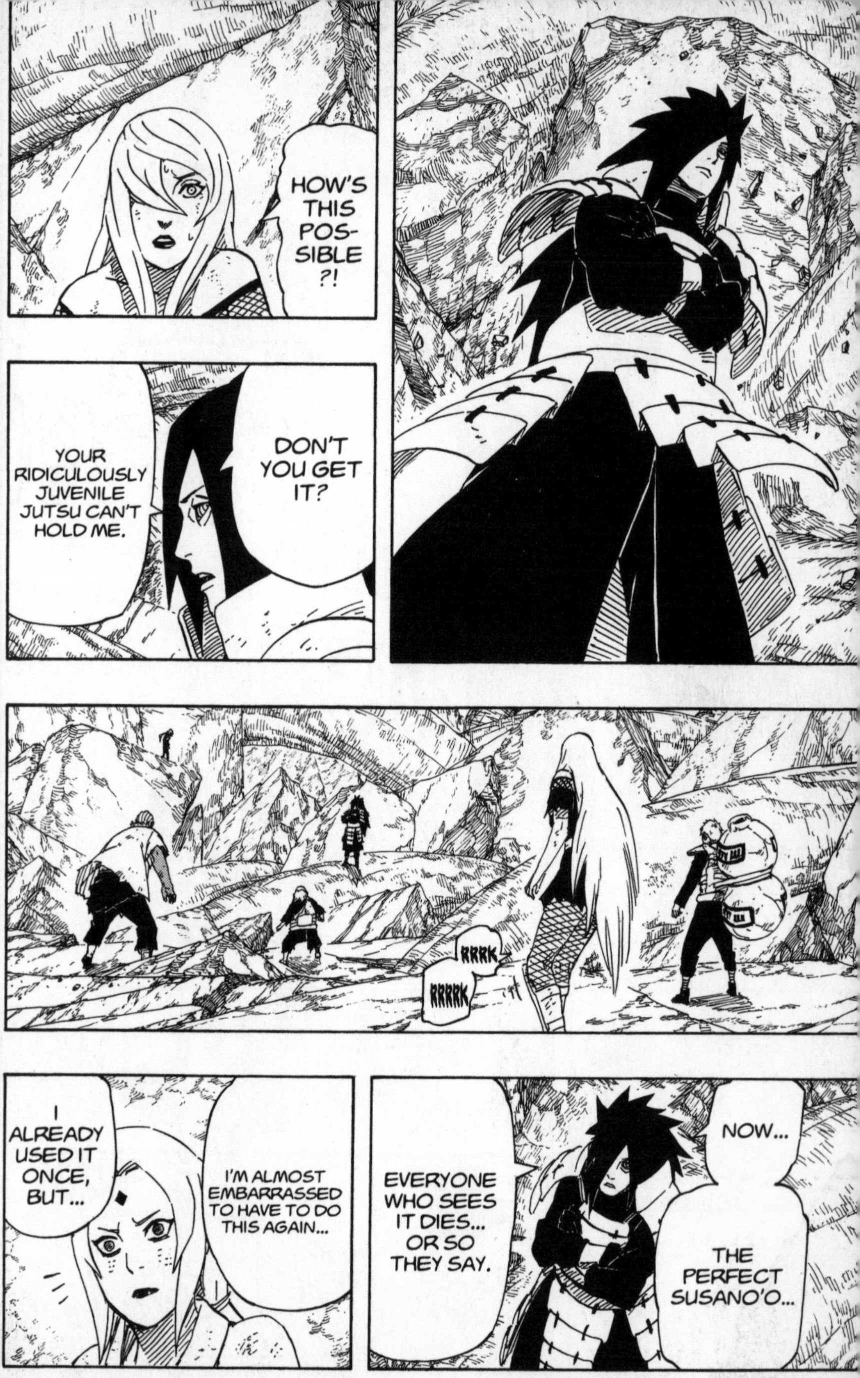
HOW'S THIS POSSIBLE?!
DON'T YOU GET IT?
YOUR RIDICULOUSLY JUVENILE JUTSU CAN'T HOLD ME.
RRRK
RRRRK
NOW...
THE PERFECT SUSANO'O...
EVERYONE WHO SEES IT DIES... OR SO THEY SAY.
I'M ALMOST EMBARRASSED TO HAVE TO DO THIS AGAIN...
I ALREADY USED IT ONCE, BUT...

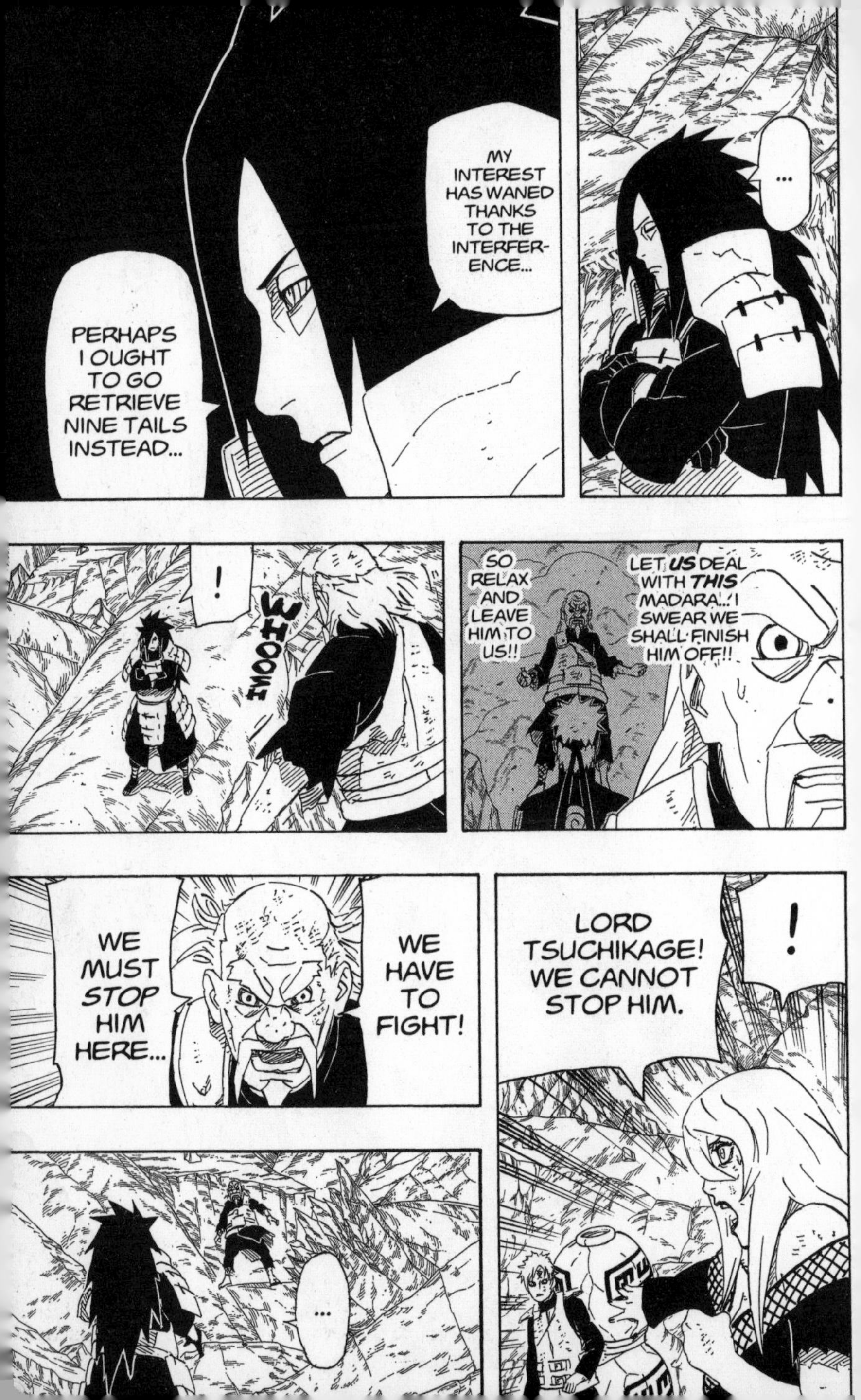
...
MY INTEREST HAS WANED THANKS TO THE INTERFERENCE...
PERHAPS I OUGHT TO GO RETRIEVE NINE TAILS INSTEAD...
LET **US** DEAL WITH **THIS** MADARA...! I SWEAR WE SHALL FINISH HIM OFF!!
SO RELAX AND LEAVE HIM TO US!!
!
WHOOSH
!
LORD TSUCHIKAGE! WE CANNOT STOP HIM.
WE HAVE TO FIGHT!
WE MUST *STOP* HIM HERE...
...

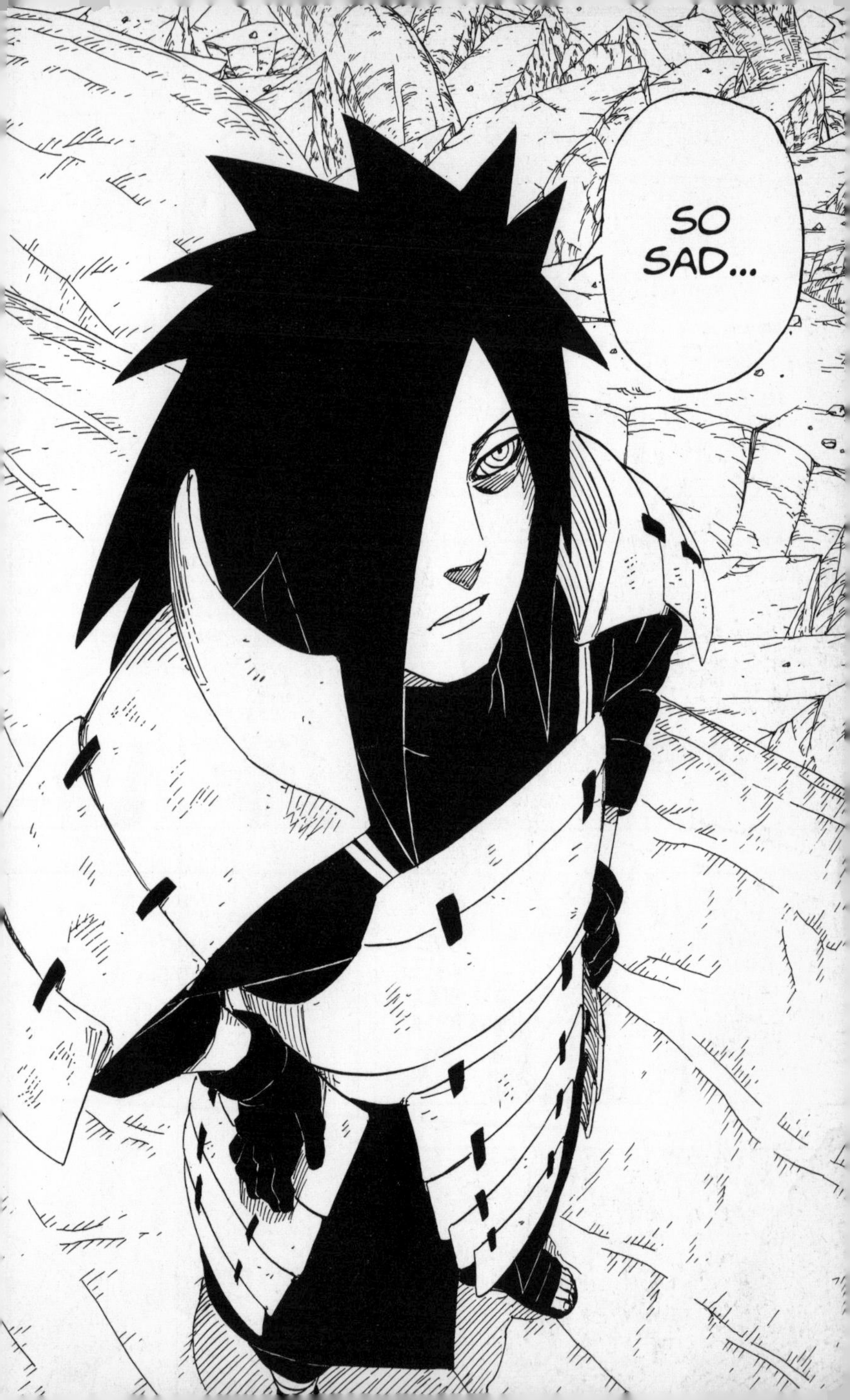
SO SAD...

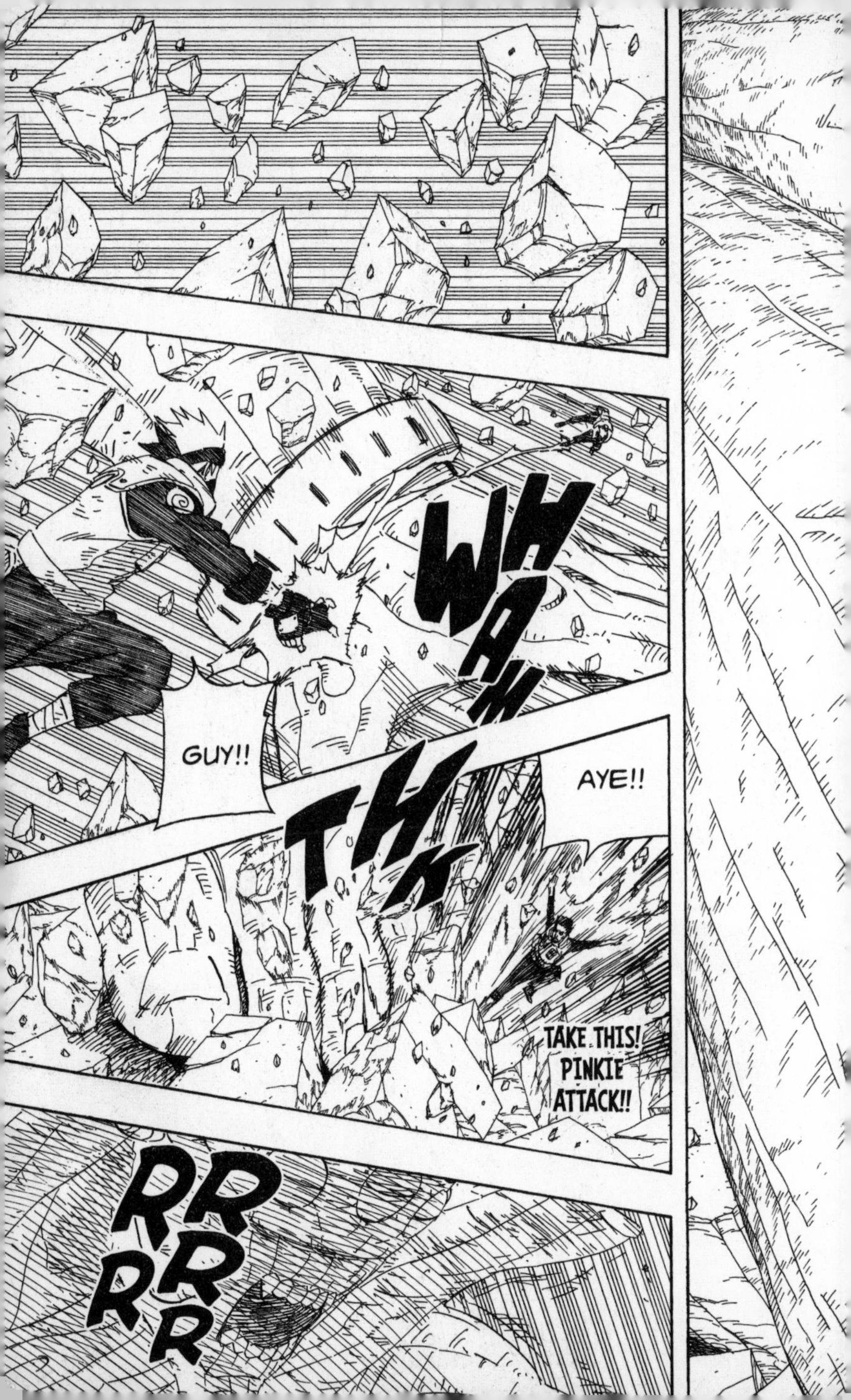
WHAM
GUY!!
AYE!!
TAKE THIS! PINKIE ATTACK!!
THK
RRRRR

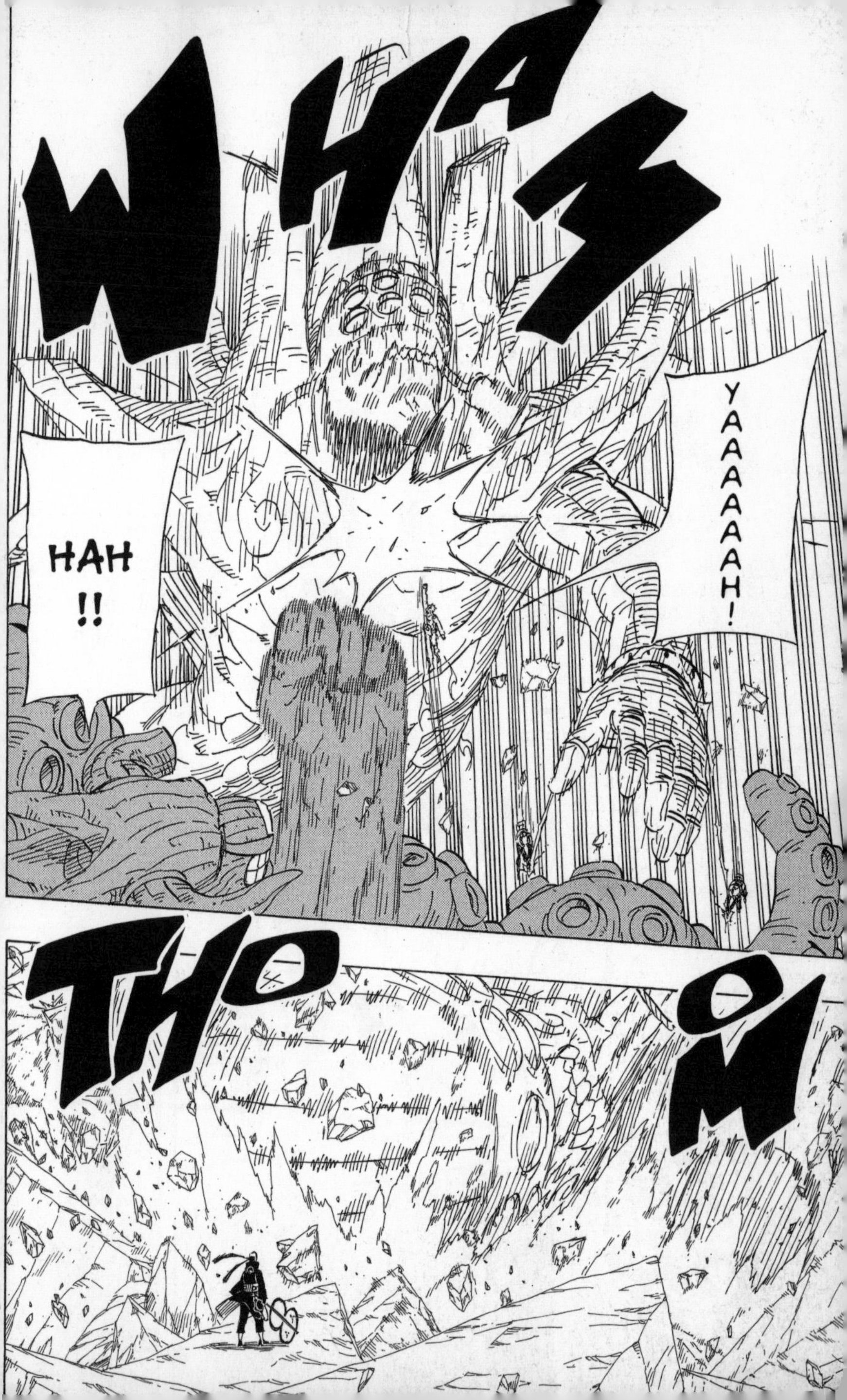
WHAM
YAAAAAAAH!
HAH !!
THOOM

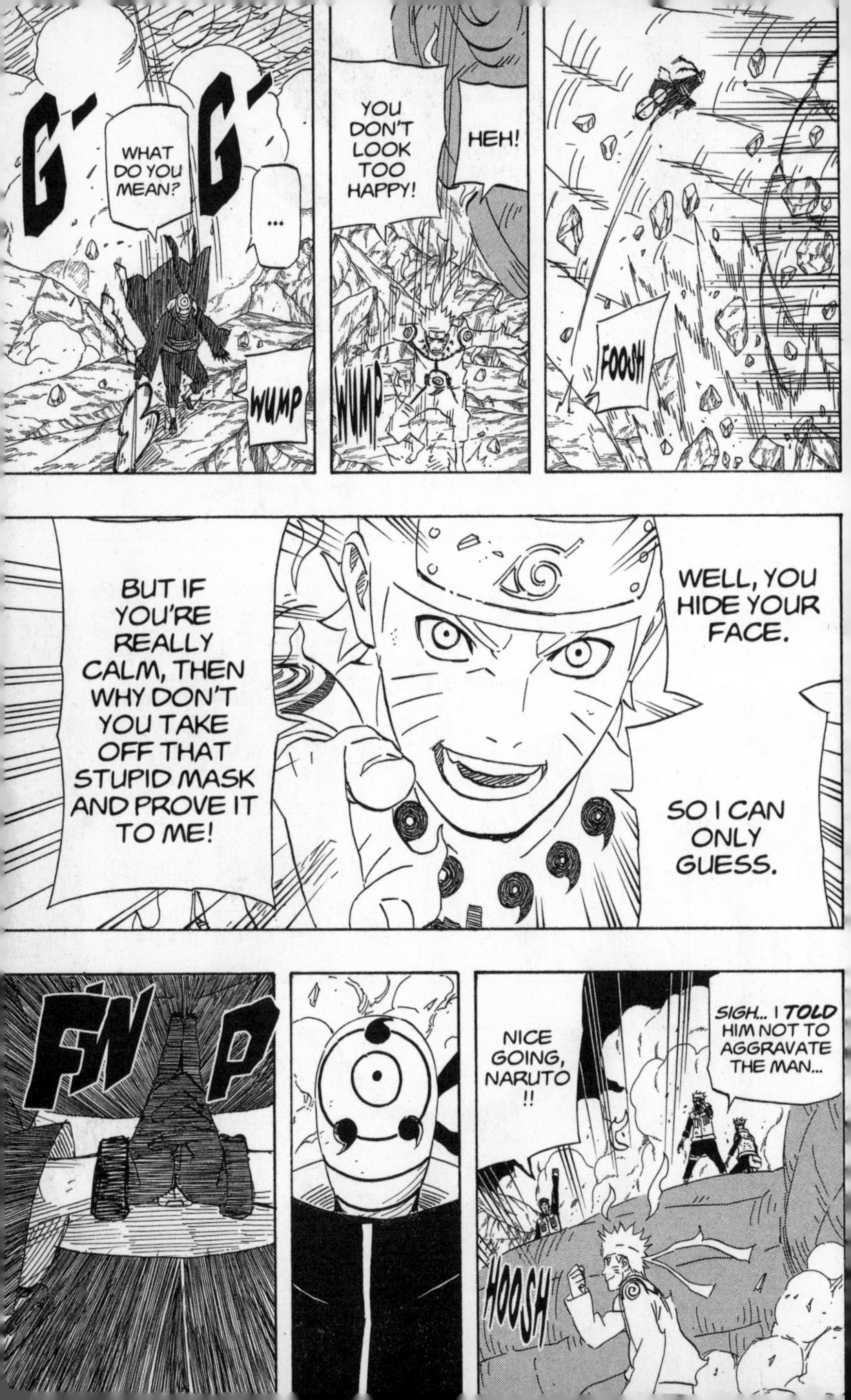
FOOSH
HEH!
YOU DON'T LOOK TOO HAPPY!
WUMP
...
WHAT DO YOU MEAN?
G- G-
WUMP
WELL, YOU HIDE YOUR FACE.
SO I CAN ONLY GUESS.
BUT IF YOU'RE REALLY CALM, THEN WHY DON'T YOU TAKE OFF THAT STUPID MASK AND PROVE IT TO ME!
SIGH... I **TOLD** HIM NOT TO AGGRAVATE THE MAN...
NICE GOING, NARUTO!!
HOOSH
FWIP

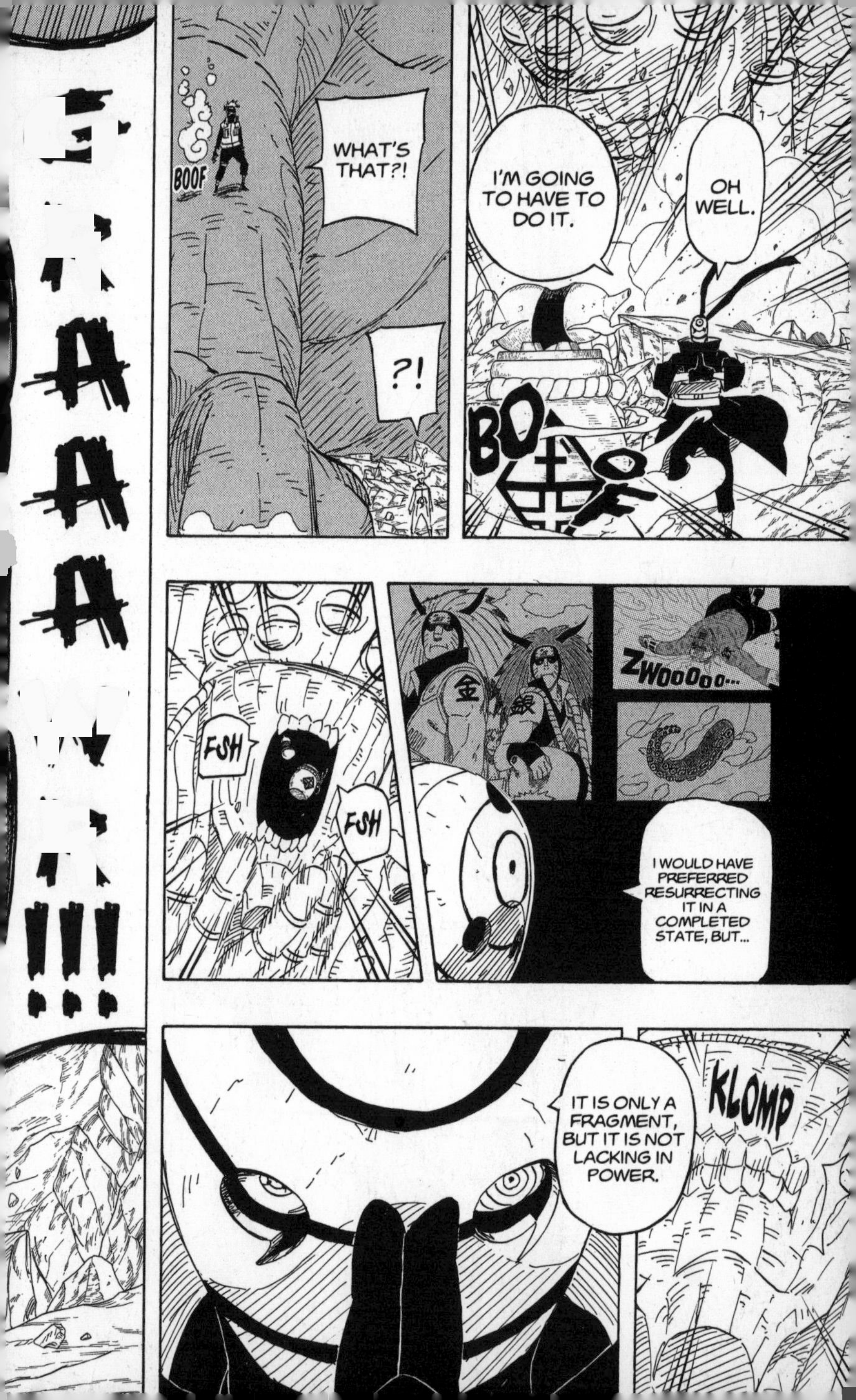
OH WELL.
I'M GOING TO HAVE TO DO IT.
BOOF
WHAT'S THAT?!
?!
BOOF
ZWOOOOOO...
I WOULD HAVE PREFERRED RESURRECTING IT IN A COMPLETED STATE, BUT...
金
銀
FSH
FSH
KLOMP
IT IS ONLY A FRAGMENT, BUT IT IS NOT LACKING IN POWER.

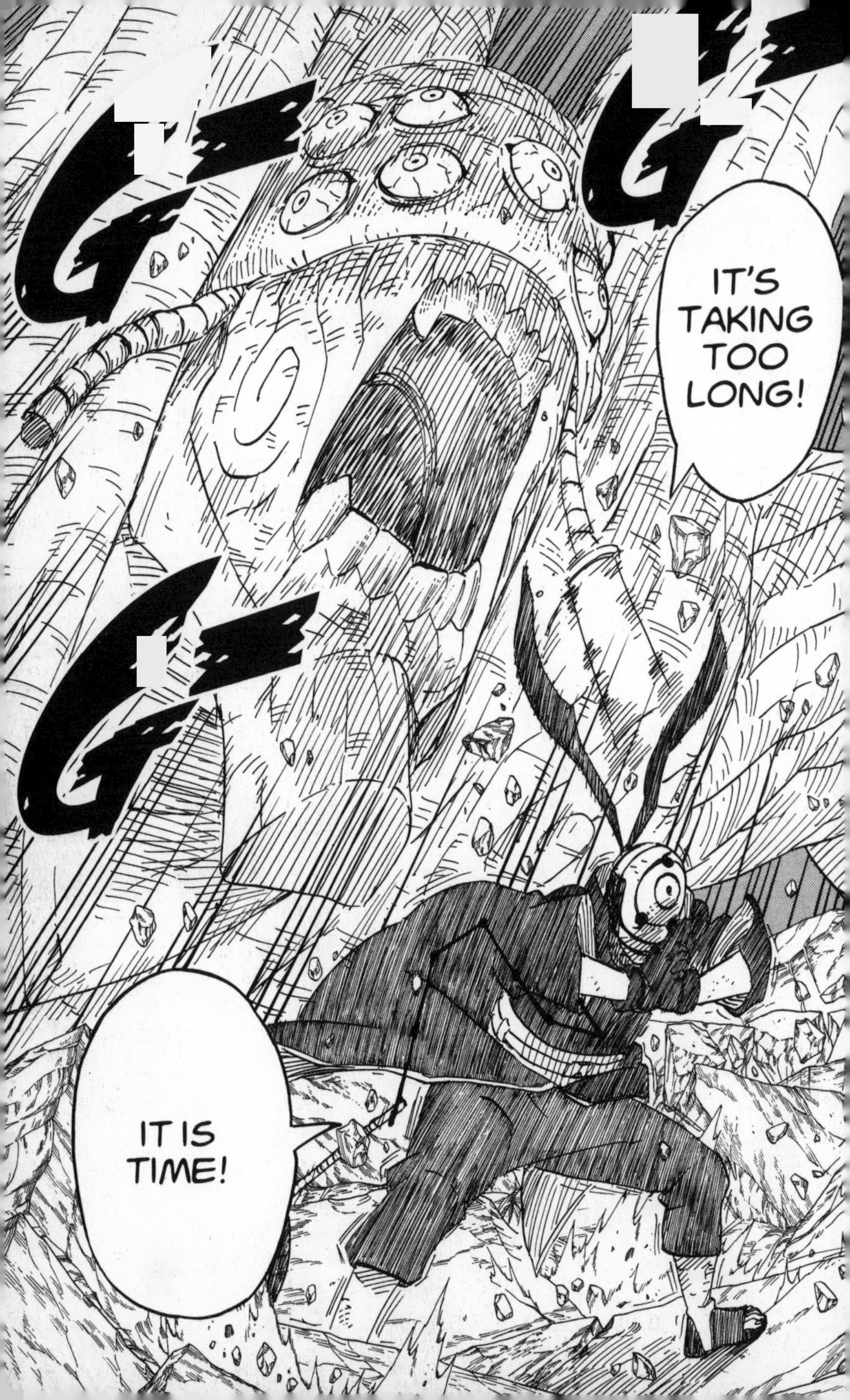
IT'S TAKING TOO LONG!
IT IS TIME!

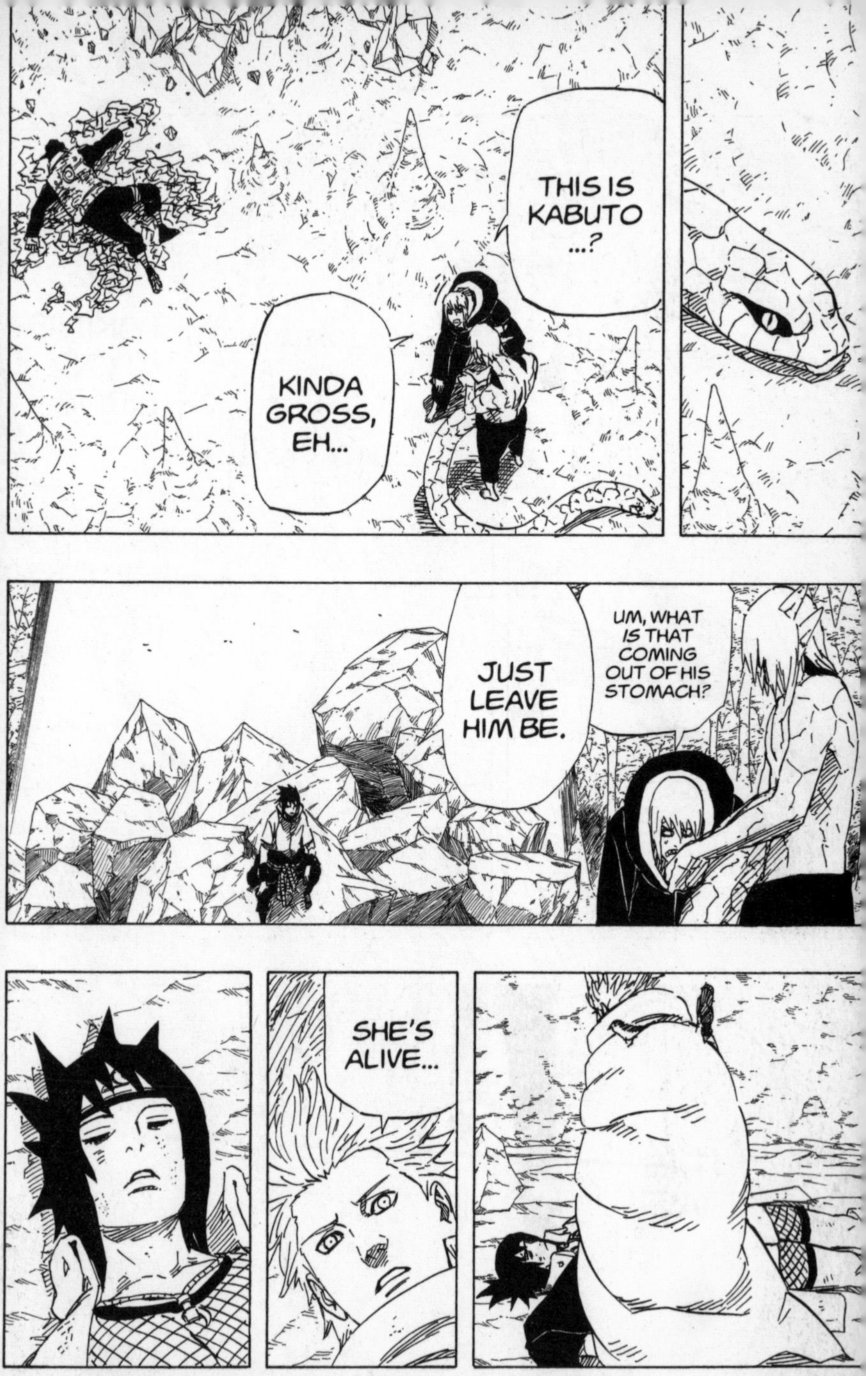
THIS IS KABUTO ...?
KINDA GROSS, EH...
UM, WHAT IS THAT COMING OUT OF HIS STOMACH?
JUST LEAVE HIM BE.
SHE'S ALIVE...

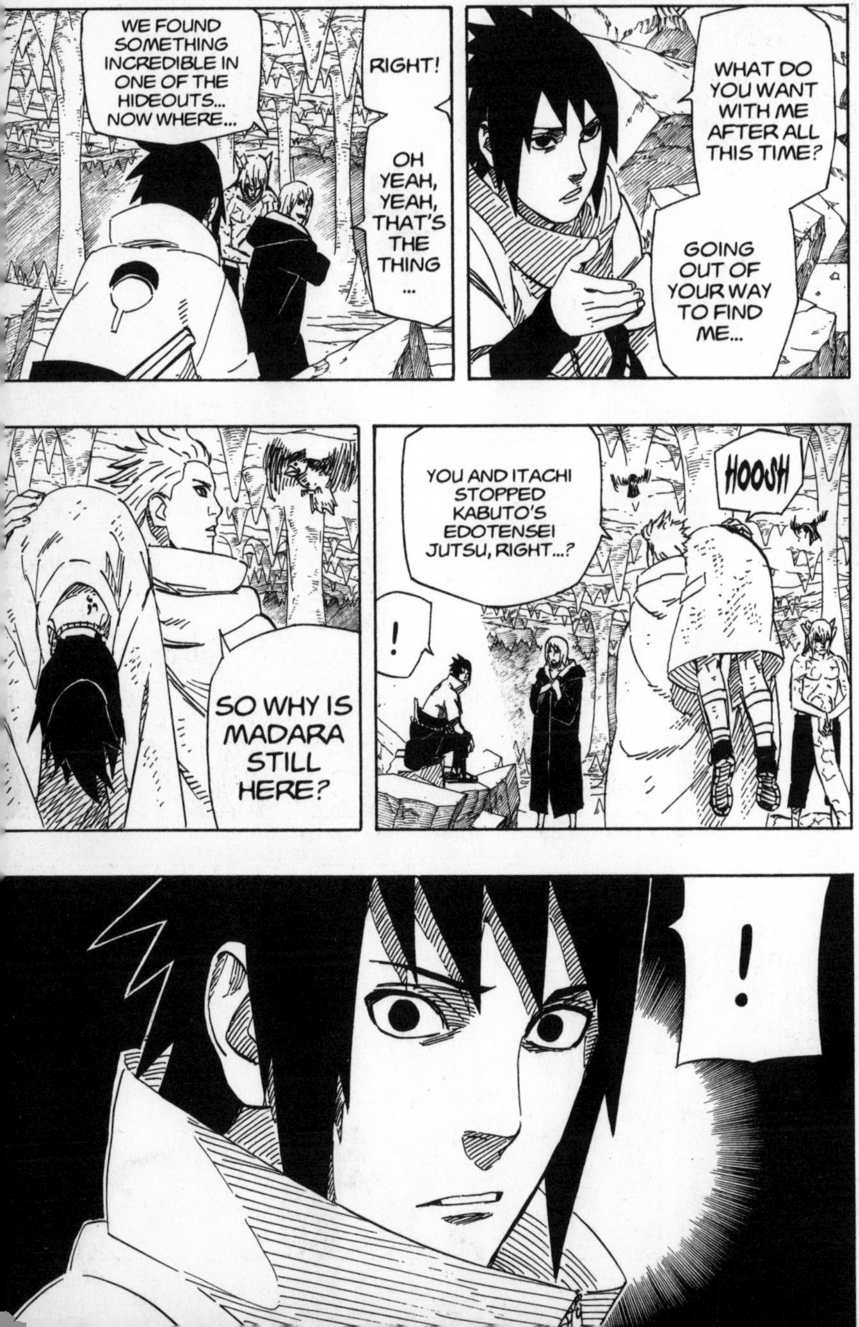
WHAT DO YOU WANT WITH ME AFTER ALL THIS TIME?
GOING OUT OF YOUR WAY TO FIND ME...
RIGHT!
OH YEAH, YEAH, THAT'S THE THING ...
WE FOUND SOMETHING INCREDIBLE IN ONE OF THE HIDEOUTS... NOW WHERE...
HOOSH
YOU AND ITACHI STOPPED KABUTO'S EDOTENSEI JUTSU, RIGHT...?
!
SO WHY IS MADARA STILL HERE?
!

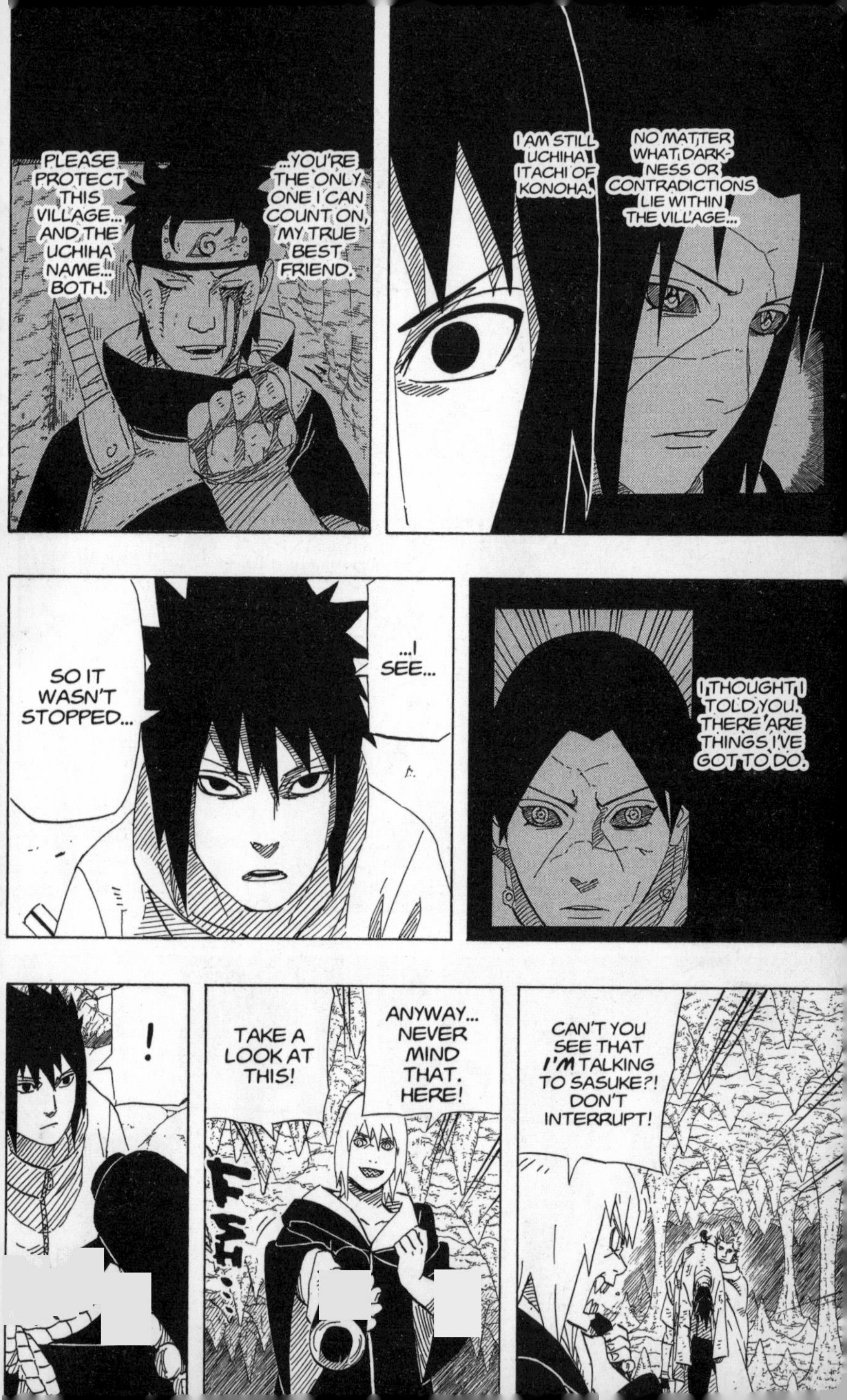
NO MATTER WHAT DARKNESS OR CONTRADICTIONS LIE WITHIN THE VILLAGE...
I AM STILL UCHIHA ITACHI OF KONOHA.
...YOU'RE THE ONLY ONE I CAN COUNT ON, MY TRUE BEST FRIEND.
PLEASE PROTECT THIS VILLAGE... AND THE UCHIHA NAME... BOTH.
I THOUGHT I TOLD YOU. THERE ARE THINGS I'VE GOT TO DO.
...I SEE...
SO IT WASN'T STOPPED...
CAN'T YOU SEE THAT *I'M* TALKING TO SASUKE?! DON'T INTERRUPT!
ANYWAY... NEVER MIND THAT. HERE!
TAKE A LOOK AT THIS!
!

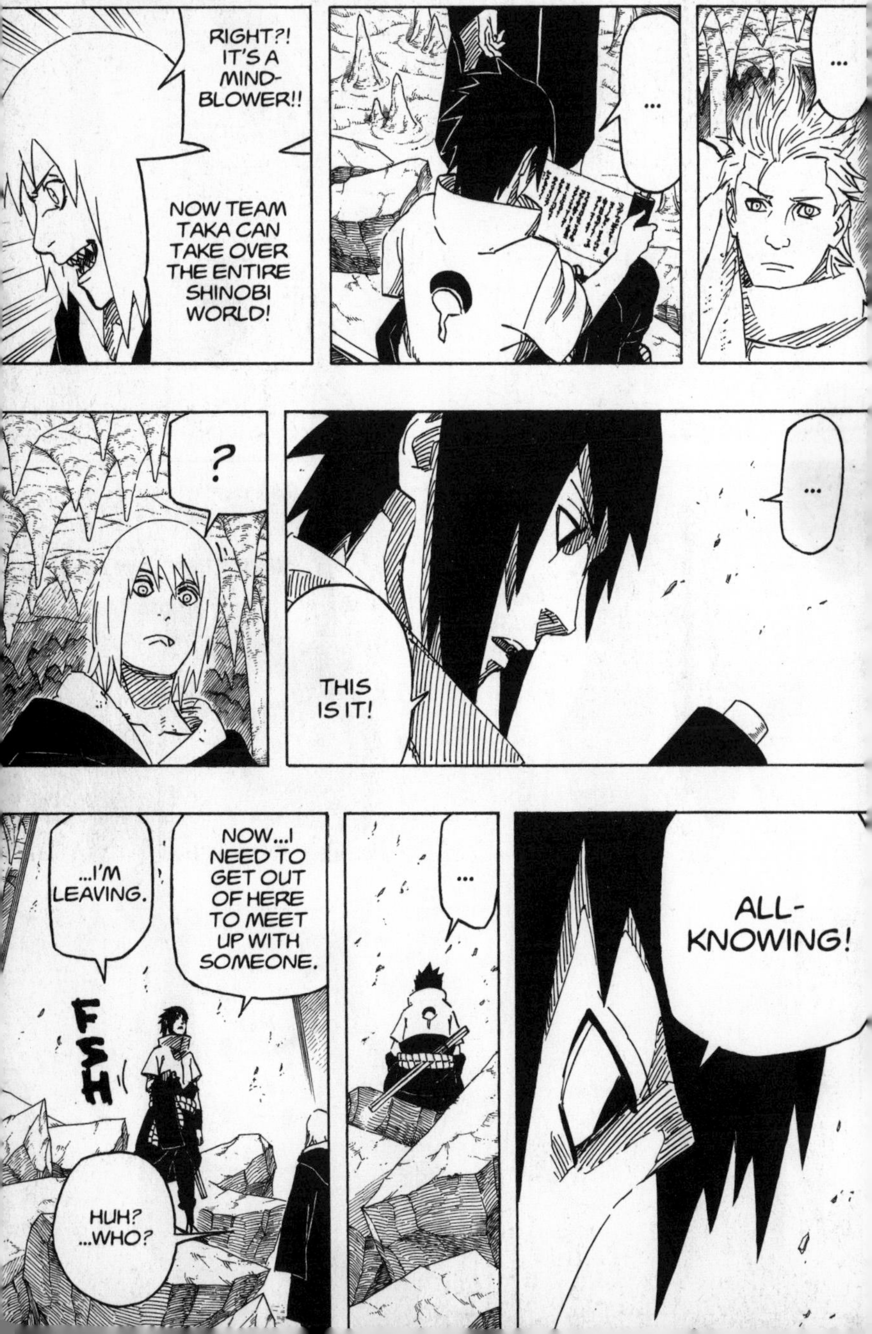
...
...
RIGHT?! IT'S A MIND-BLOWER!!
NOW TEAM TAKA CAN TAKE OVER THE ENTIRE SHINOBI WORLD!
...
THIS IS IT!
?
ALL-KNOWING!
...
NOW...I NEED TO GET OUT OF HERE TO MEET UP WITH SOMEONE.
...I'M LEAVING.
FSH
HUH? ...WHO?

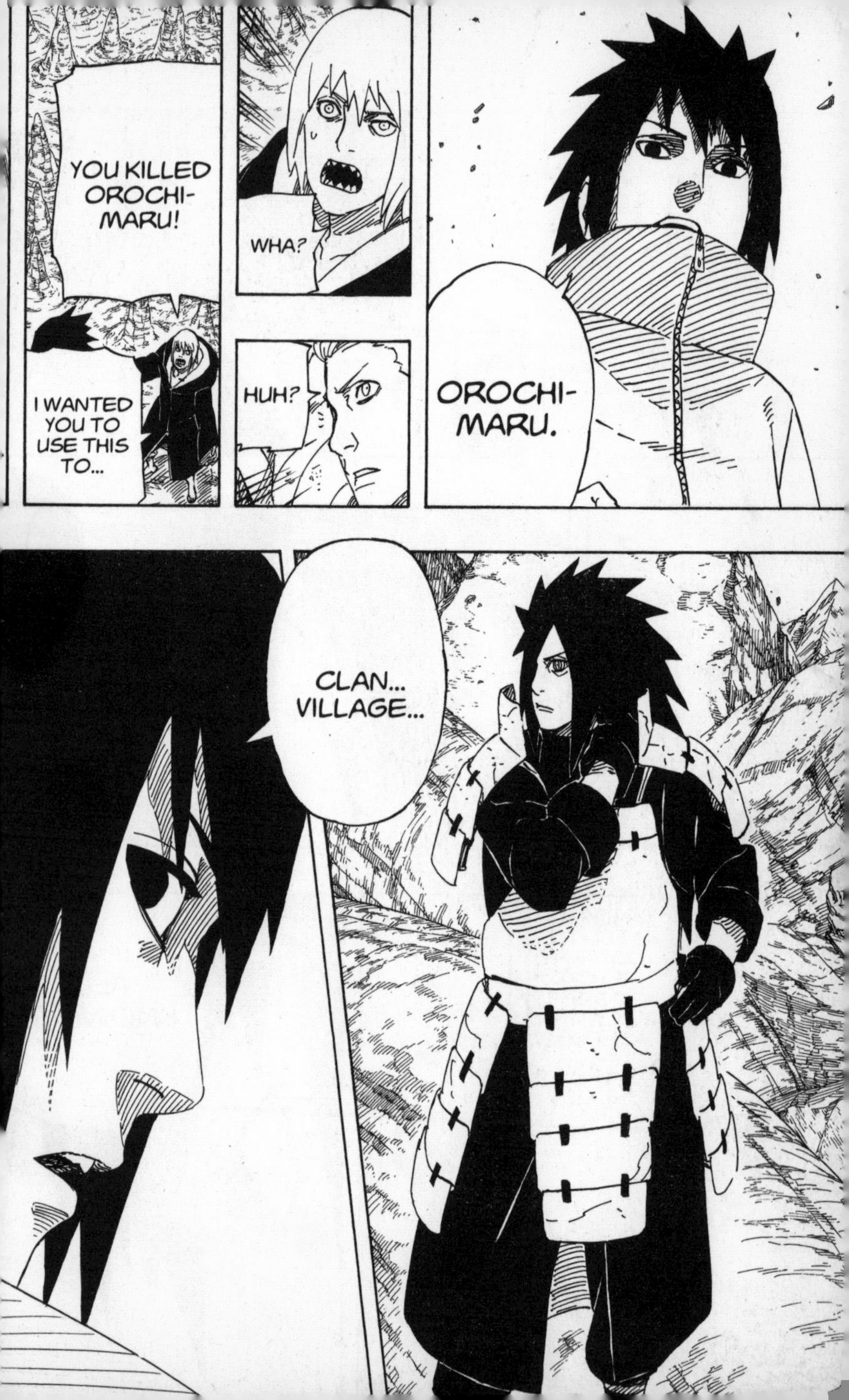
OROCHI-MARU.
WHA?
HUH?
YOU KILLED OROCHI-MARU!
I WANTED YOU TO USE THIS TO...
CLAN... VILLAGE...

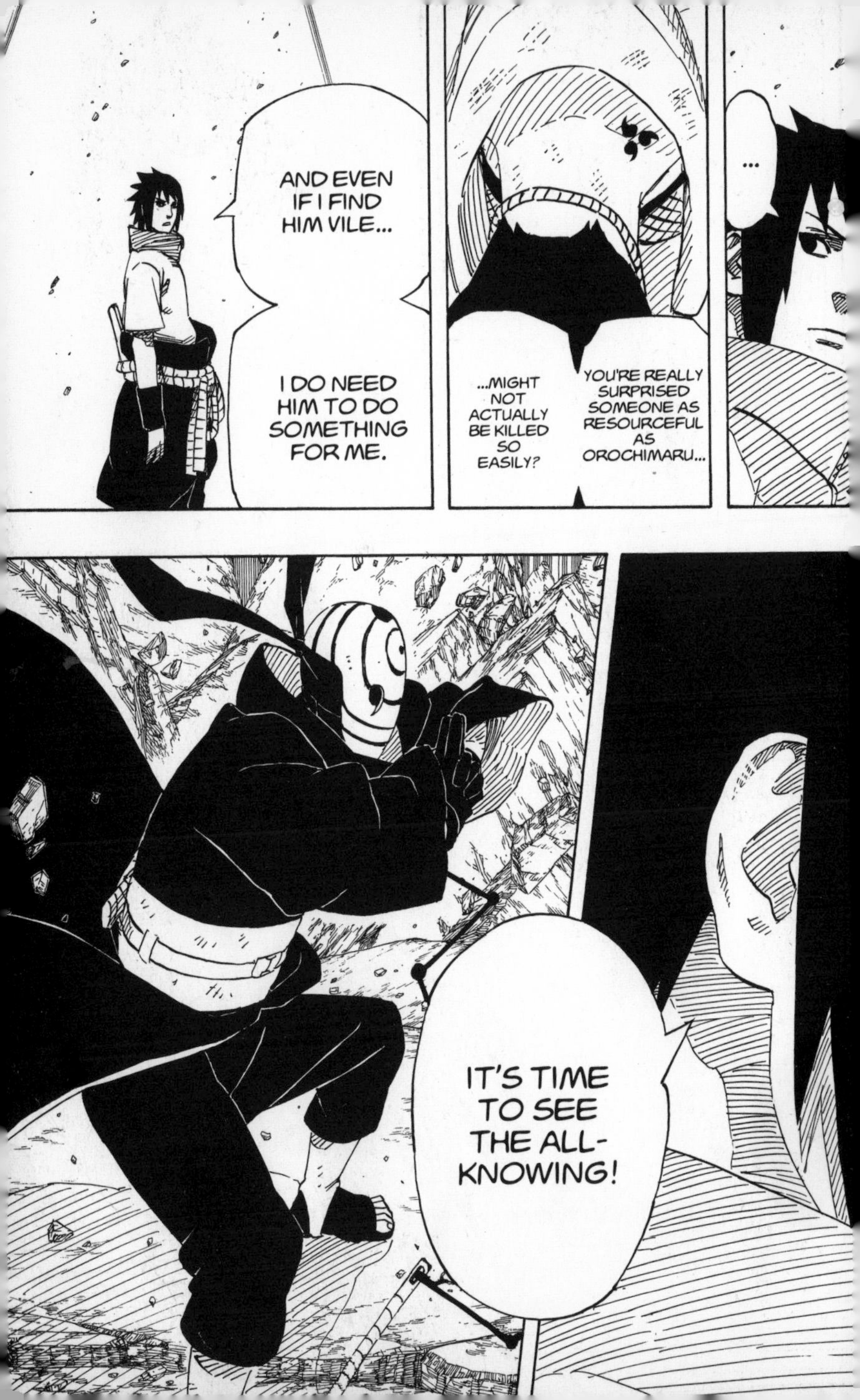
...
YOU'RE REALLY SURPRISED SOMEONE AS RESOURCEFUL AS OROCHIMARU...
...MIGHT NOT ACTUALLY BE KILLED SO EASILY?
AND EVEN IF I FIND HIM VILE...
I DO NEED HIM TO DO SOMETHING FOR ME.
IT'S TIME TO SEE THE ALL-KNOWING!

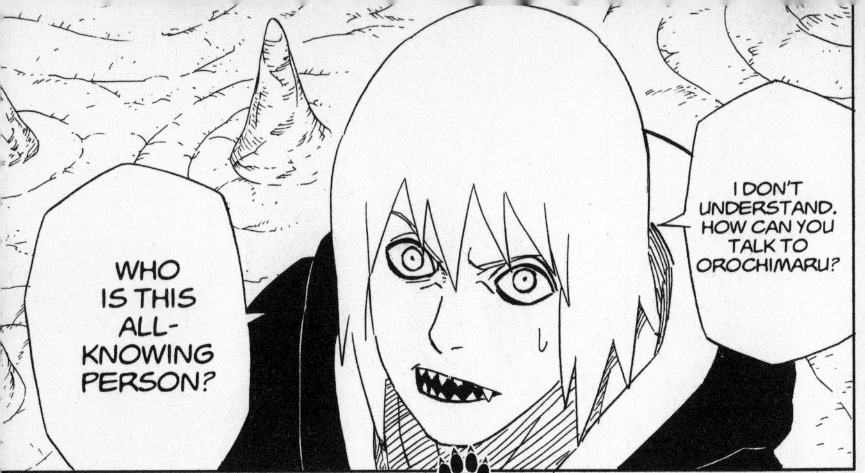
I DON'T UNDERSTAND. HOW CAN YOU TALK TO OROCHIMARU?
WHO IS THIS ALL-KNOWING PERSON?

Number 593: Orochimaru's Return

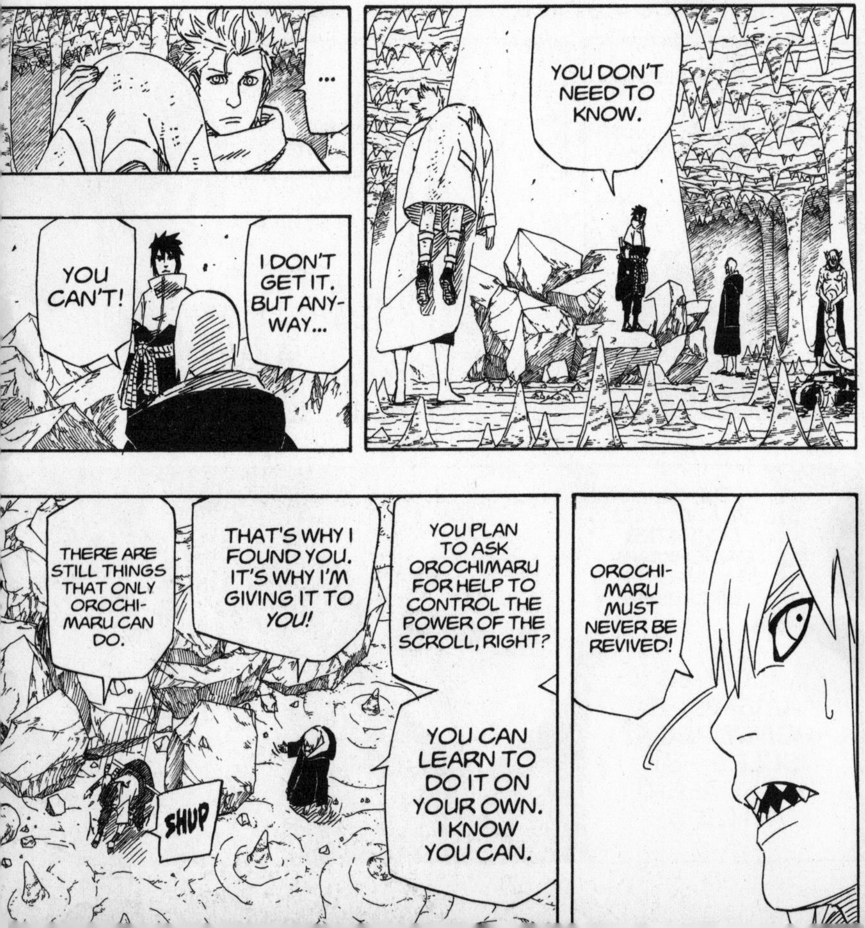
YOU DON'T NEED TO KNOW.
...
I DON'T GET IT. BUT ANYWAY...
YOU CAN'T!
OROCHIMARU MUST NEVER BE REVIVED!
YOU PLAN TO ASK OROCHIMARU FOR HELP TO CONTROL THE POWER OF THE SCROLL, RIGHT?
YOU CAN LEARN TO DO IT ON YOUR OWN. I KNOW YOU CAN.
THAT'S WHY I FOUND YOU. IT'S WHY I'M GIVING IT TO YOU!
THERE ARE STILL THINGS THAT ONLY OROCHIMARU CAN DO.
SHUP

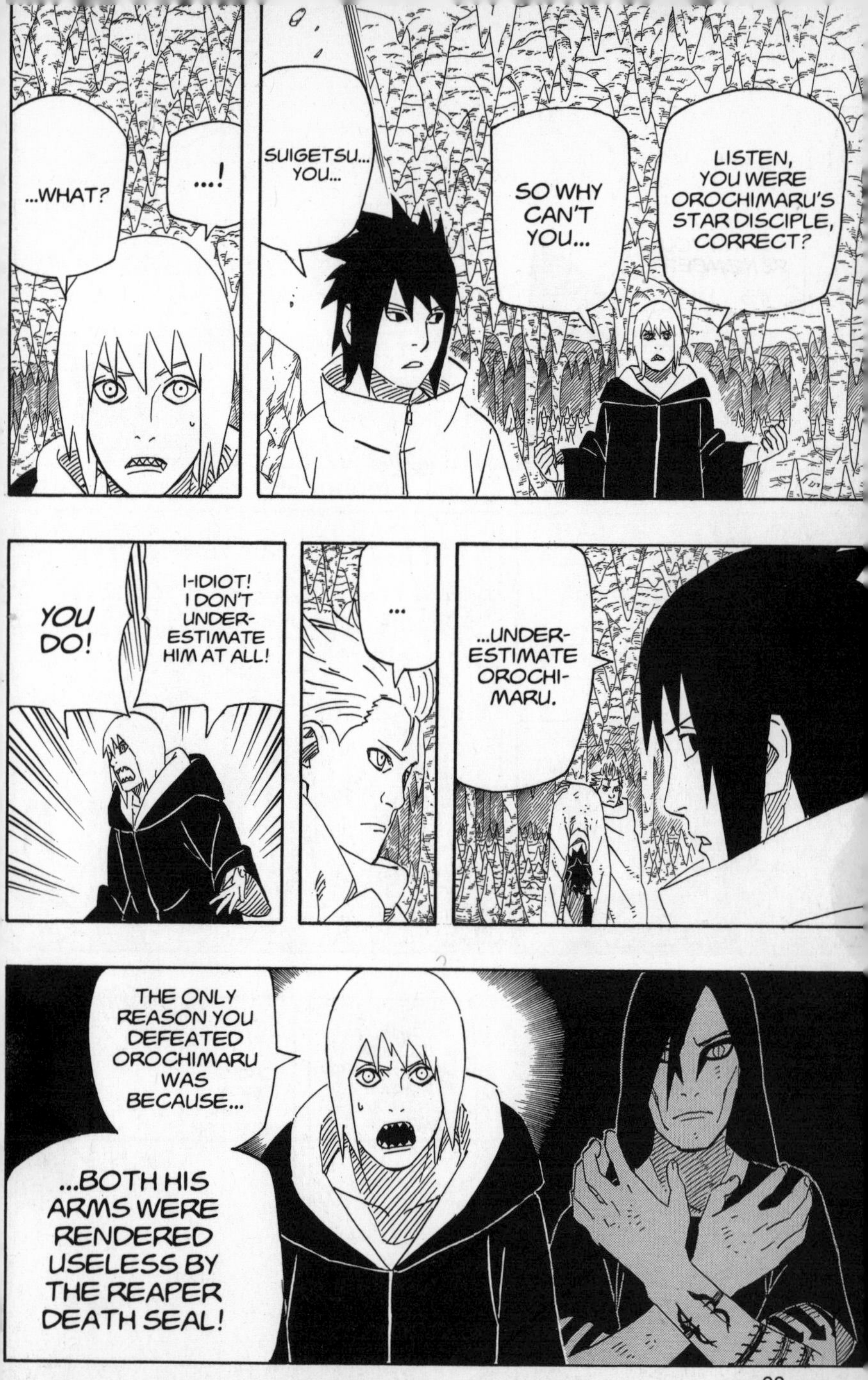
LISTEN, YOU WERE OROCHIMARU'S STAR DISCIPLE, CORRECT?
SO WHY CAN'T YOU...
SUIGETSU... YOU...
...!
...WHAT?
...UNDER-ESTIMATE OROCHI-MARU.
...
I-IDIOT! I DON'T UNDER-ESTIMATE HIM AT ALL!
YOU DO!
THE ONLY REASON YOU DEFEATED OROCHIMARU WAS BECAUSE...
...BOTH HIS ARMS WERE RENDERED USELESS BY THE REAPER DEATH SEAL!

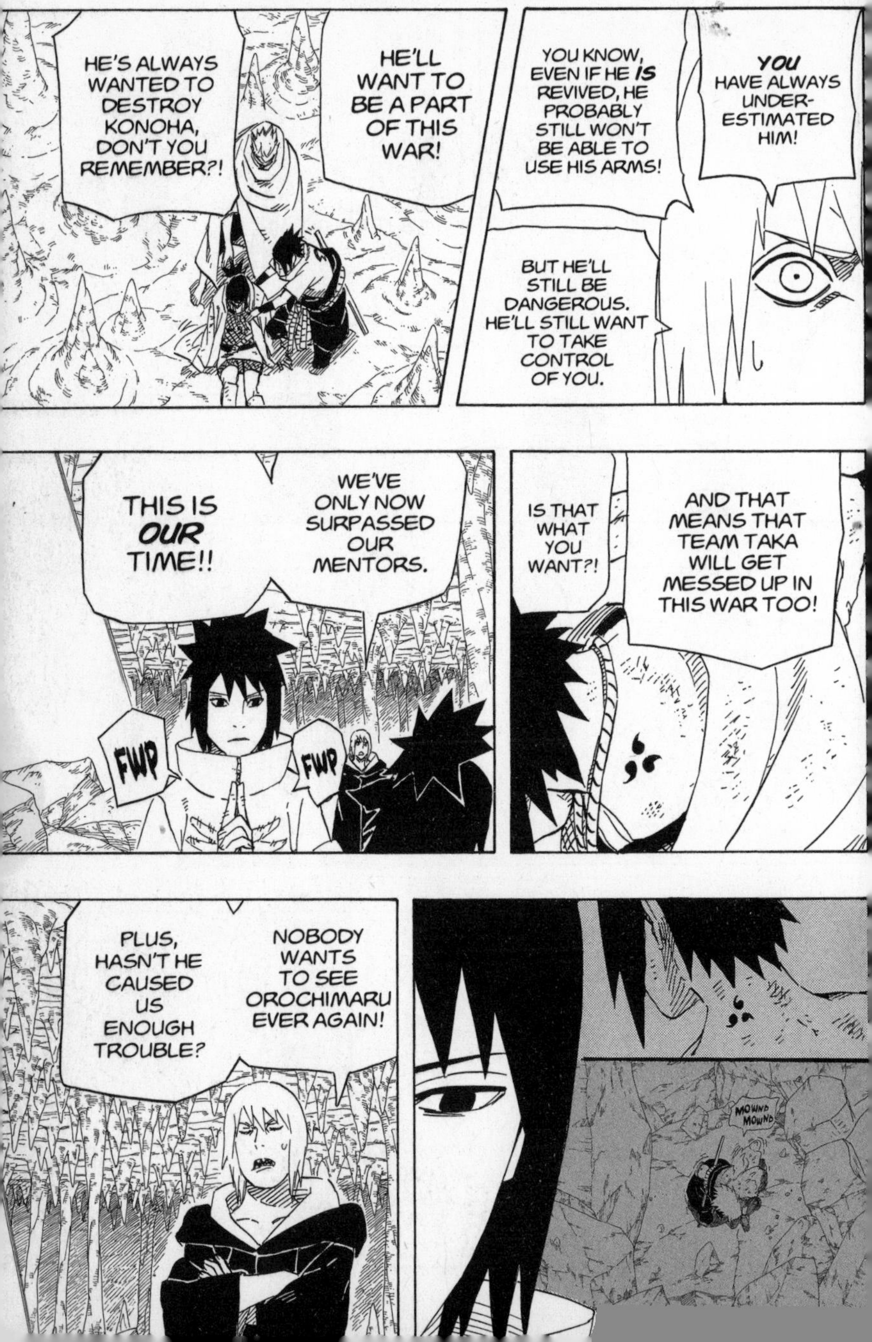
YOU HAVE ALWAYS UNDER-ESTIMATED HIM!
YOU KNOW, EVEN IF HE IS REVIVED, HE PROBABLY STILL WON'T BE ABLE TO USE HIS ARMS!
BUT HE'LL STILL BE DANGEROUS. HE'LL STILL WANT TO TAKE CONTROL OF YOU.
HE'LL WANT TO BE A PART OF THIS WAR!
HE'S ALWAYS WANTED TO DESTROY KONOHA, DON'T YOU REMEMBER?!
AND THAT MEANS THAT TEAM TAKA WILL GET MESSED UP IN THIS WAR TOO!
IS THAT WHAT YOU WANT?!
WE'VE ONLY NOW SURPASSED OUR MENTORS.
THIS IS OUR TIME!!
FWP
FWP
MOWND MOWND
NOBODY WANTS TO SEE OROCHIMARU EVER AGAIN!
PLUS, HASN'T HE CAUSED US ENOUGH TROUBLE?

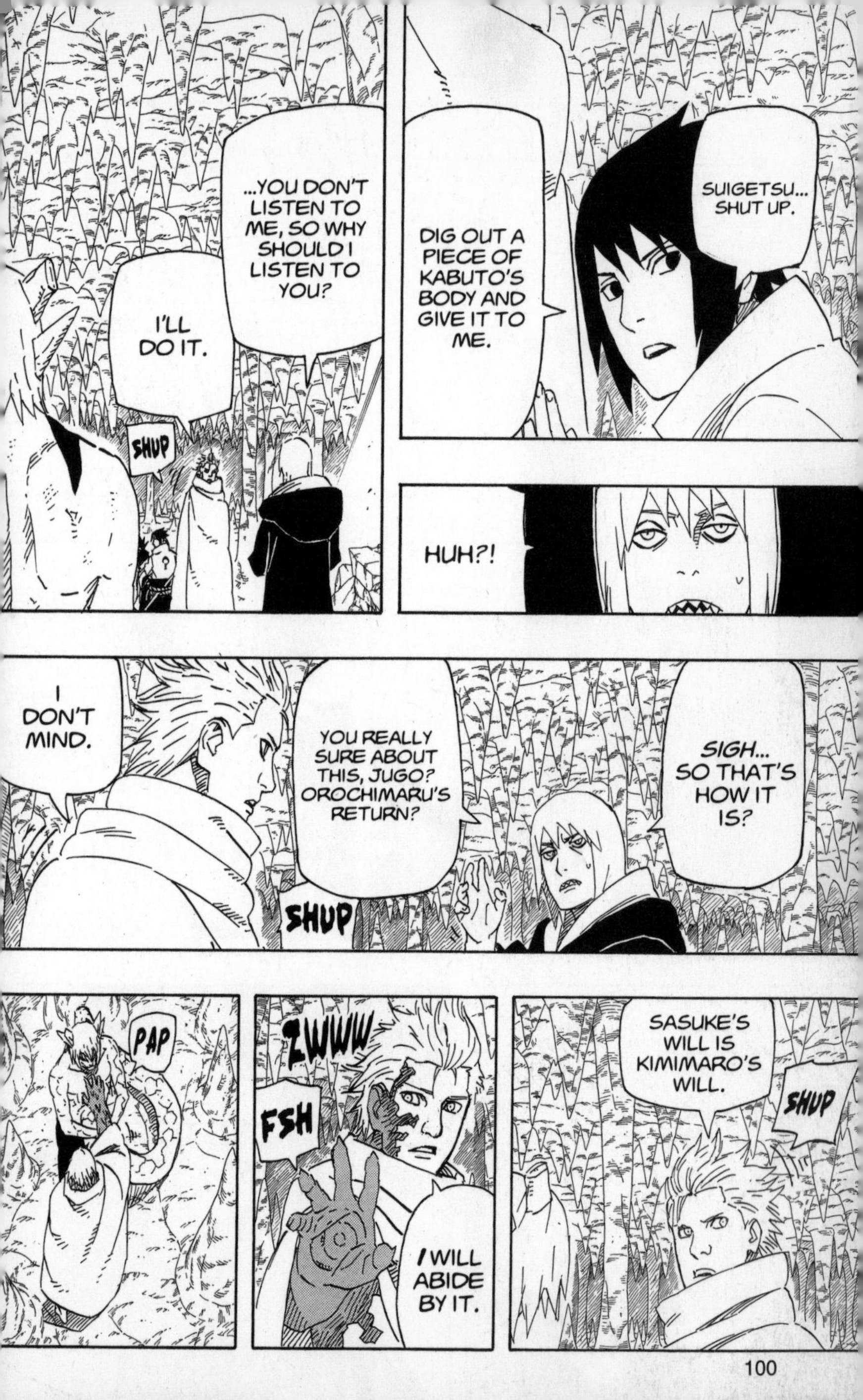
SUIGETSU... SHUT UP.
DIG OUT A PIECE OF KABUTO'S BODY AND GIVE IT TO ME.
HUH?!
...YOU DON'T LISTEN TO ME, SO WHY SHOULD I LISTEN TO YOU?
I'LL DO IT.
SHUP
SIGH... SO THAT'S HOW IT IS?
YOU REALLY SURE ABOUT THIS, JUGO? OROCHIMARU'S RETURN?
SHUP
I DON'T MIND.
SASUKE'S WILL IS KIMIMARO'S WILL.
SHUP
ZWWW
FSH
I WILL ABIDE BY IT.
PAP

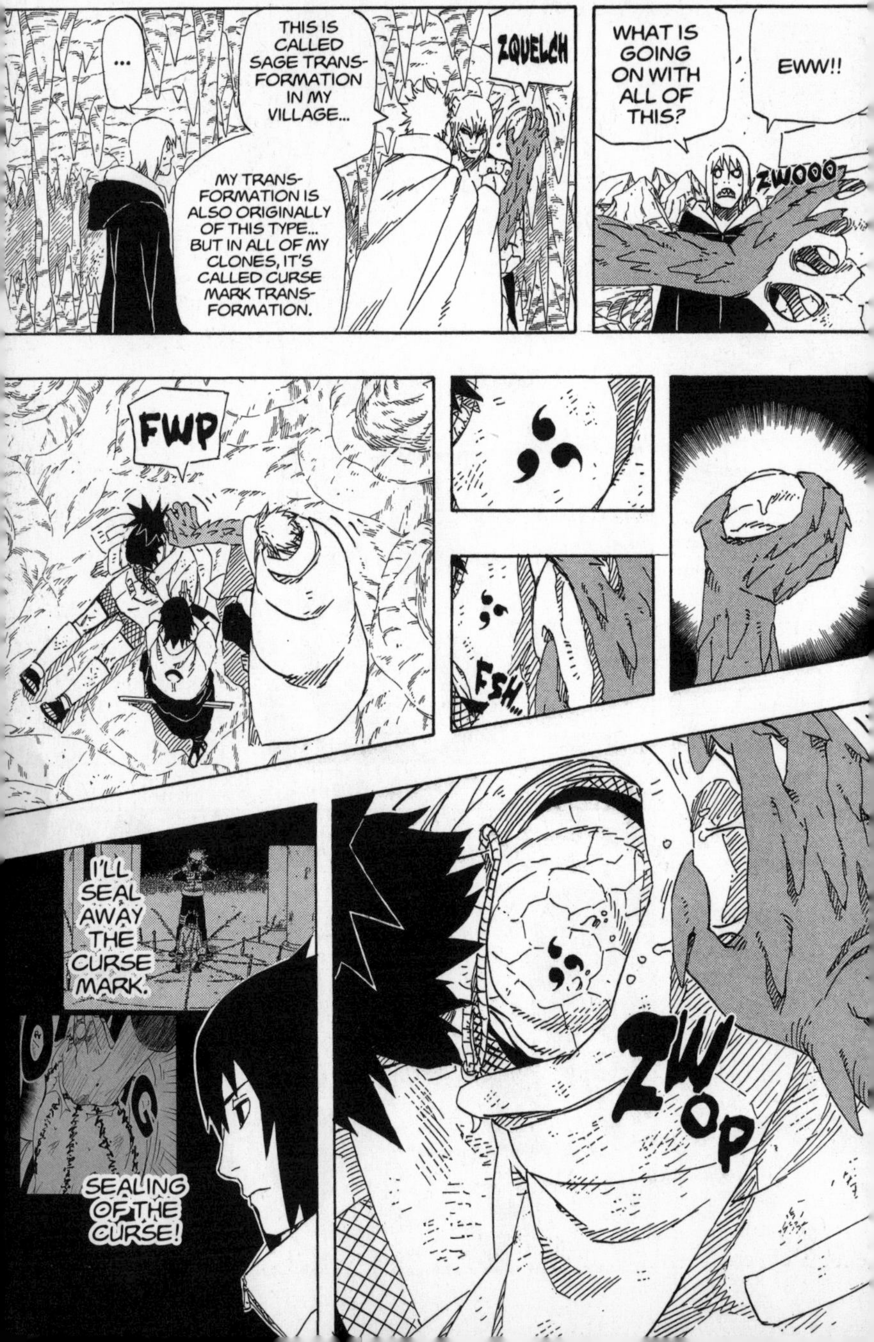
EWW!!
WHAT IS GOING ON WITH ALL OF THIS?
ZWOOO
ZQUELCH
THIS IS CALLED SAGE TRANSFORMATION IN MY VILLAGE...
...
MY TRANSFORMATION IS ALSO ORIGINALLY OF THIS TYPE... BUT IN ALL OF MY CLONES, IT'S CALLED CURSE MARK TRANSFORMATION.
FSH...
FWP
ZWOOP
I'LL SEAL AWAY THE CURSE MARK.
SEALING OF THE CURSE!

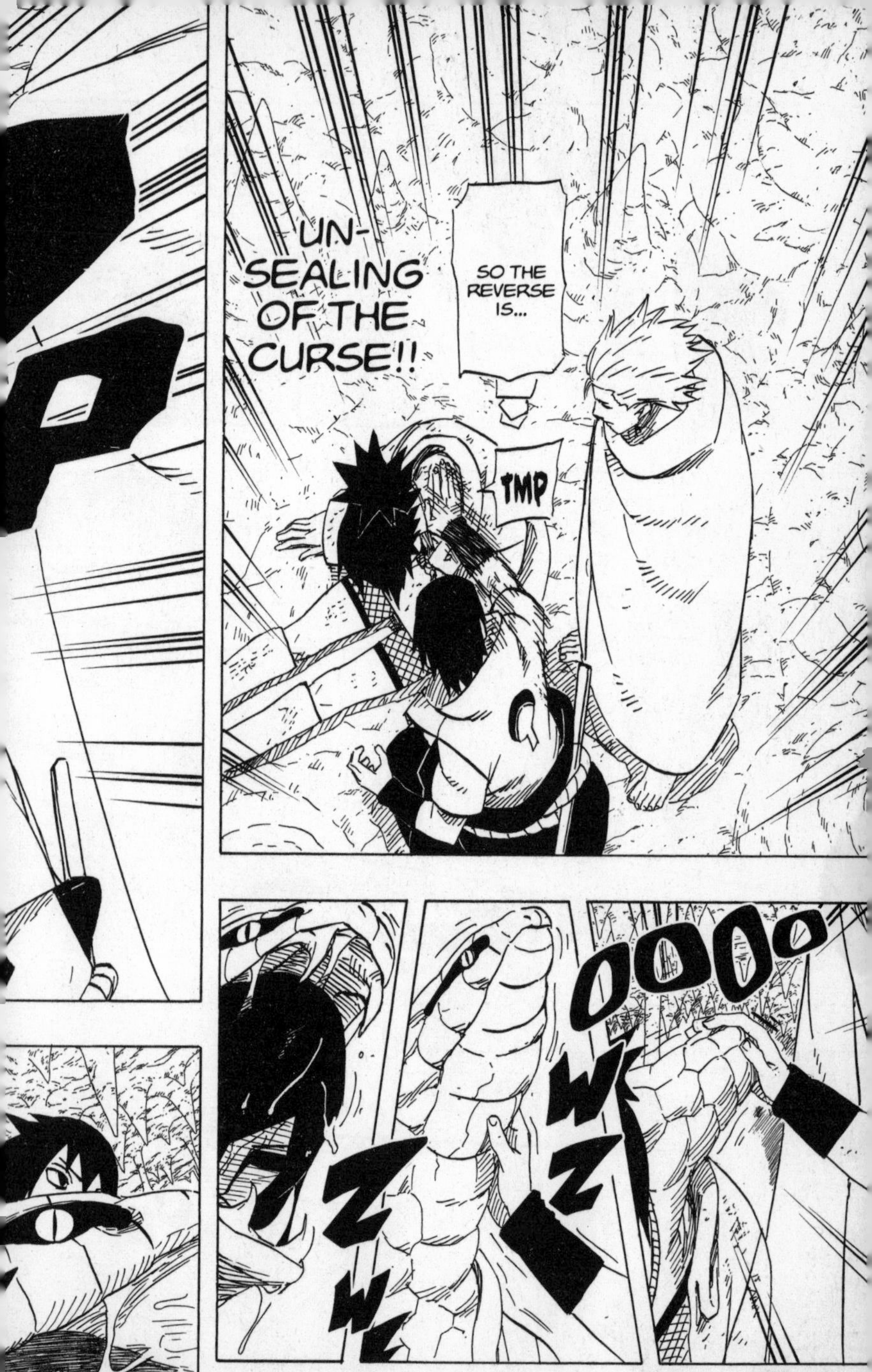
UN-SEALING OF THE CURSE!!
SO THE REVERSE IS...
TMP

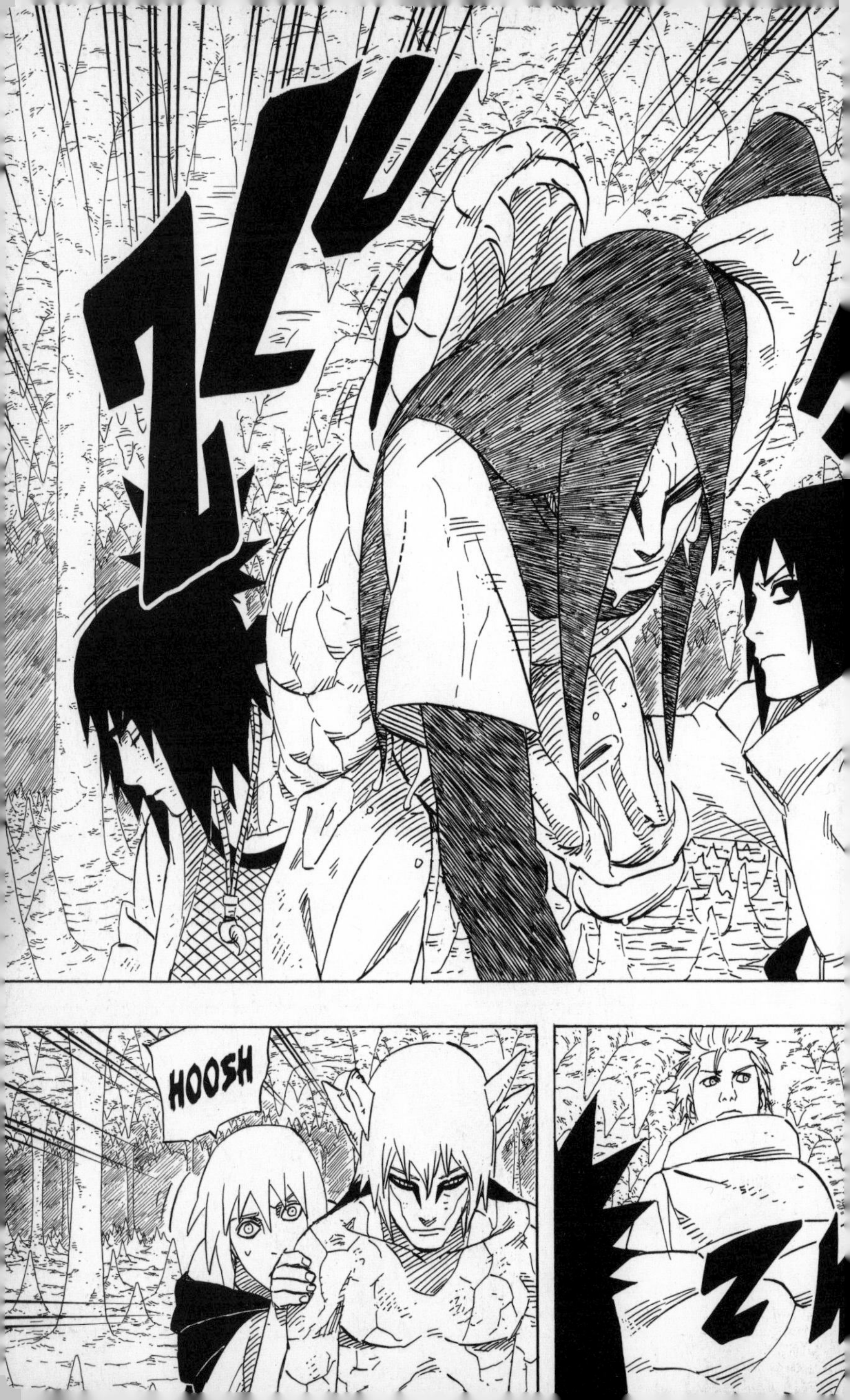
HOOSH

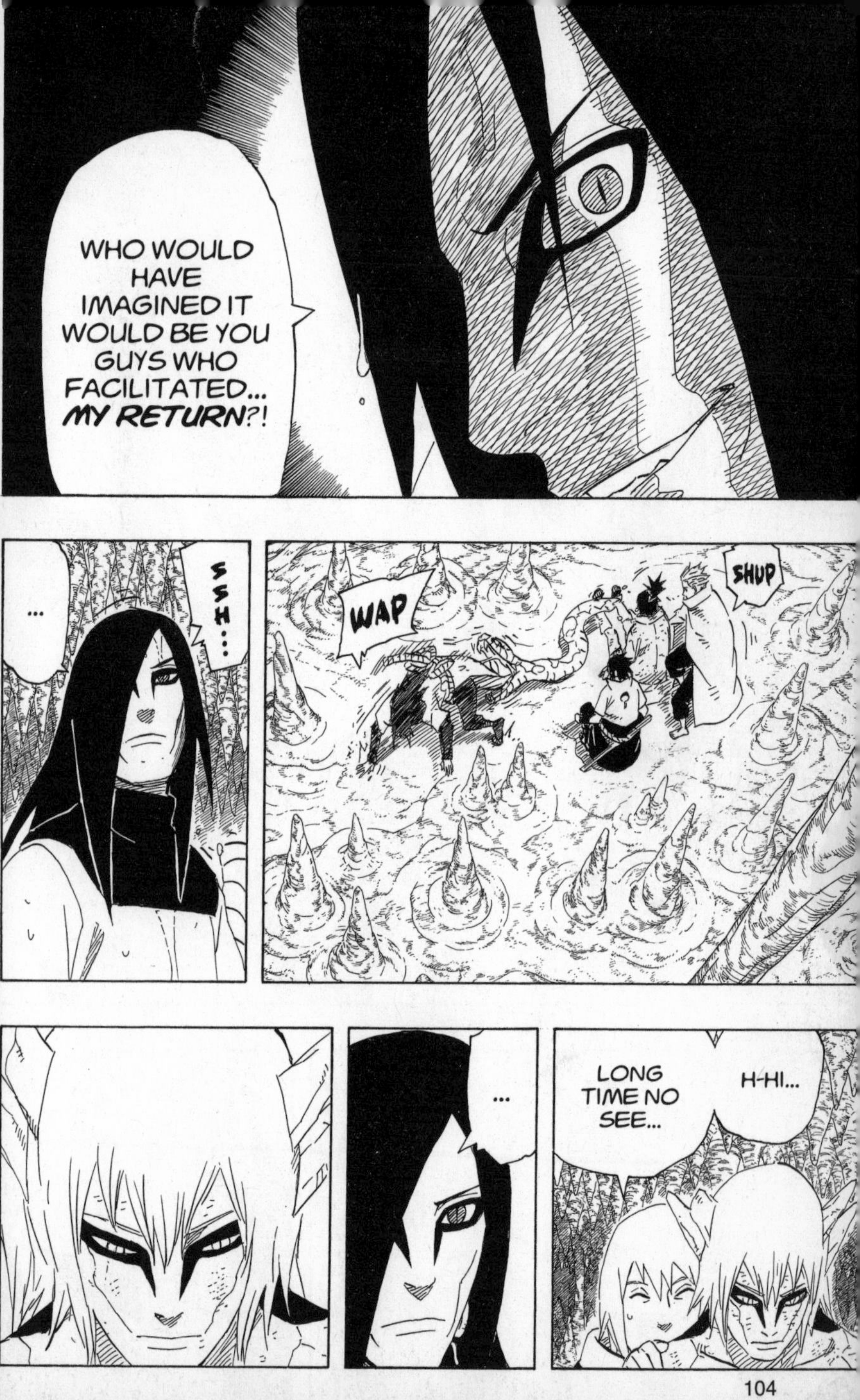
WHO WOULD HAVE IMAGINED IT WOULD BE YOU GUYS WHO FACILITATED... MY RETURN?!
SHUP
WAP
SSH...
...
H-HI...
LONG TIME NO SEE...
...

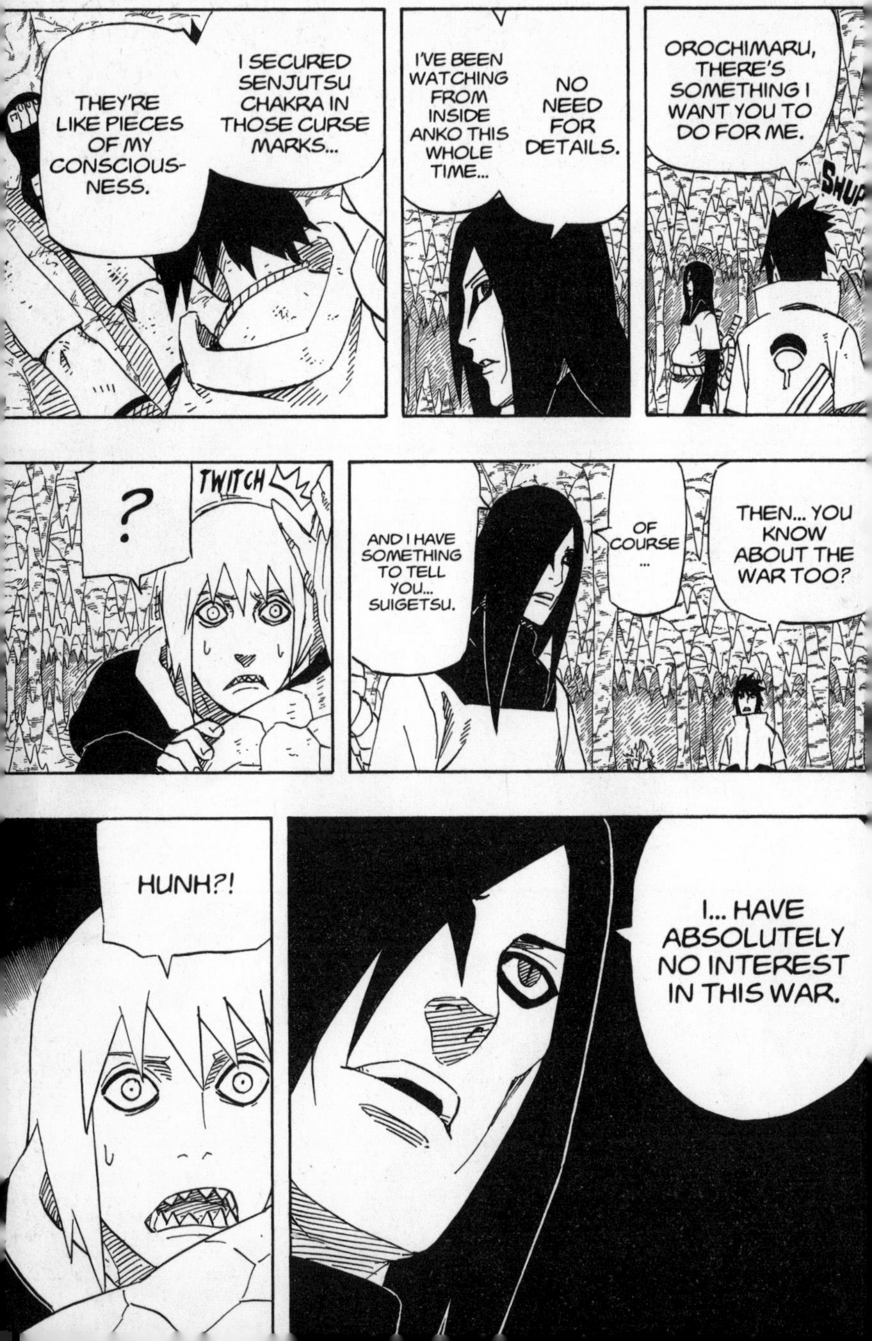
OROCHIMARU, THERE'S SOMETHING I WANT YOU TO DO FOR ME.
SHUP
NO NEED FOR DETAILS.
I'VE BEEN WATCHING FROM INSIDE ANKO THIS WHOLE TIME...
I SECURED SENJUTSU CHAKRA IN THOSE CURSE MARKS...
THEY'RE LIKE PIECES OF MY CONSCIOUS-NESS.
THEN... YOU KNOW ABOUT THE WAR TOO?
OF COURSE ...
AND I HAVE SOMETHING TO TELL YOU... SUIGETSU.
TWITCH
?
I... HAVE ABSOLUTELY NO INTEREST IN THIS WAR.
HUNH?!

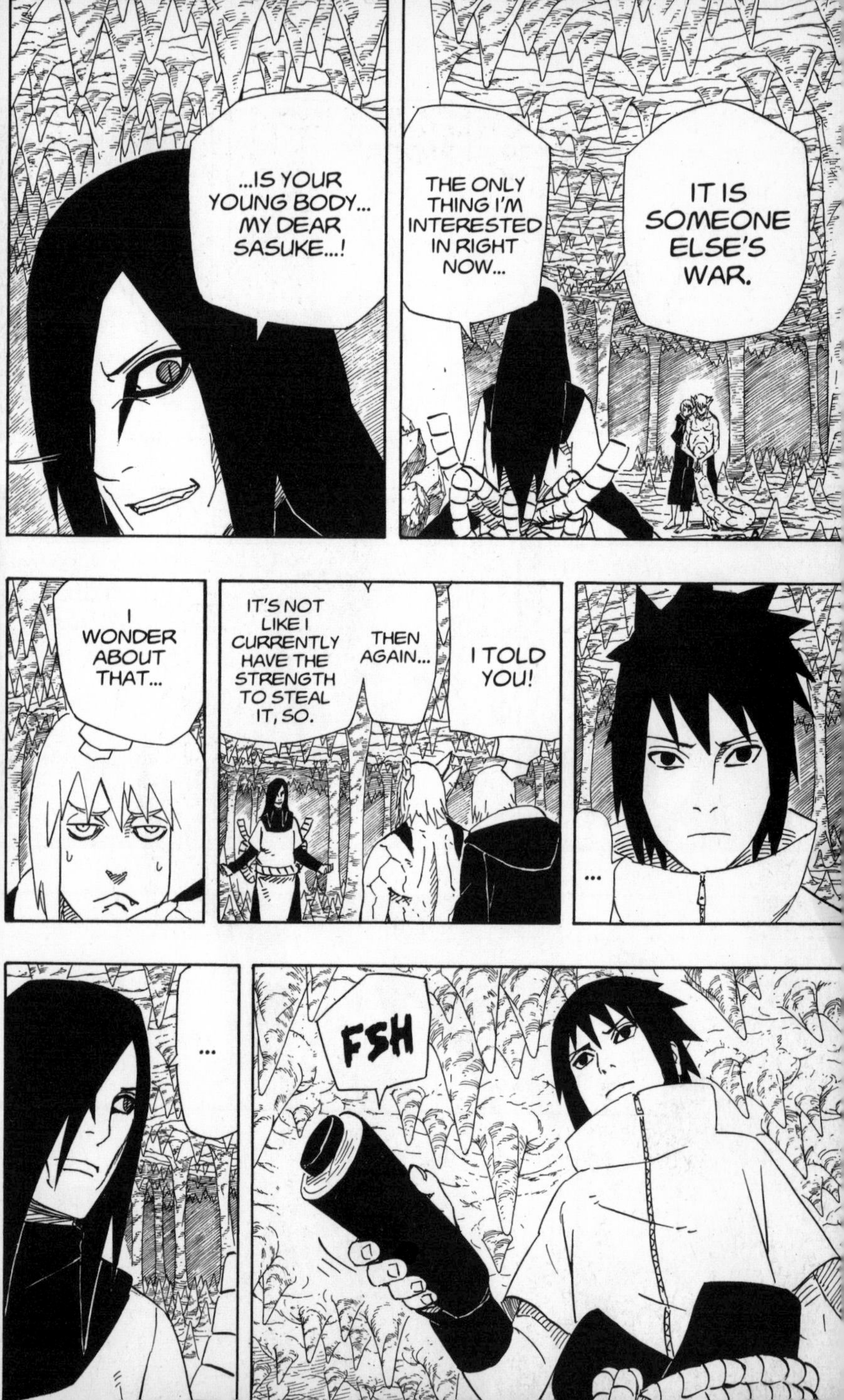
IT IS SOMEONE ELSE'S WAR.
THE ONLY THING I'M INTERESTED IN RIGHT NOW...
...IS YOUR YOUNG BODY... MY DEAR SASUKE...!
...
I TOLD YOU!
THEN AGAIN...
IT'S NOT LIKE I CURRENTLY HAVE THE STRENGTH TO STEAL IT, SO.
I WONDER ABOUT THAT...
FSH
...

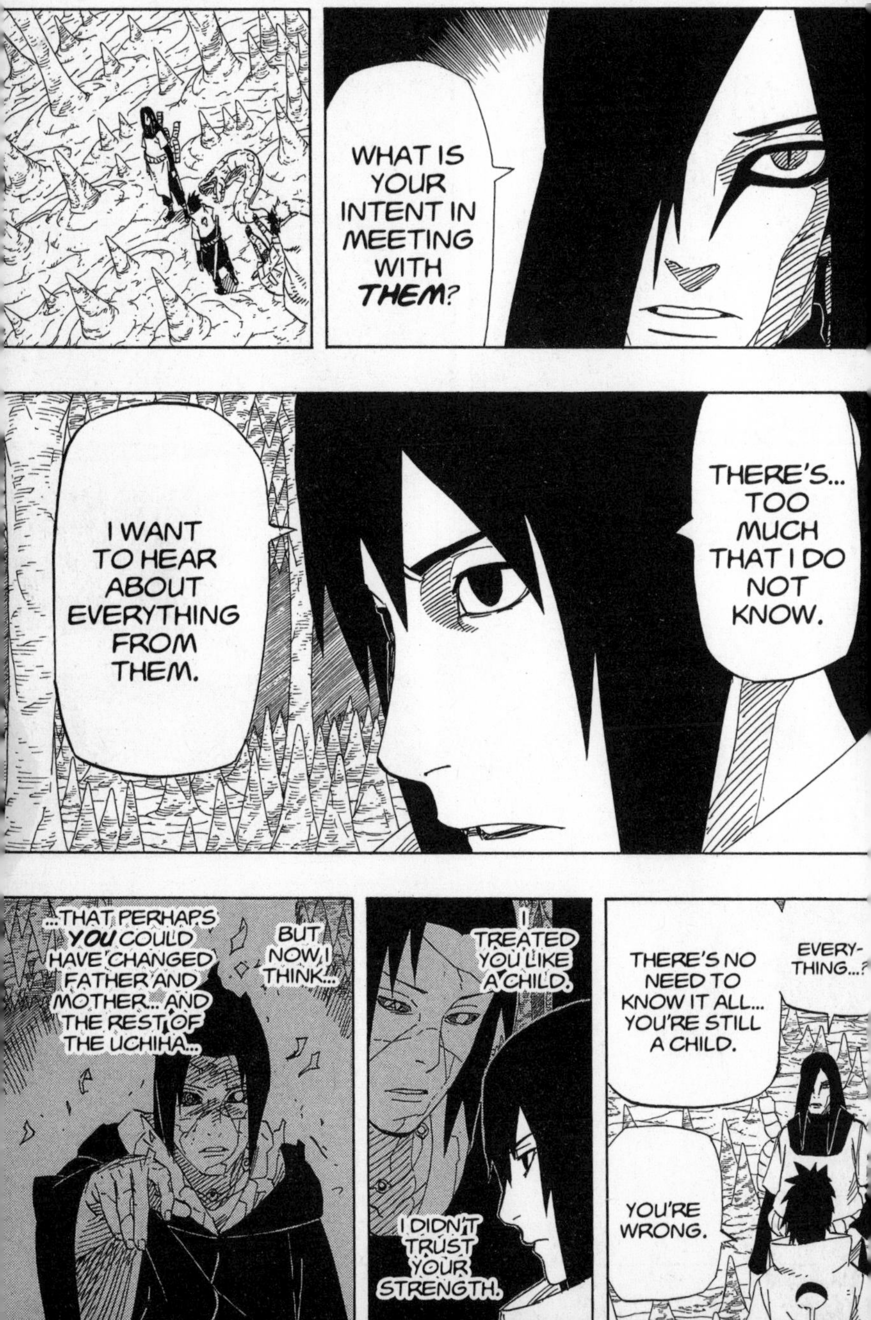
WHAT IS YOUR INTENT IN MEETING WITH *THEM*?
THERE'S... TOO MUCH THAT I DO NOT KNOW.
I WANT TO HEAR ABOUT EVERYTHING FROM THEM.
EVERY-THING...?
THERE'S NO NEED TO KNOW IT ALL... YOU'RE STILL A CHILD.
YOU'RE WRONG.
I TREATED YOU LIKE A CHILD.
I DIDN'T TRUST YOUR STRENGTH.
BUT NOW, I THINK...
...THAT PERHAPS *YOU* COULD HAVE CHANGED FATHER AND MOTHER... AND THE REST OF THE UCHIHA...

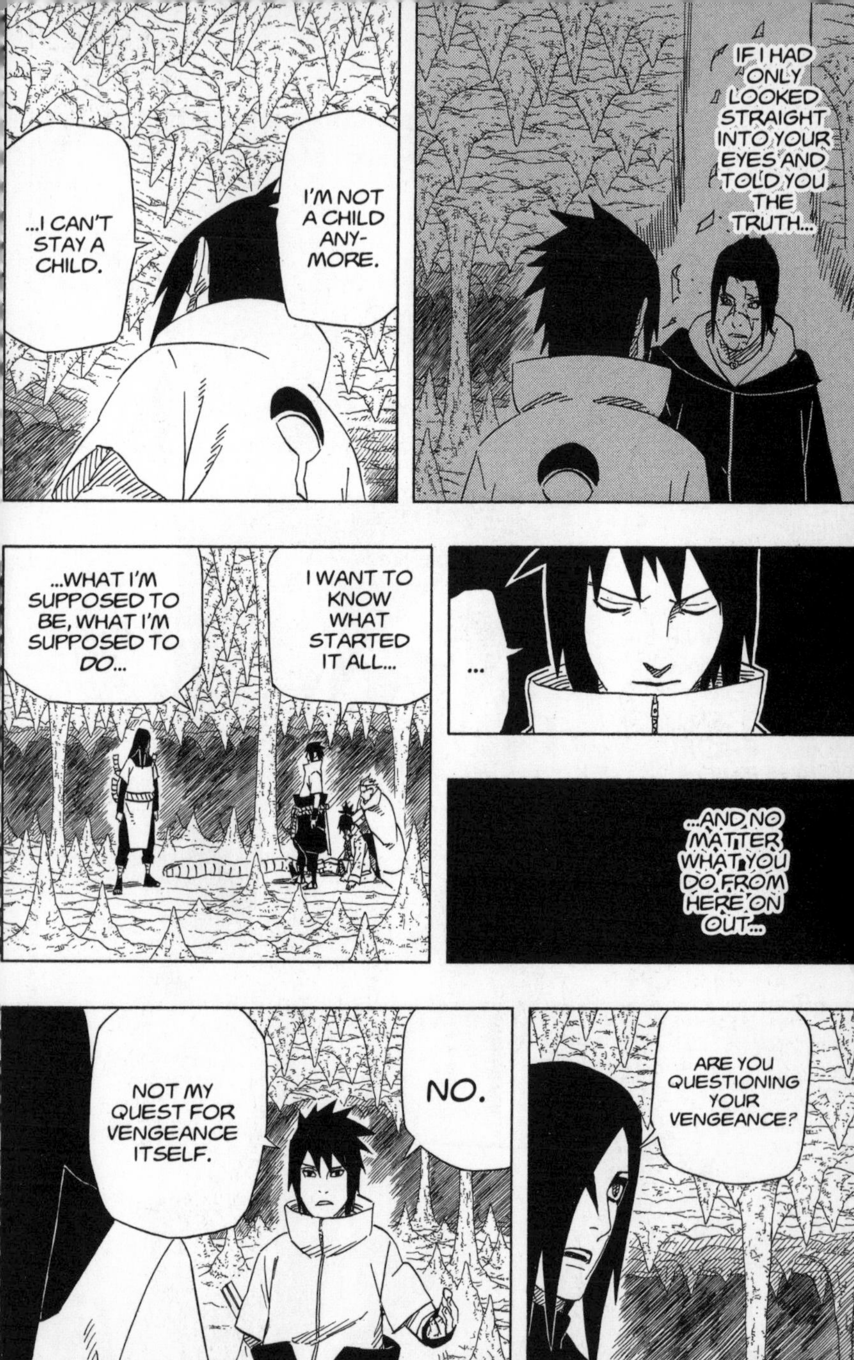
IF I HAD ONLY LOOKED STRAIGHT INTO YOUR EYES AND TOLD YOU THE TRUTH...
I'M NOT A CHILD ANYMORE.
...I CAN'T STAY A CHILD.
...
...AND NO MATTER WHAT YOU DO FROM HERE ON OUT...
I WANT TO KNOW WHAT STARTED IT ALL...
...WHAT I'M SUPPOSED TO BE, WHAT I'M SUPPOSED TO DO...
ARE YOU QUESTIONING YOUR VENGEANCE?
NO.
NOT MY QUEST FOR VENGEANCE ITSELF.

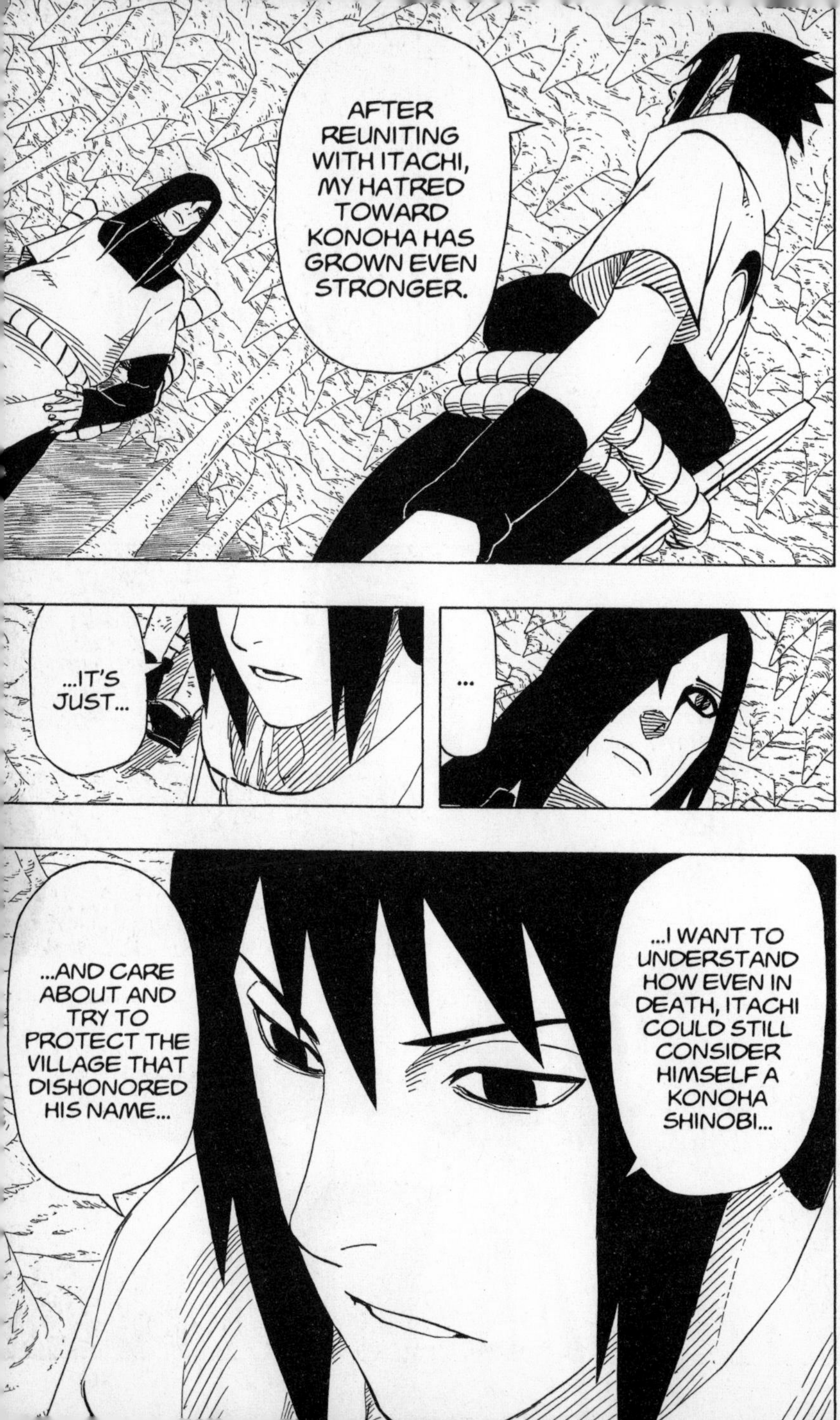
AFTER REUNITING WITH ITACHI, MY HATRED TOWARD KONOHA HAS GROWN EVEN STRONGER.
...
...IT'S JUST...
...I WANT TO UNDERSTAND HOW EVEN IN DEATH, ITACHI COULD STILL CONSIDER HIMSELF A KONOHA SHINOBI...
...AND CARE ABOUT AND TRY TO PROTECT THE VILLAGE THAT DISHONORED HIS NAME...

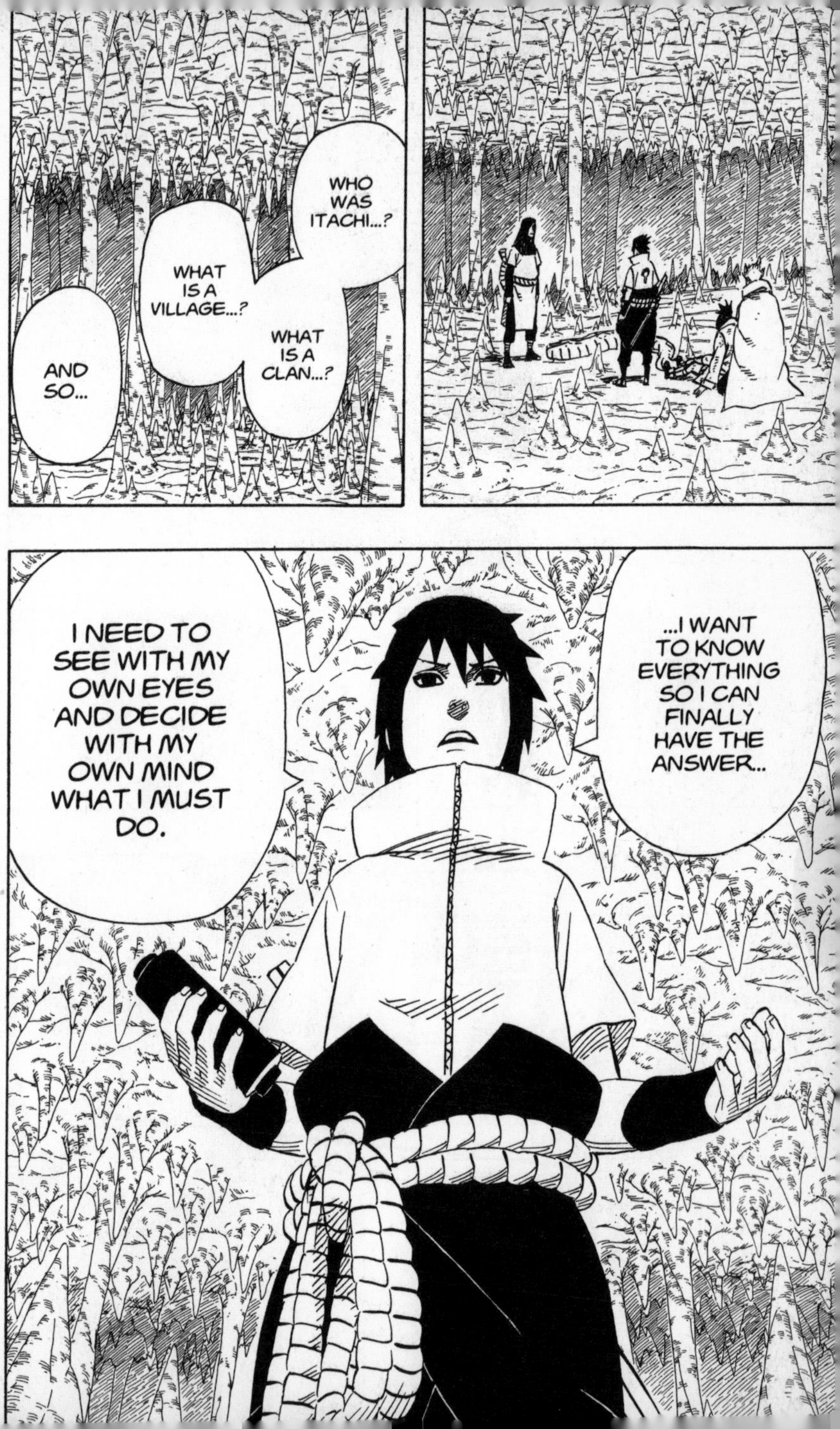
WHO WAS ITACHI...?
WHAT IS A CLAN...?
WHAT IS A VILLAGE...?
AND SO...
...I WANT TO KNOW EVERYTHING SO I CAN FINALLY HAVE THE ANSWER...
I NEED TO SEE WITH MY OWN EYES AND DECIDE WITH MY OWN MIND WHAT I MUST DO.

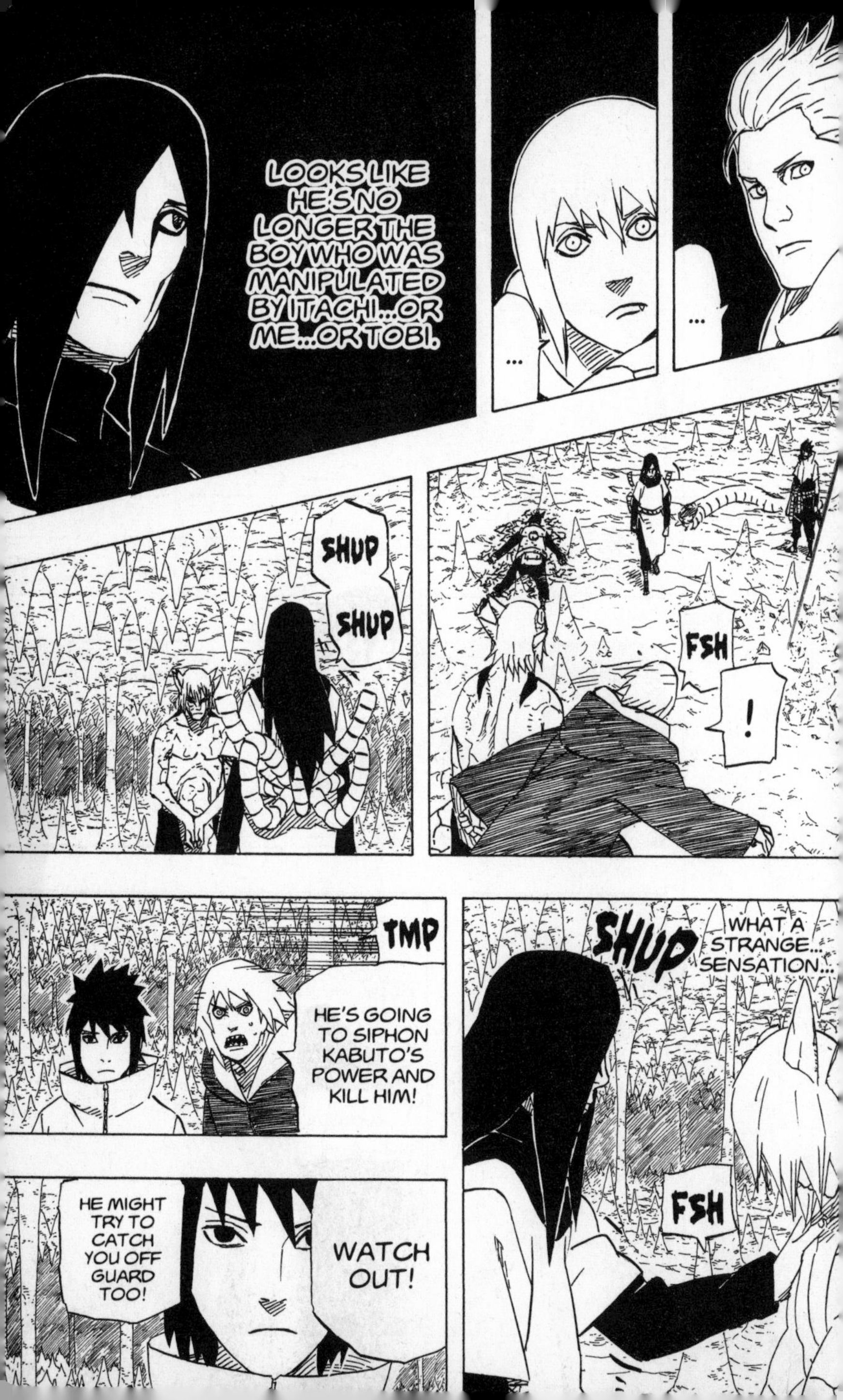
...
...
LOOKS LIKE HE'S NO LONGER THE BOY WHO WAS MANIPULATED BY ITACHI...OR ME...OR TOBI.
FSH
!
SHUP
SHUP
SHUP
WHAT A STRANGE... SENSATION...
FSH
TMP
HE'S GOING TO SIPHON KABUTO'S POWER AND KILL HIM!
WATCH OUT!
HE MIGHT TRY TO CATCH YOU OFF GUARD TOO!

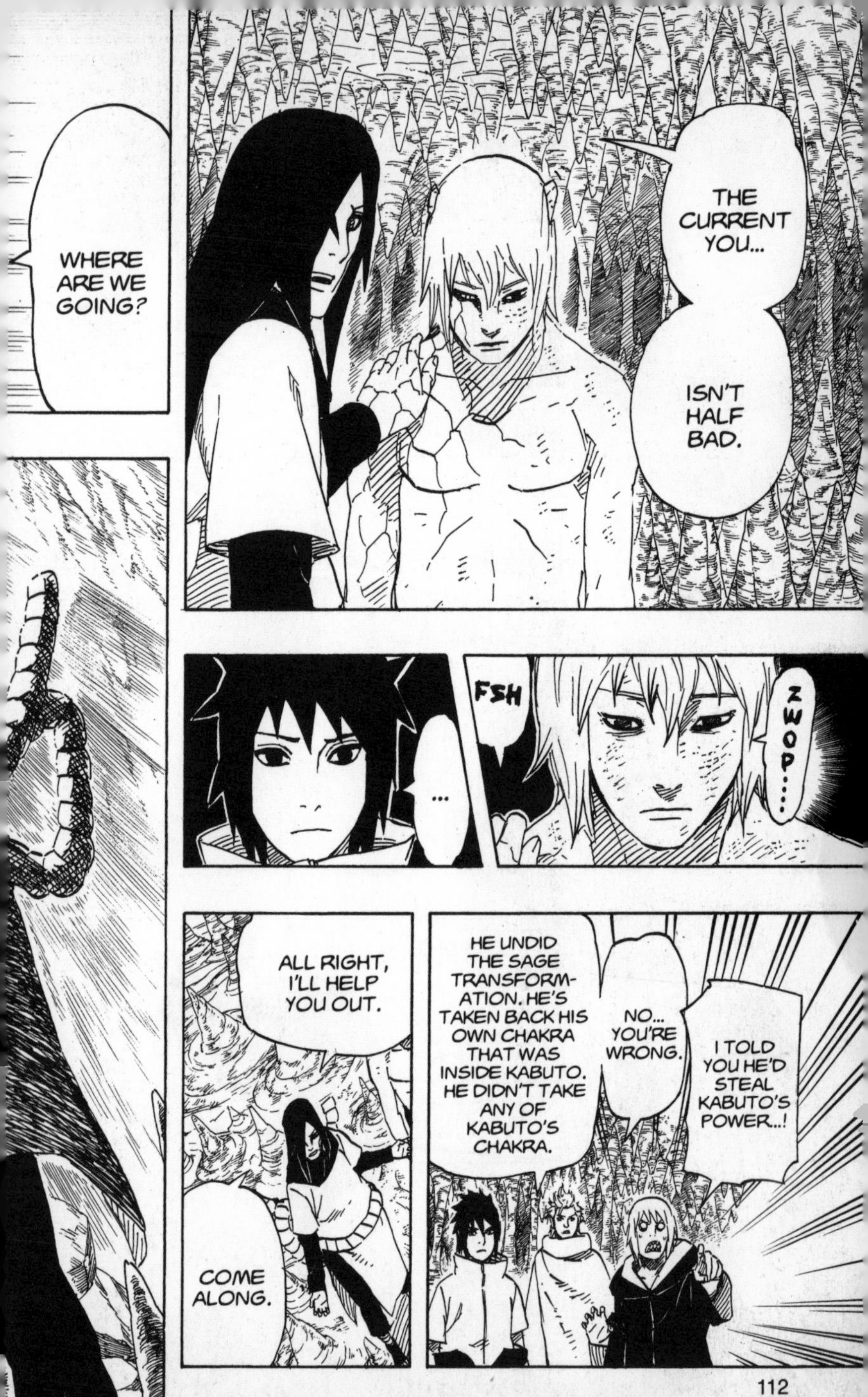
THE CURRENT YOU...
ISN'T HALF BAD.
ZWOP....
FSH
...
I TOLD YOU HE'D STEAL KABUTO'S POWER...!
NO... YOU'RE WRONG.
HE UNDID THE SAGE TRANSFORM-ATION. HE'S TAKEN BACK HIS OWN CHAKRA THAT WAS INSIDE KABUTO. HE DIDN'T TAKE ANY OF KABUTO'S CHAKRA.
ALL RIGHT, I'LL HELP YOU OUT.
COME ALONG.
WHERE ARE WE GOING?

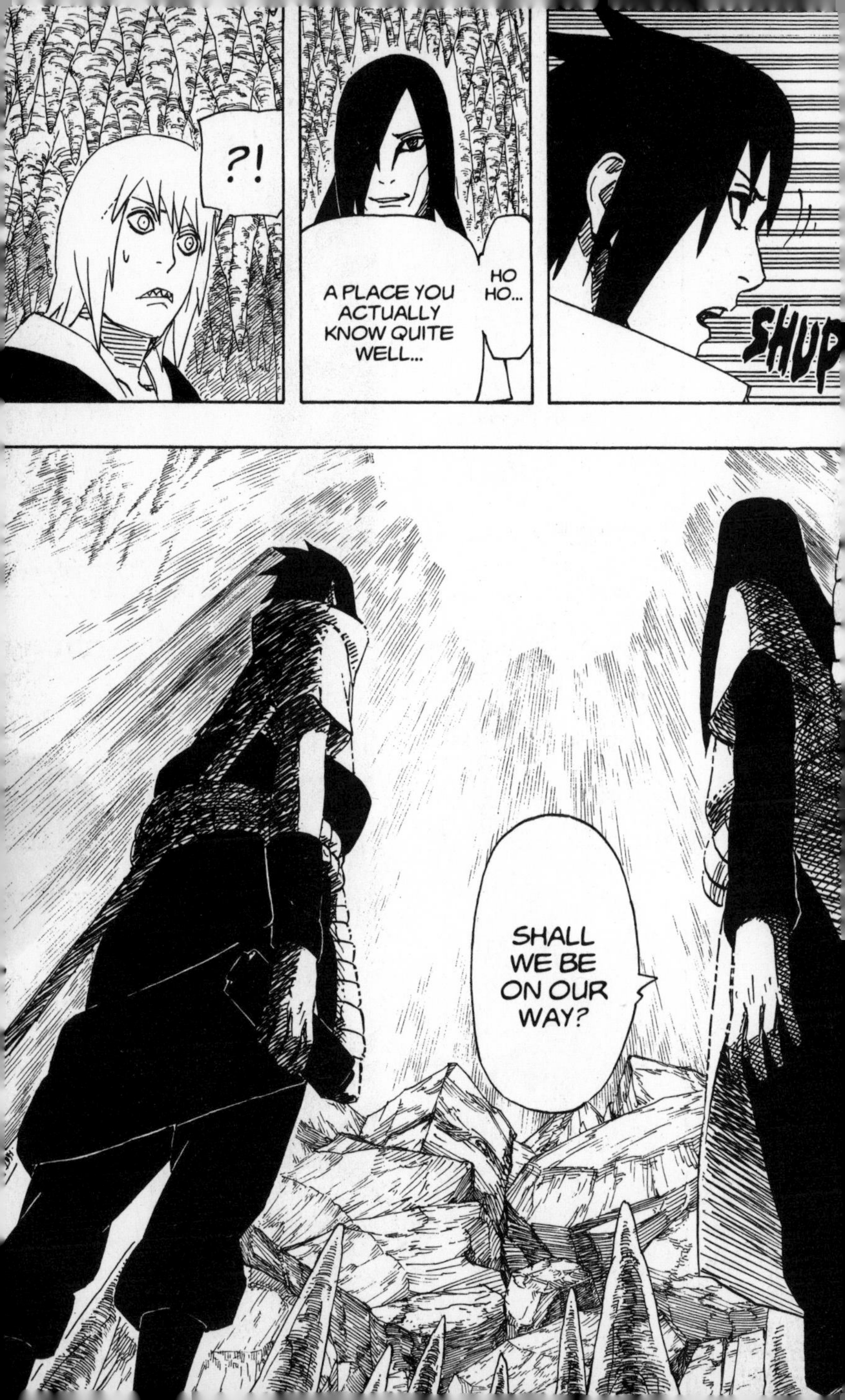
SHUP
HO HO...
A PLACE YOU ACTUALLY KNOW QUITE WELL...
?!
SHALL WE BE ON OUR WAY?

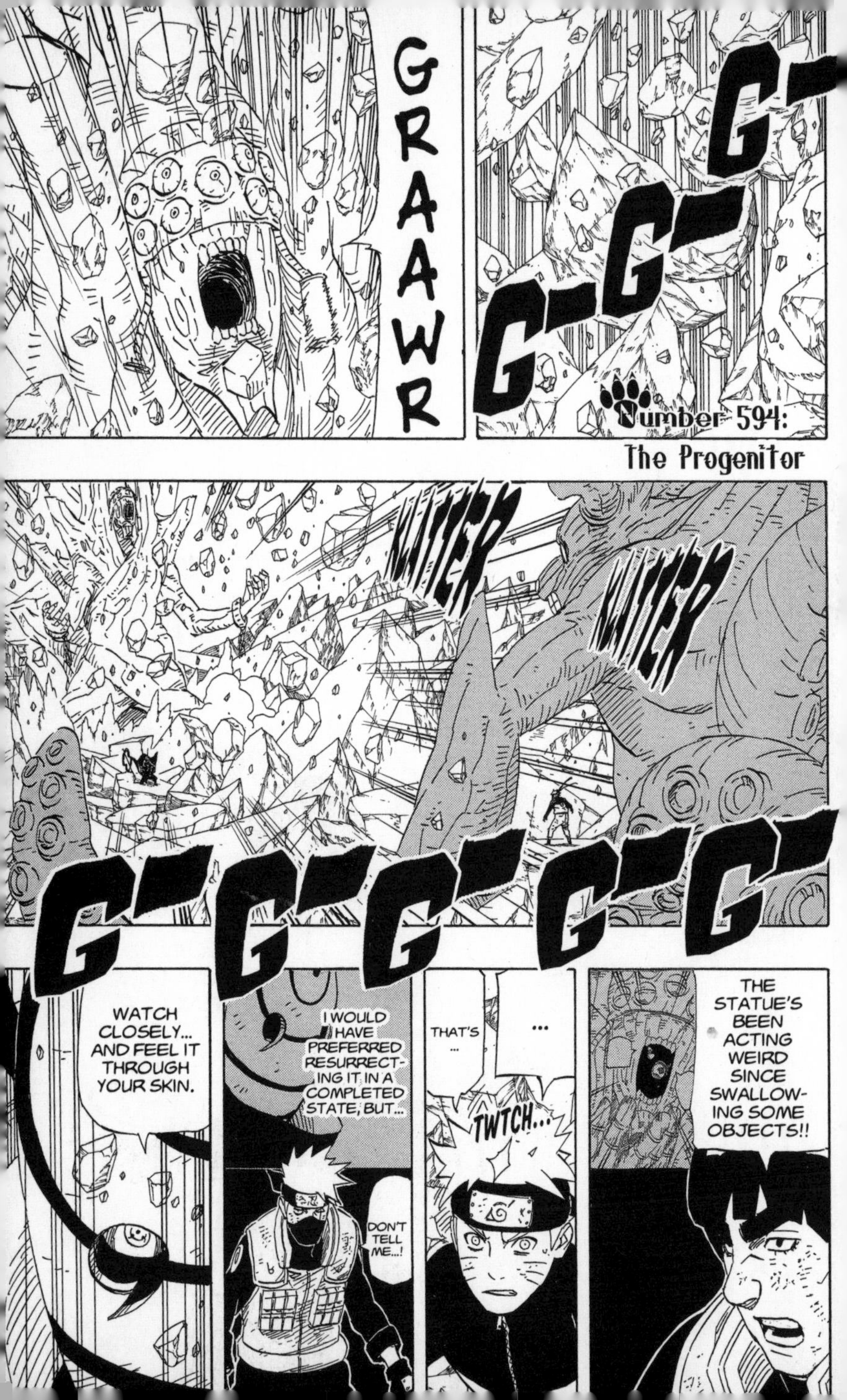
G-G-G-
Number 594:
The Progenitor
GRAWR
G'G'G'G'G'G'
THE STATUE'S BEEN ACTING WEIRD SINCE SWALLOWING SOME OBJECTS!!
...
THAT'S ...
TWTCH...
I WOULD HAVE PREFERRED RESURRECTING IT IN A COMPLETED STATE, BUT...
DON'T TELL ME...!
WATCH CLOSELY... AND FEEL IT THROUGH YOUR SKIN.

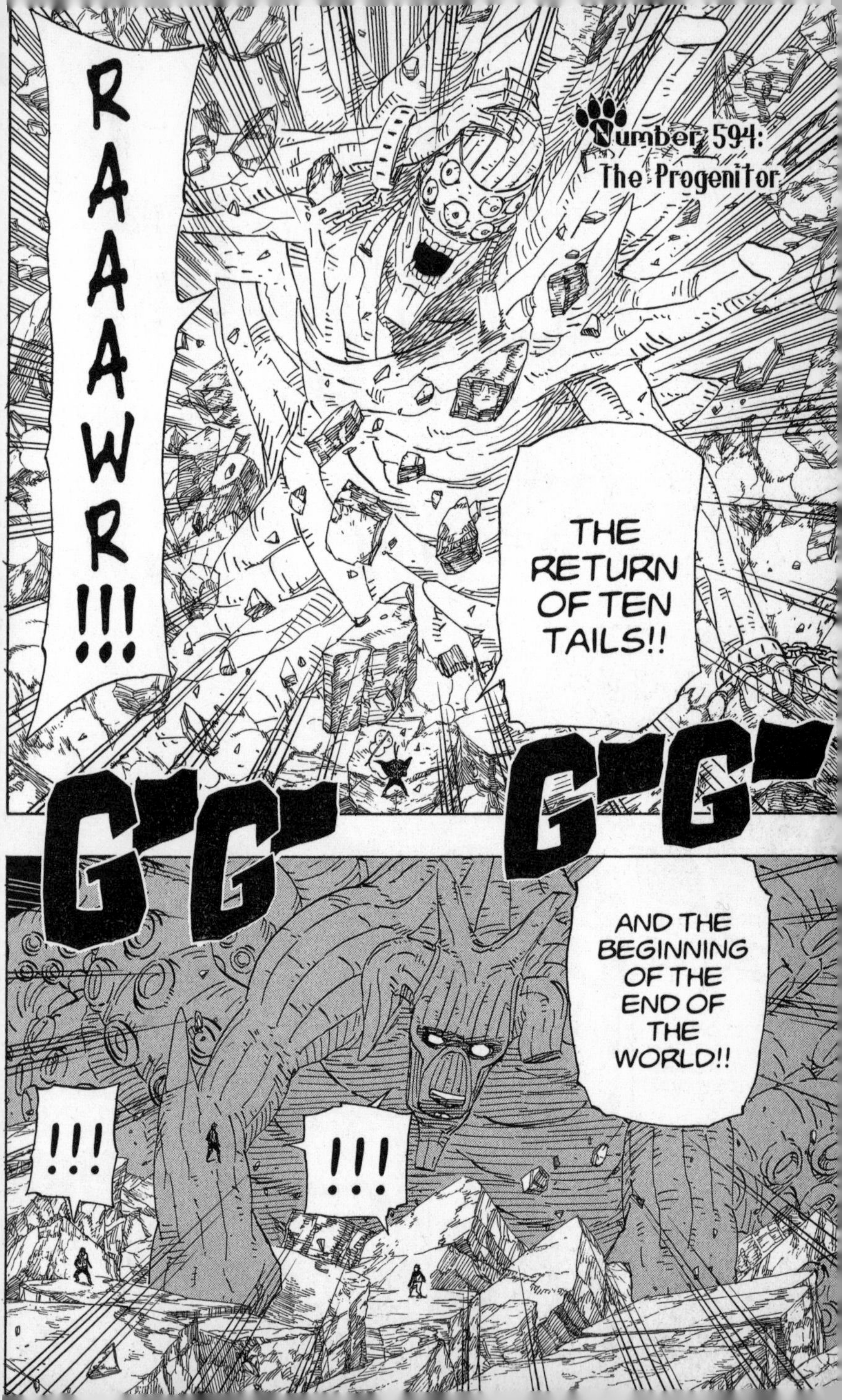
Number 594:
The Progenitor
THE RETURN OF TEN TAILS!!
RAAAWR!!!
GG GG
AND THE BEGINNING OF THE END OF THE WORLD!!
!!!
!!!

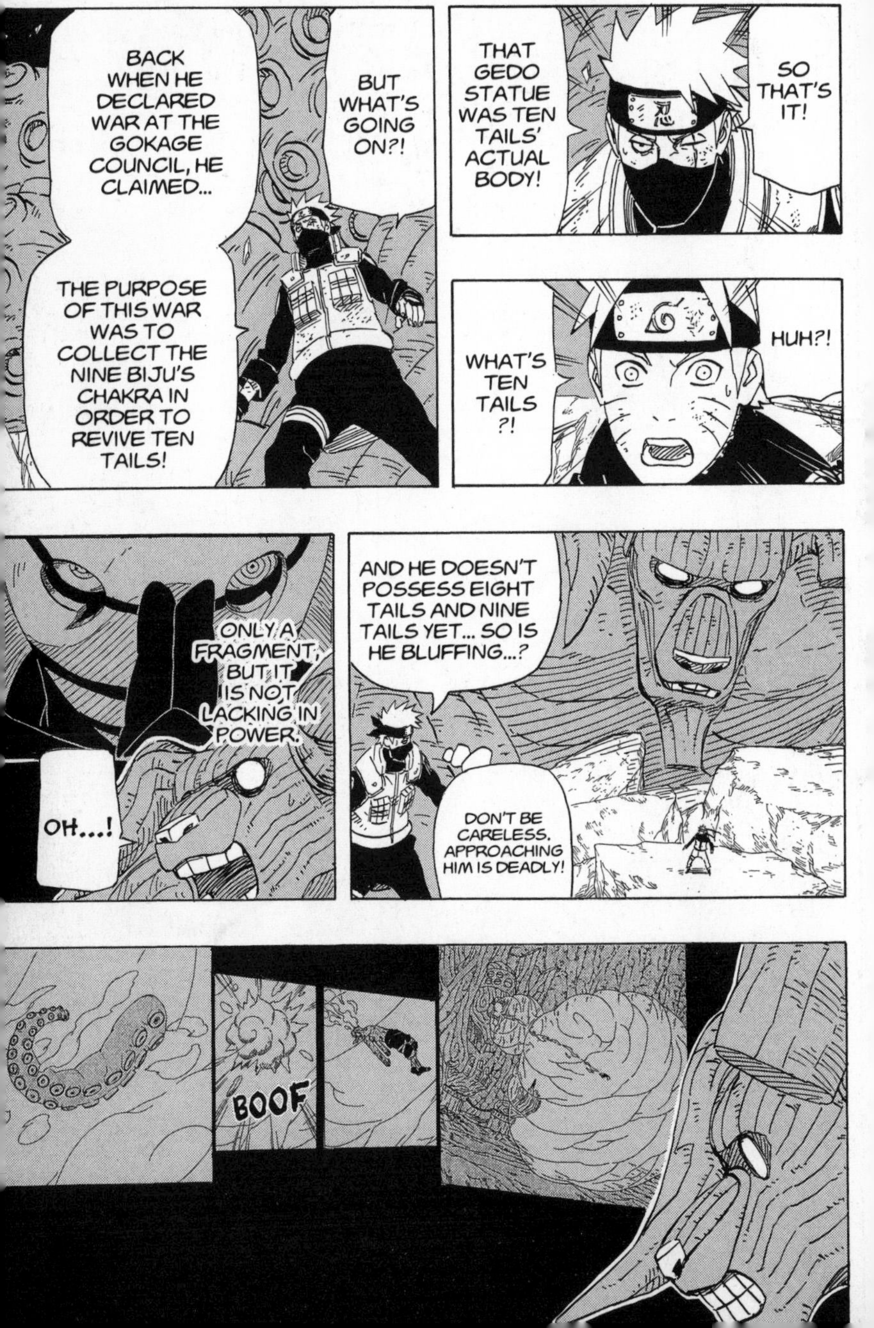
SO THAT'S IT!
THAT GEDO STATUE WAS TEN TAILS' ACTUAL BODY!
HUH?!
WHAT'S TEN TAILS ?!
BUT WHAT'S GOING ON?!
BACK WHEN HE DECLARED WAR AT THE GOKAGE COUNCIL, HE CLAIMED...
THE PURPOSE OF THIS WAR WAS TO COLLECT THE NINE BIJU'S CHAKRA IN ORDER TO REVIVE TEN TAILS!
AND HE DOESN'T POSSESS EIGHT TAILS AND NINE TAILS YET... SO IS HE BLUFFING...?
DON'T BE CARELESS. APPROACHING HIM IS DEADLY!
ONLY A FRAGMENT, BUT IT IS NOT LACKING IN POWER.
OH...!
BOOF

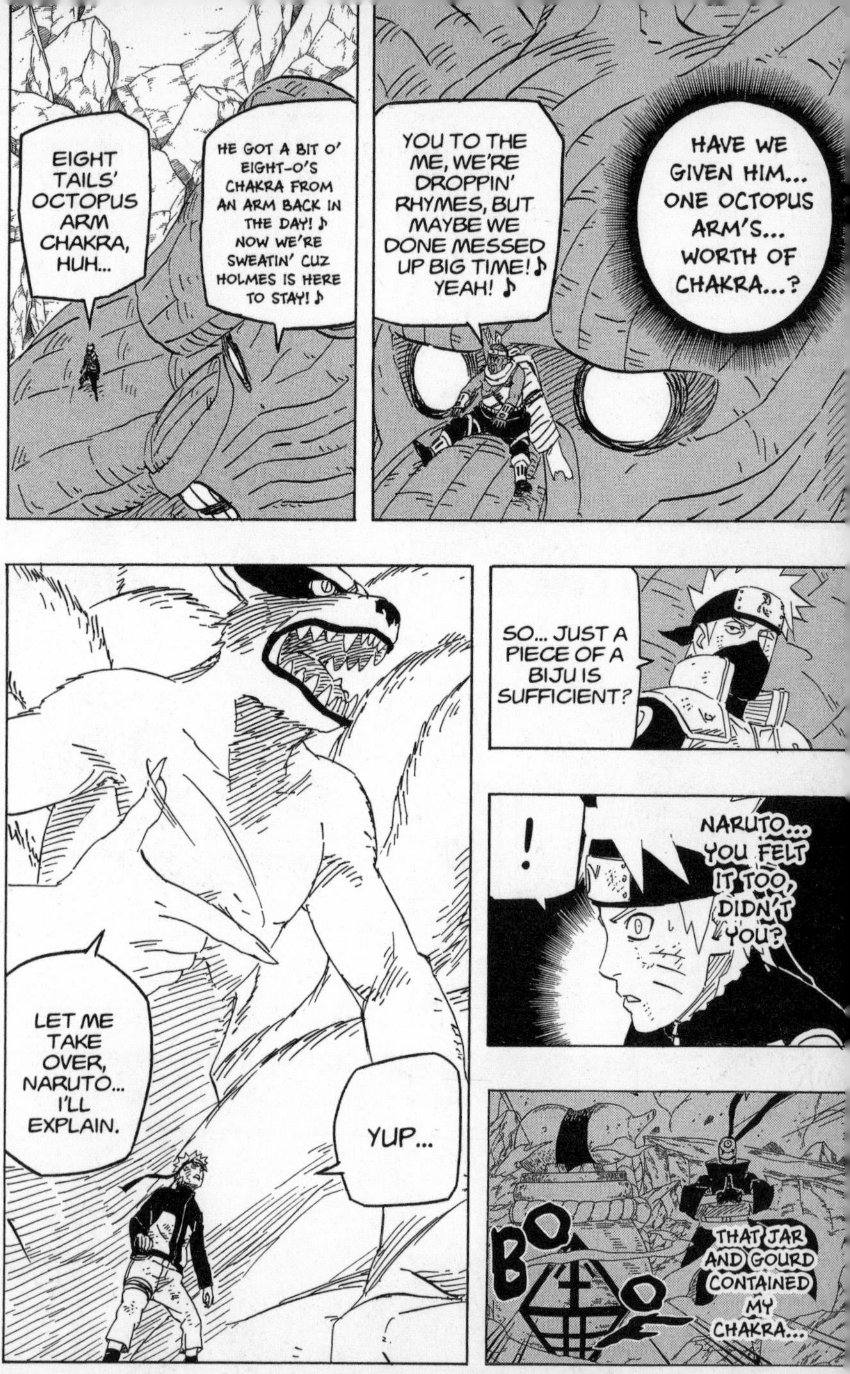
HAVE WE GIVEN HIM... ONE OCTOPUS ARM'S... WORTH OF CHAKRA...?
YOU TO THE ME, WE'RE DROPPIN' RHYMES, BUT MAYBE WE DONE MESSED UP BIG TIME! ♪ YEAH! ♪
HE GOT A BIT O' EIGHT-O'S CHAKRA FROM AN ARM BACK IN THE DAY! ♪ NOW WE'RE SWEATIN' CUZ HOLMES IS HERE TO STAY! ♪
EIGHT TAILS' OCTOPUS ARM CHAKRA, HUH...
SO... JUST A PIECE OF A BIJU IS SUFFICIENT?
!
NARUTO... YOU FELT IT TOO, DIDN'T YOU?
THAT JAR AND GOURD CONTAINED MY CHAKRA...
YUP...
LET ME TAKE OVER, NARUTO... I'LL EXPLAIN.

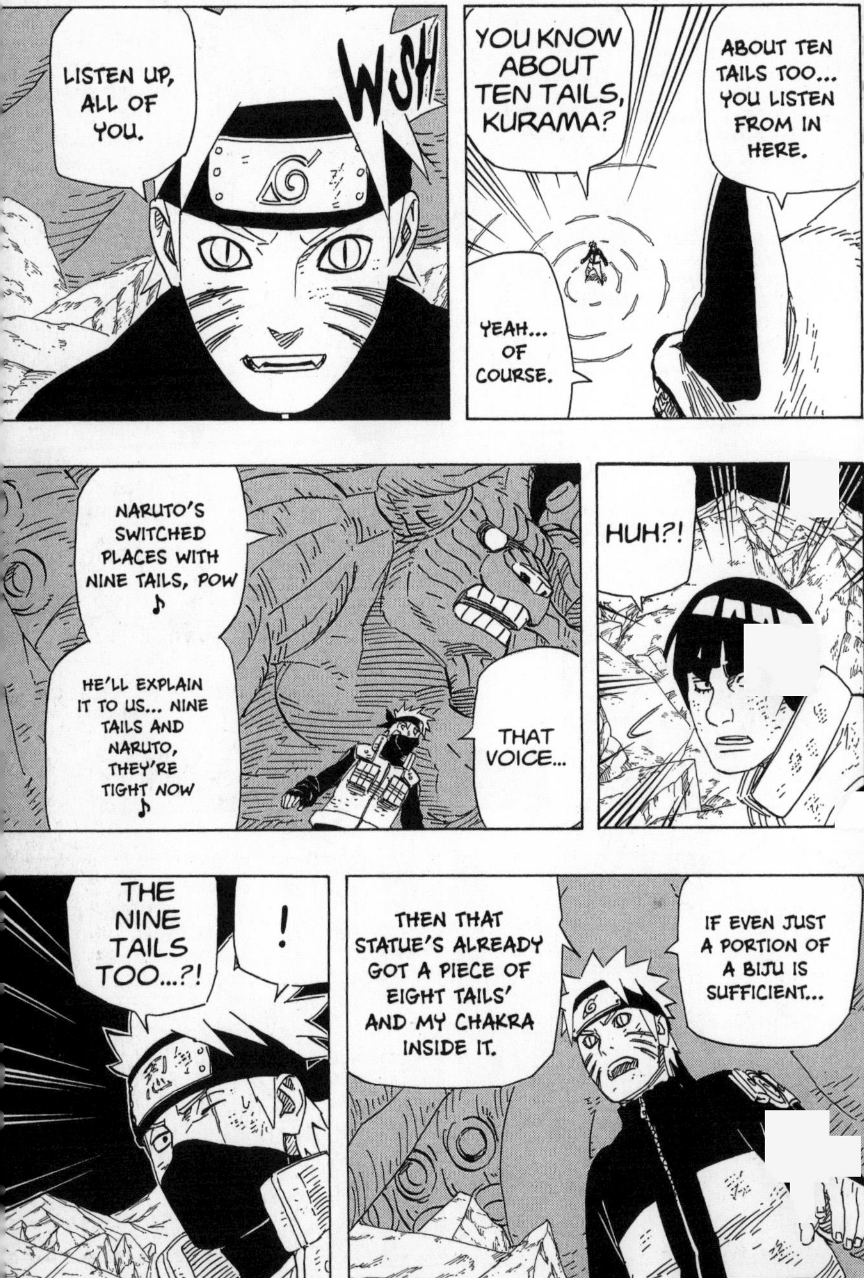
ABOUT TEN TAILS TOO... YOU LISTEN FROM IN HERE.
YOU KNOW ABOUT TEN TAILS, KURAMA?
YEAH... OF COURSE.
WSH
LISTEN UP, ALL OF YOU.
HUH?!
NARUTO'S SWITCHED PLACES WITH NINE TAILS, POW ♪
THAT VOICE...
HE'LL EXPLAIN IT TO US... NINE TAILS AND NARUTO, THEY'RE TIGHT NOW ♪
IF EVEN JUST A PORTION OF A BIJU IS SUFFICIENT...
THEN THAT STATUE'S ALREADY GOT A PIECE OF EIGHT TAILS' AND MY CHAKRA INSIDE IT.
!
THE NINE TAILS TOO...?!

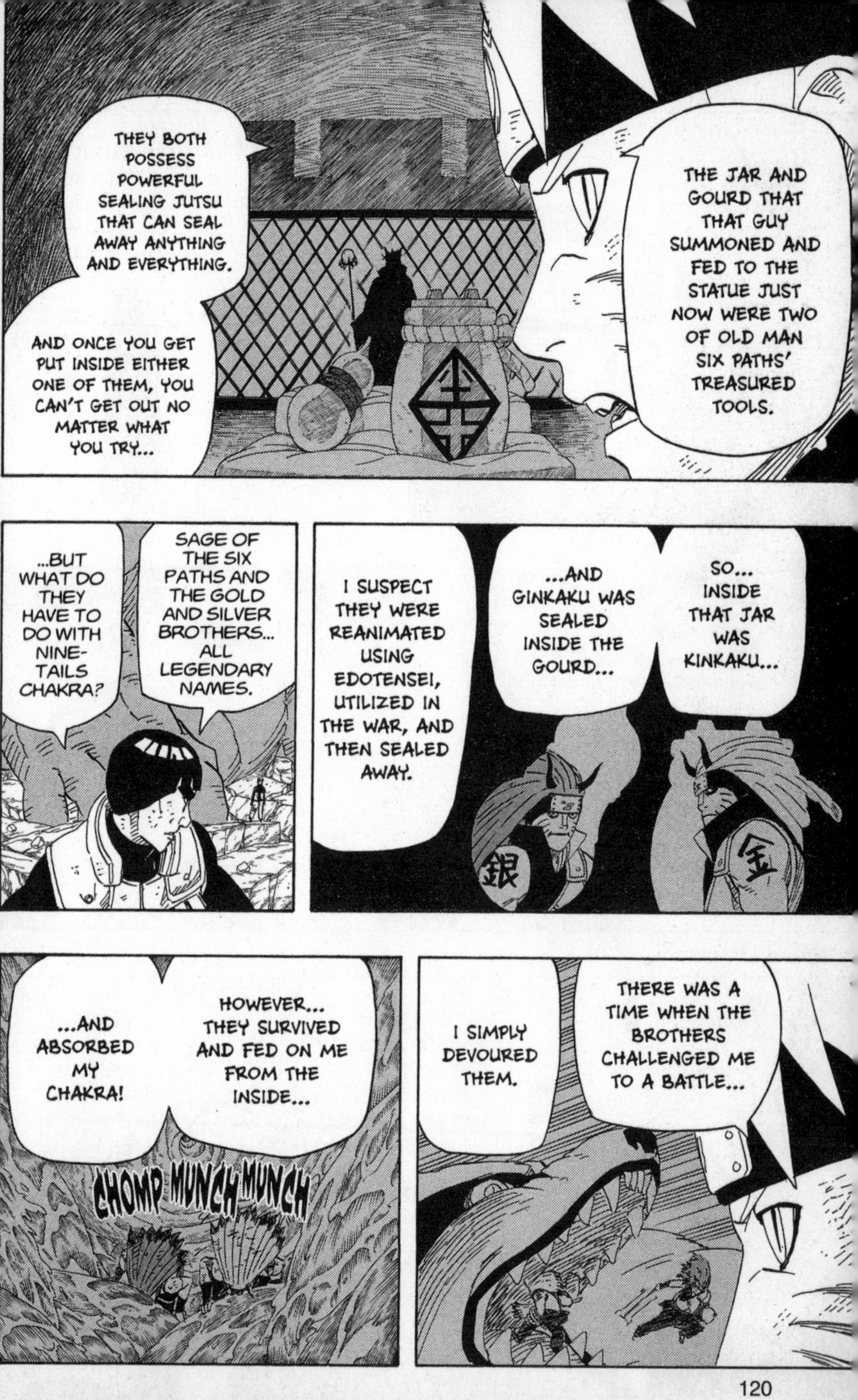
THE JAR AND GOURD THAT THAT GUY SUMMONED AND FED TO THE STATUE JUST NOW WERE TWO OF OLD MAN SIX PATHS' TREASURED TOOLS.
THEY BOTH POSSESS POWERFUL SEALING JUTSU THAT CAN SEAL AWAY ANYTHING AND EVERYTHING.
AND ONCE YOU GET PUT INSIDE EITHER ONE OF THEM, YOU CAN'T GET OUT NO MATTER WHAT YOU TRY...
SO... INSIDE THAT JAR WAS KINKAKU...
...AND GINKAKU WAS SEALED INSIDE THE GOURD...
I SUSPECT THEY WERE REANIMATED USING EDOTENSEI, UTILIZED IN THE WAR, AND THEN SEALED AWAY.
SAGE OF THE SIX PATHS AND THE GOLD AND SILVER BROTHERS... ALL LEGENDARY NAMES.
...BUT WHAT DO THEY HAVE TO DO WITH NINE-TAILS CHAKRA?
THERE WAS A TIME WHEN THE BROTHERS CHALLENGED ME TO A BATTLE...
I SIMPLY DEVOURED THEM.
HOWEVER... THEY SURVIVED AND FED ON ME FROM THE INSIDE...
...AND ABSORBED MY CHAKRA!
CHOMP MUNCH MUNCH

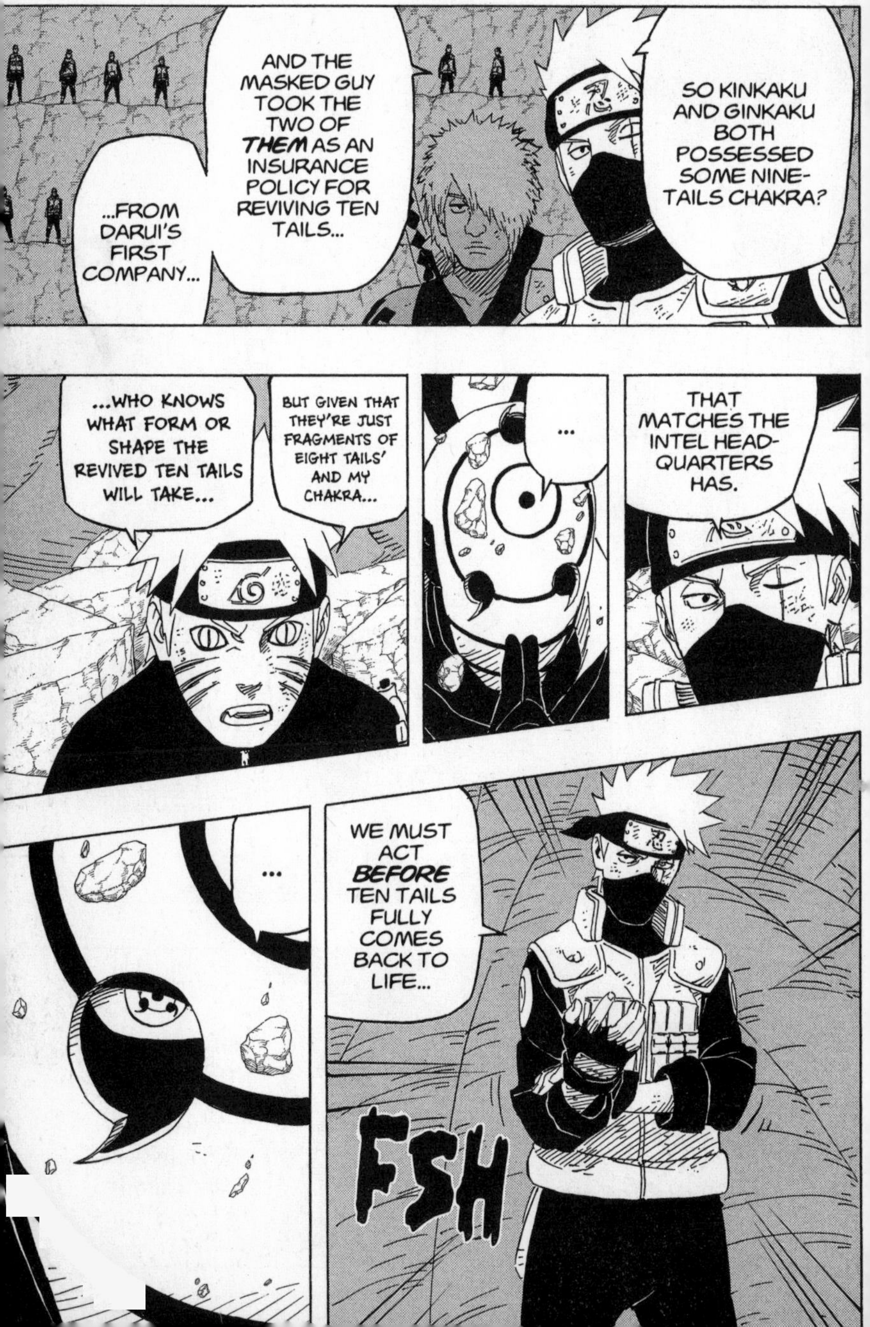
SO KINKAKU AND GINKAKU BOTH POSSESSED SOME NINE-TAILS CHAKRA?
AND THE MASKED GUY TOOK THE TWO OF *THEM* AS AN INSURANCE POLICY FOR REVIVING TEN TAILS...
...FROM DARUI'S FIRST COMPANY...
THAT MATCHES THE INTEL HEAD-QUARTERS HAS.
...
BUT GIVEN THAT THEY'RE JUST FRAGMENTS OF EIGHT TAILS' AND MY CHAKRA...
...WHO KNOWS WHAT FORM OR SHAPE THE REVIVED TEN TAILS WILL TAKE...
WE MUST ACT *BEFORE* TEN TAILS FULLY COMES BACK TO LIFE...
FSH
...

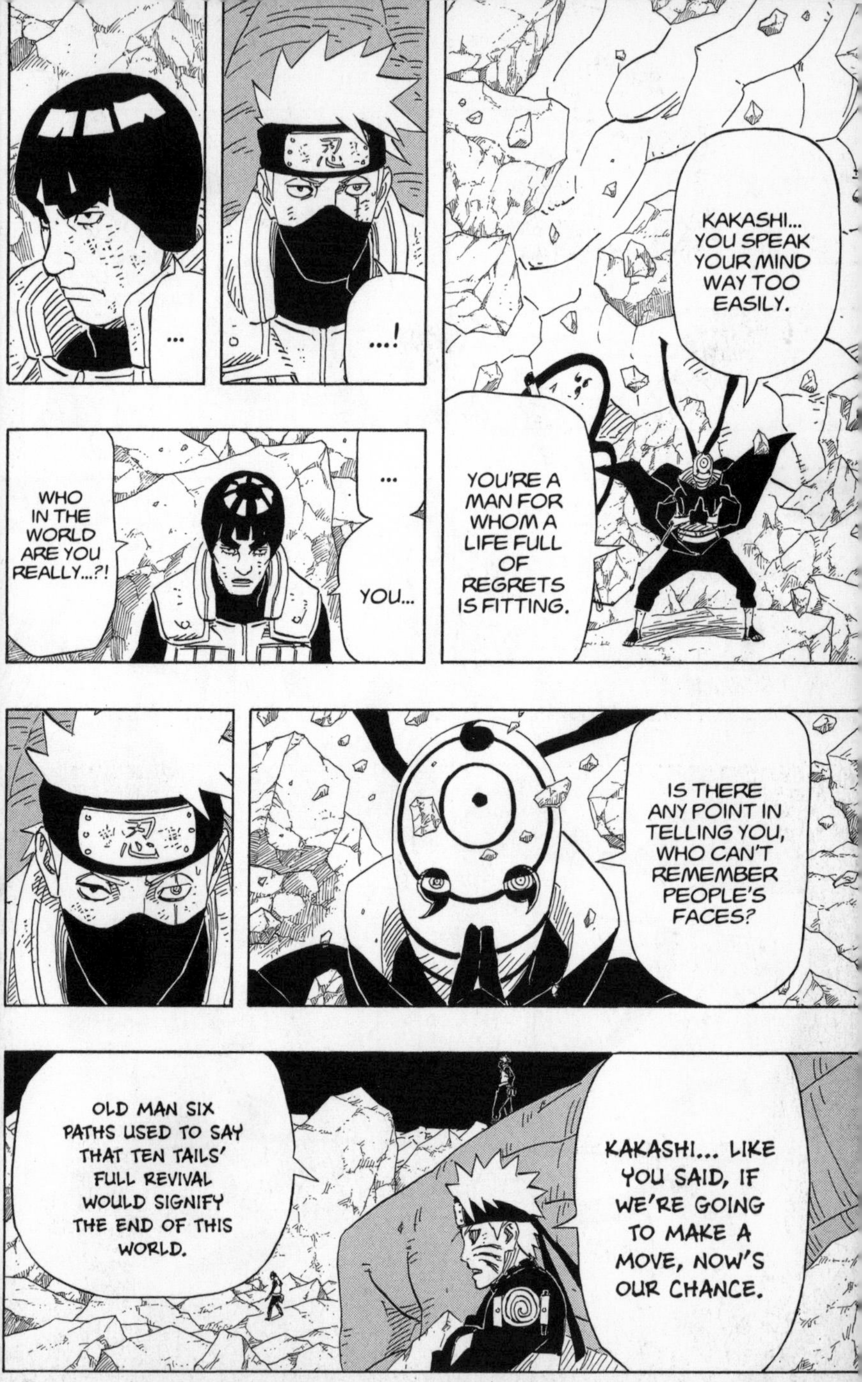
KAKASHI... YOU SPEAK YOUR MIND WAY TOO EASILY.
YOU'RE A MAN FOR WHOM A LIFE FULL OF REGRETS IS FITTING.
...!
...
...
YOU...
WHO IN THE WORLD ARE YOU REALLY...?!
IS THERE ANY POINT IN TELLING YOU, WHO CAN'T REMEMBER PEOPLE'S FACES?
KAKASHI... LIKE YOU SAID, IF WE'RE GOING TO MAKE A MOVE, NOW'S OUR CHANCE.
OLD MAN SIX PATHS USED TO SAY THAT TEN TAILS' FULL REVIVAL WOULD SIGNIFY THE END OF THIS WORLD.

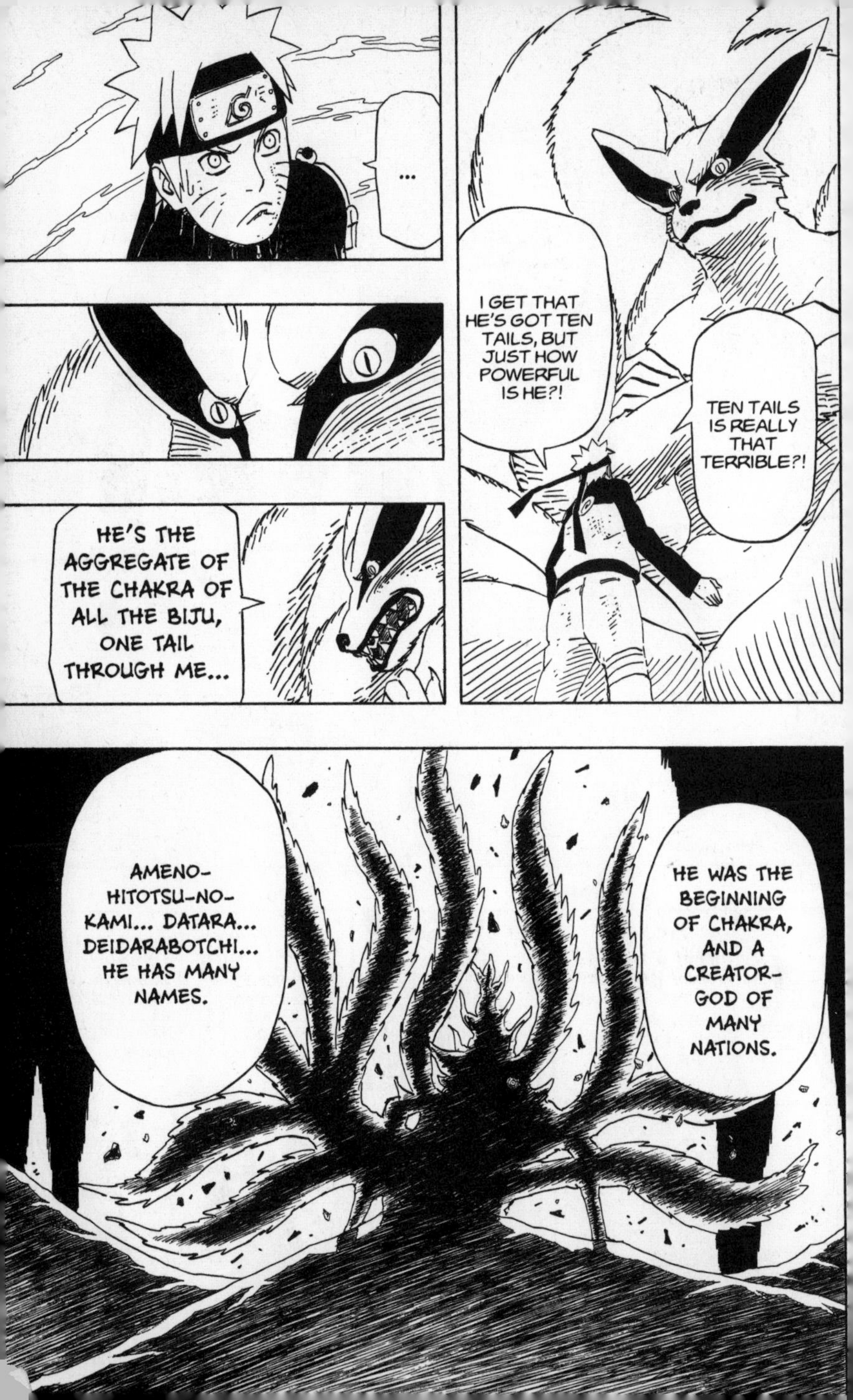
TEN TAILS IS REALLY THAT TERRIBLE?!
I GET THAT HE'S GOT TEN TAILS, BUT JUST HOW POWERFUL IS HE?!
...
HE'S THE AGGREGATE OF THE CHAKRA OF ALL THE BIJU, ONE TAIL THROUGH ME...
HE WAS THE BEGINNING OF CHAKRA, AND A CREATOR-GOD OF MANY NATIONS.
AMENO-HITOTSU-NO-KAMI... DATARA... DEIDARABOTCHI... HE HAS MANY NAMES.

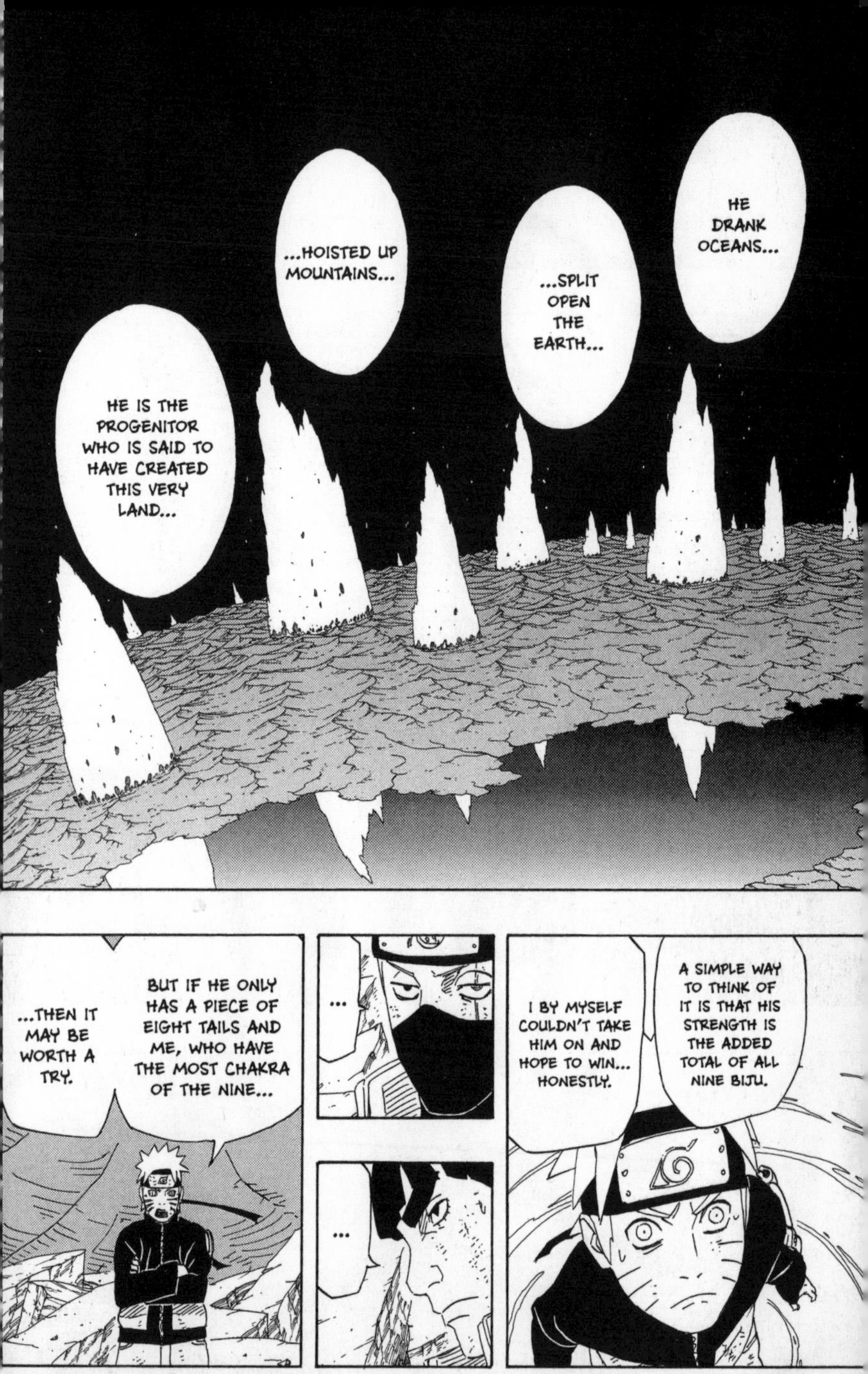
HE DRANK OCEANS...
...SPLIT OPEN THE EARTH...
...HOISTED UP MOUNTAINS...
HE IS THE PROGENITOR WHO IS SAID TO HAVE CREATED THIS VERY LAND...
A SIMPLE WAY TO THINK OF IT IS THAT HIS STRENGTH IS THE ADDED TOTAL OF ALL NINE BIJU.
I BY MYSELF COULDN'T TAKE HIM ON AND HOPE TO WIN... HONESTLY.
...
...
BUT IF HE ONLY HAS A PIECE OF EIGHT TAILS AND ME, WHO HAVE THE MOST CHAKRA OF THE NINE...
...THEN IT MAY BE WORTH A TRY.

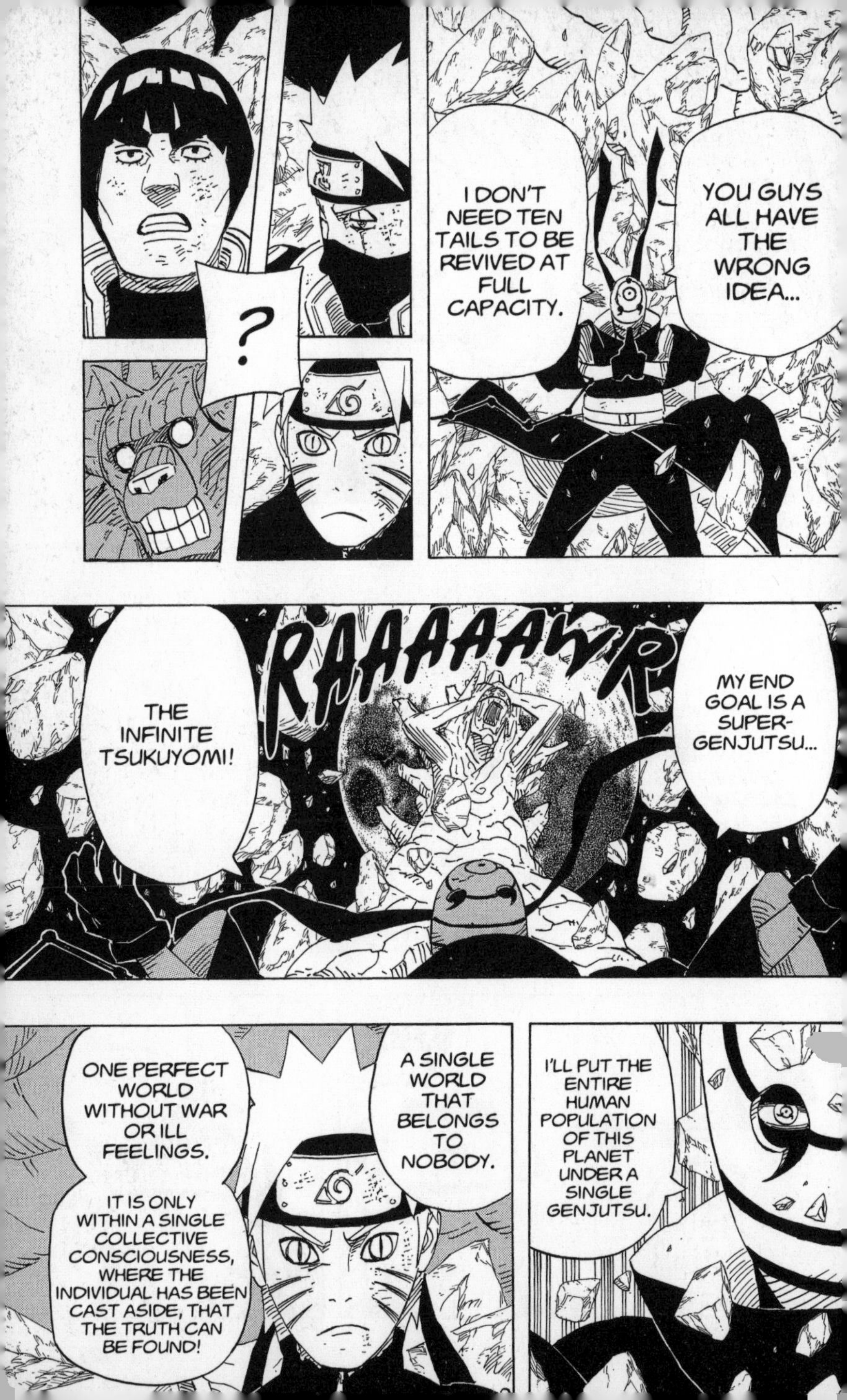
YOU GUYS ALL HAVE THE WRONG IDEA...
I DON'T NEED TEN TAILS TO BE REVIVED AT FULL CAPACITY.
?
MY END GOAL IS A SUPER-GENJUTSU...
RAAAAAWR
THE INFINITE TSUKUYOMI!
I'LL PUT THE ENTIRE HUMAN POPULATION OF THIS PLANET UNDER A SINGLE GENJUTSU.
A SINGLE WORLD THAT BELONGS TO NOBODY.
ONE PERFECT WORLD WITHOUT WAR OR ILL FEELINGS.
IT IS ONLY WITHIN A SINGLE COLLECTIVE CONSCIOUSNESS, WHERE THE INDIVIDUAL HAS BEEN CAST ASIDE, THAT THE TRUTH CAN BE FOUND!

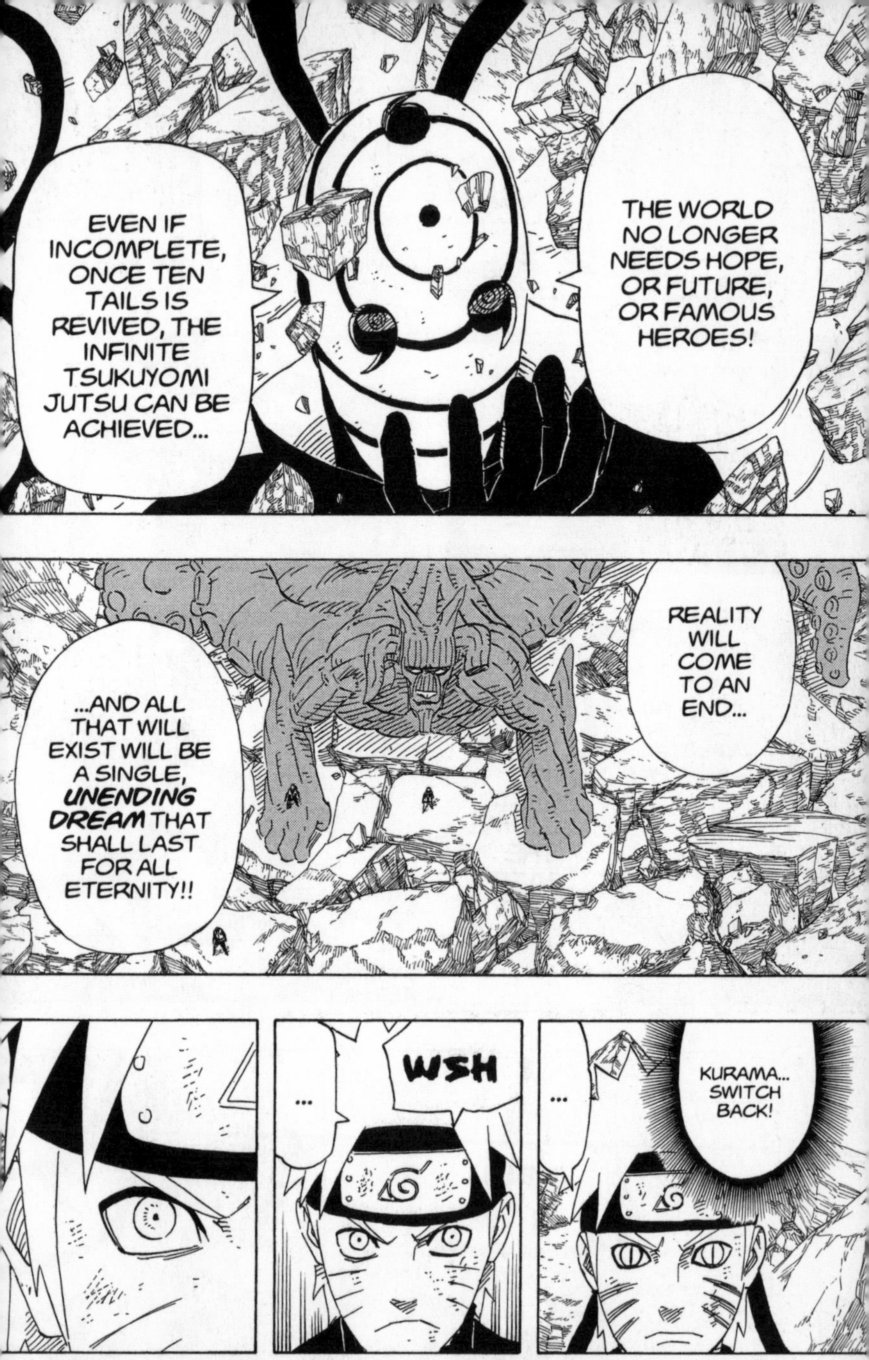
THE WORLD NO LONGER NEEDS HOPE, OR FUTURE, OR FAMOUS HEROES!
EVEN IF INCOMPLETE, ONCE TEN TAILS IS REVIVED, THE INFINITE TSUKUYOMI JUTSU CAN BE ACHIEVED...
REALITY WILL COME TO AN END...
...AND ALL THAT WILL EXIST WILL BE A SINGLE, UNENDING DREAM THAT SHALL LAST FOR ALL ETERNITY!!
...
KURAMA... SWITCH BACK!
WSH
...

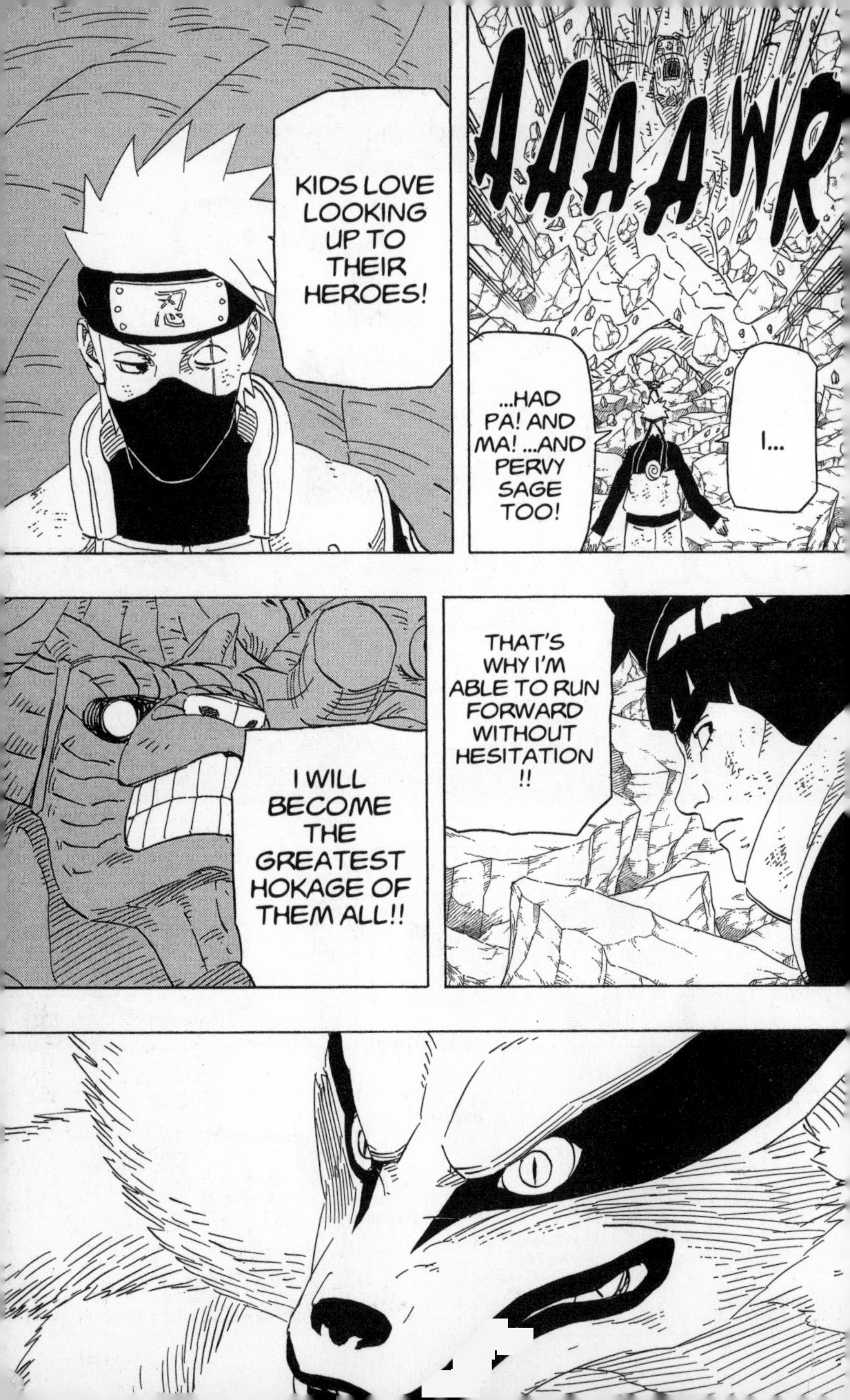
AAAAWR
I...
...HAD PA! AND MA! ...AND PERVY SAGE TOO!
KIDS LOVE LOOKING UP TO THEIR HEROES!
THAT'S WHY I'M ABLE TO RUN FORWARD WITHOUT HESITATION!!
I WILL BECOME THE GREATEST HOKAGE OF THEM ALL!!

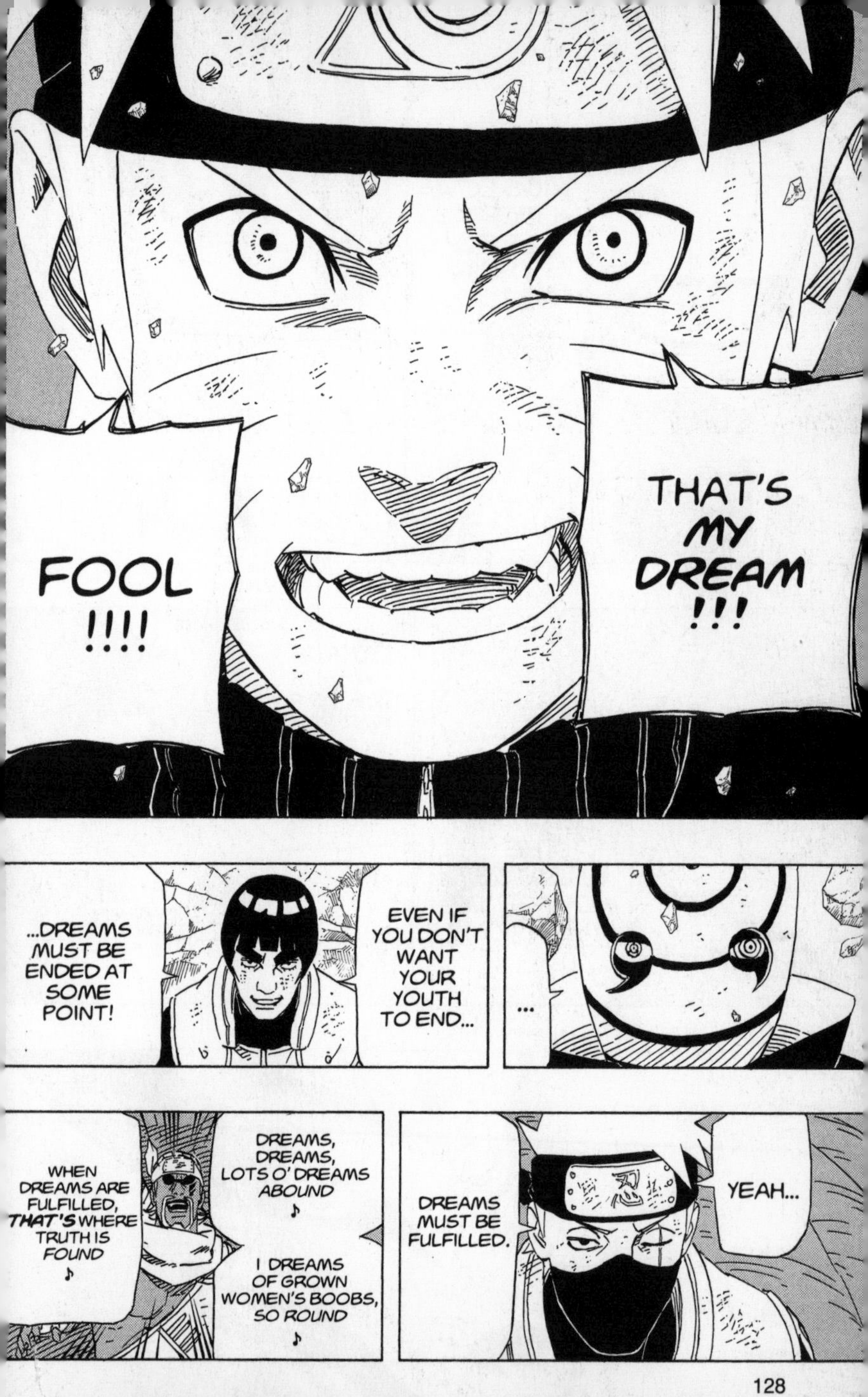

THAT'S MY DREAM!!!
FOOL!!!!
...
EVEN IF YOU DON'T WANT YOUR YOUTH TO END...
...DREAMS MUST BE ENDED AT SOME POINT!
YEAH...
DREAMS MUST BE FULFILLED.
DREAMS, DREAMS, LOTS O' DREAMS ABOUND ♪
WHEN DREAMS ARE FULFILLED, ***THAT'S*** WHERE TRUTH IS FOUND ♪
I DREAMS OF GROWN WOMEN'S BOOBS, SO ROUND ♪

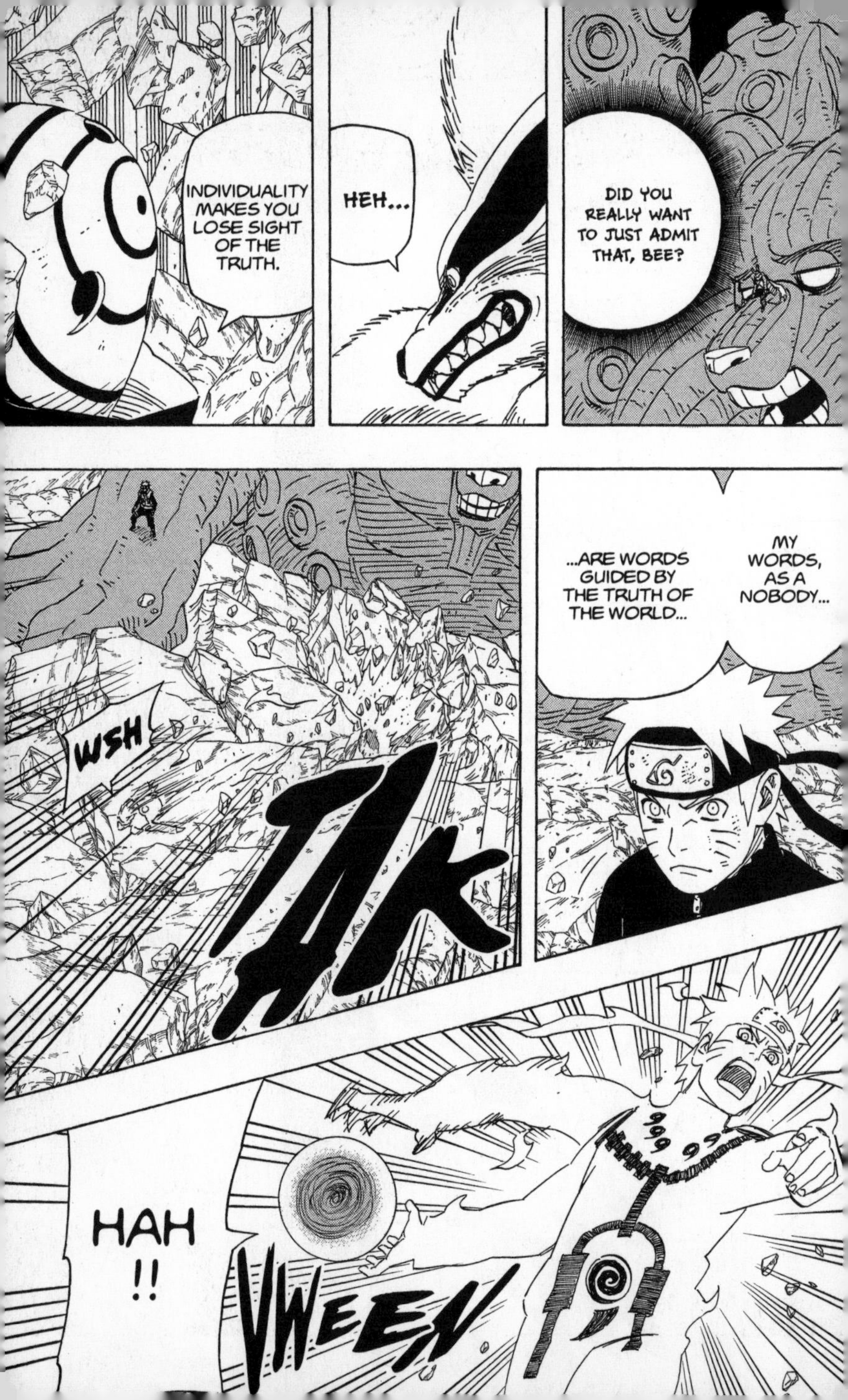
DID YOU REALLY WANT TO JUST ADMIT THAT, BEE?
HEH...
INDIVIDUALITY MAKES YOU LOSE SIGHT OF THE TRUTH.
MY WORDS, AS A NOBODY...
...ARE WORDS GUIDED BY THE TRUTH OF THE WORLD...
WSH
TAK
VWEEN
HAH !!

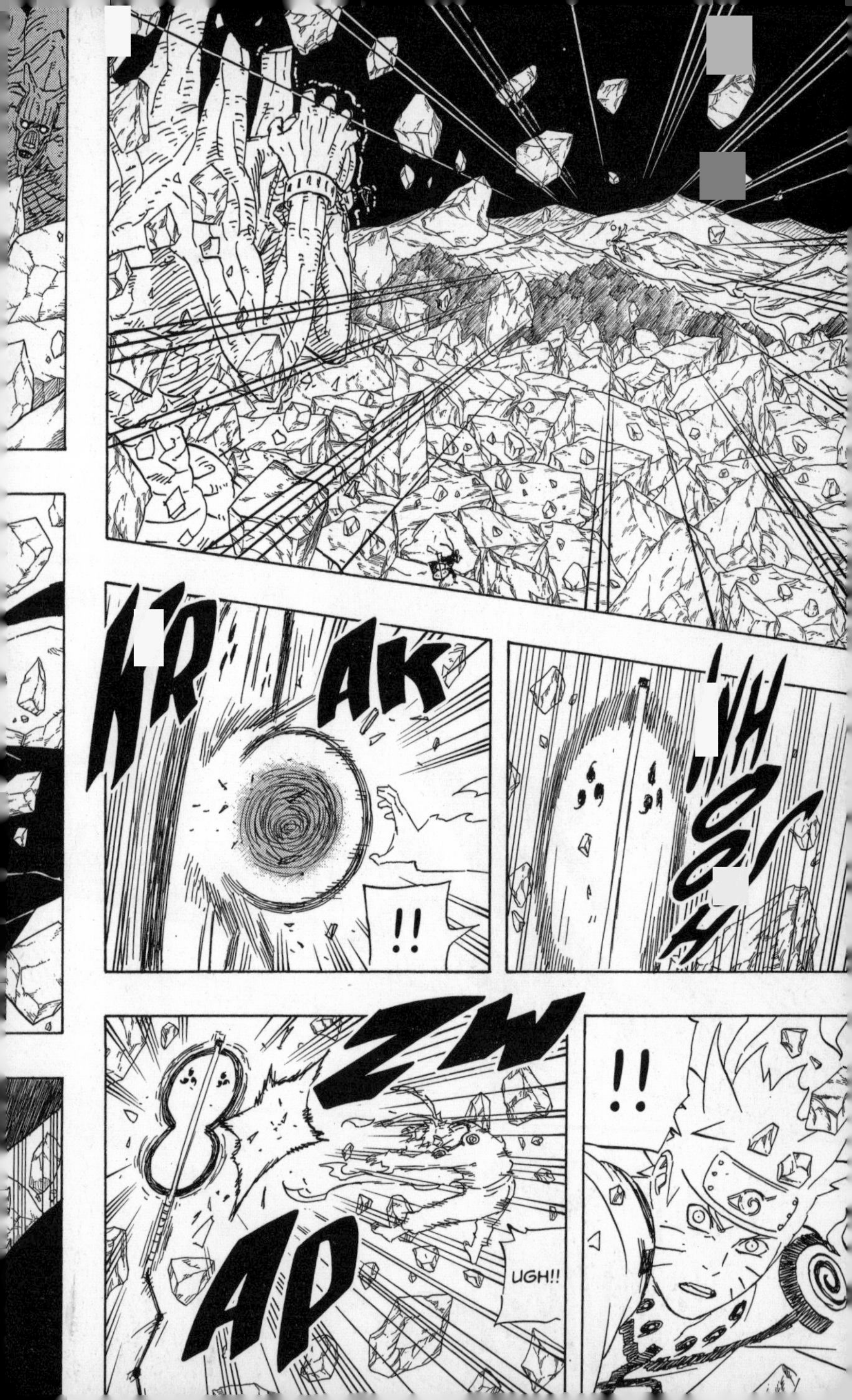
WH
O
S
H
KR
AK
!!
!!
ZW
AP
UGH!!

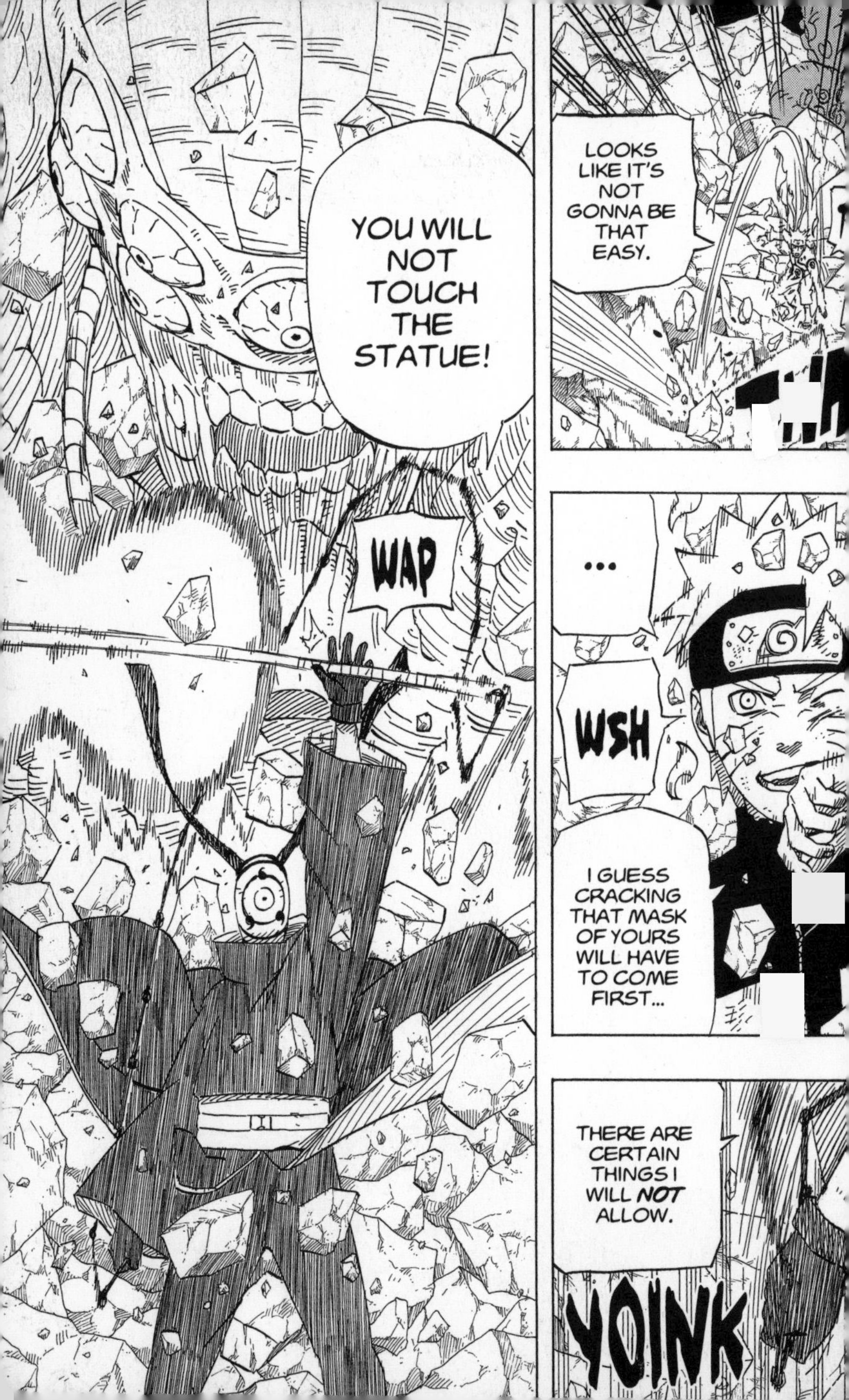
LOOKS LIKE IT'S NOT GONNA BE THAT EASY.
...
WSH
I GUESS CRACKING THAT MASK OF YOURS WILL HAVE TO COME FIRST...
THERE ARE CERTAIN THINGS I WILL *NOT* ALLOW.
YOINK
YOU WILL NOT TOUCH THE STATUE!
WAP

NARUTO

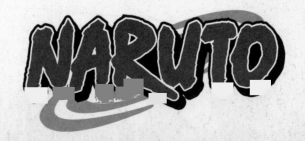

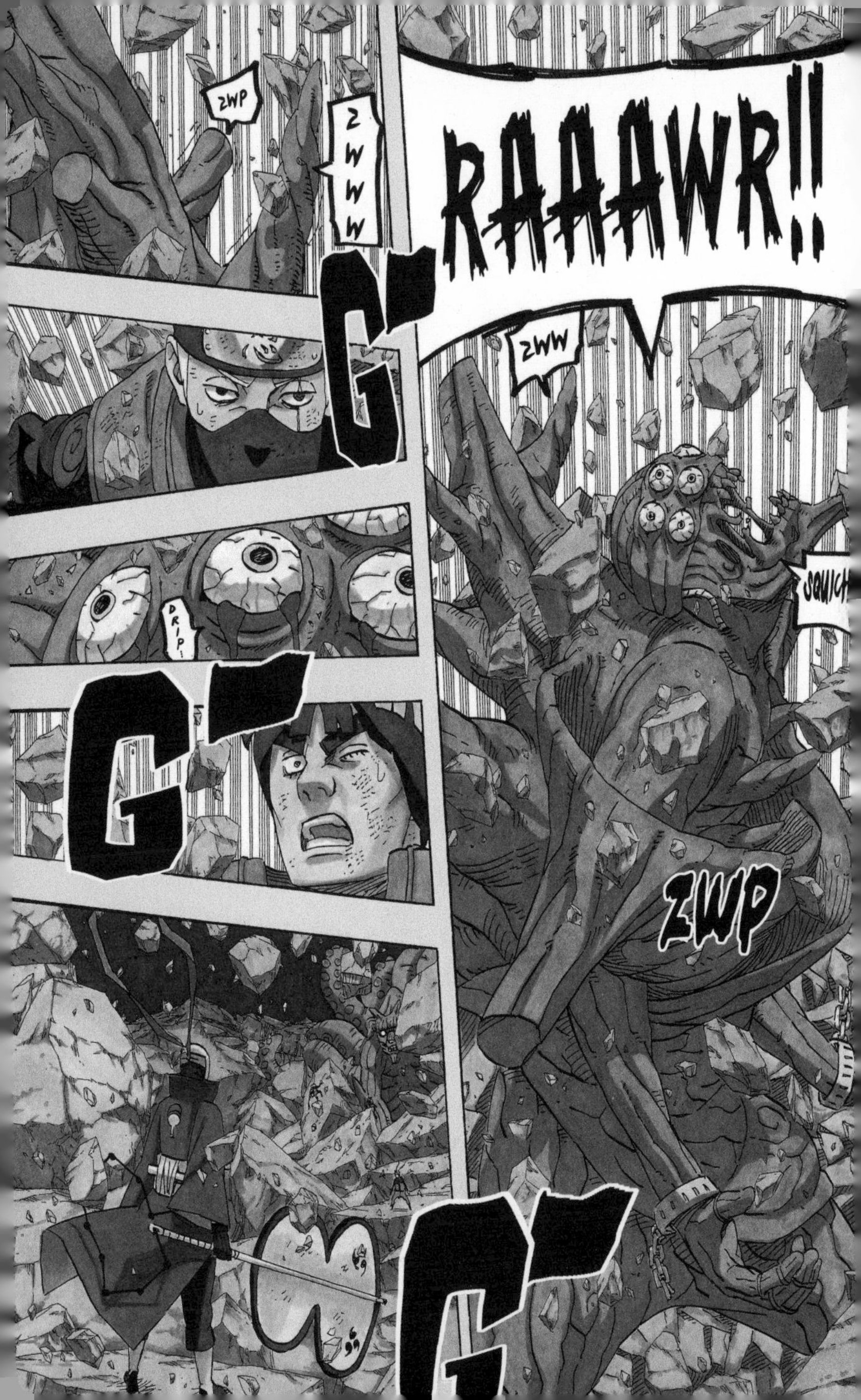
RAAAWR!!
ZWW
SQUICH
ZWP
G'
ZWP
ZWWWW
G'
DRIP...
G'

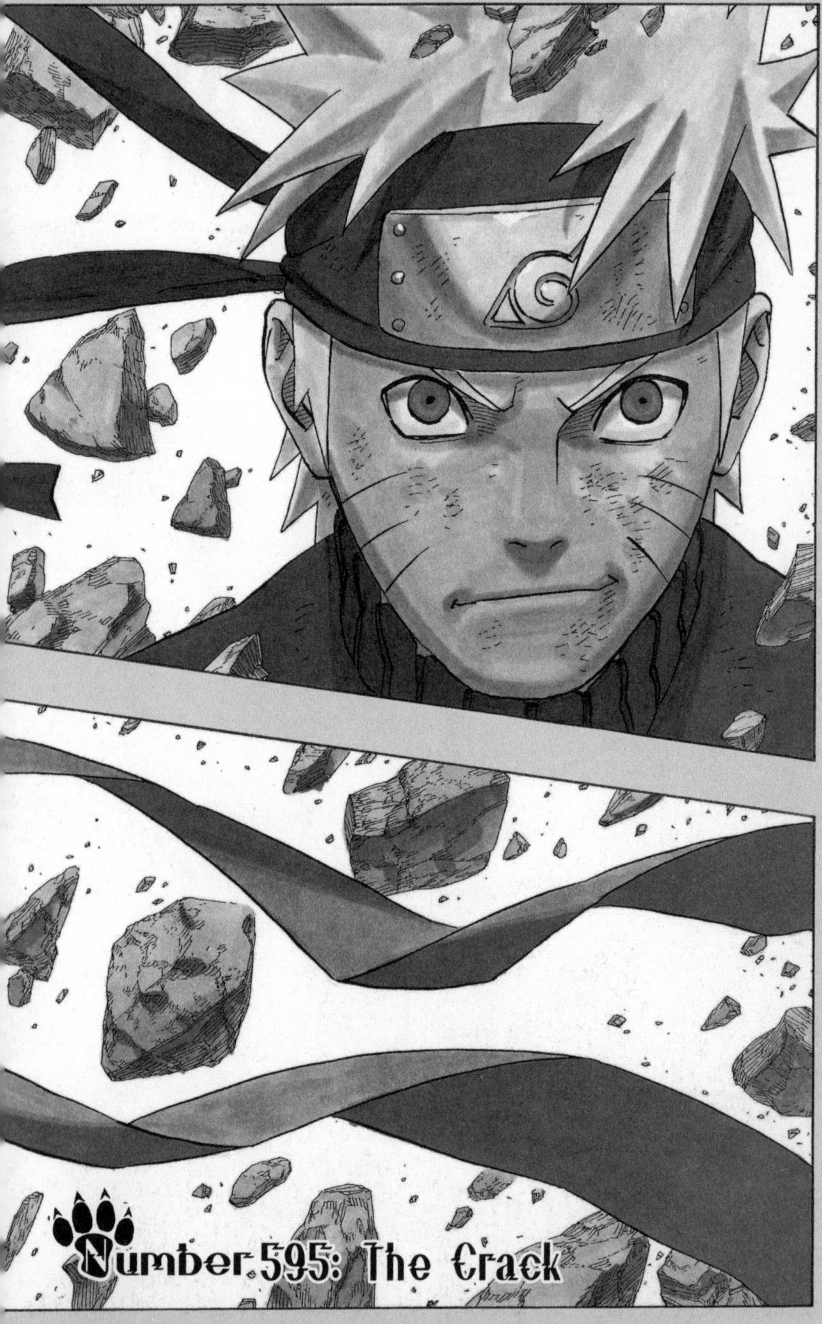

Number 595: The Crack

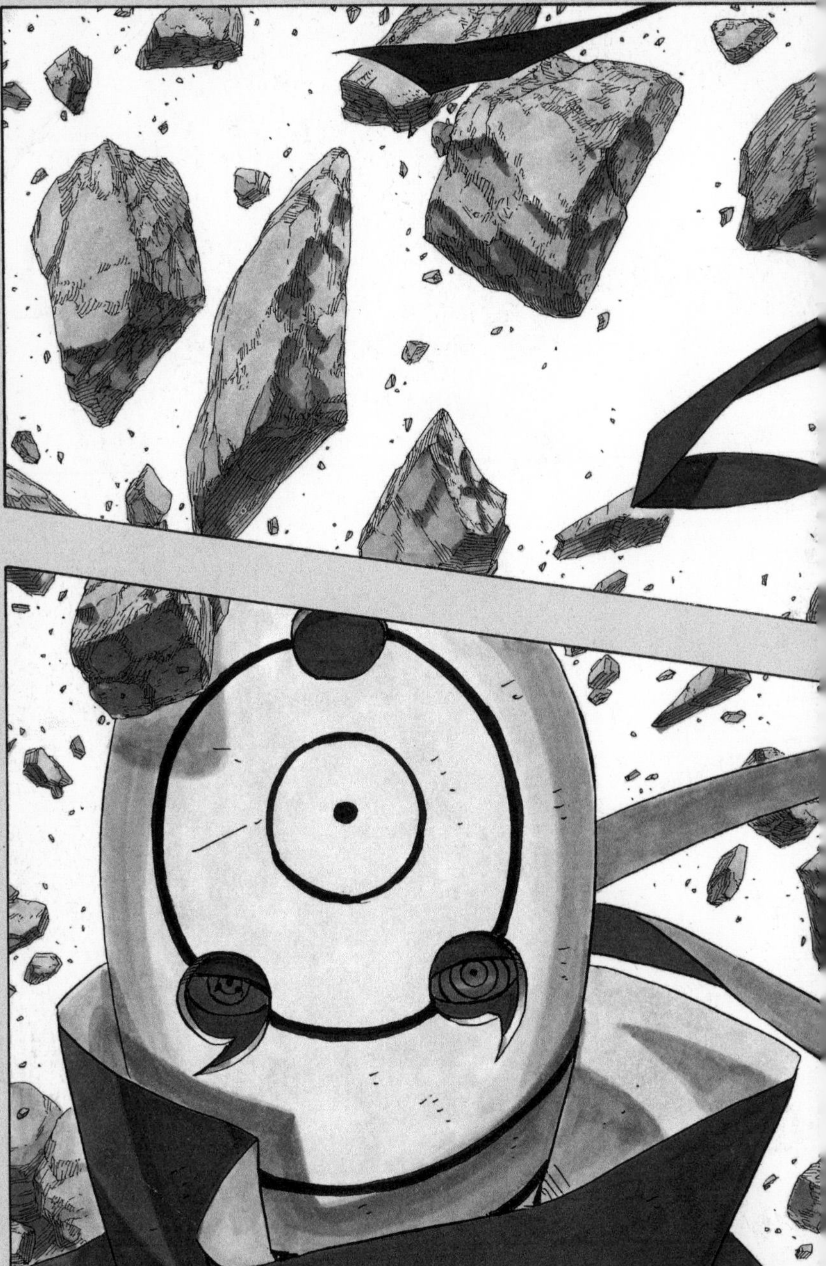

NARUTO

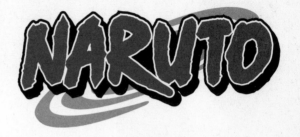

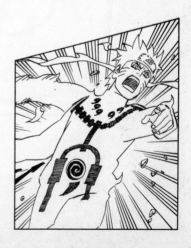

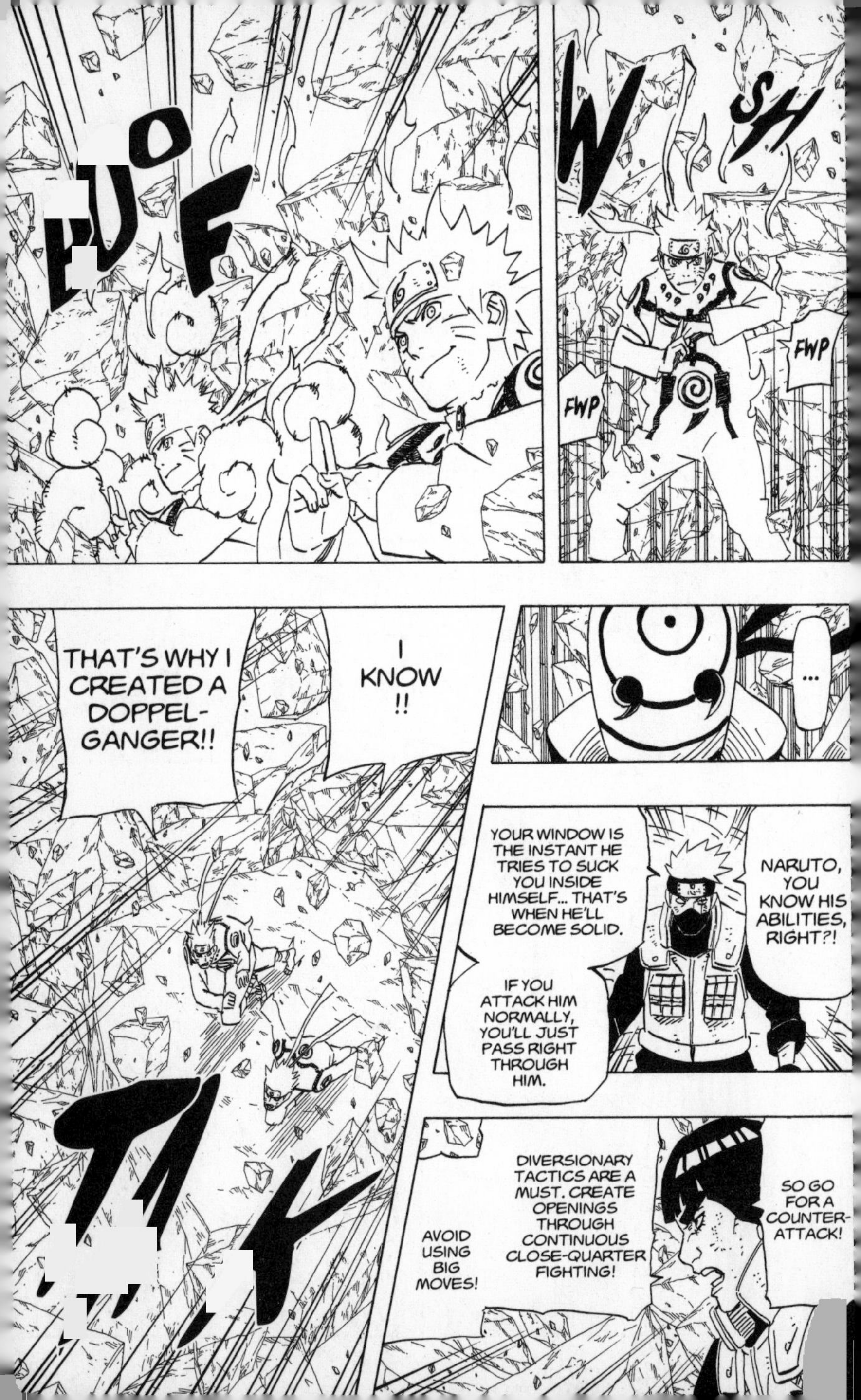
WSH
FWP
FWP
...
NARUTO, YOU KNOW HIS ABILITIES, RIGHT?!
YOUR WINDOW IS THE INSTANT HE TRIES TO SUCK YOU INSIDE HIMSELF... THAT'S WHEN HE'LL BECOME SOLID.
IF YOU ATTACK HIM NORMALLY, YOU'LL JUST PASS RIGHT THROUGH HIM.
SO GO FOR A COUNTER-ATTACK!
DIVERSIONARY TACTICS ARE A MUST. CREATE OPENINGS THROUGH CONTINUOUS CLOSE-QUARTER FIGHTING!
AVOID USING BIG MOVES!
I KNOW!!
THAT'S WHY I CREATED A DOPPEL-GANGER!!

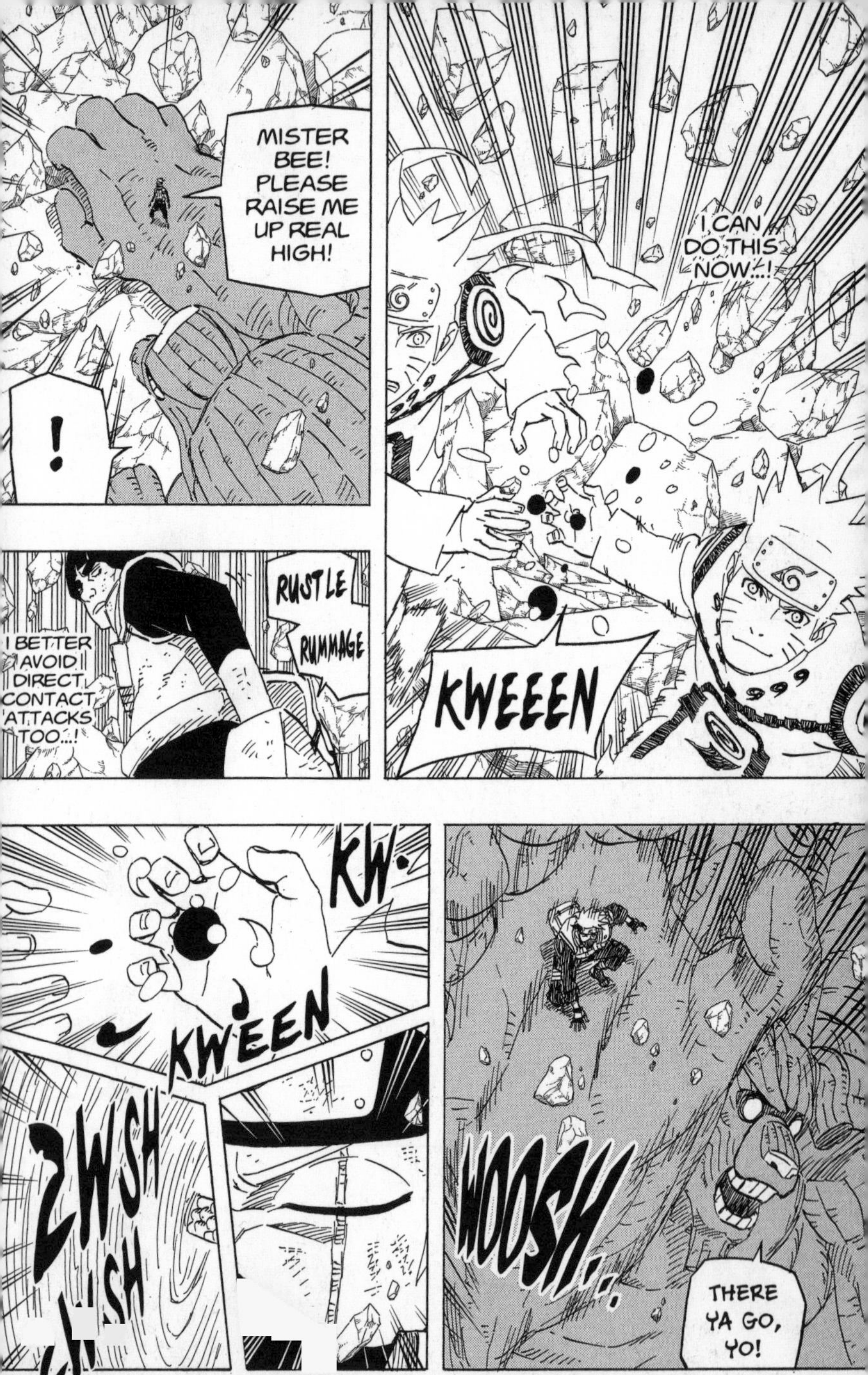
I CAN DO THIS NOW...!
KWEEEN
MISTER BEE! PLEASE RAISE ME UP REAL HIGH!
!
RUSTLE
RUMMAGE
I BETTER AVOID DIRECT CONTACT ATTACKS TOO...!
WOOSH
THERE YA GO, YO!
KW
KWEEN
ZWSH
ZWSH

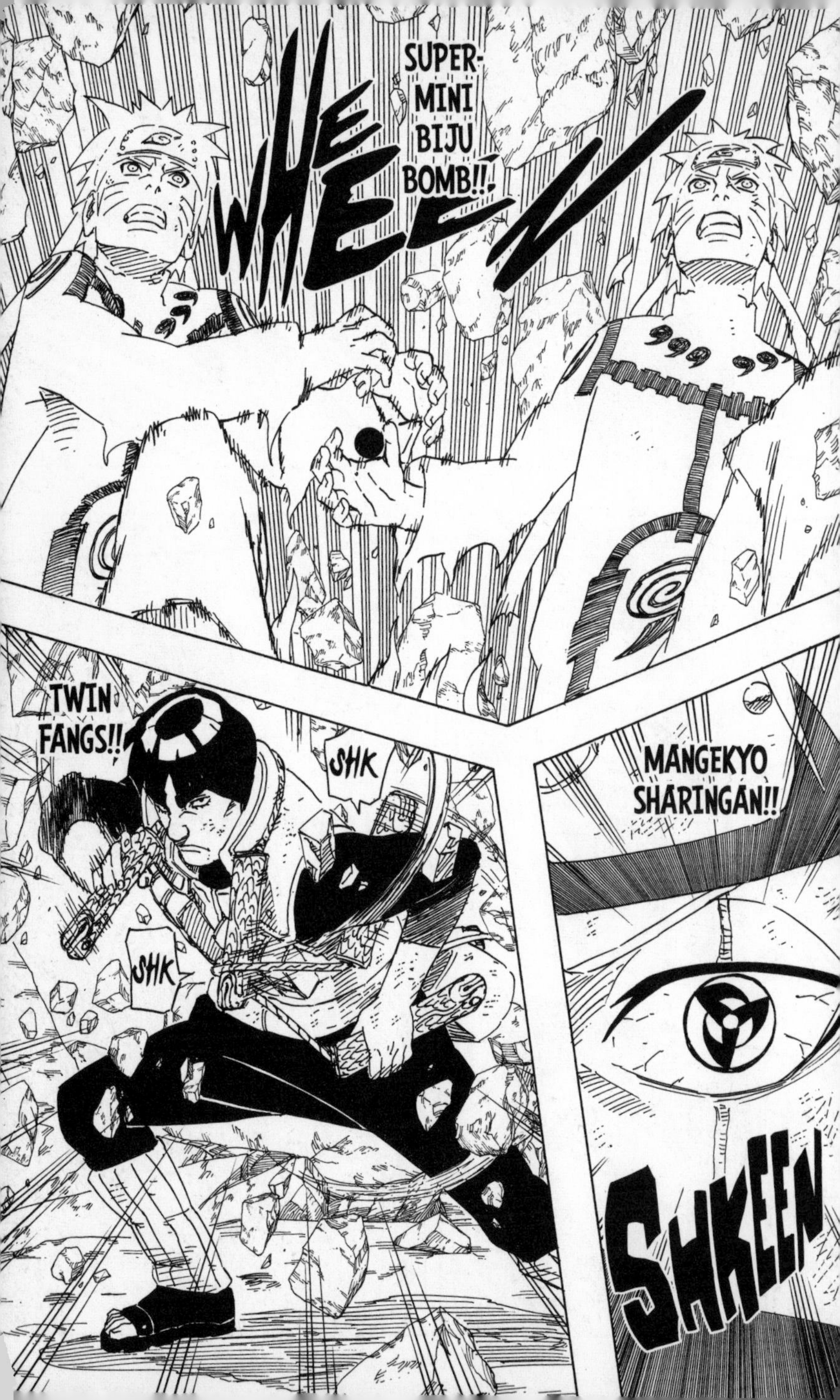
SUPER-MINI BIJU BOMB!!
WHEEEN
MANGEKYO SHARINGAN!!
SHKEEN
TWIN FANGS!!
SHK
SHK

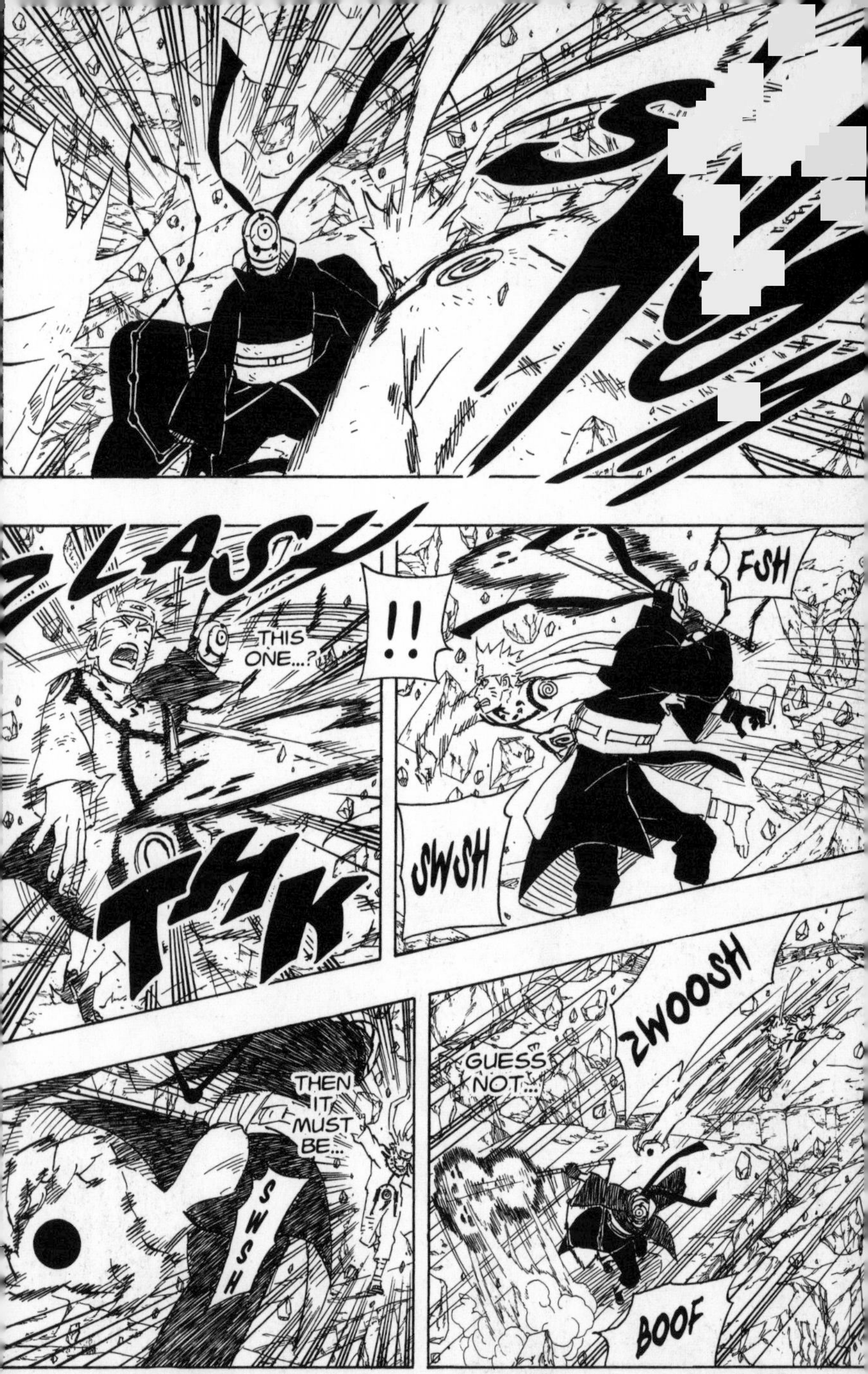
FSH
!!
SWSH
SLASH
THIS ONE...?
TNK
ZWOOSH
GUESS NOT...
BOOF
THEN IT MUST BE...
SWSH

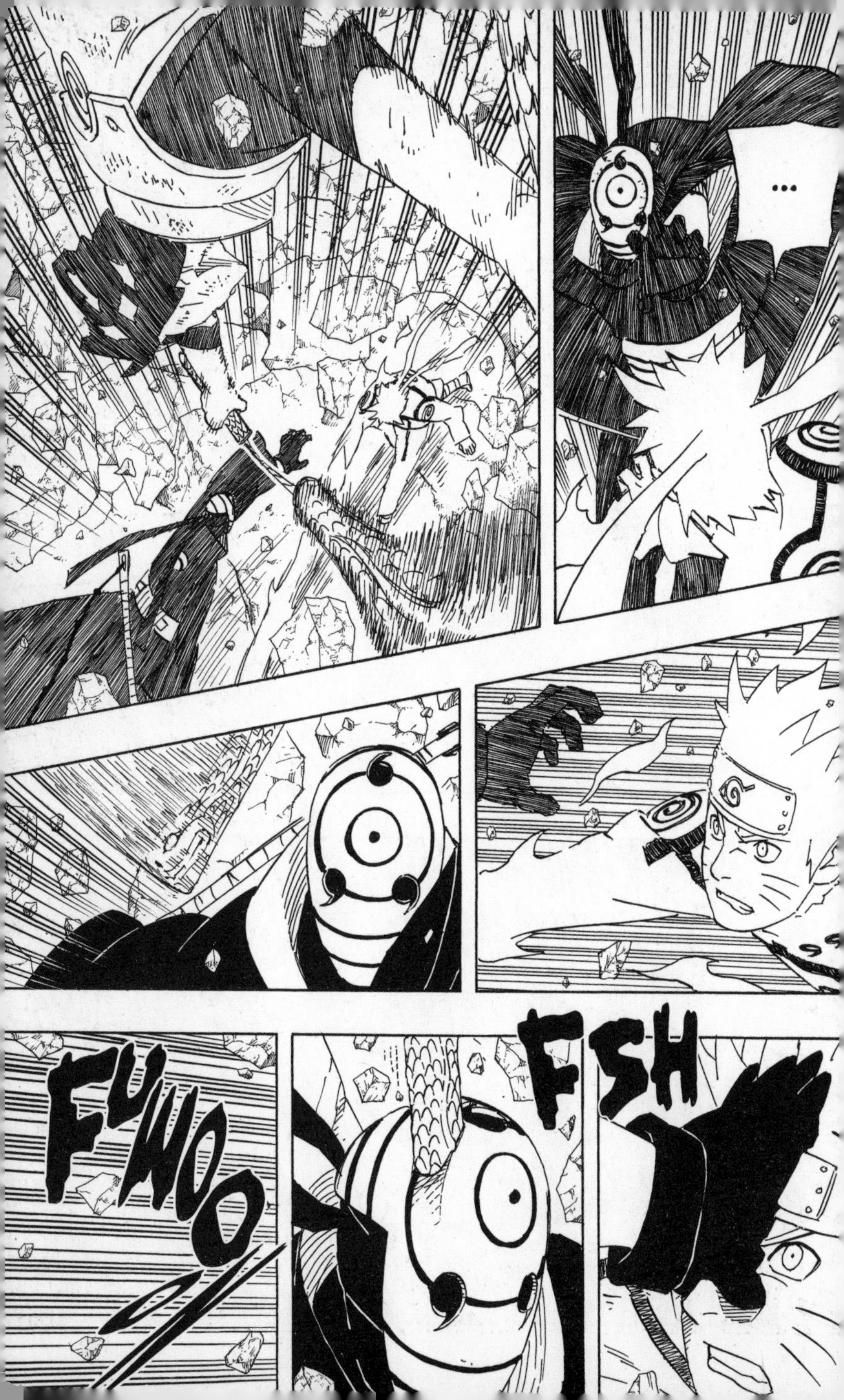
...
FSH
FWOO

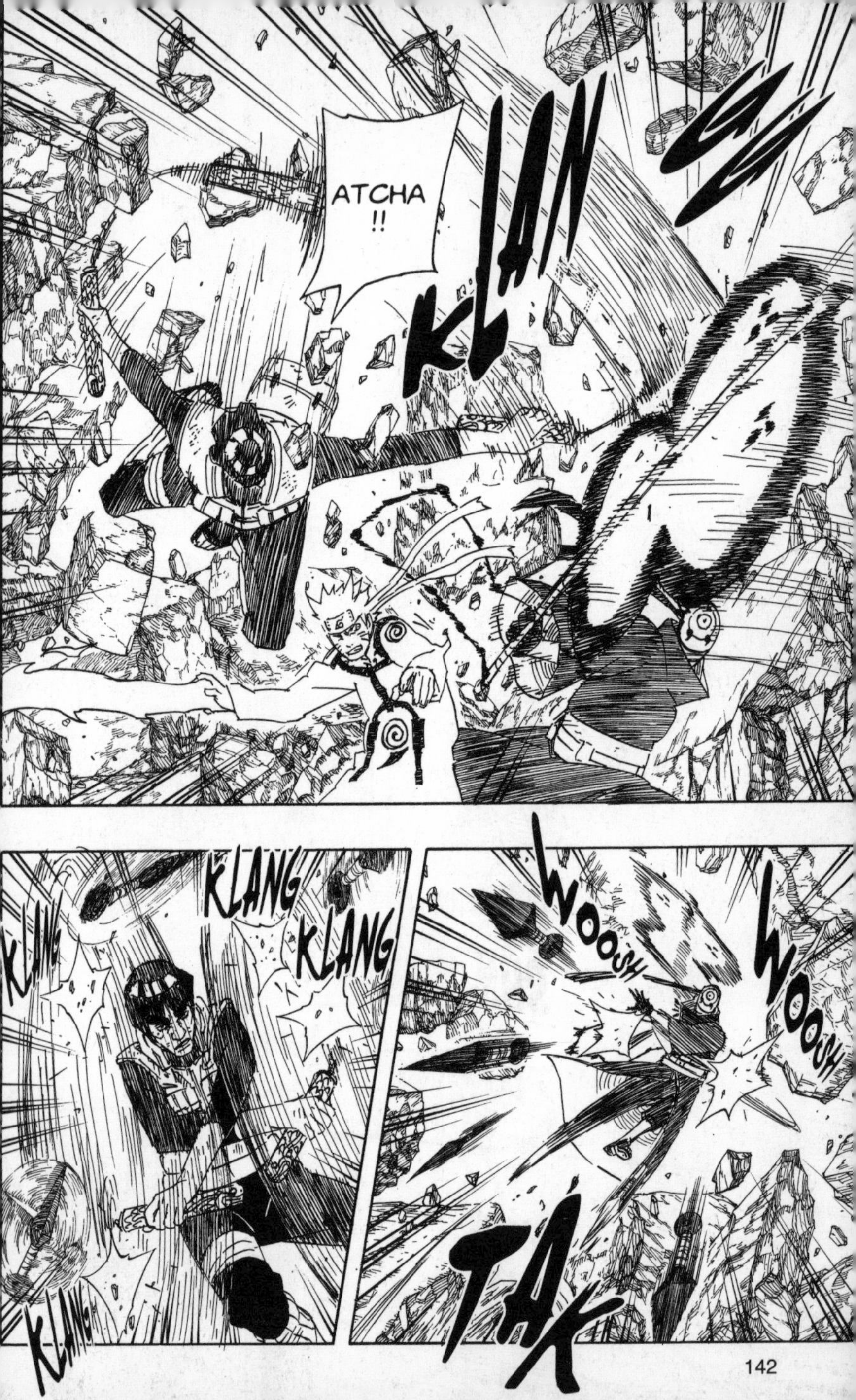

KLAN
ATCHA !!
WOOSH
WOOSH
TAK
KLANG
KLANG
KLANG
KLANG
KLANG

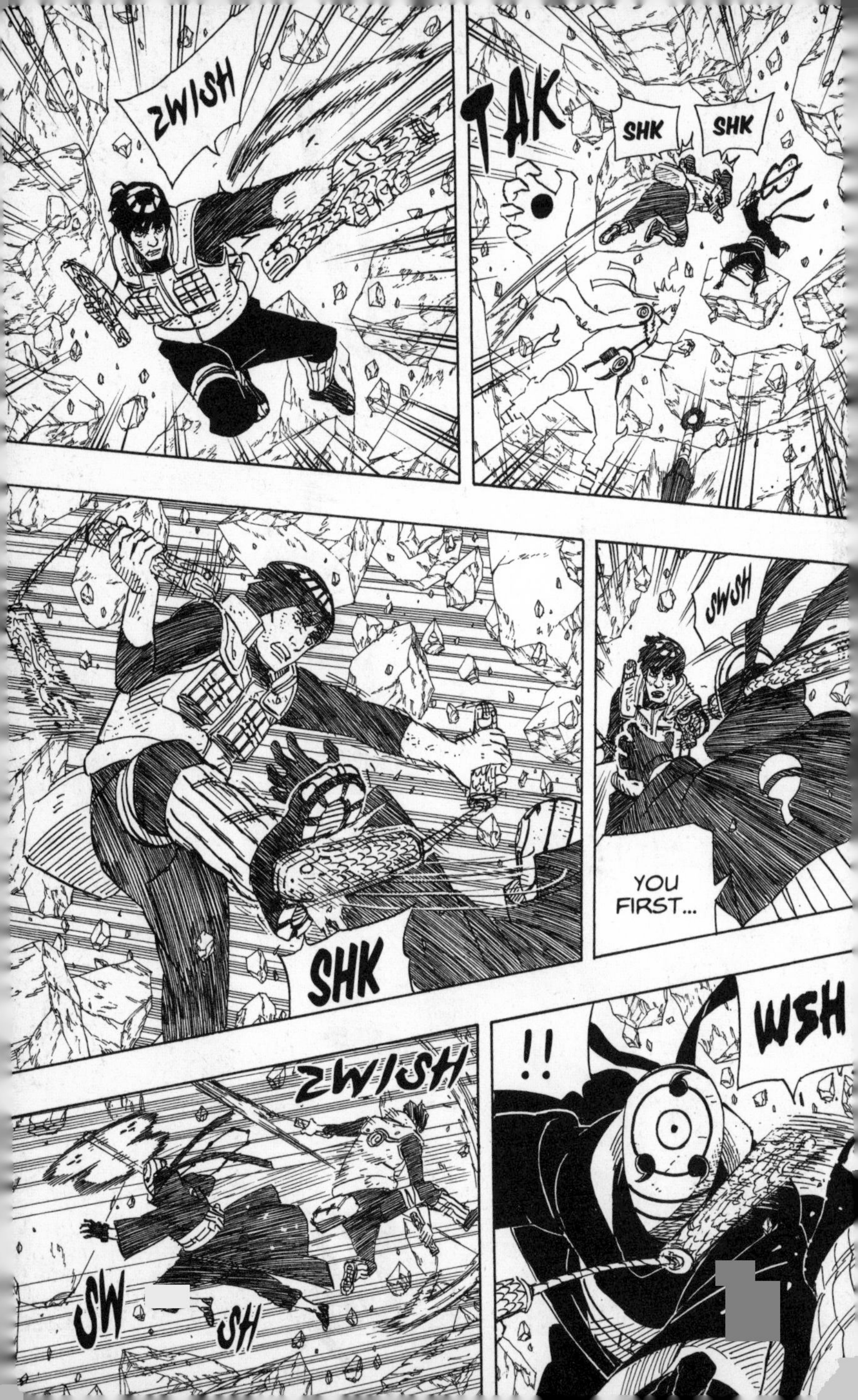
TAK
SHK
SHK
ZWISH
SWSH
YOU FIRST...
SHK
WSH
!!
ZWISH
SW
SH

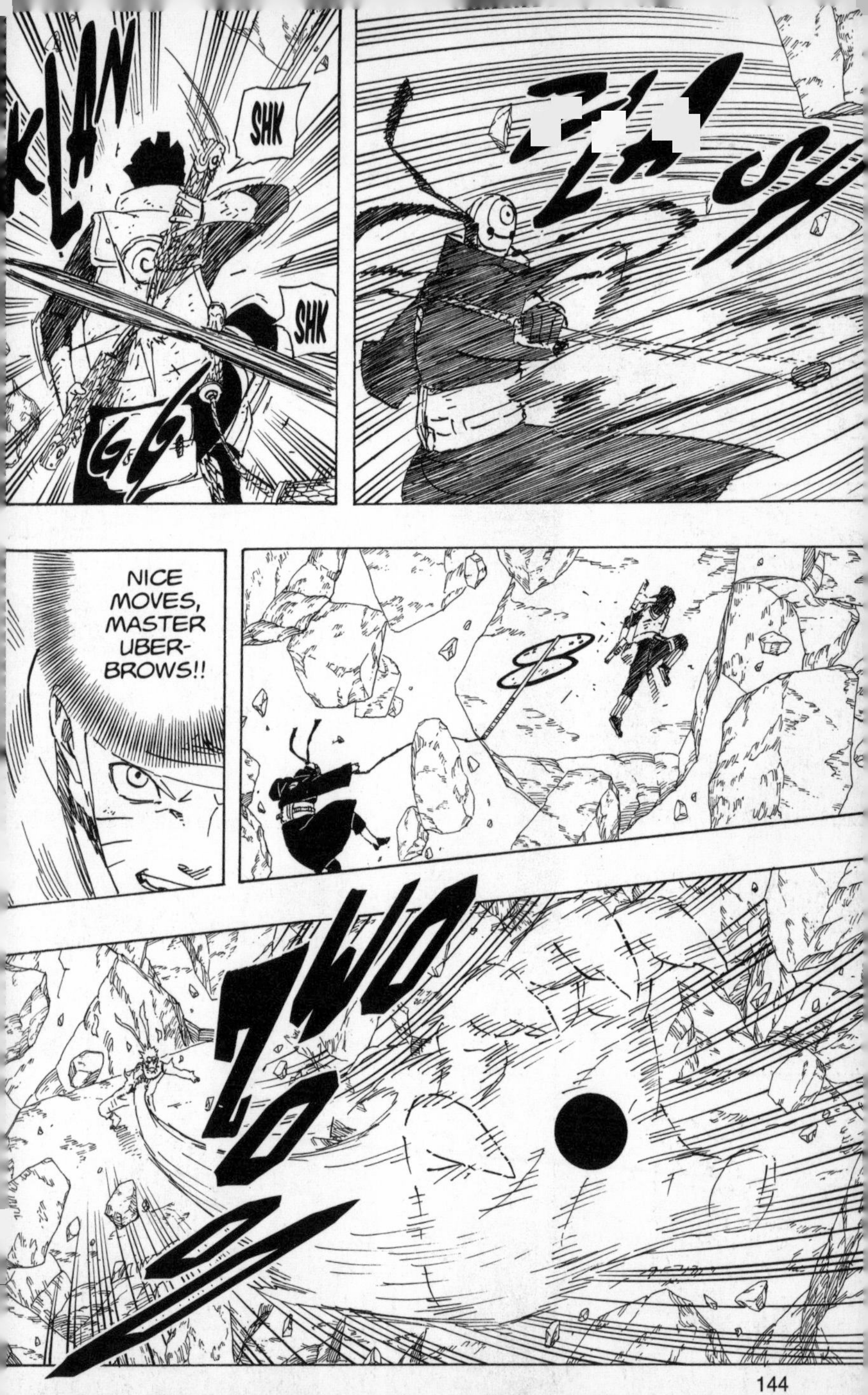
KLAN
SHK
SHK
NICE MOVES, MASTER UBER-BROWS!!

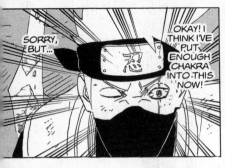

SORRY, BUT...

OKAY!! I THINK I'VE PUT ENOUGH CHAKRA INTO THIS NOW!

?!

!!

TWITCH

KAMUI!!

I'M GOING AFTER THE GEDO STATUE!!

IF I GOUGE OUT ITS HEAD, IT SHOULDN'T BE ABLE TO SURVIVE, GEDO STATUE OR NOT!

ZWWW

FWIP

FWIP

KR

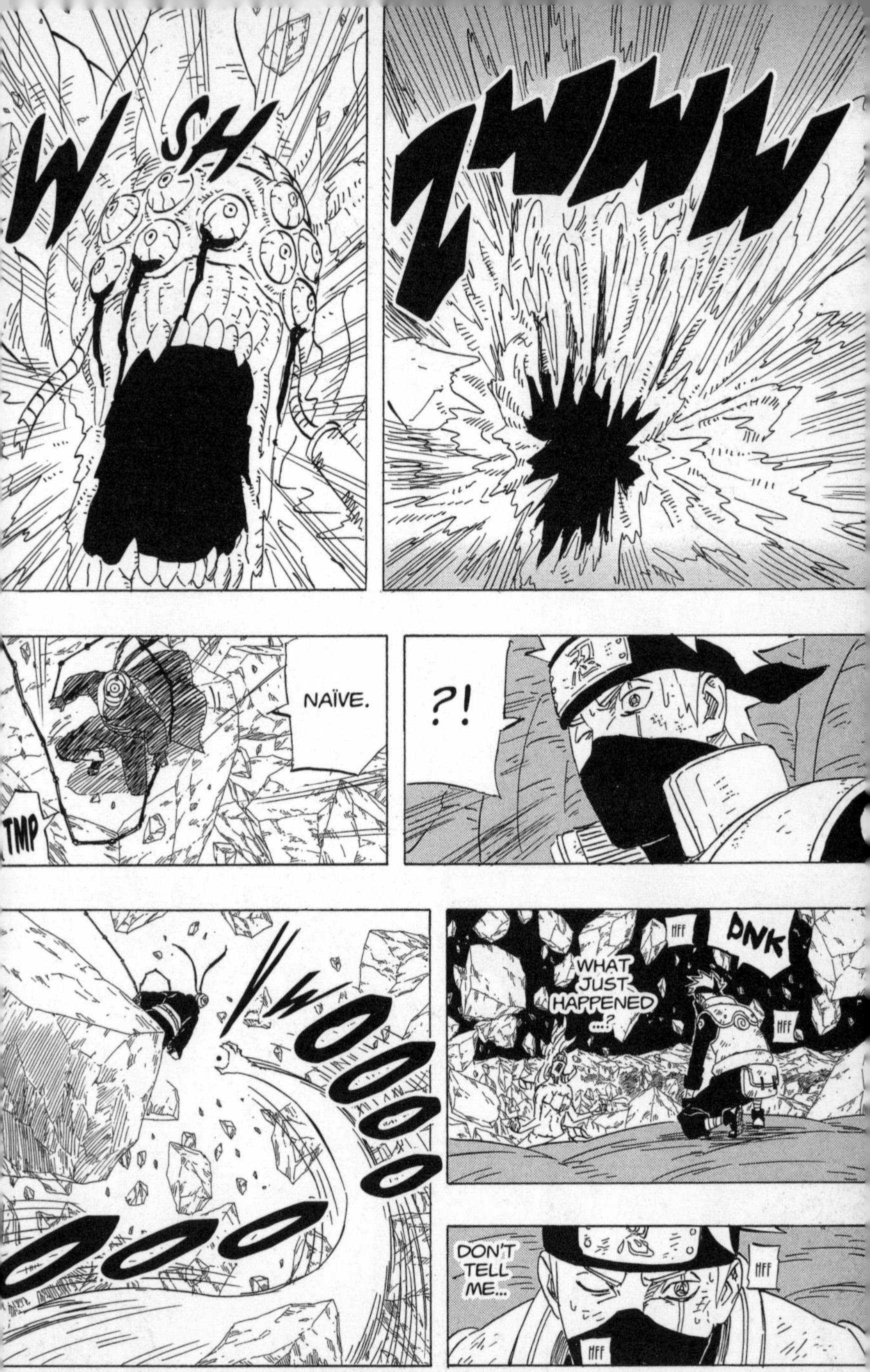
WSH
?!
NAÏVE.
TMP
DNK
HFF
WHAT JUST HAPPENED ...?
HFF
HFF
DON'T TELL ME...
HFF

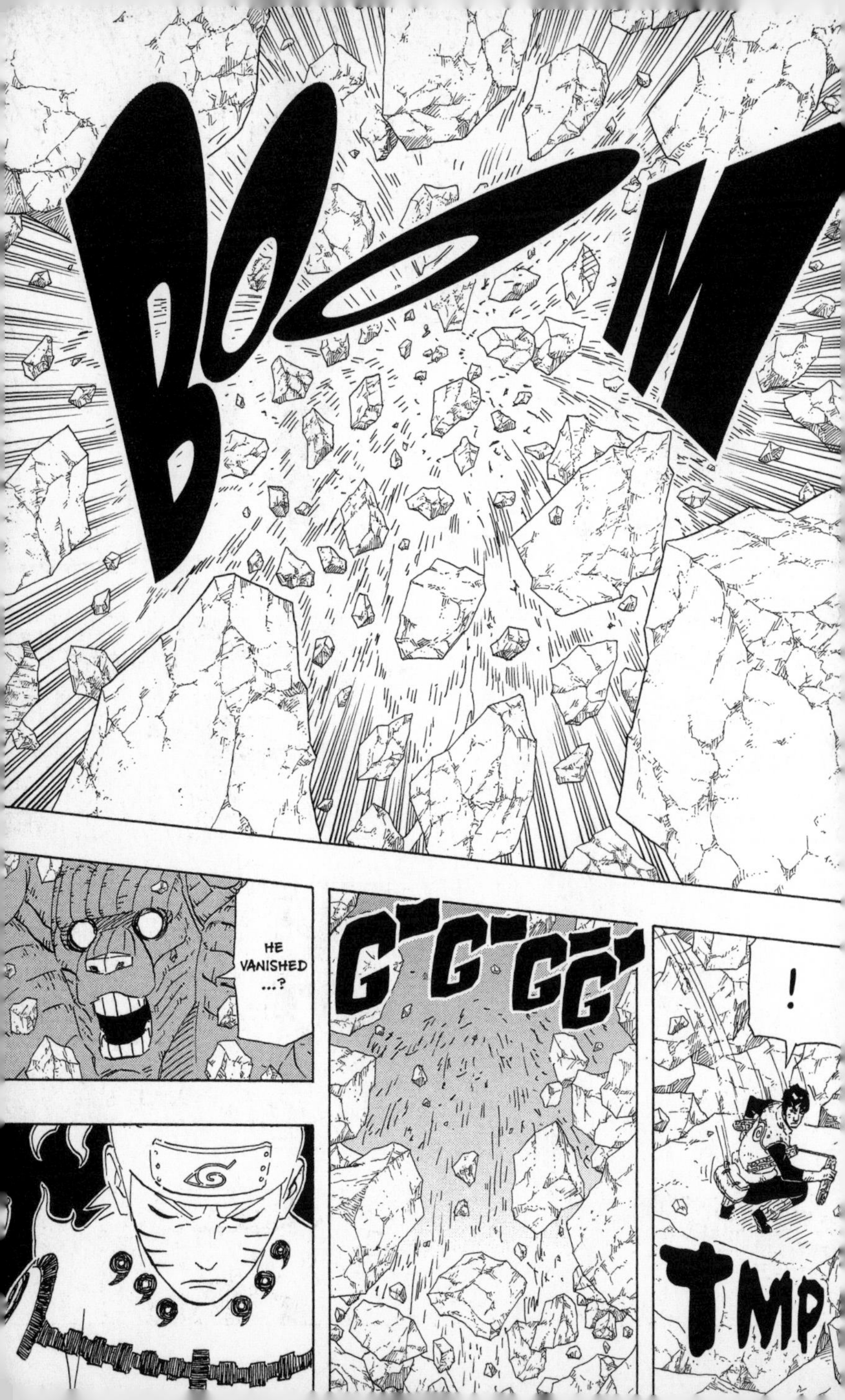
BOOM
!
TMP
G G GG
HE VANISHED ...?

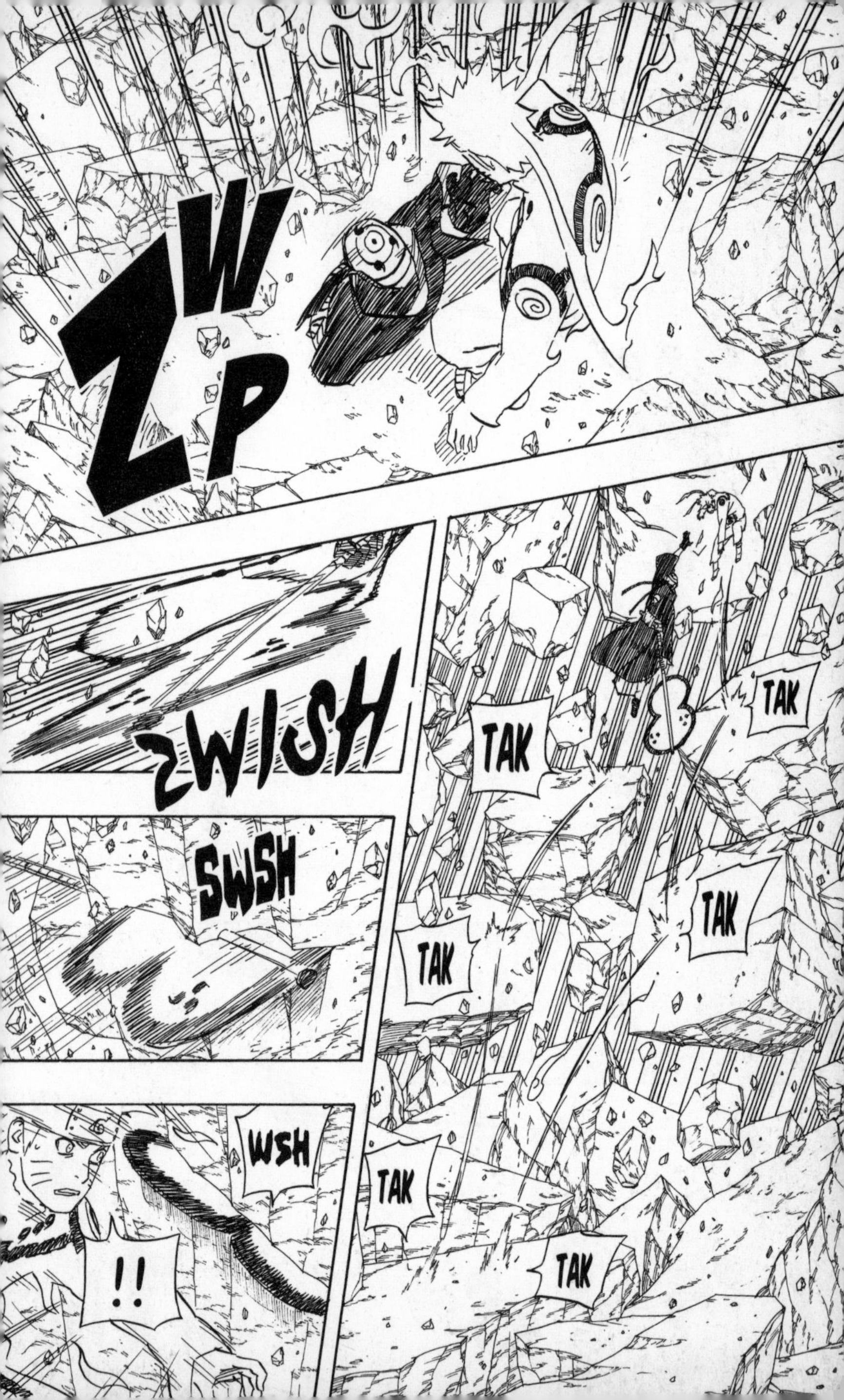
ZWZP
TAK
TAK
TAK
TAK
TAK
TAK
ZWISH
SWSH
WSH
!!

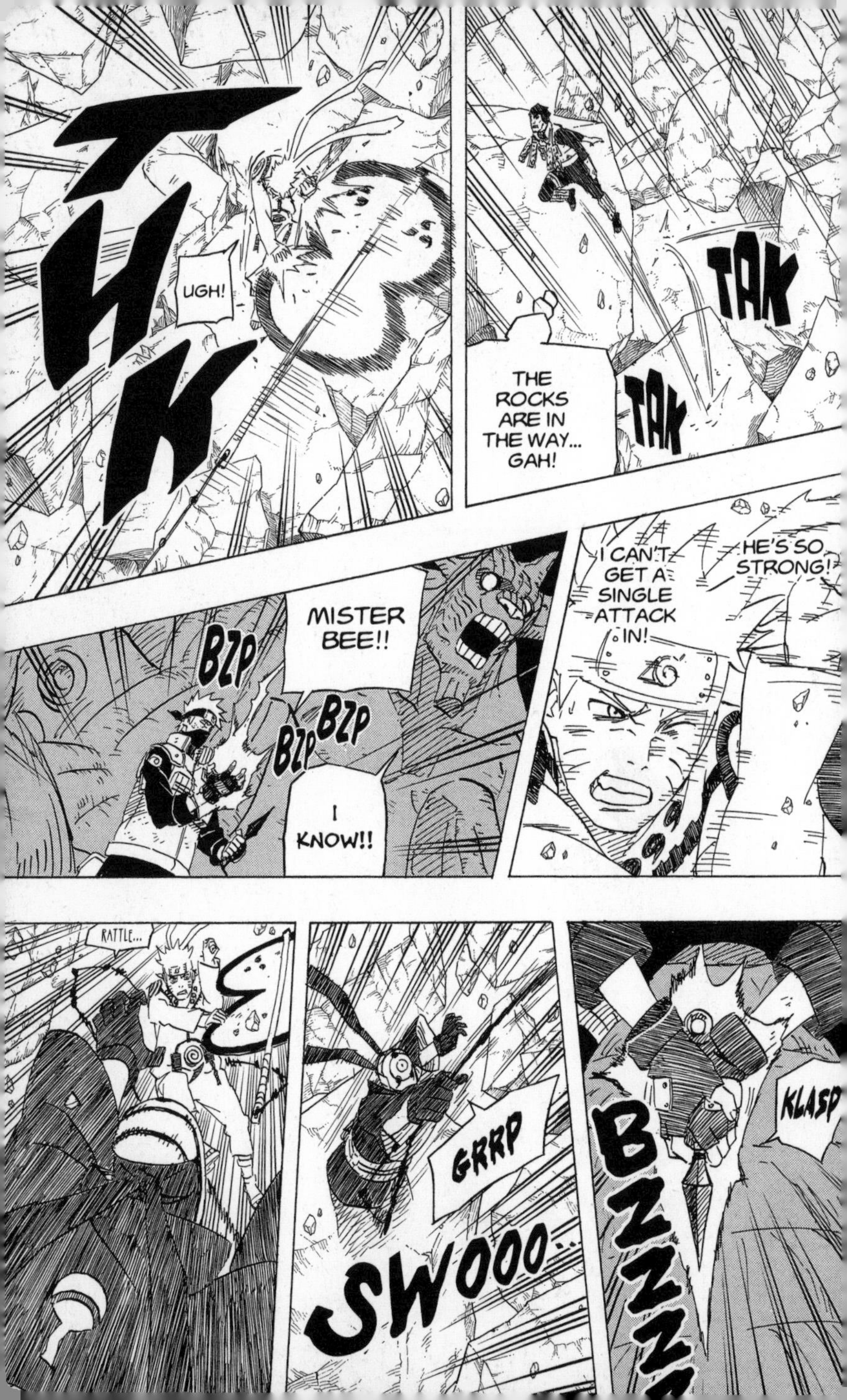
TAK
TAK
THE ROCKS ARE IN THE WAY... GAH!
THWK
UGH!
HE'S SO STRONG!
I CAN'T GET A SINGLE ATTACK IN!
MISTER BEE!!
BZP
BZP
BZP
I KNOW!!
KLASP
BZNN
GRRP
SWOOO...
RATTLE...

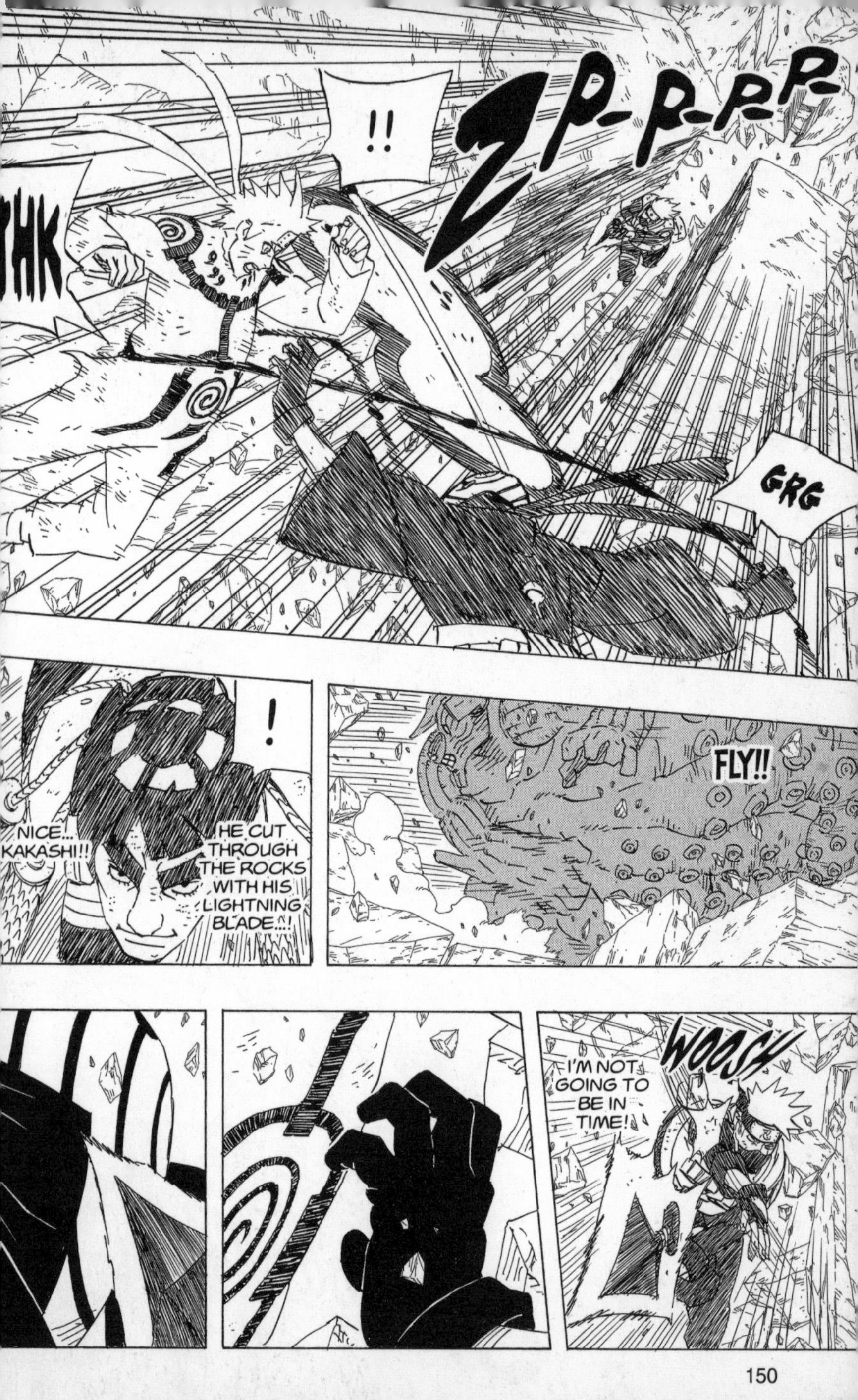
ZR-R-R-R
!!
THK
GRG
FLY!!
!
HE CUT THROUGH THE ROCKS WITH HIS LIGHTNING BLADE...!
NICE... KAKASHI!!
WOOSH
I'M NOT GOING TO BE IN TIME!

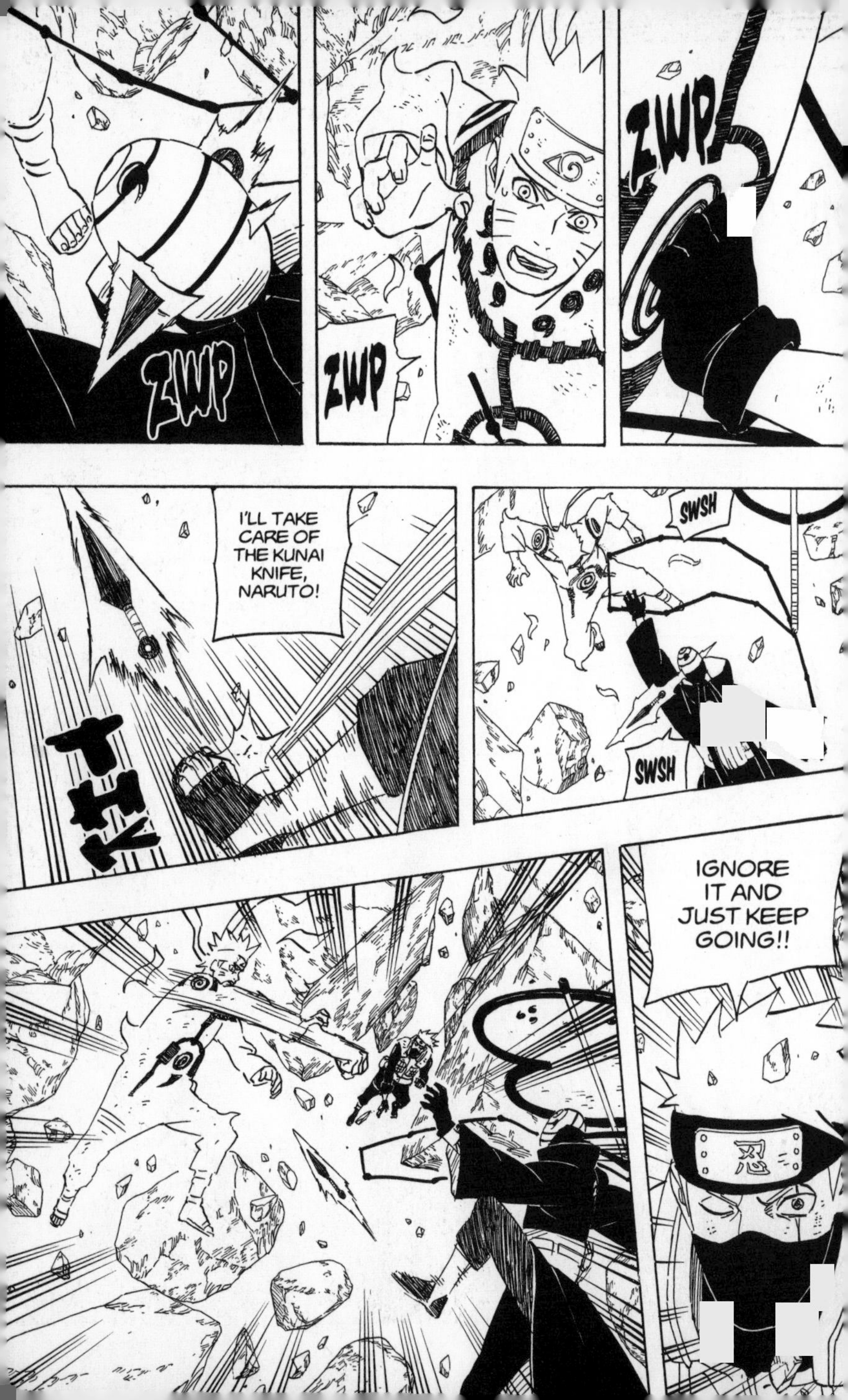
ZWP!
ZWP
ZWP
SWSH
SWSH
I'LL TAKE CARE OF THE KUNAI KNIFE, NARUTO!
THK
IGNORE IT AND JUST KEEP GOING!!

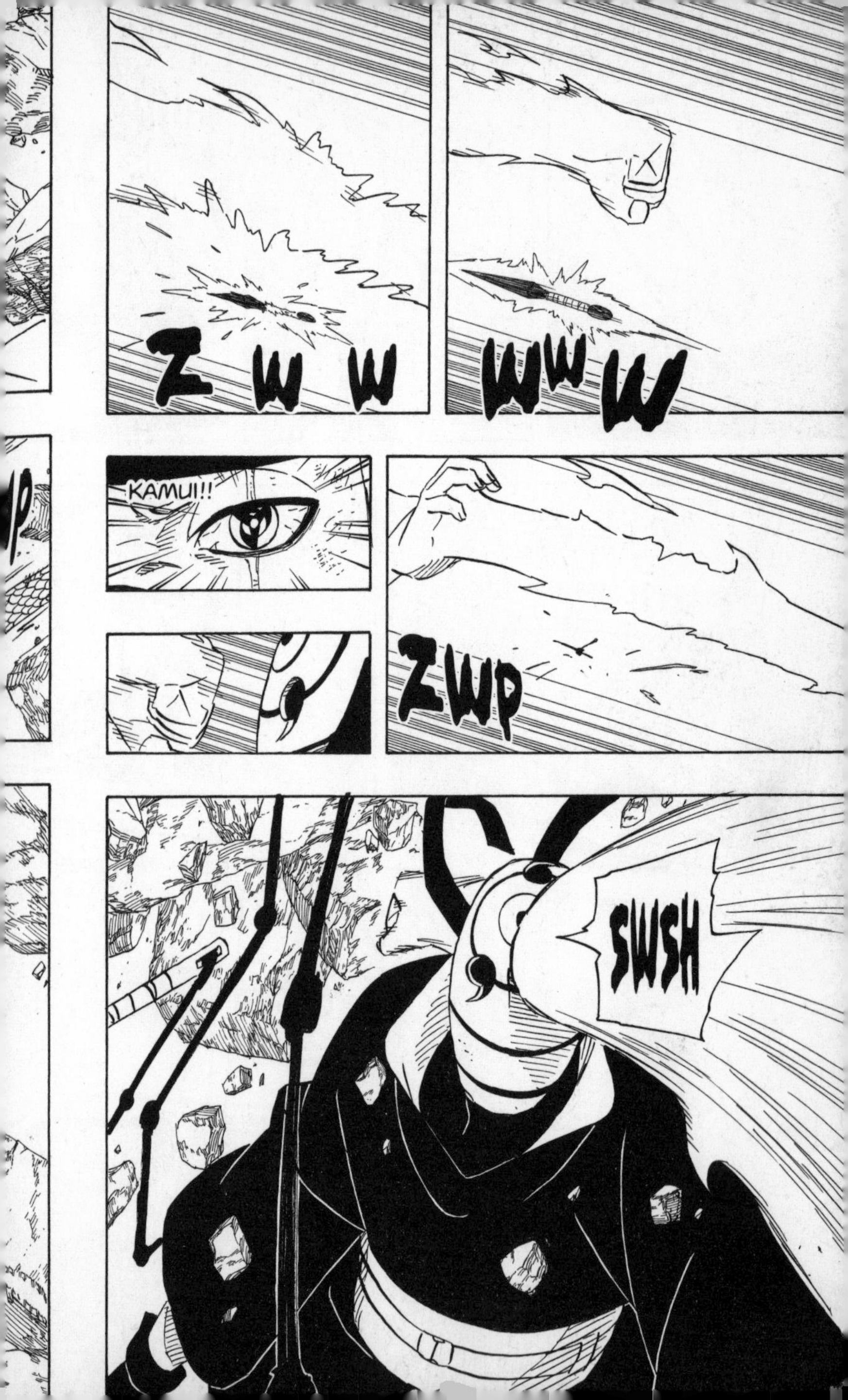
ZWWWWWW
ZWP
KAMUI!!
SWSH

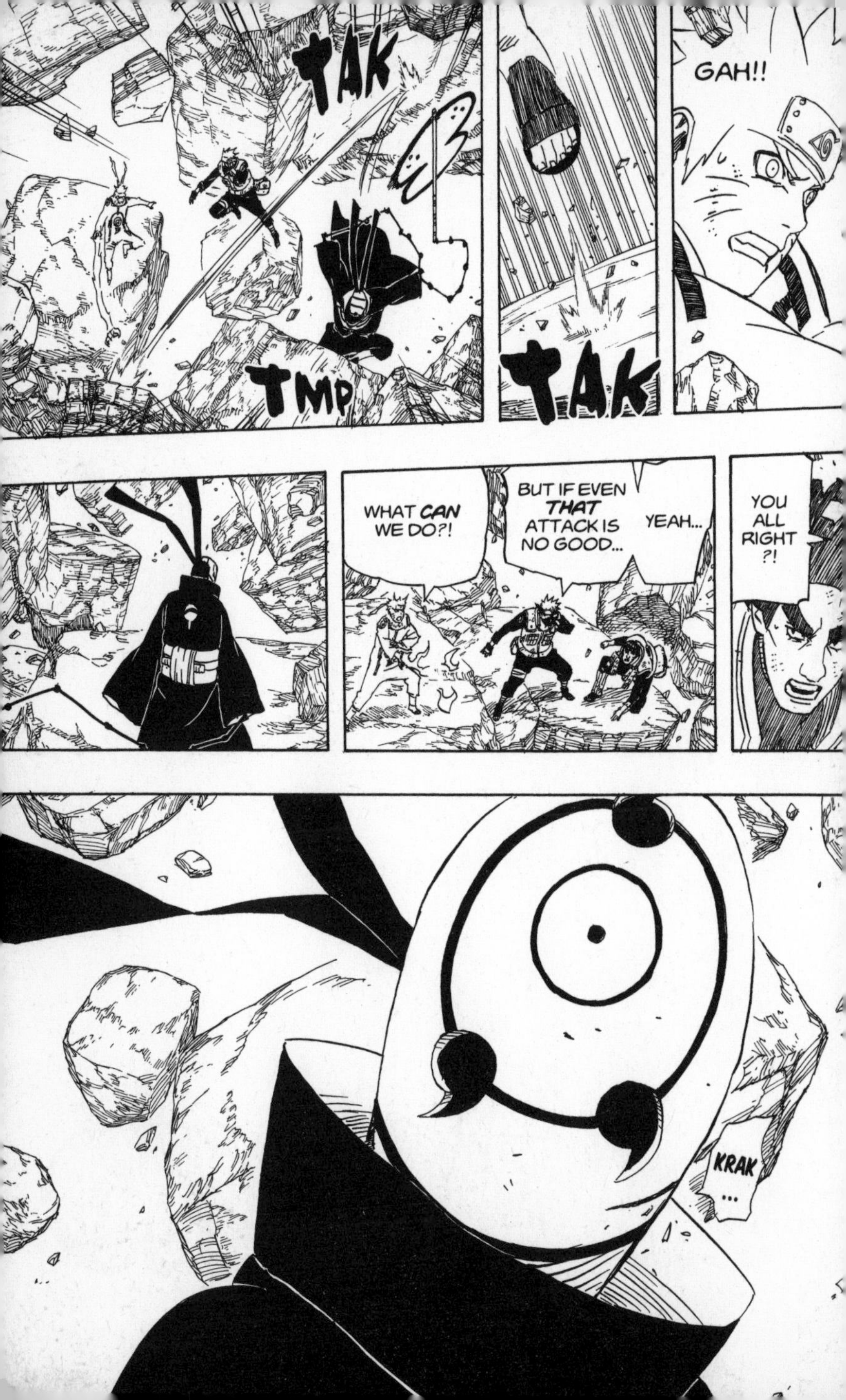
GAH!!
TAK
TAK
TMP
YOU ALL RIGHT ?!
YEAH...
BUT IF EVEN THAT ATTACK IS NO GOOD...
WHAT CAN WE DO?!
KRAK
...

NARUTO

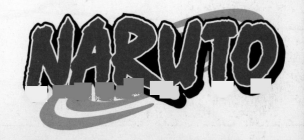

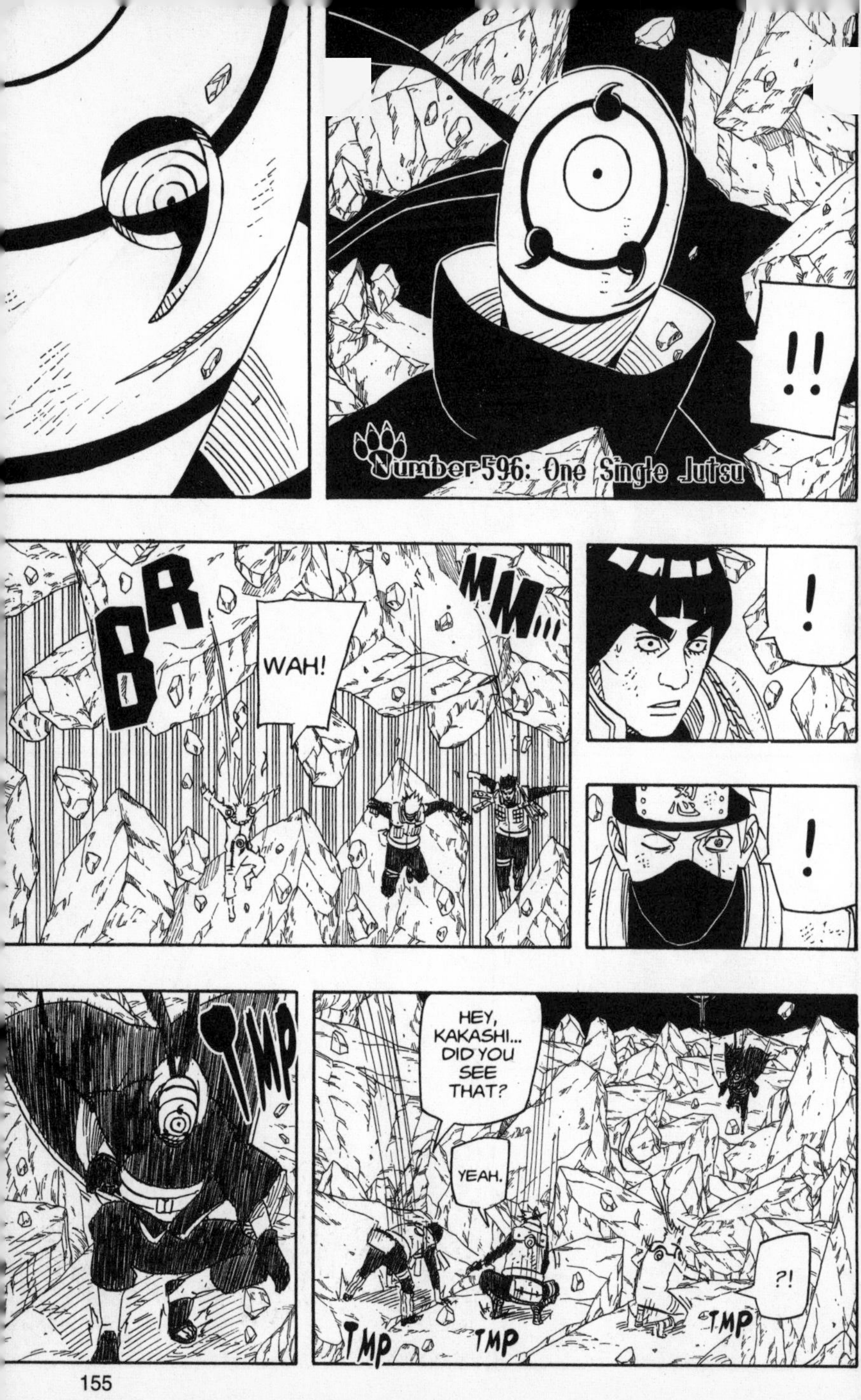

!!
Number 596: One Single Jutsu
!
!
BRMM...
WAH!
HEY, KAKASHI... DID YOU SEE THAT?
YEAH.
?!
TMP
TMP
TMP
TMP

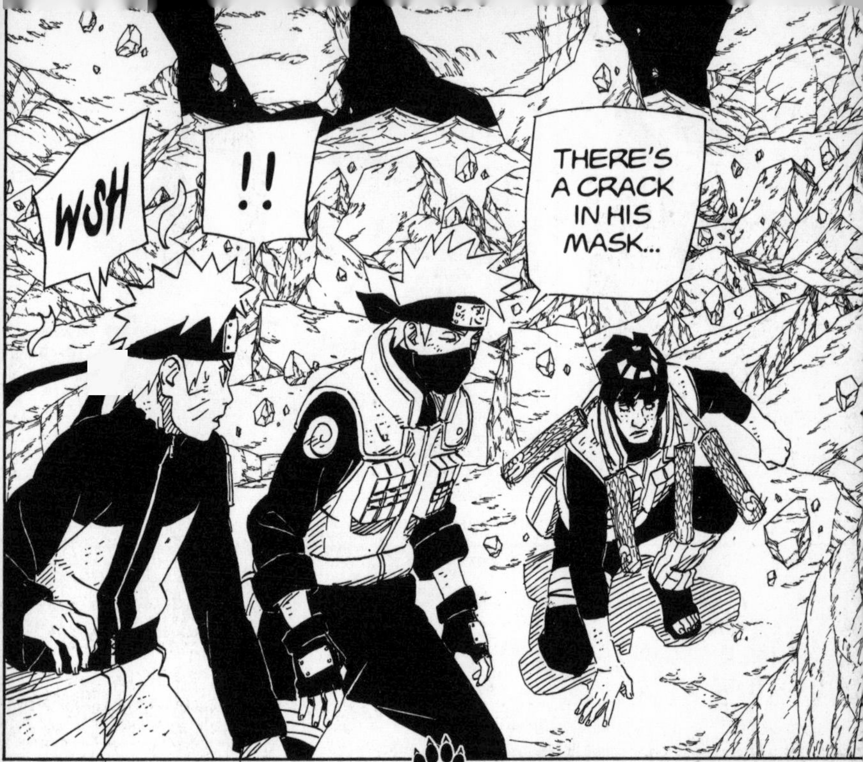
THERE'S A CRACK IN HIS MASK...
!!
WSH

Number 596: One Single Jutsu

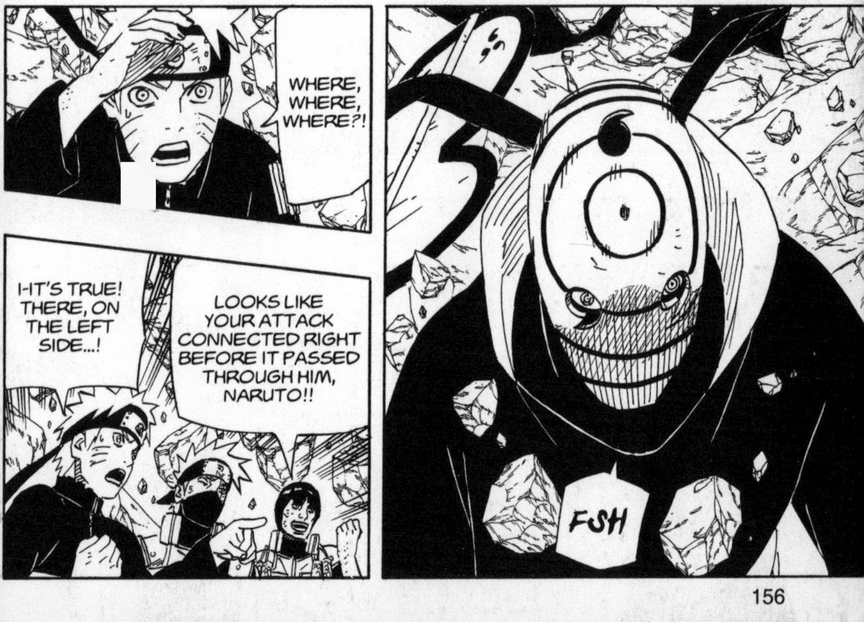
FSH
WHERE, WHERE, WHERE?!
LOOKS LIKE YOUR ATTACK CONNECTED RIGHT BEFORE IT PASSED THROUGH HIM, NARUTO!!
I-IT'S TRUE! THERE, ON THE LEFT SIDE...!

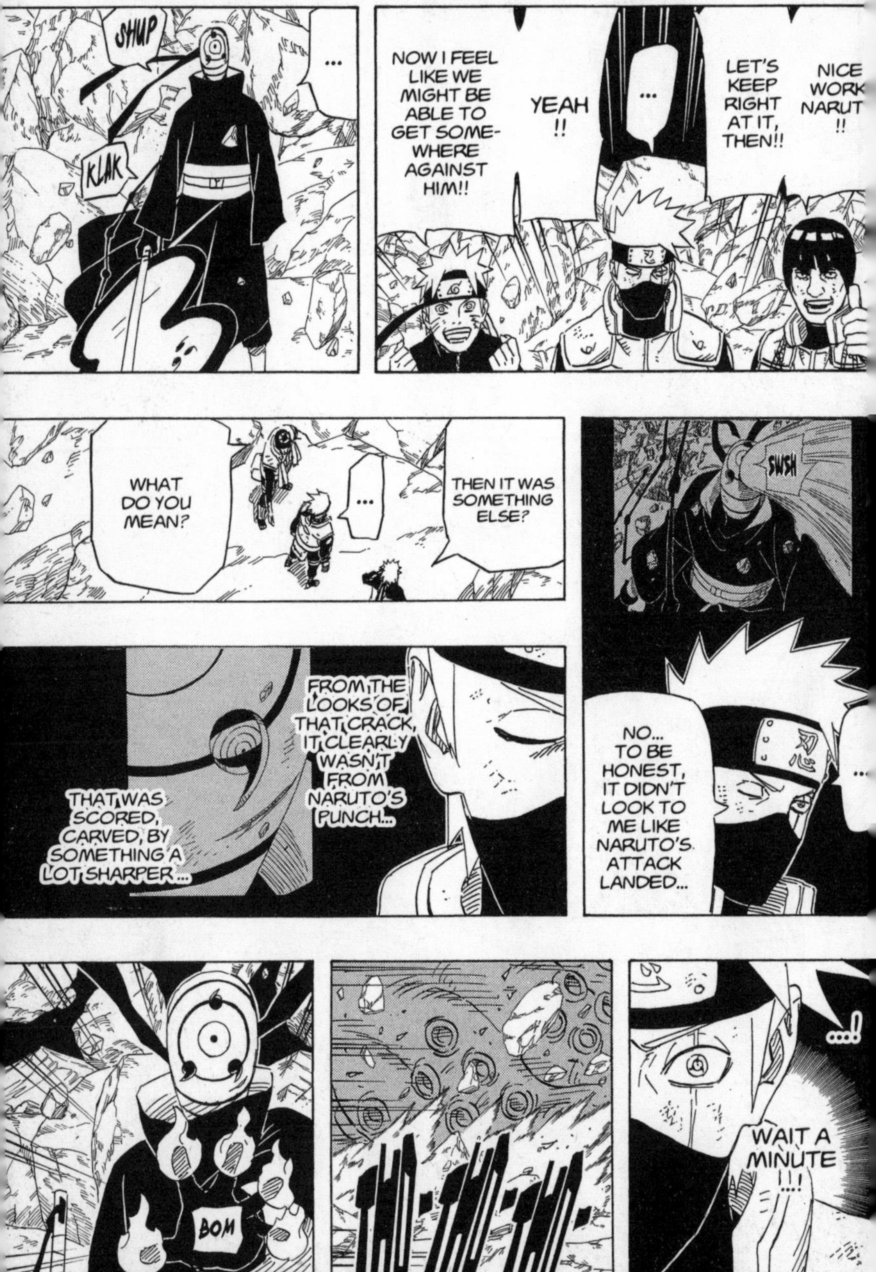
NICE WORK NARUT !!
LET'S KEEP RIGHT AT IT, THEN!!
...
YEAH !!
NOW I FEEL LIKE WE MIGHT BE ABLE TO GET SOME-WHERE AGAINST HIM!!
...
SHUP
KLAK
SWSH
...
NO... TO BE HONEST, IT DIDN'T LOOK TO ME LIKE NARUTO'S ATTACK LANDED...
THEN IT WAS SOMETHING ELSE?
...
WHAT DO YOU MEAN?
FROM THE LOOKS OF THAT CRACK, IT CLEARLY WASN'T FROM NARUTO'S PUNCH...
THAT WAS SCORED, CARVED, BY SOMETHING A LOT SHARPER...
...!
WAIT A MINUTE !!!...
THD-THD-THD
BOM

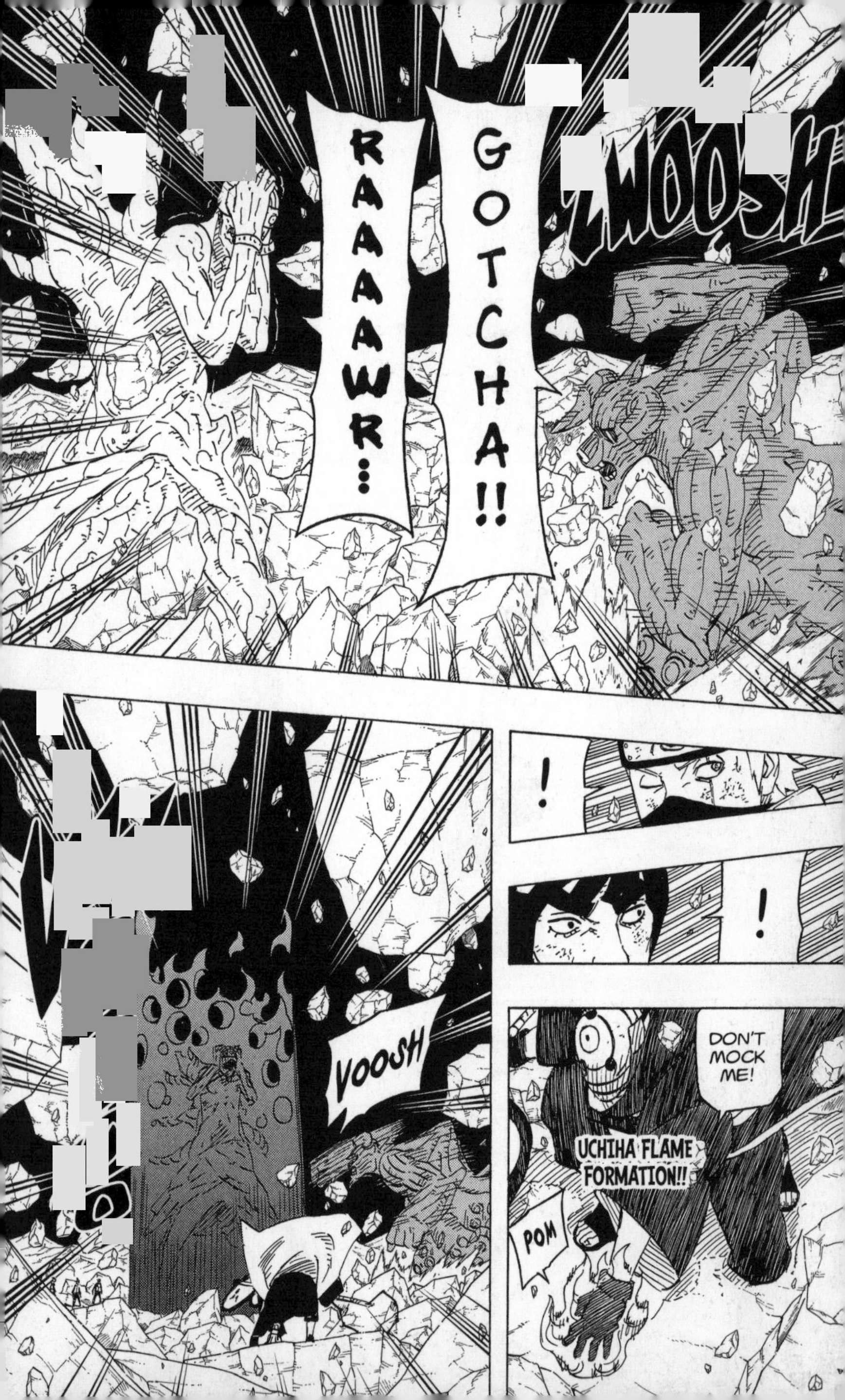
ZWOOSH
GOTCHA!!
RAAAAWR...
!
!
DON'T MOCK ME!
UCHIHA FLAME FORMATION!!
POM
VOOSH

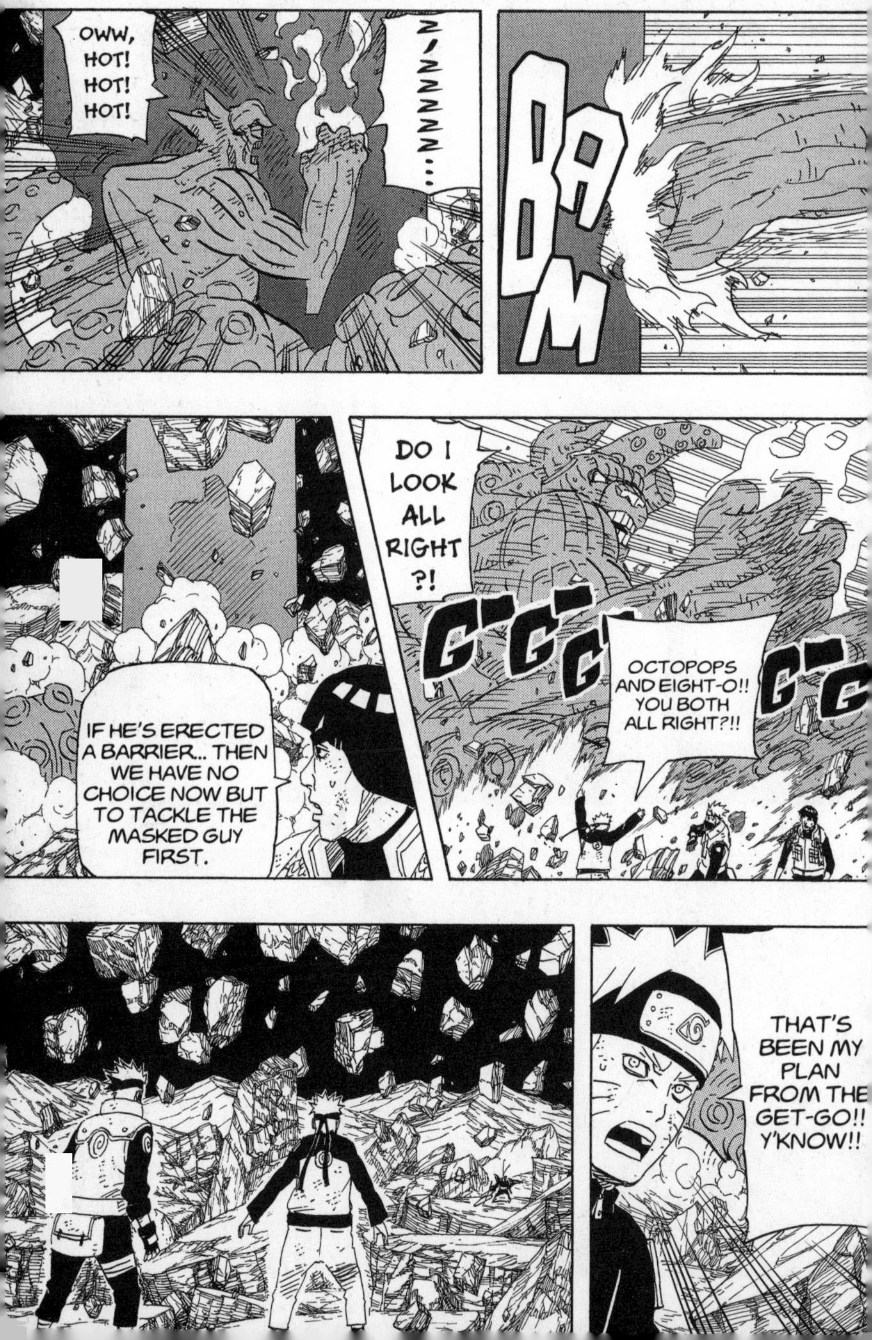
BAM
ZZZZZZ...
OWW, HOT! HOT! HOT!
DO I LOOK ALL RIGHT?!
G-G
OCTOPOPS AND EIGHT-O!! YOU BOTH ALL RIGHT?!!
G-G-G
IF HE'S ERECTED A BARRIER... THEN WE HAVE NO CHOICE NOW BUT TO TACKLE THE MASKED GUY FIRST.
THAT'S BEEN MY PLAN FROM THE GET-GO!! Y'KNOW!!

EXCEPT...

...

NO... IT CAN'T BE...

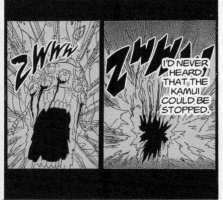

ZWnn

ZWHA!

I'D NEVER HEARD THAT THE KAMUI COULD BE STOPPED.

WW ///

ZWP

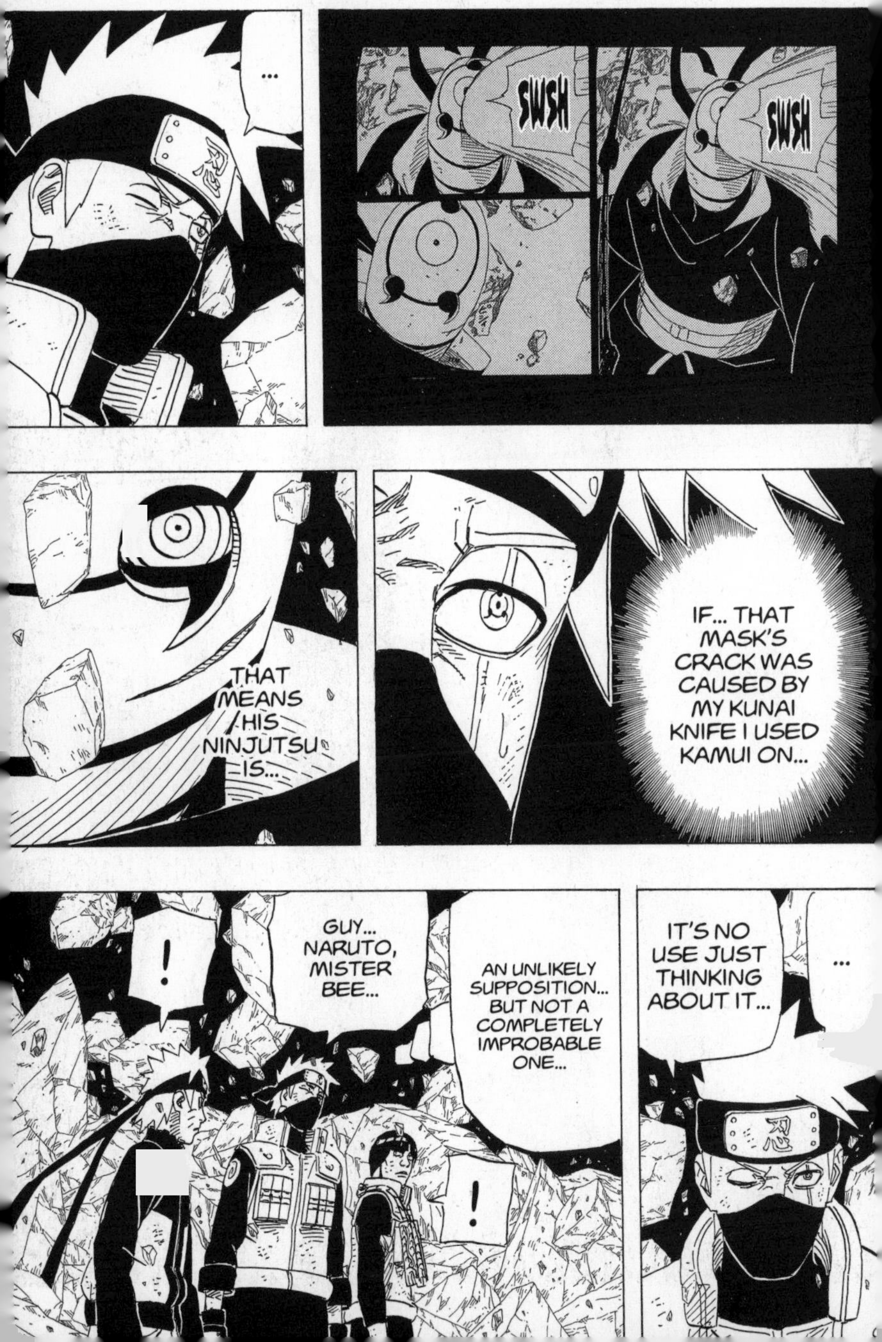
SWSH
SWSH
...
IF... THAT MASK'S CRACK WAS CAUSED BY MY KUNAI KNIFE I USED KAMUI ON...
THAT MEANS HIS NINJUTSU IS...
...
IT'S NO USE JUST THINKING ABOUT IT...
AN UNLIKELY SUPPOSITION... BUT NOT A COMPLETELY IMPROBABLE ONE...
GUY... NARUTO, MISTER BEE...
!
!

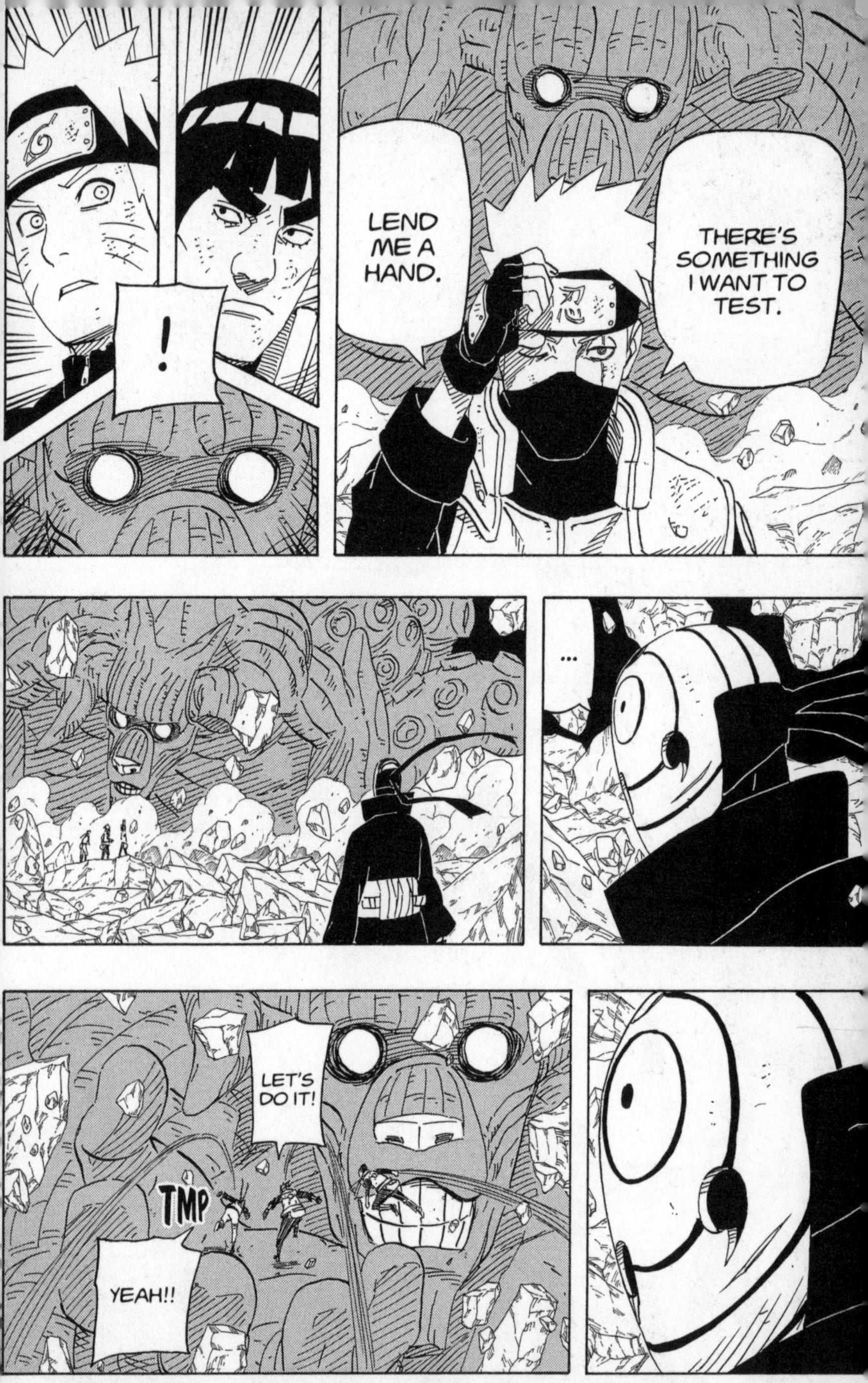
THERE'S SOMETHING I WANT TO TEST.
LEND ME A HAND.
!
...
LET'S DO IT!
TMP
YEAH!!

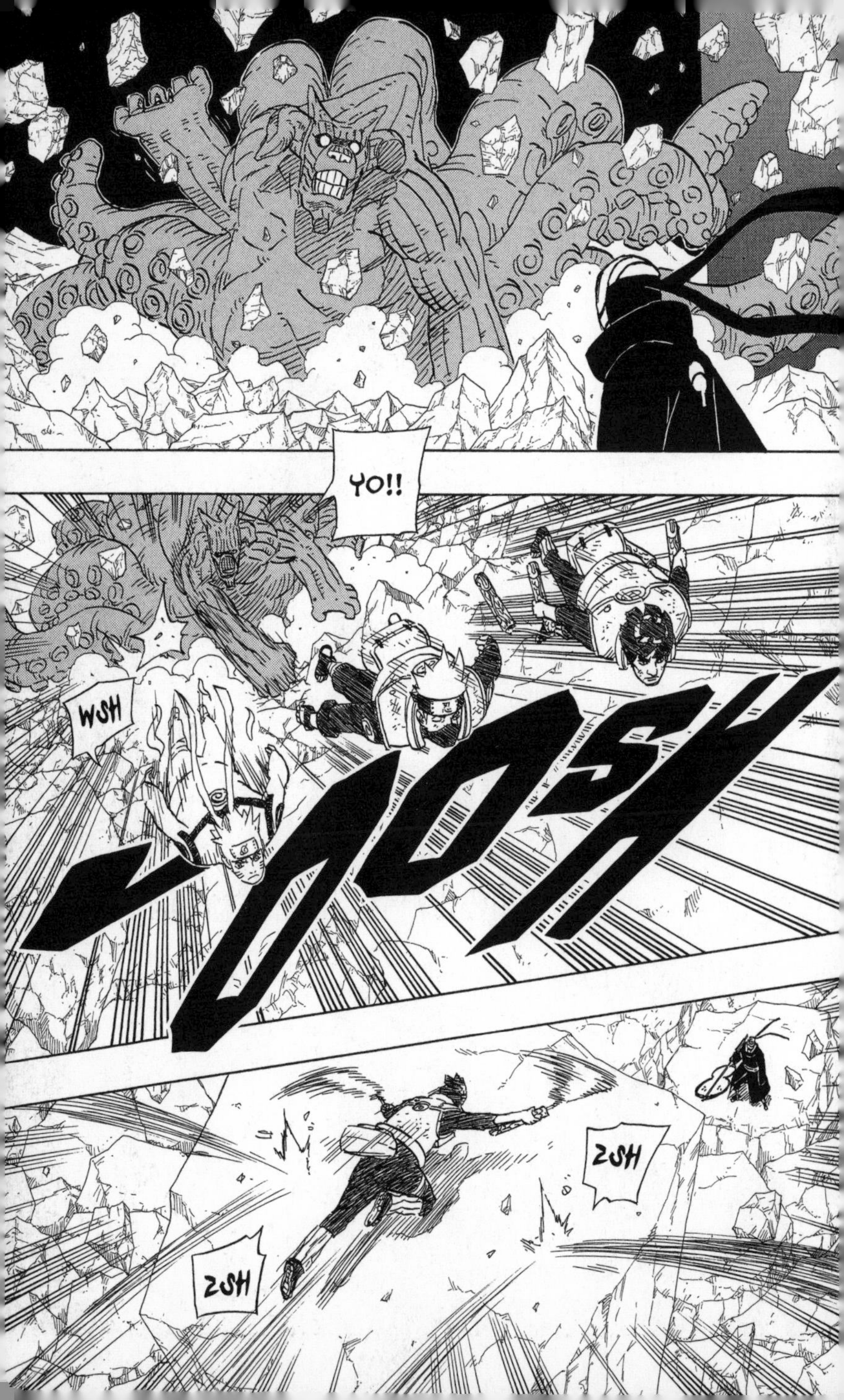
YO!!
WSH
ZSH
ZSH

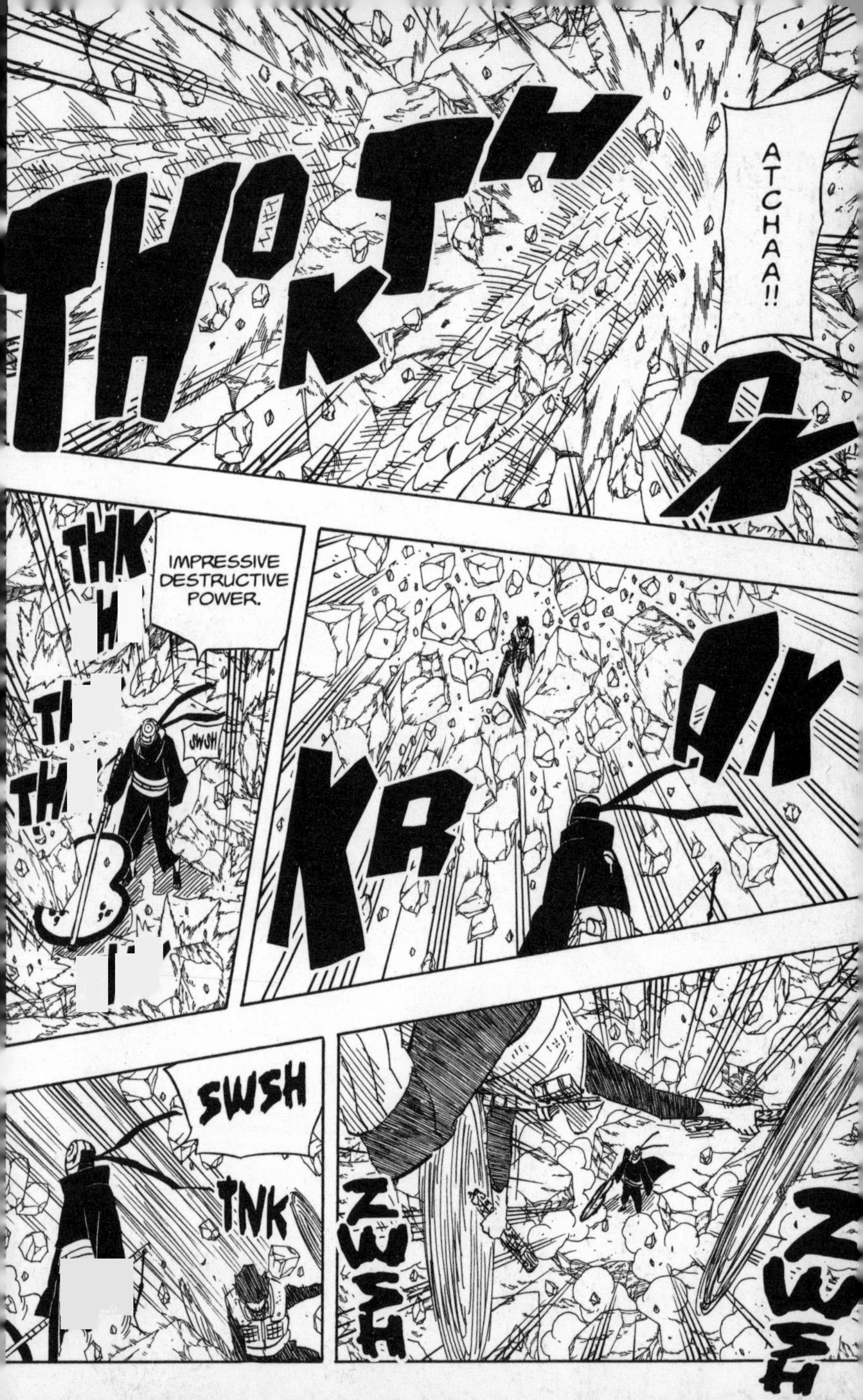
ATCHAA!!
KRAK
IMPRESSIVE DESTRUCTIVE POWER.
SWSH
THK
ZWSH
ZWSH
SWSH
TNK

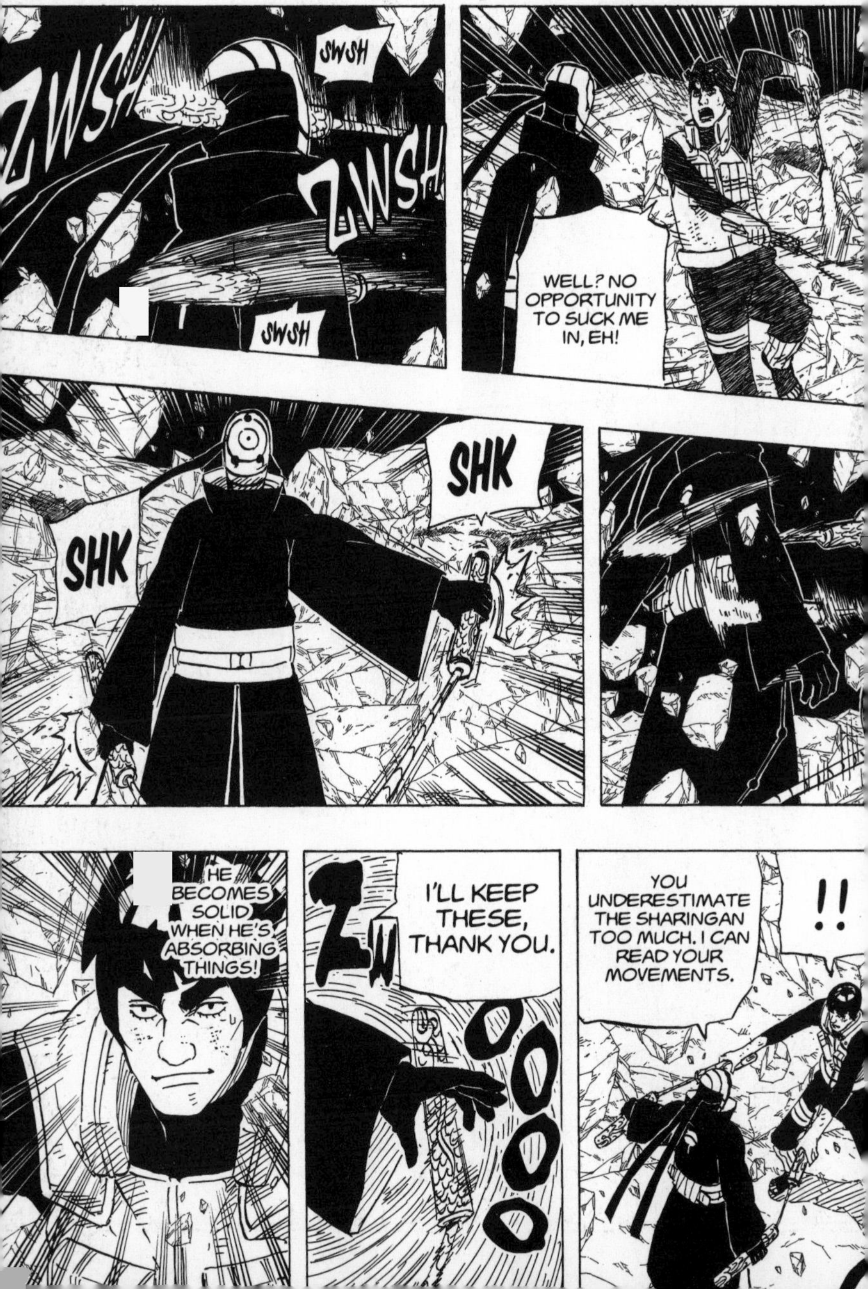
WELL? NO OPPORTUNITY TO SUCK ME IN, EH!
SWSH
ZWSH
ZWSH
SWSH
SHK
SHK
!!
YOU UNDERESTIMATE THE SHARINGAN TOO MUCH. I CAN READ YOUR MOVEMENTS.
I'LL KEEP THESE, THANK YOU.
ZU
HE BECOMES SOLID WHEN HE'S ABSORBING THINGS!

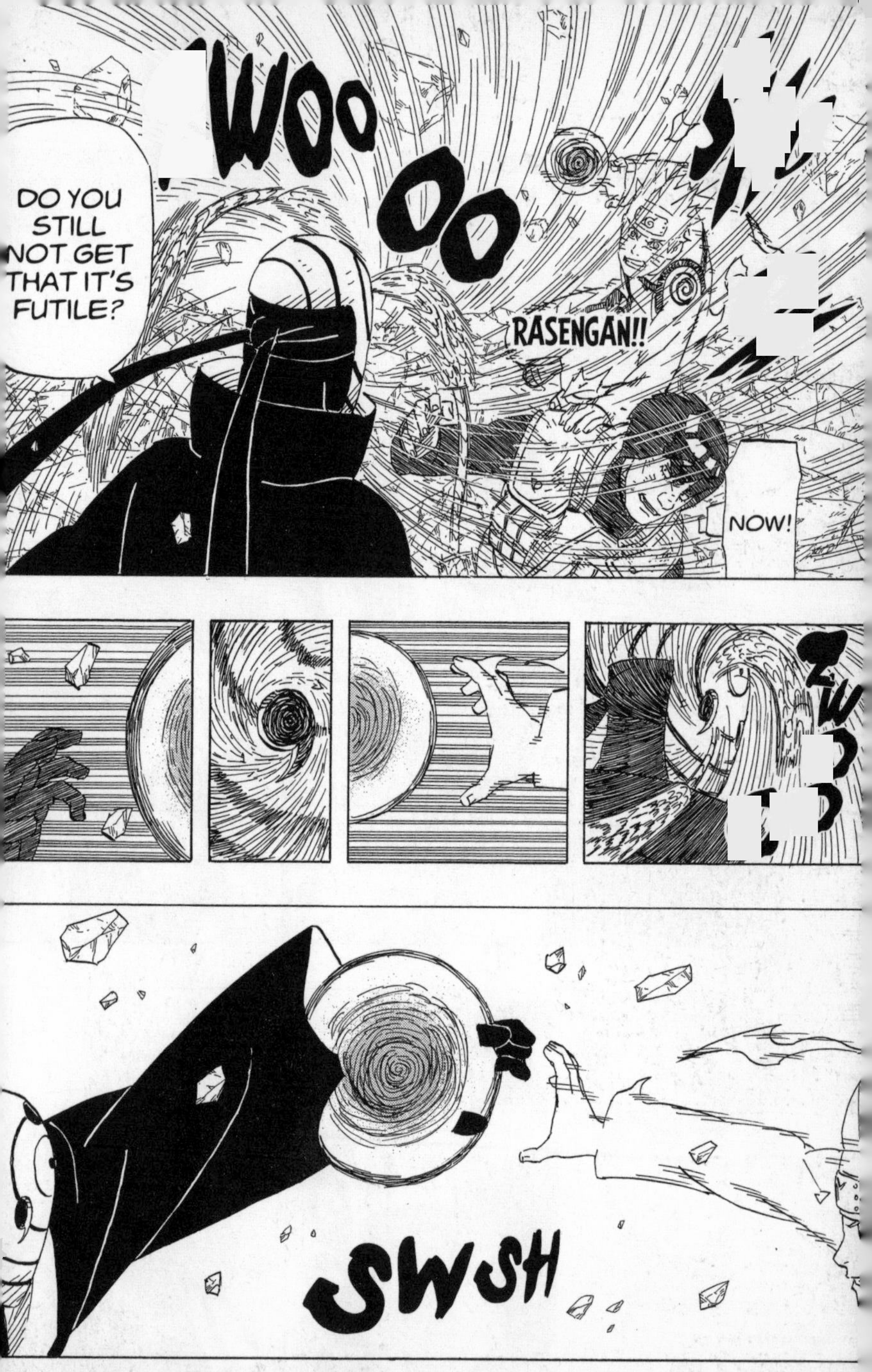
WOO OO
RASENGAN!!
NOW!
DO YOU STILL NOT GET THAT IT'S FUTILE?
SWSH

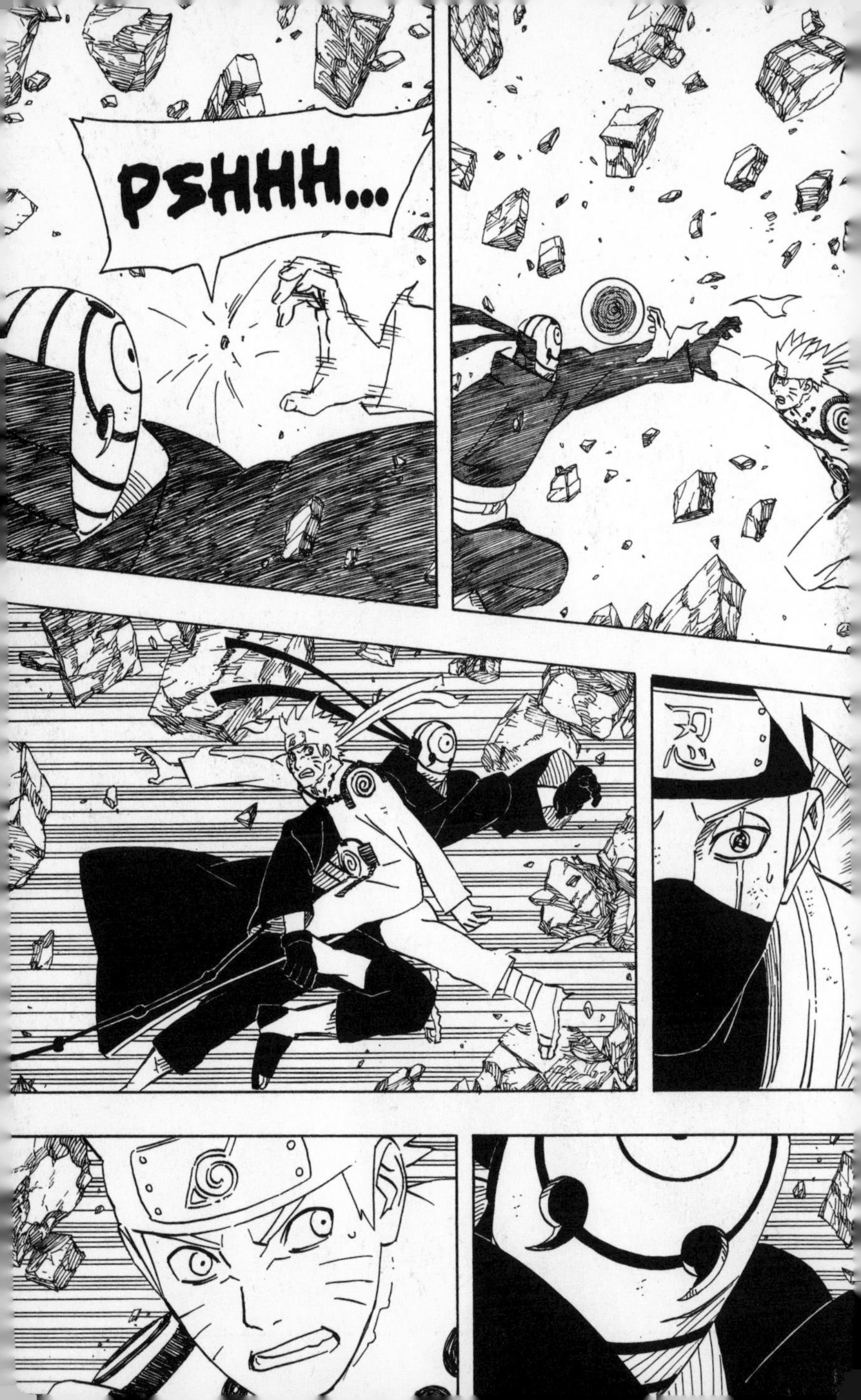
PSHHH...

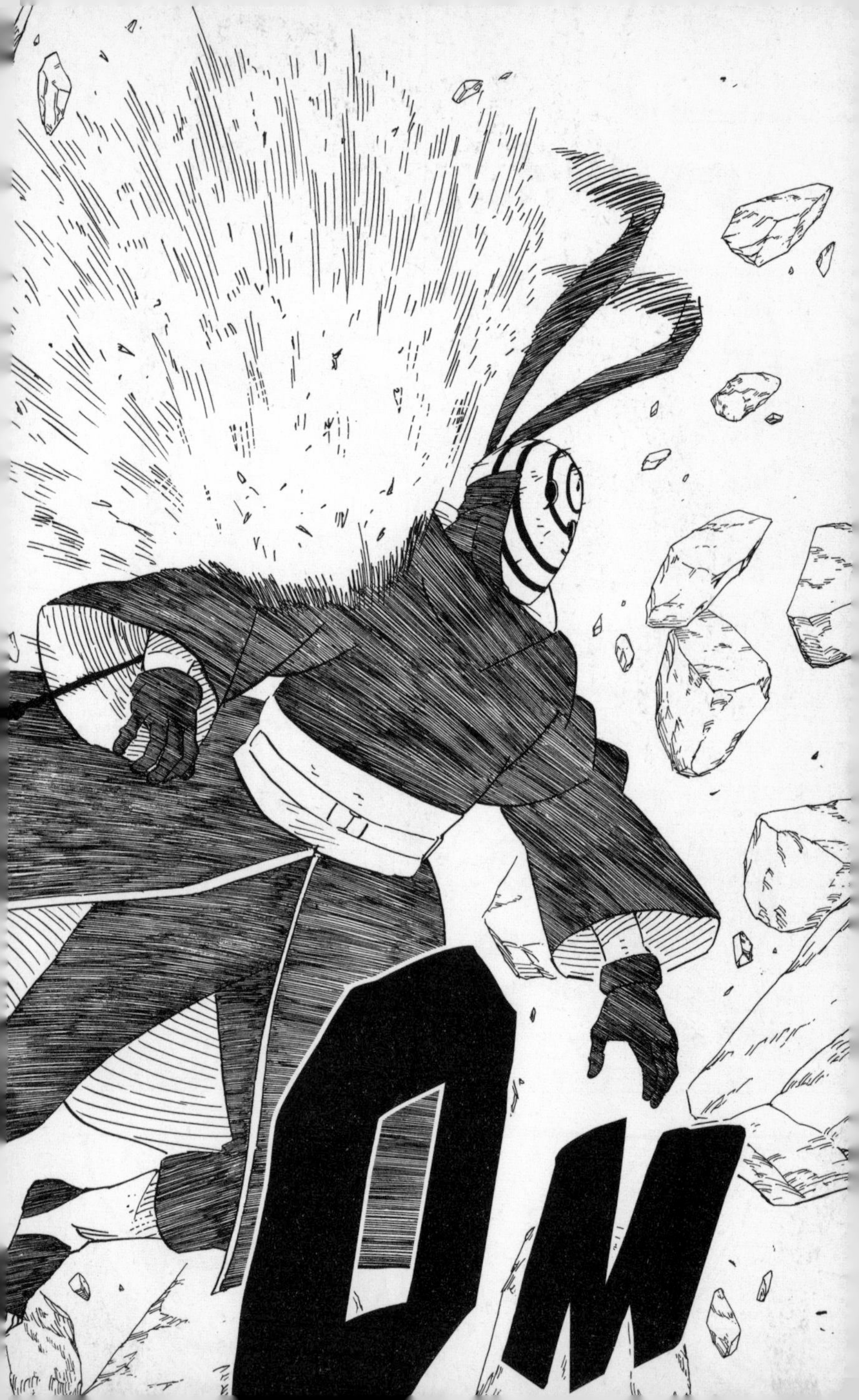

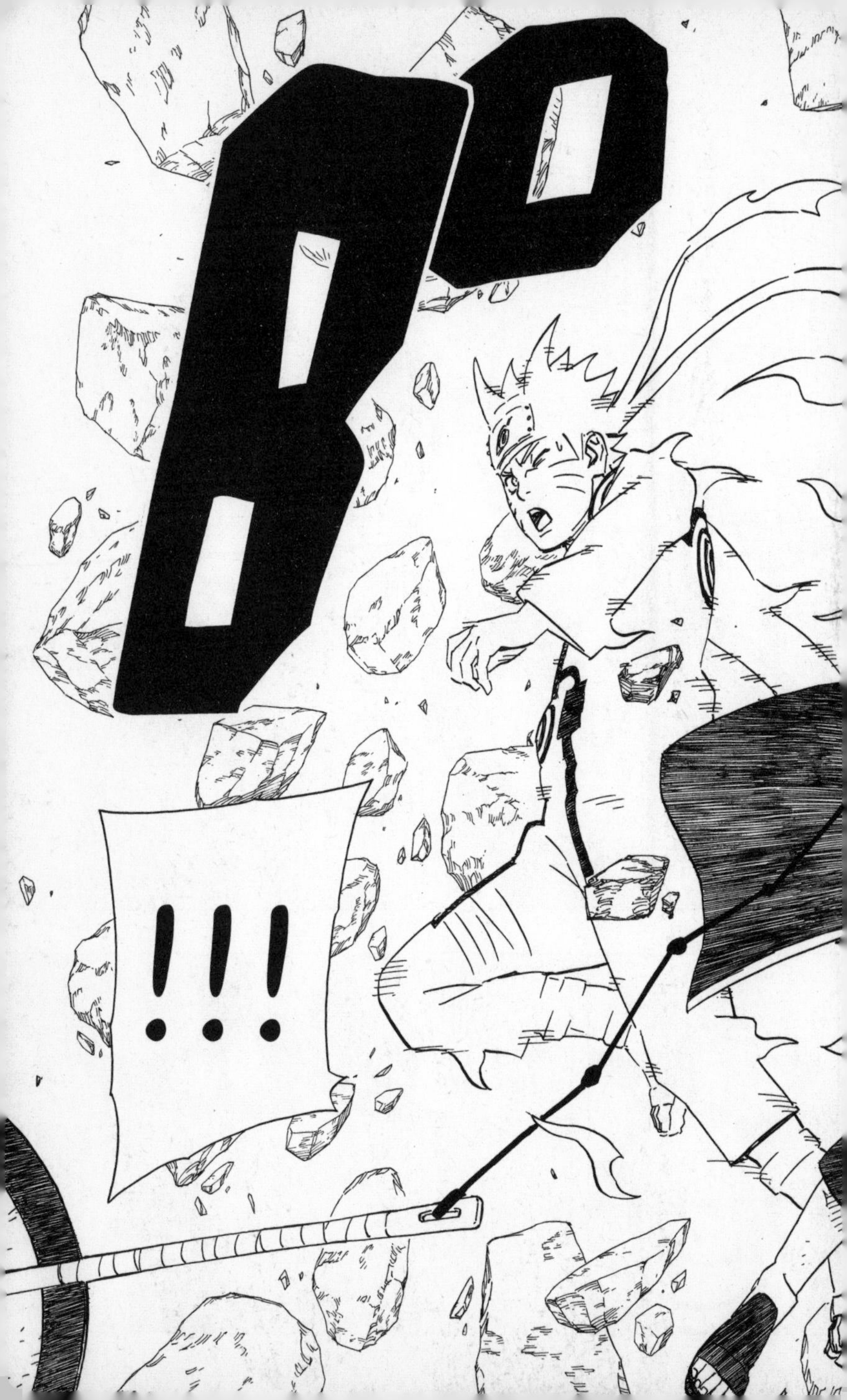
BOOM
!!!

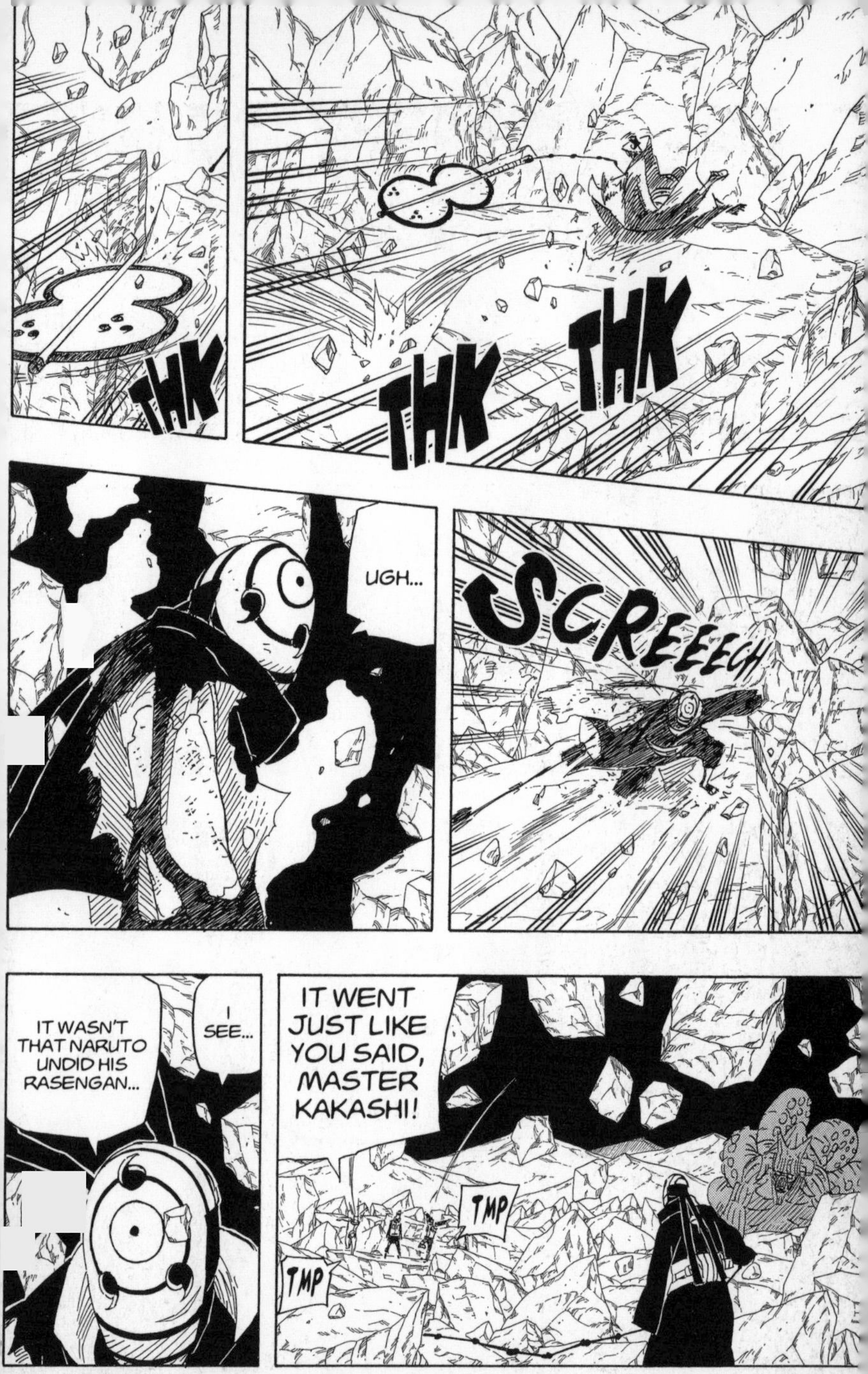
THK
THK
THK
SCREEECH
UGH...
IT WENT JUST LIKE YOU SAID, MASTER KAKASHI!
TMP
TMP
I SEE...
IT WASN'T THAT NARUTO UNDID HIS RASENGAN...

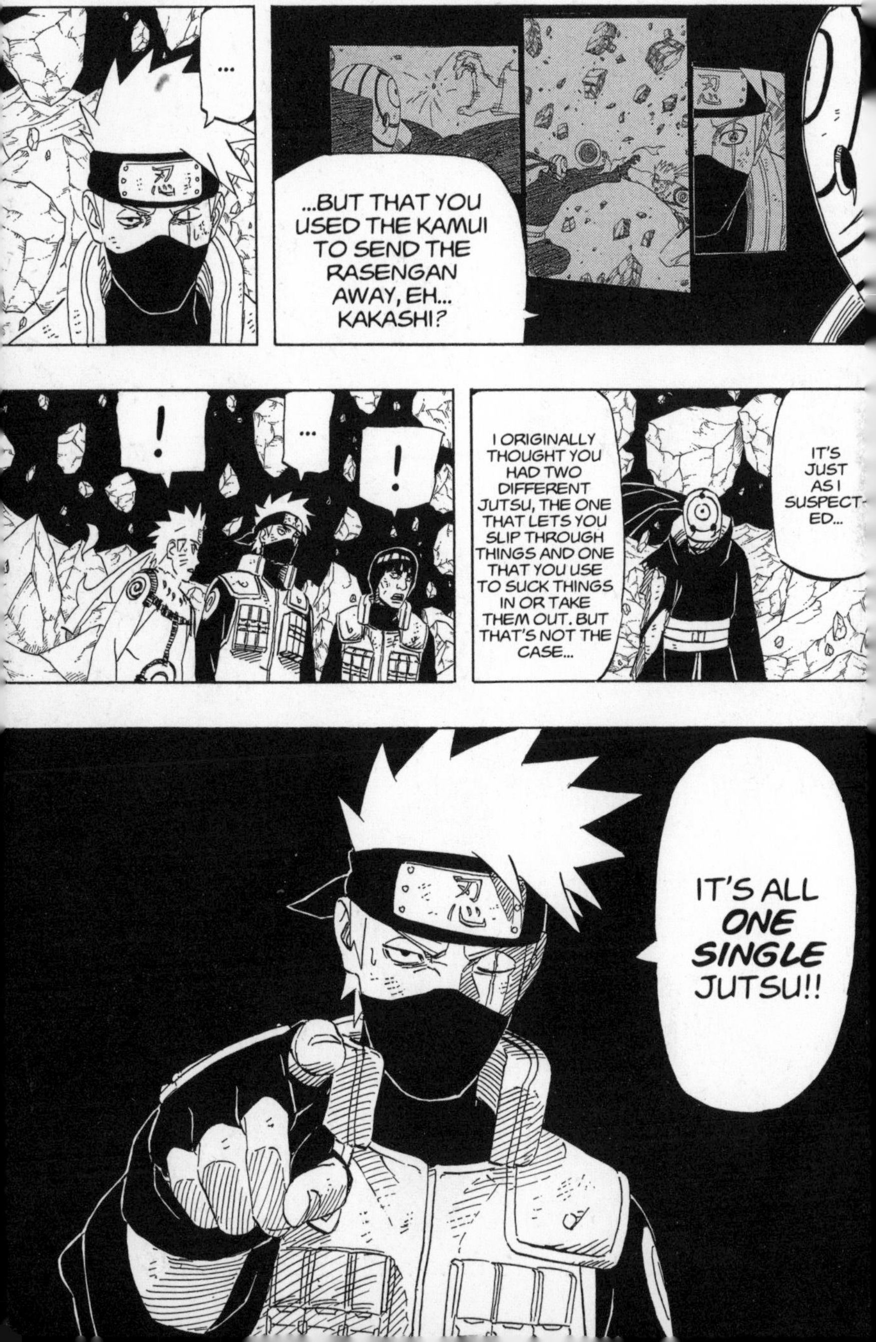
...BUT THAT YOU USED THE KAMUI TO SEND THE RASENGAN AWAY, EH... KAKASHI?
...
IT'S JUST AS I SUSPECTED...
I ORIGINALLY THOUGHT YOU HAD TWO DIFFERENT JUTSU, THE ONE THAT LETS YOU SLIP THROUGH THINGS AND ONE THAT YOU USE TO SUCK THINGS IN OR TAKE THEM OUT. BUT THAT'S NOT THE CASE...
!
...
!
IT'S ALL *ONE SINGLE* JUTSU!!

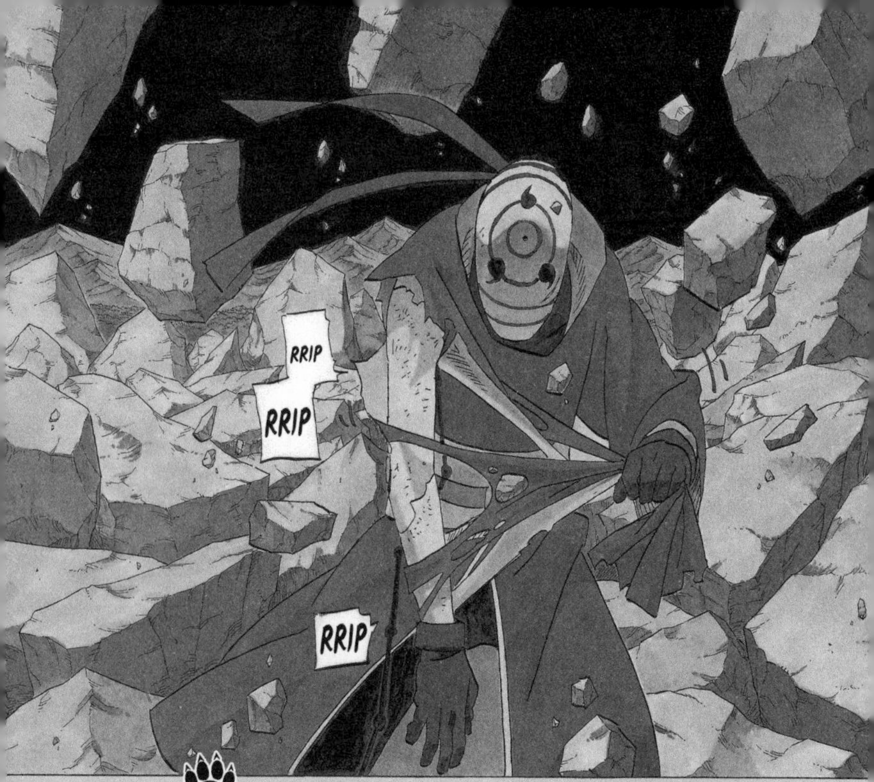
RRIP
RRIP
RRIP

Number 597: The Secret of Teleportation Ninjutsu

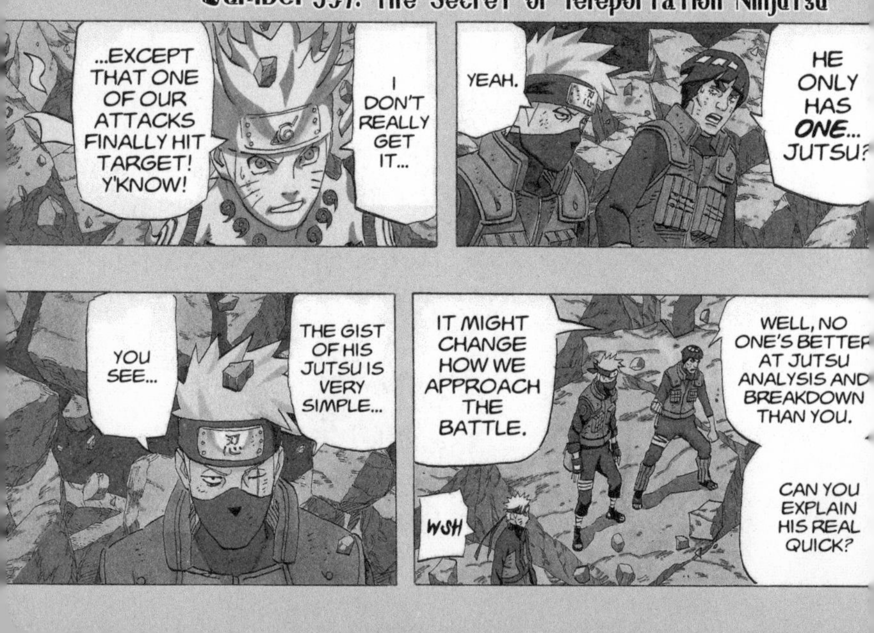
HE ONLY HAS ONE... JUTSU?
YEAH.
I DON'T REALLY GET IT...
...EXCEPT THAT ONE OF OUR ATTACKS FINALLY HIT TARGET! Y'KNOW!
WELL, NO ONE'S BETTER AT JUTSU ANALYSIS AND BREAKDOWN THAN YOU.
CAN YOU EXPLAIN HIS REAL QUICK?
IT MIGHT CHANGE HOW WE APPROACH THE BATTLE.
WSH
THE GIST OF HIS JUTSU IS VERY SIMPLE...
YOU SEE...

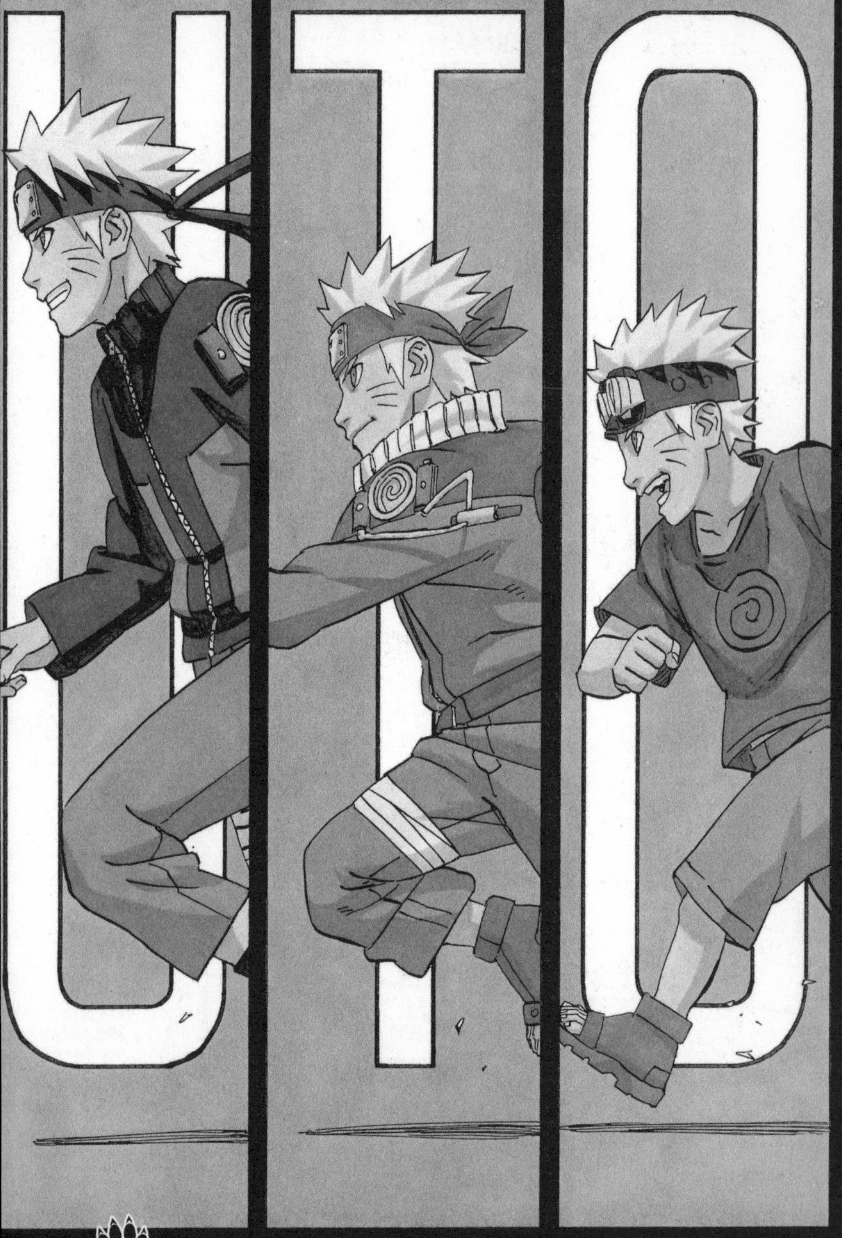

Number 597: The Secret of Teleportation Ninjutsu

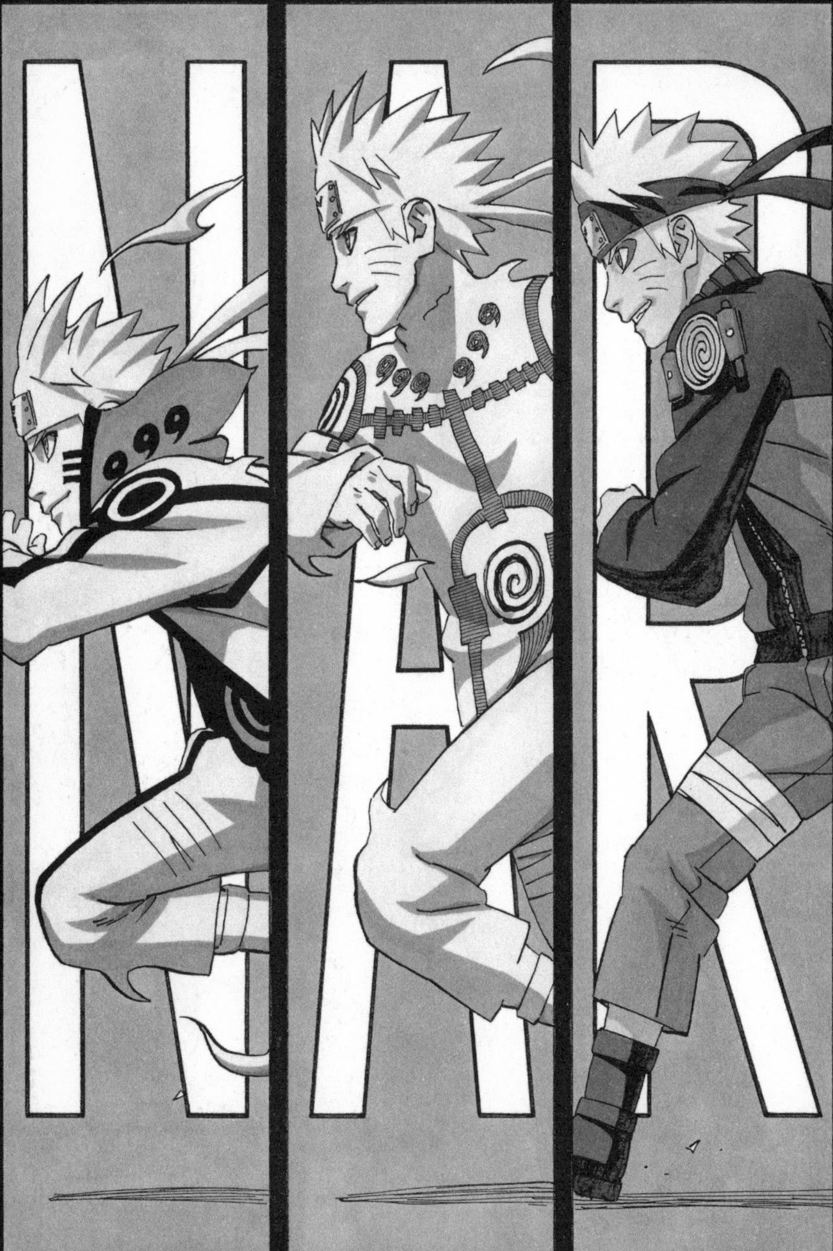

NARUTO

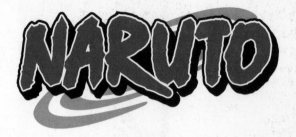

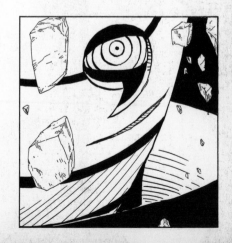

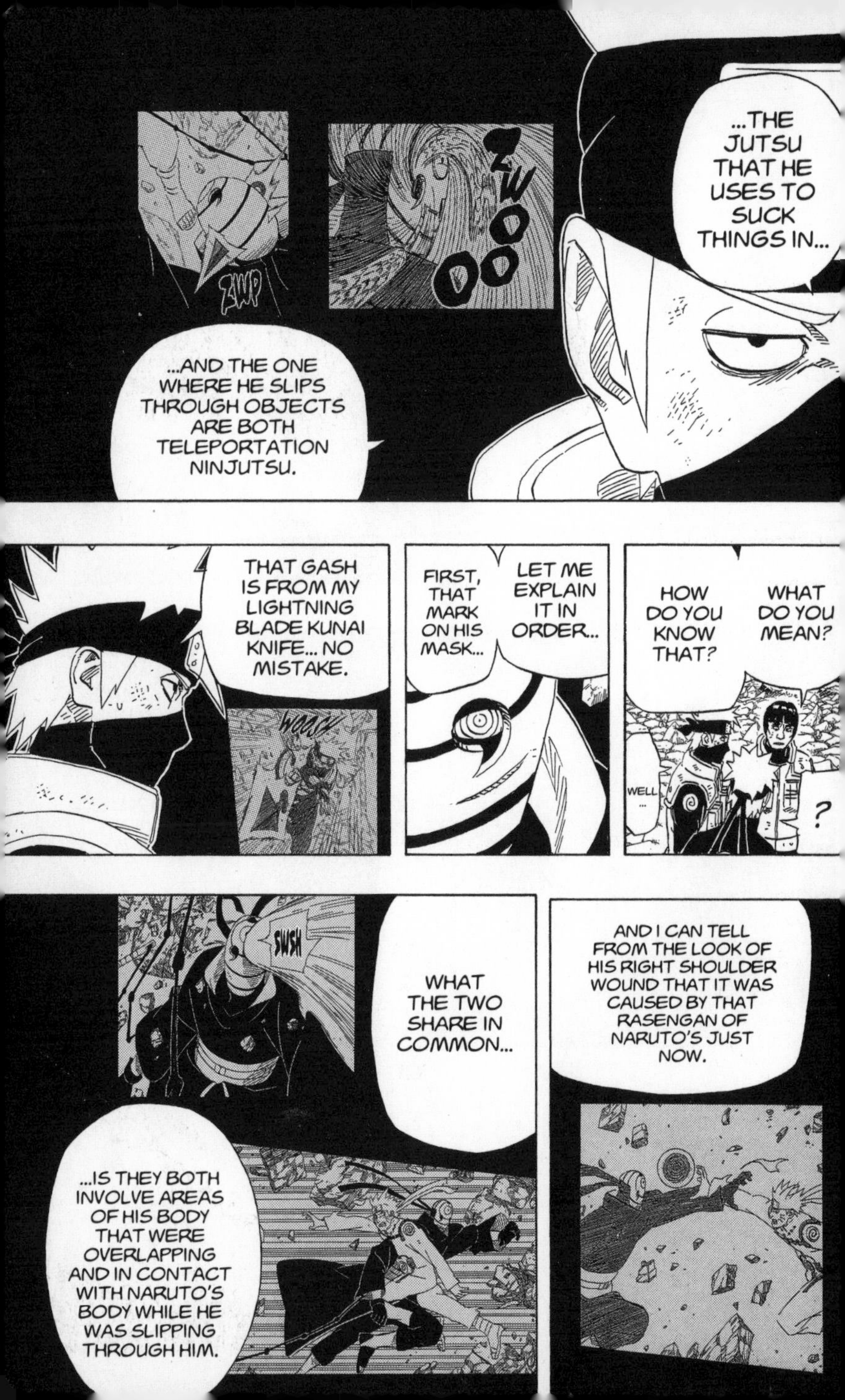
...THE JUTSU THAT HE USES TO SUCK THINGS IN...
ZWOOOO
ZWP
...AND THE ONE WHERE HE SLIPS THROUGH OBJECTS ARE BOTH TELEPORTATION NINJUTSU.
WHAT DO YOU MEAN?
HOW DO YOU KNOW THAT?
WELL...
?
LET ME EXPLAIN IT IN ORDER...
FIRST, THAT MARK ON HIS MASK...
THAT GASH IS FROM MY LIGHTNING BLADE KUNAI KNIFE... NO MISTAKE.
AND I CAN TELL FROM THE LOOK OF HIS RIGHT SHOULDER WOUND THAT IT WAS CAUSED BY THAT RASENGAN OF NARUTO'S JUST NOW.
SWSH
WHAT THE TWO SHARE IN COMMON...
...IS THEY BOTH INVOLVE AREAS OF HIS BODY THAT WERE OVERLAPPING AND IN CONTACT WITH NARUTO'S BODY WHILE HE WAS SLIPPING THROUGH HIM.

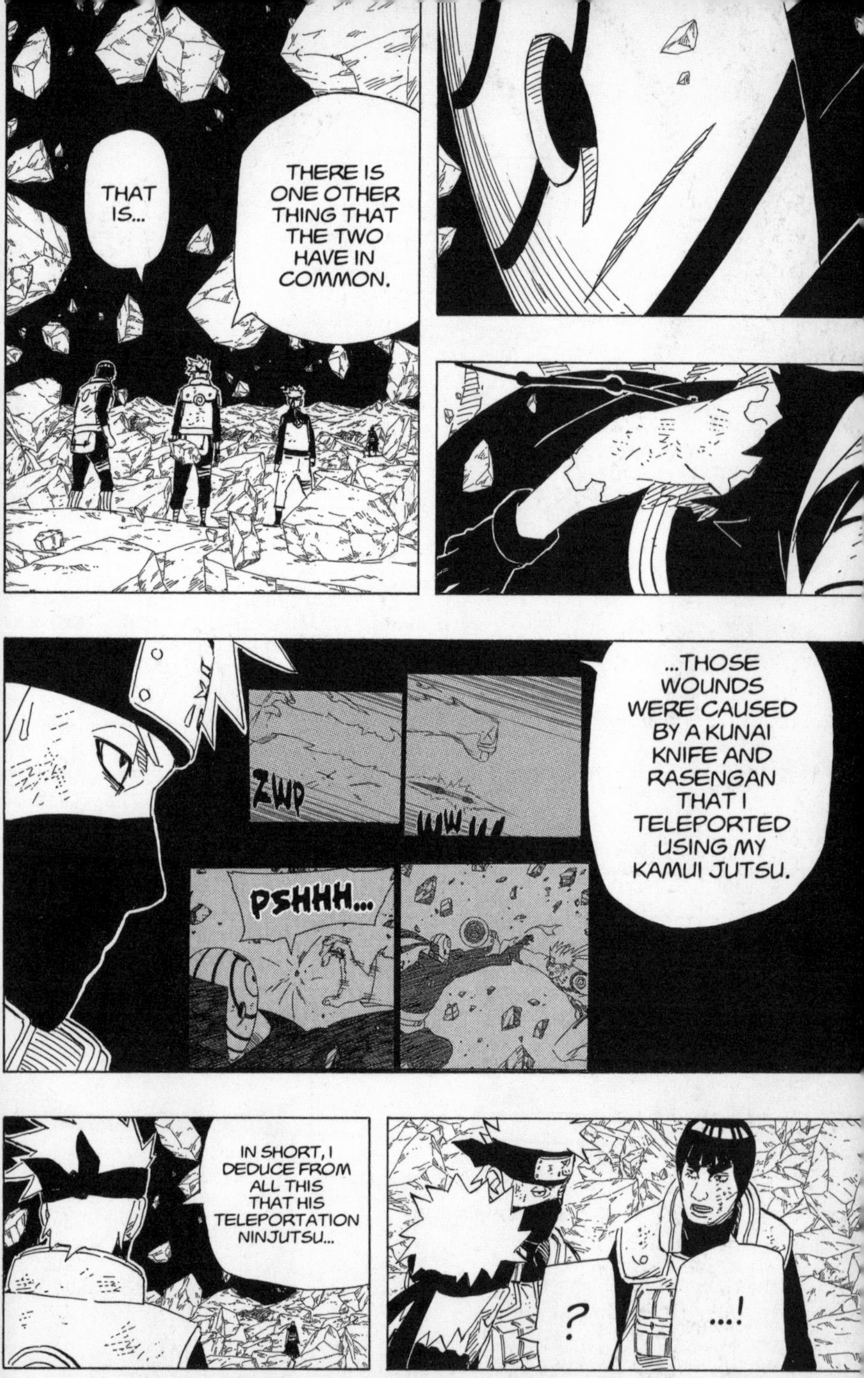
THERE IS ONE OTHER THING THAT THE TWO HAVE IN COMMON.
THAT IS...
...THOSE WOUNDS WERE CAUSED BY A KUNAI KNIFE AND RASENGAN THAT I TELEPORTED USING MY KAMUI JUTSU.
ZWP
PSHHH...
...!
?
IN SHORT, I DEDUCE FROM ALL THIS THAT HIS TELEPORTATION NINJUTSU...

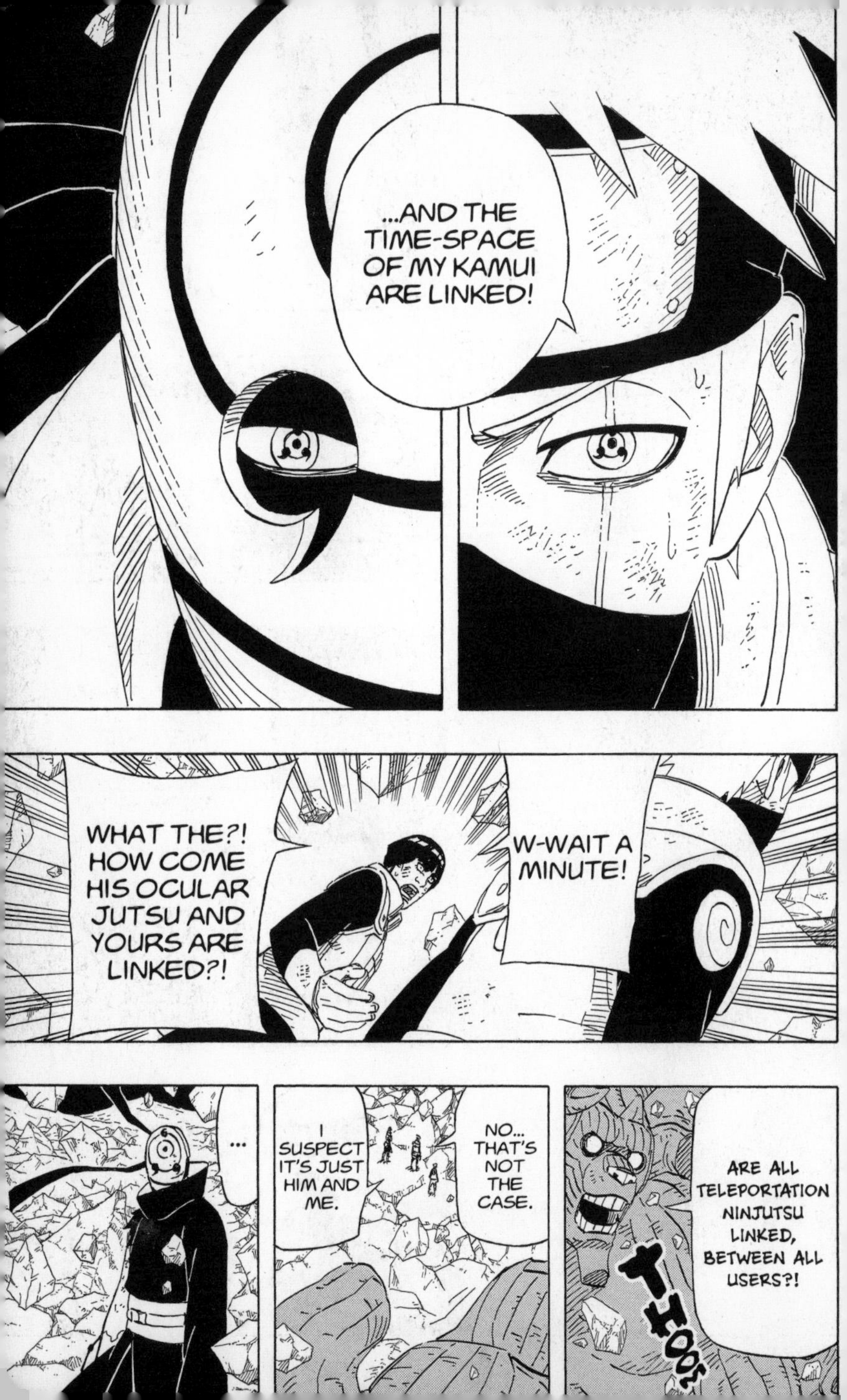
...AND THE TIME-SPACE OF MY KAMUI ARE LINKED!
W-WAIT A MINUTE!
WHAT THE?! HOW COME HIS OCULAR JUTSU AND YOURS ARE LINKED?!
ARE ALL TELEPORTATION NINJUTSU LINKED, BETWEEN ALL USERS?!
THOO
NO... THAT'S NOT THE CASE.
I SUSPECT IT'S JUST HIM AND ME.
...

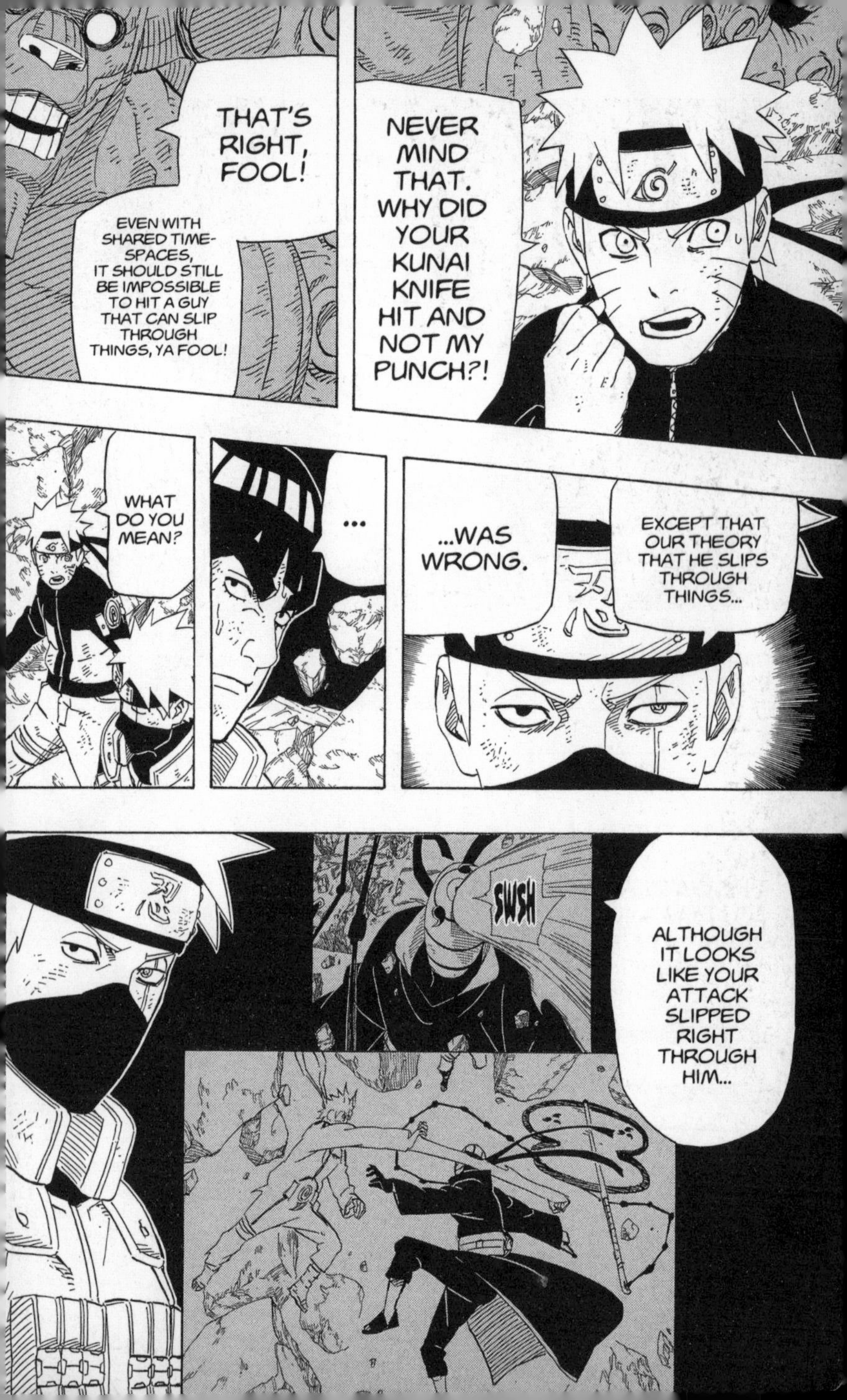
NEVER MIND THAT. WHY DID YOUR KUNAI KNIFE HIT AND NOT MY PUNCH?!
THAT'S RIGHT, FOOL!
EVEN WITH SHARED TIME-SPACES, IT SHOULD STILL BE IMPOSSIBLE TO HIT A GUY THAT CAN SLIP THROUGH THINGS, YA FOOL!
EXCEPT THAT OUR THEORY THAT HE SLIPS THROUGH THINGS...
...WAS WRONG.
...
WHAT DO YOU MEAN?
ALTHOUGH IT LOOKS LIKE YOUR ATTACK SLIPPED RIGHT THROUGH HIM...
SWSH

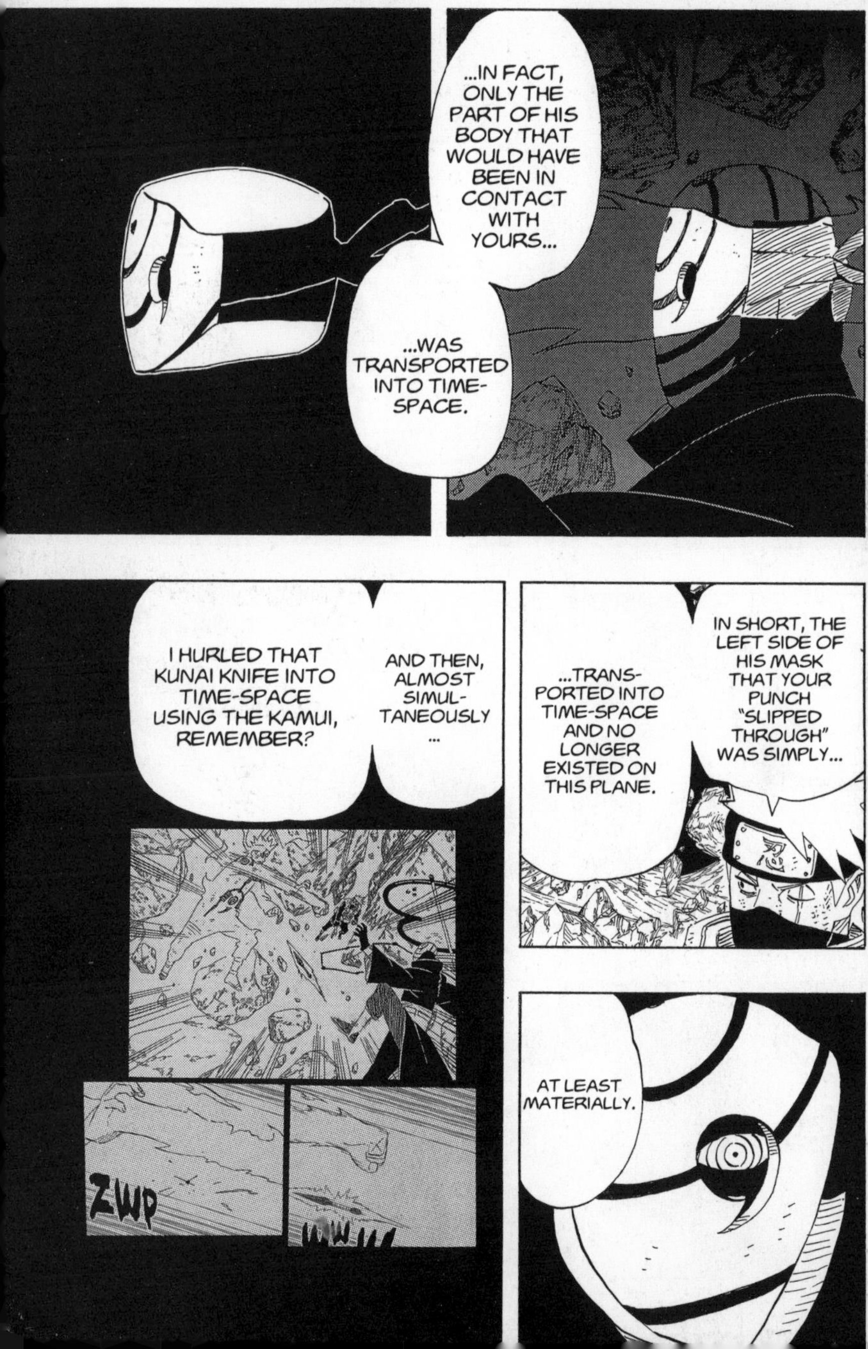
...IN FACT, ONLY THE PART OF HIS BODY THAT WOULD HAVE BEEN IN CONTACT WITH YOURS...
...WAS TRANSPORTED INTO TIME-SPACE.
IN SHORT, THE LEFT SIDE OF HIS MASK THAT YOUR PUNCH "SLIPPED THROUGH" WAS SIMPLY...
...TRANS-PORTED INTO TIME-SPACE AND NO LONGER EXISTED ON THIS PLANE.
AT LEAST MATERIALLY.
I HURLED THAT KUNAI KNIFE INTO TIME-SPACE USING THE KAMUI, REMEMBER?
AND THEN, ALMOST SIMUL-TANEOUSLY ...
ZWP

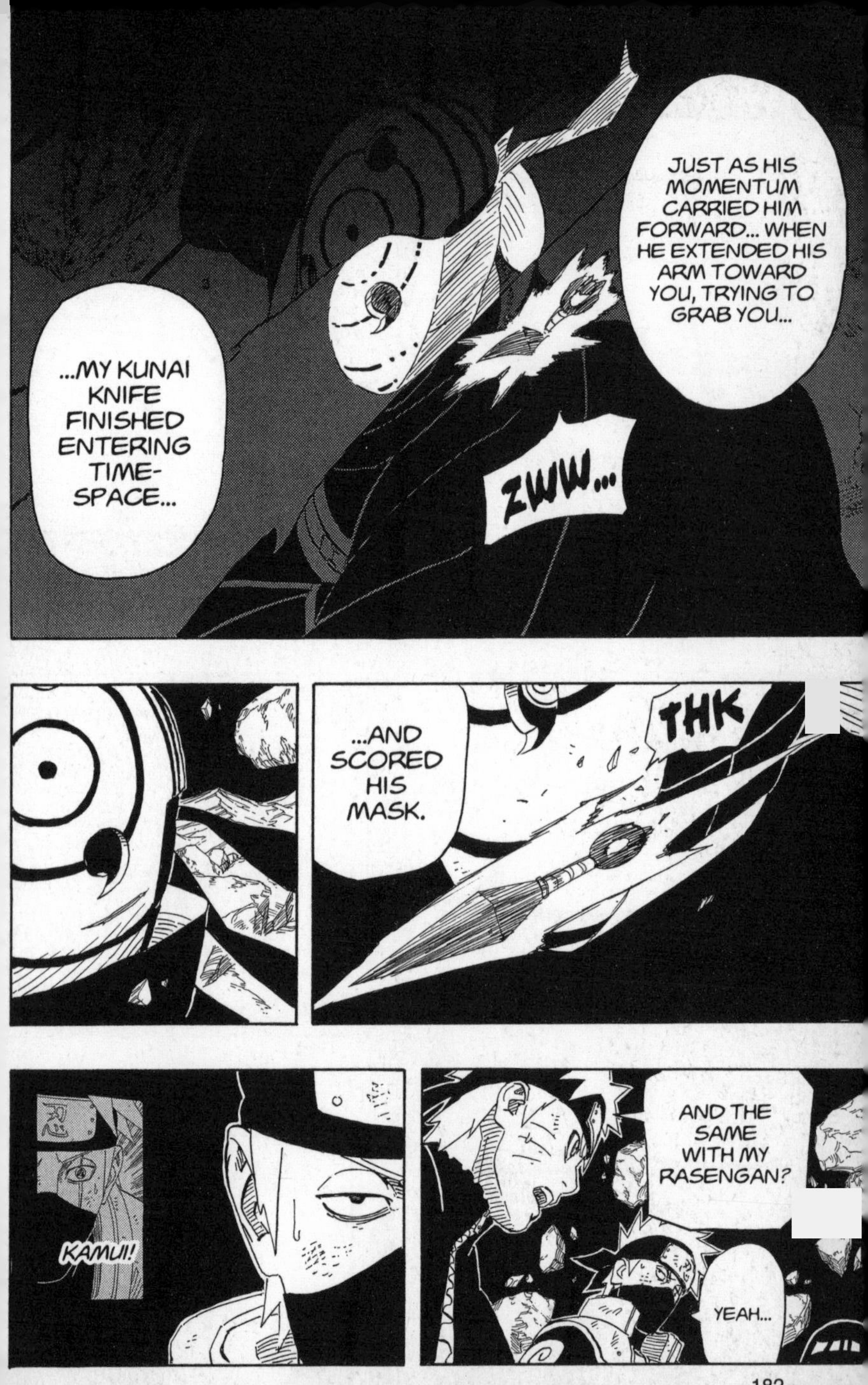
JUST AS HIS MOMENTUM CARRIED HIM FORWARD... WHEN HE EXTENDED HIS ARM TOWARD YOU, TRYING TO GRAB YOU...
...MY KUNAI KNIFE FINISHED ENTERING TIME-SPACE...
ZWW...
THK
...AND SCORED HIS MASK.
AND THE SAME WITH MY RASENGAN?
YEAH...
KAMUI!

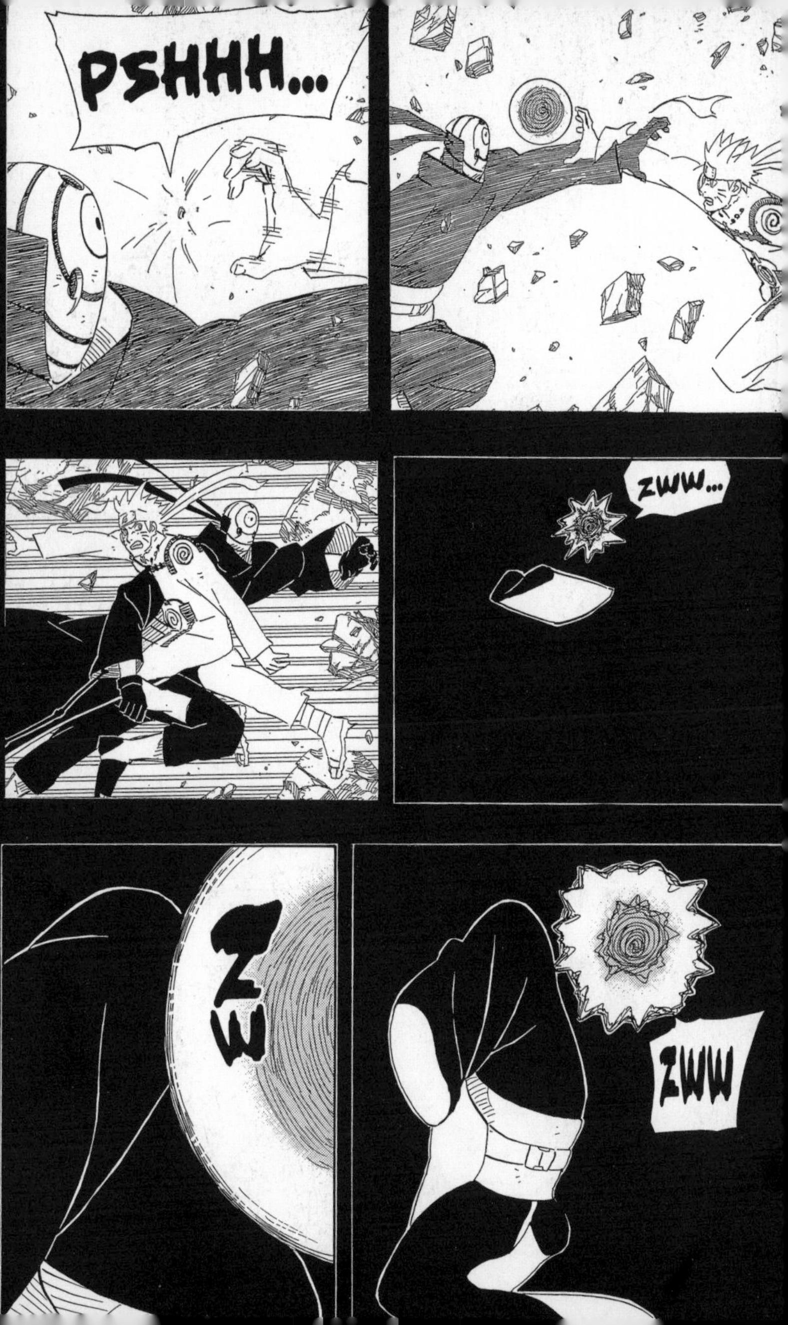
PSHHH...
ZWW...
ZWW
ZWW

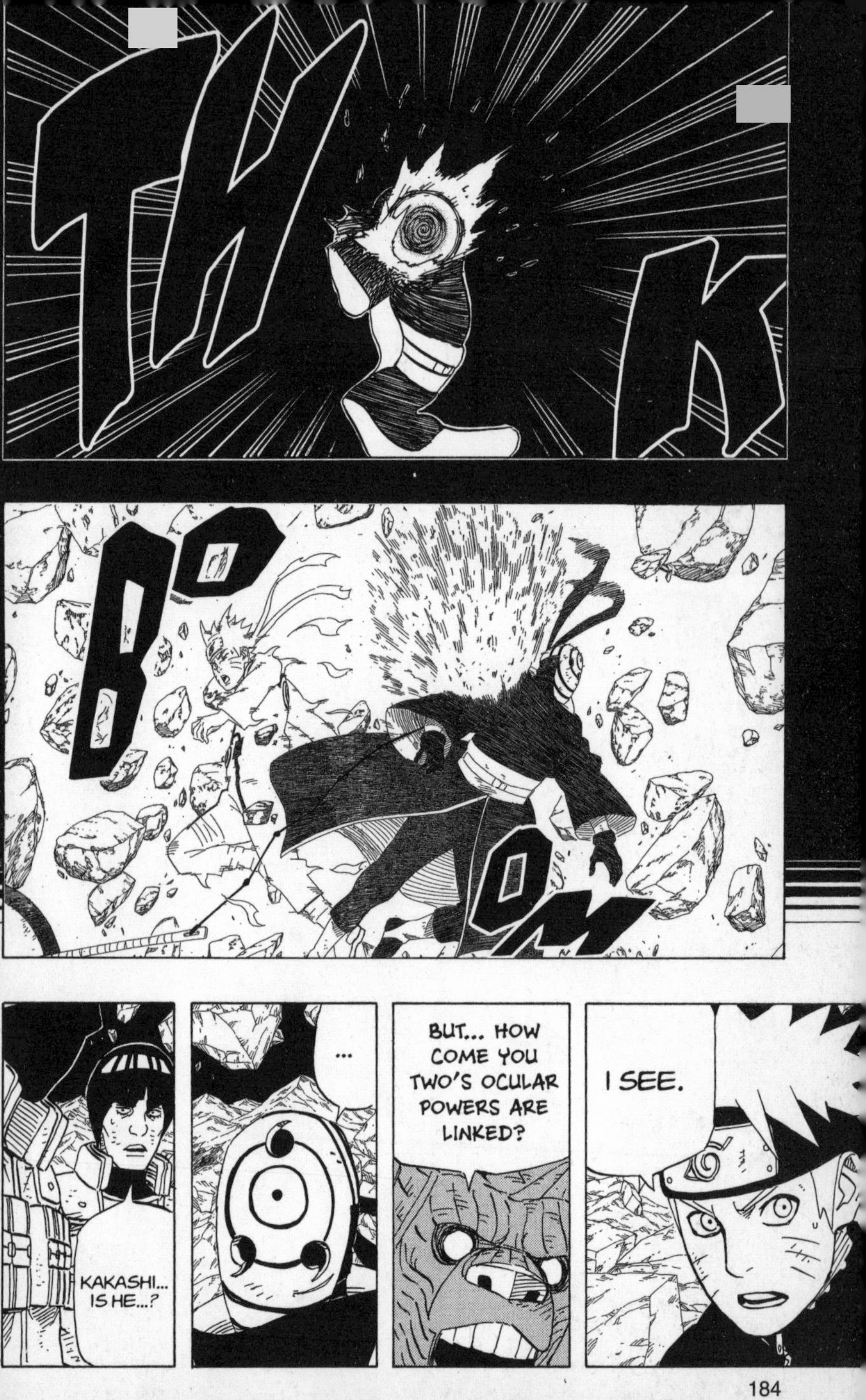
THK
BOOM
I SEE.
BUT... HOW COME YOU TWO'S OCULAR POWERS ARE LINKED?
...
KAKASHI... IS HE...?

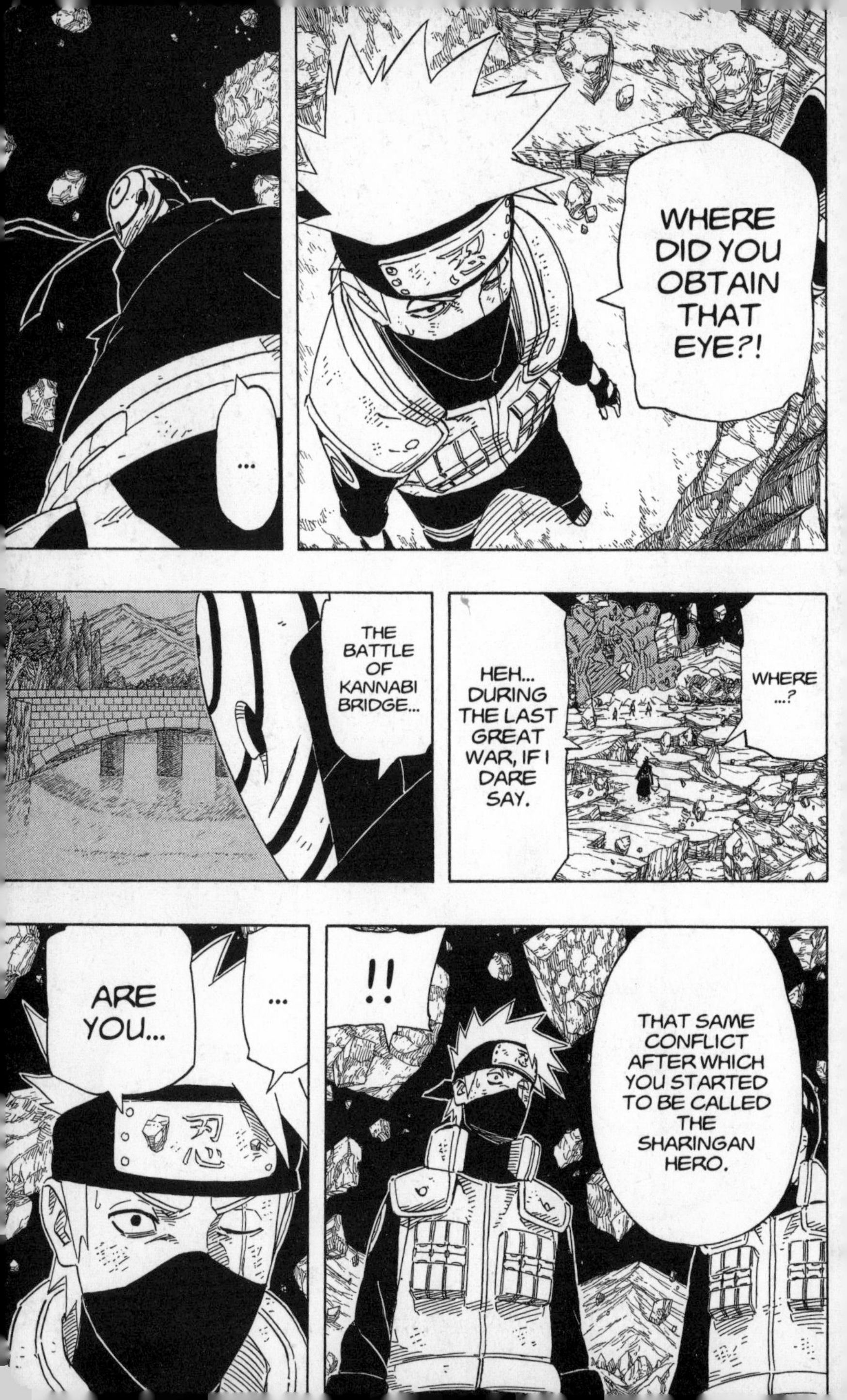
WHERE DID YOU OBTAIN THAT EYE?!
...
WHERE ...?
HEH... DURING THE LAST GREAT WAR, IF I DARE SAY.
THE BATTLE OF KANNABI BRIDGE...
THAT SAME CONFLICT AFTER WHICH YOU STARTED TO BE CALLED THE SHARINGAN HERO.
!!
...
ARE YOU...

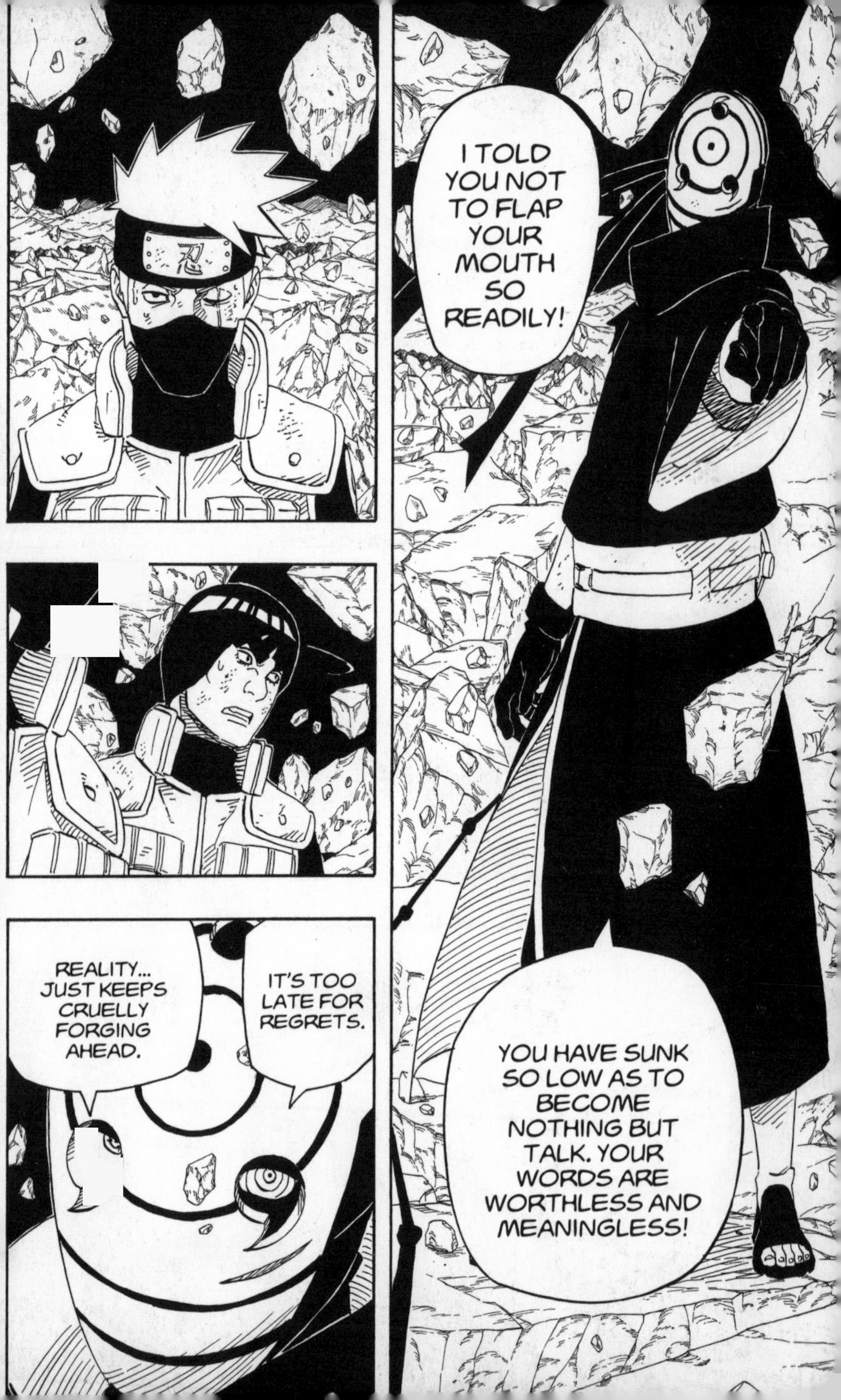
I TOLD YOU NOT TO FLAP YOUR MOUTH SO READILY!
YOU HAVE SUNK SO LOW AS TO BECOME NOTHING BUT TALK. YOUR WORDS ARE WORTHLESS AND MEANINGLESS!
IT'S TOO LATE FOR REGRETS.
REALITY... JUST KEEPS CRUELLY FORGING AHEAD.

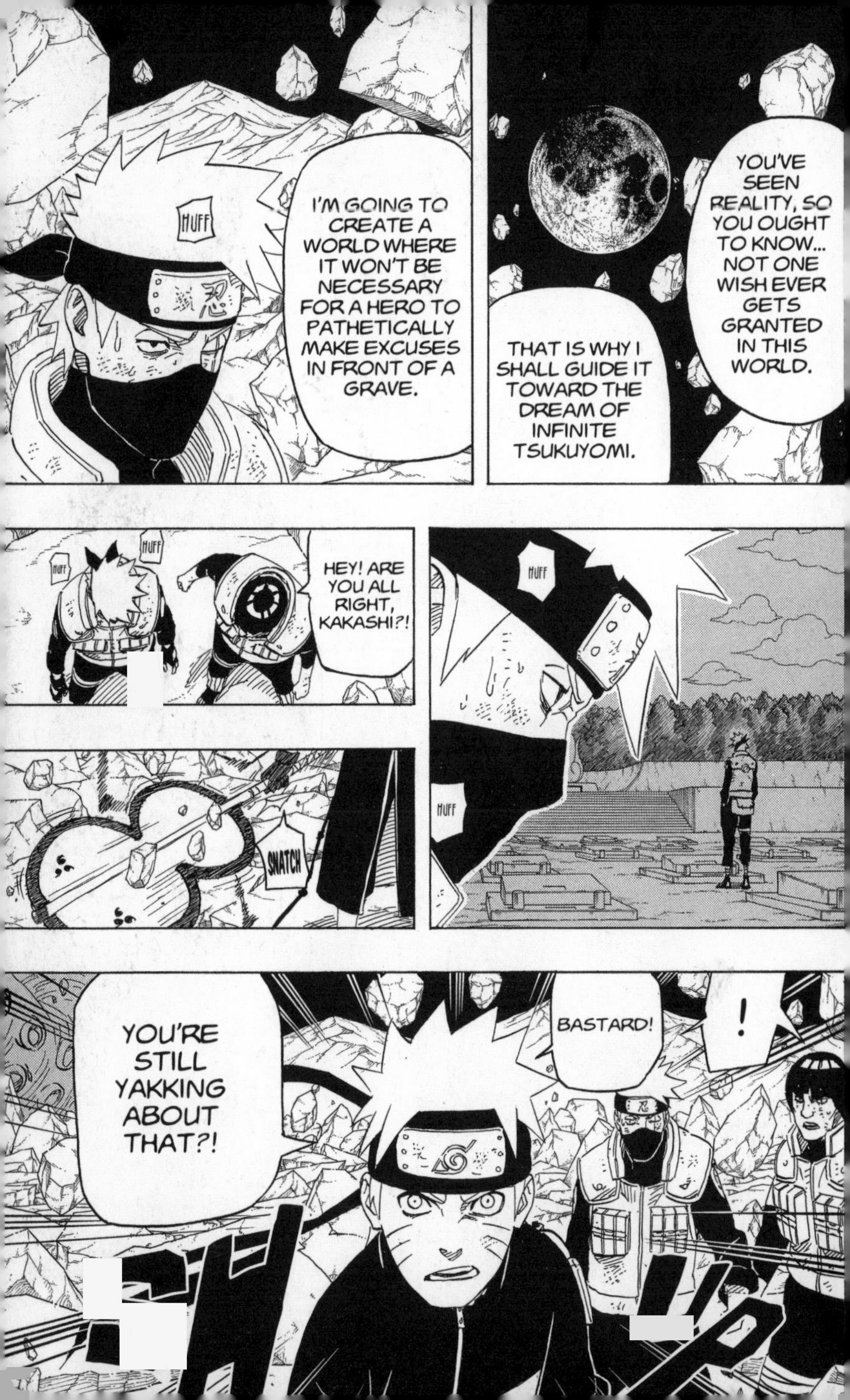
YOU'VE SEEN REALITY, SO YOU OUGHT TO KNOW... NOT ONE WISH EVER GETS GRANTED IN THIS WORLD.
THAT IS WHY I SHALL GUIDE IT TOWARD THE DREAM OF INFINITE TSUKUYOMI.
HUFF
I'M GOING TO CREATE A WORLD WHERE IT WON'T BE NECESSARY FOR A HERO TO PATHETICALLY MAKE EXCUSES IN FRONT OF A GRAVE.
HUFF
HUFF
HEY! ARE YOU ALL RIGHT, KAKASHI?!
HUFF
HUFF
SNATCH
!
BASTARD!
YOU'RE STILL YAKKING ABOUT THAT?!

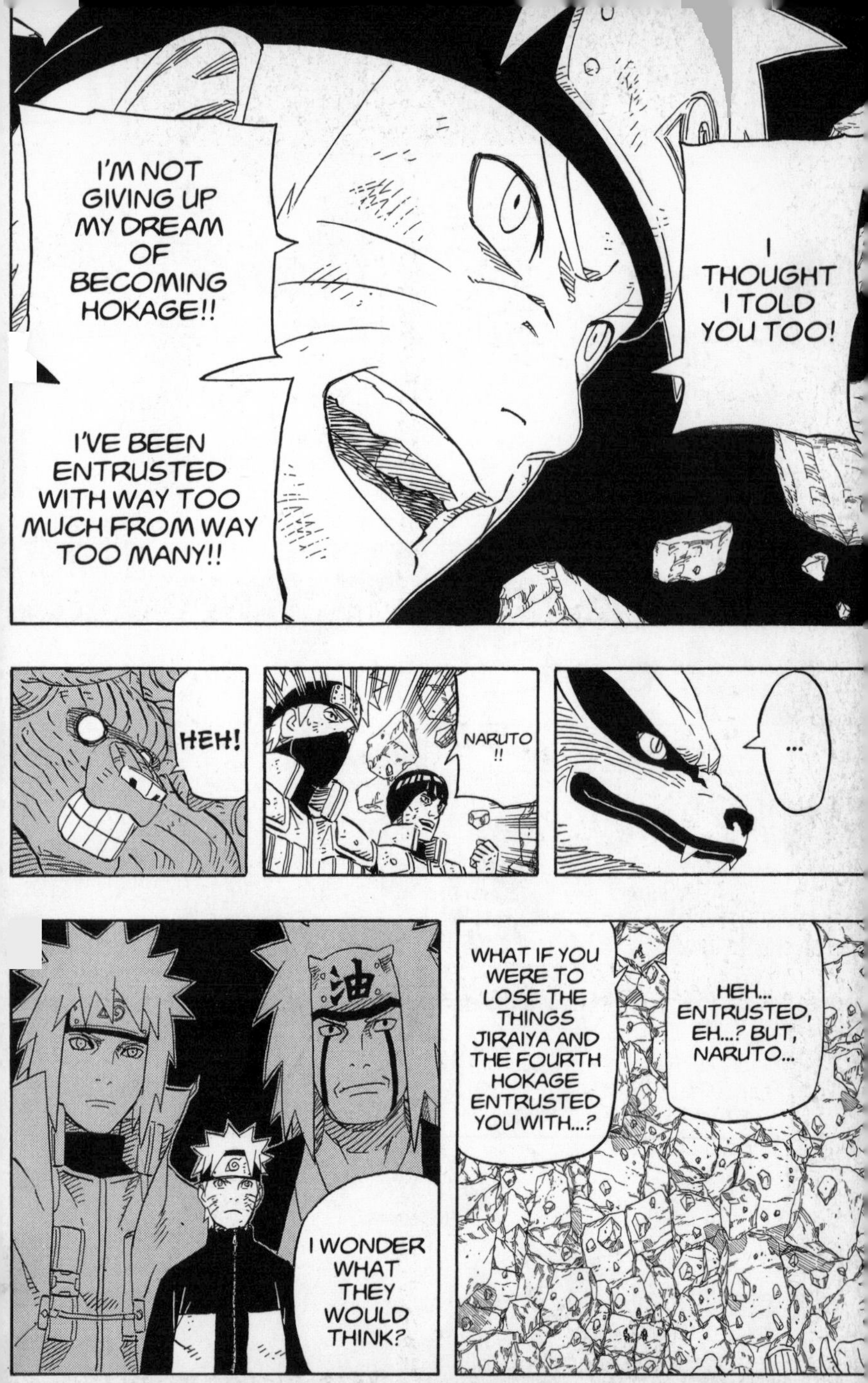
I THOUGHT I TOLD YOU TOO!
I'M NOT GIVING UP MY DREAM OF BECOMING HOKAGE!!
I'VE BEEN ENTRUSTED WITH WAY TOO MUCH FROM WAY TOO MANY!!
...
NARUTO !!
HEH!
HEH... ENTRUSTED, EH...? BUT, NARUTO...
WHAT IF YOU WERE TO LOSE THE THINGS JIRAIYA AND THE FOURTH HOKAGE ENTRUSTED YOU WITH...?
I WONDER WHAT THEY WOULD THINK?

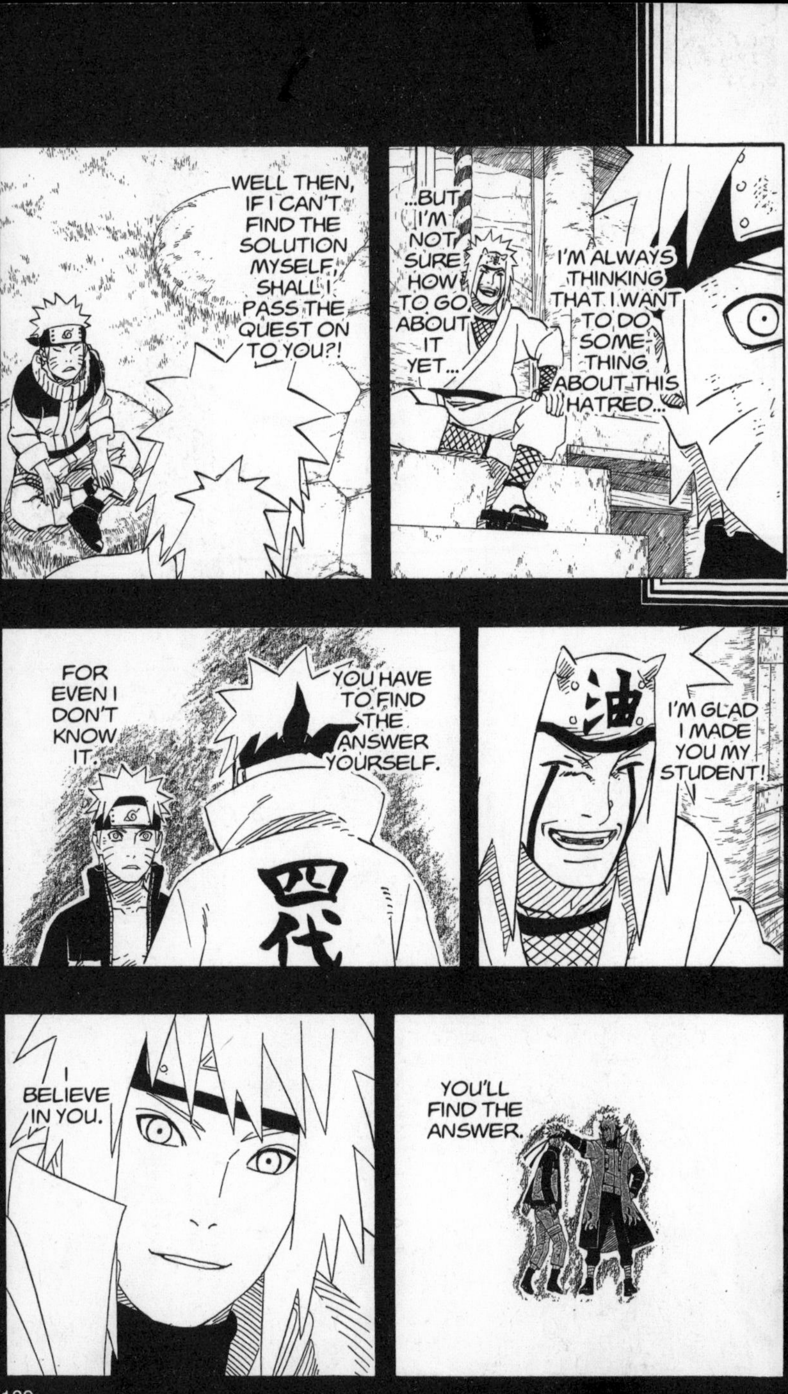
I'M ALWAYS THINKING THAT I WANT TO DO SOMETHING ABOUT THIS HATRED...
...BUT I'M NOT SURE HOW TO GO ABOUT IT YET...
WELL THEN, IF I CAN'T FIND THE SOLUTION MYSELF, SHALL I PASS THE QUEST ON TO YOU?!
I'M GLAD I MADE YOU MY STUDENT!
YOU HAVE TO FIND THE ANSWER YOURSELF.
FOR EVEN I DON'T KNOW IT.
YOU'LL FIND THE ANSWER.
I BELIEVE IN YOU.

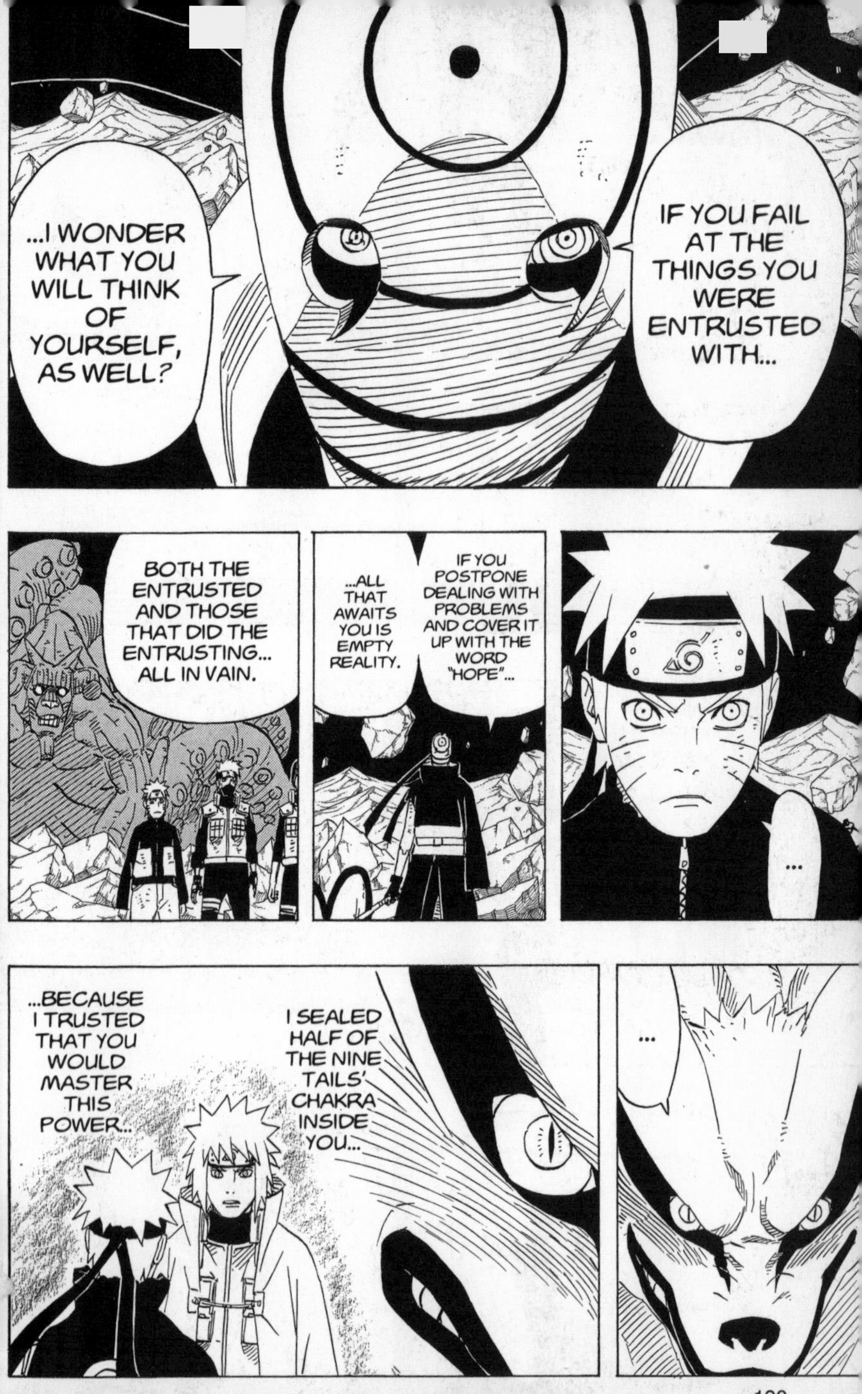
IF YOU FAIL AT THE THINGS YOU WERE ENTRUSTED WITH...
...I WONDER WHAT YOU WILL THINK OF YOURSELF, AS WELL?
...
IF YOU POSTPONE DEALING WITH PROBLEMS AND COVER IT UP WITH THE WORD "HOPE"...
...ALL THAT AWAITS YOU IS EMPTY REALITY.
BOTH THE ENTRUSTED AND THOSE THAT DID THE ENTRUSTING... ALL IN VAIN.
...
I SEALED HALF OF THE NINE TAILS' CHAKRA INSIDE YOU...
...BECAUSE I TRUSTED THAT YOU WOULD MASTER THIS POWER...

...BECAUSE YOU ARE MY SON.

NARUTO... SWITCH WITH ME! I'VE GOT SOMETHING TO SAY TO HIM.

FSH

!

...HE'S NOT THE SORT THAT YOUR WORDS APPLY TO.

SORRY, BUT...

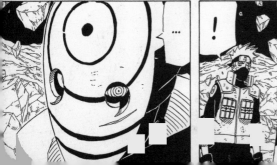

...

!

NINE TAILS...!

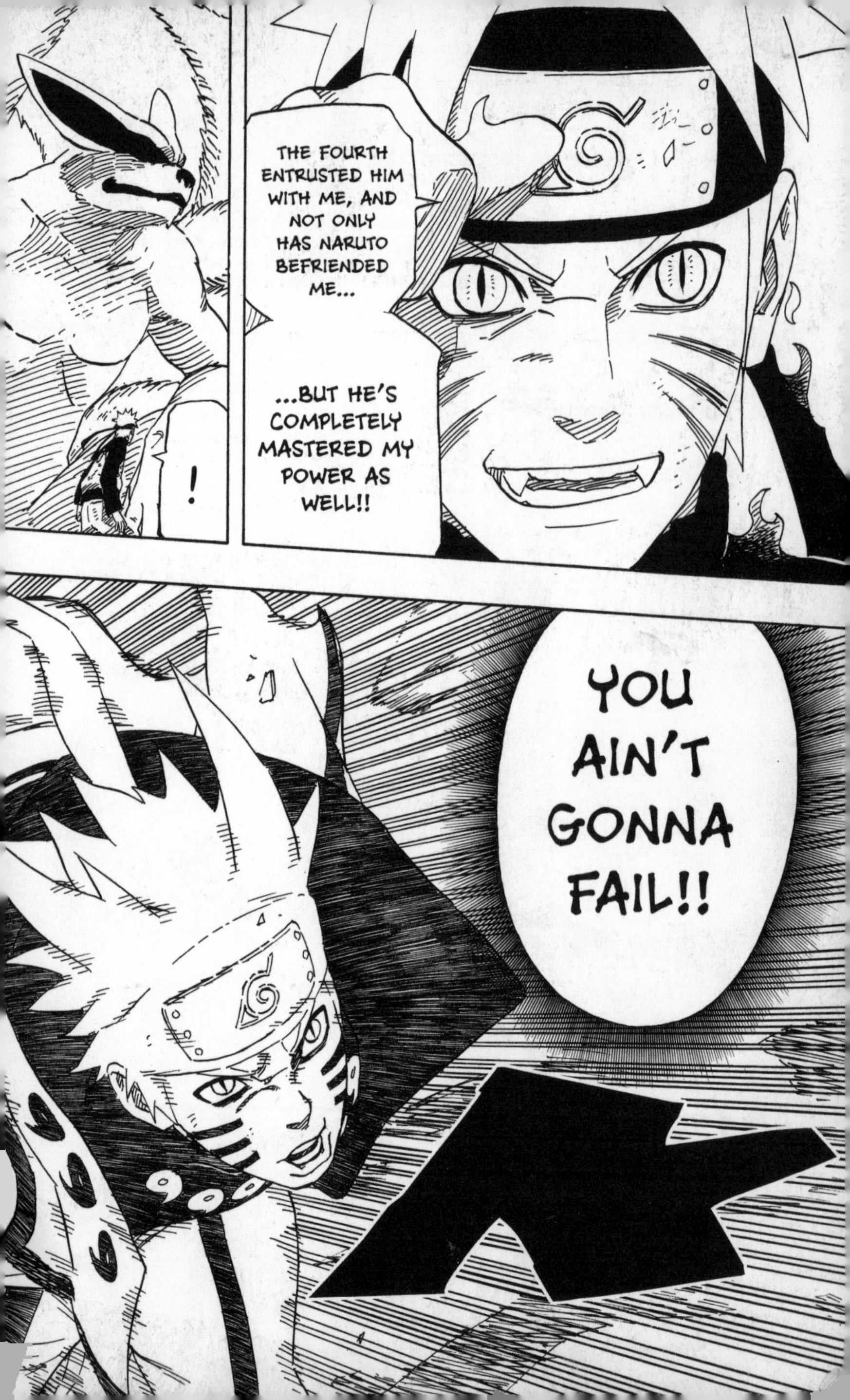
THE FOURTH ENTRUSTED HIM WITH ME, AND NOT ONLY HAS NARUTO BEFRIENDED ME...
...BUT HE'S COMPLETELY MASTERED MY POWER AS WELL!!
!
YOU AIN'T GONNA FAIL!!

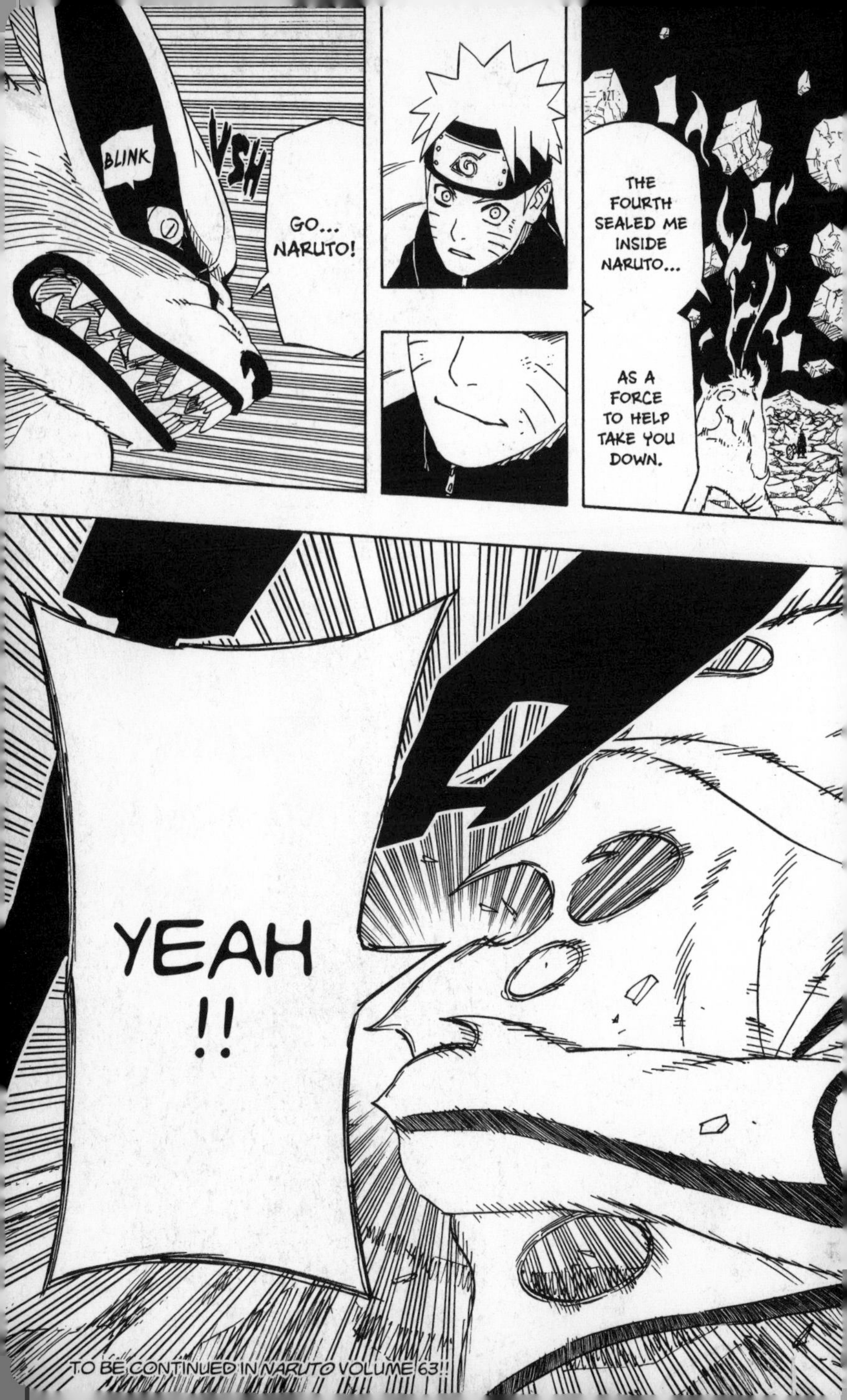
THE FOURTH SEALED ME INSIDE NARUTO...
AS A FORCE TO HELP TAKE YOU DOWN.
GO... NARUTO!
VSH
BLINK
YEAH !!
TO BE CONTINUED IN NARUTO VOLUME 63!!

IN THE NEXT VOLUME...

WORLD OF DREAMS

Naruto, Kakashi and Guy continue their relentless attacks against the powerful Tobi. As they continue to figure out Tobi's abilities, Naruto may be ready to land a deciding blow. But when Tobi's identity is revealed, the results will shock everyone!

AVAILABLE NOVEMBER 2013!

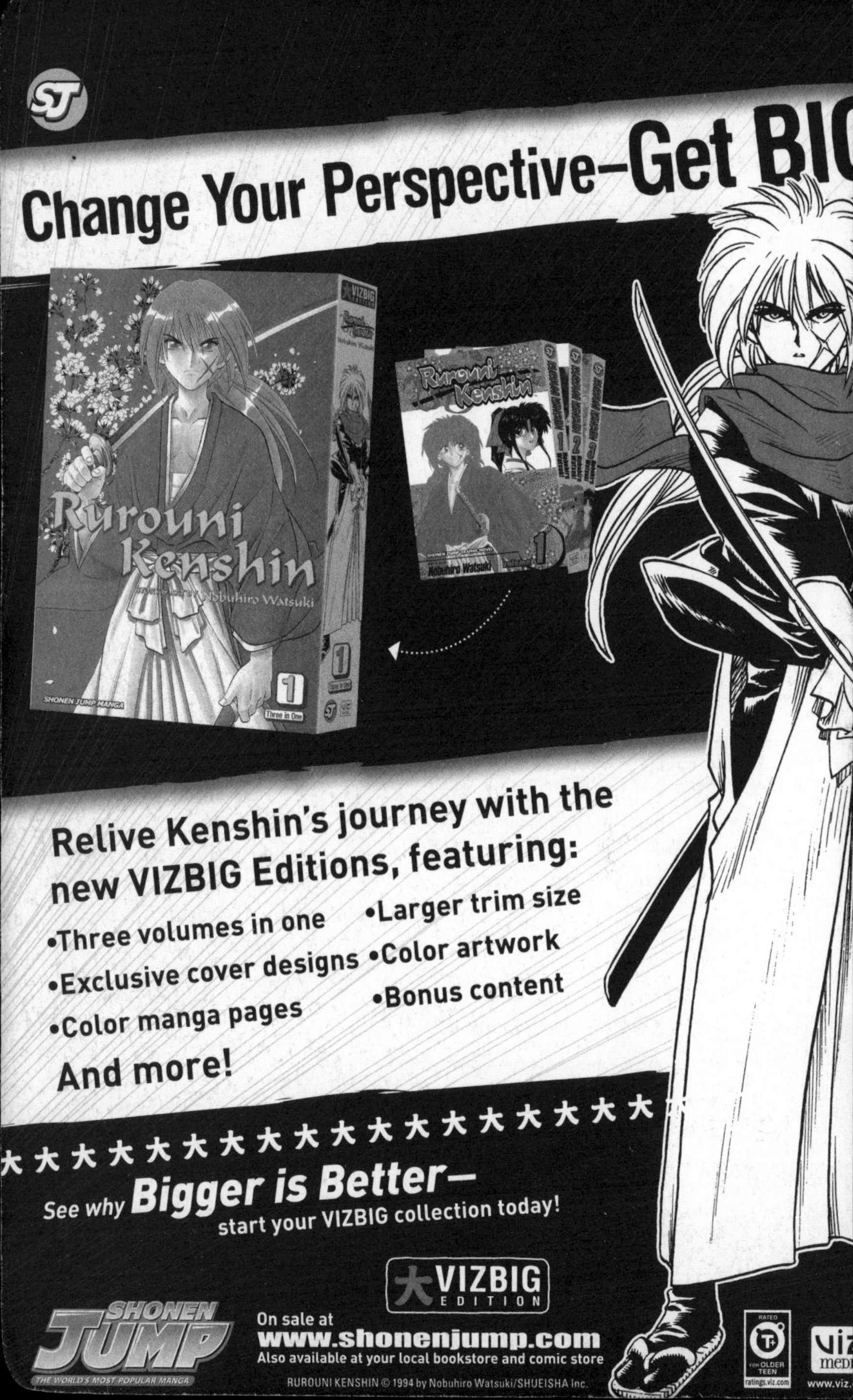
Change Your Perspective—Get BIG
Rurouni Kenshin
Nobuhiro Watsuki
SHONEN JUMP MANGA
1
Three in One
Rurouni Kenshin
Nobuhiro Watsuki
Relive Kenshin's journey with the new VIZBIG Editions, featuring:
•Three volumes in one
•Larger trim size
•Exclusive cover designs
•Color artwork
•Color manga pages
•Bonus content
And more!
See why Bigger is Better—
start your VIZBIG collection today!
VIZBIG EDITION
SHONEN JUMP
THE WORLD'S MOST POPULAR MANGA
On sale at
www.shonenjump.com
Also available at your local bookstore and comic store
RUROUNI KENSHIN © 1994 by Nobuhiro Watsuki/SHUEISHA Inc.
RATED T+ FOR OLDER TEEN
ratings.viz.com

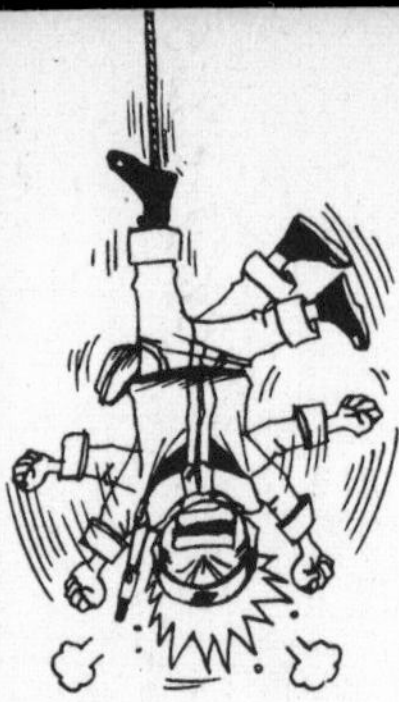

You're Reading in the Wrong Direction!!

Whoops! Guess what? You're starting at the wrong end of the comic!

...It's true! In keeping with the original Japanese format, **Naruto** is meant to be read from right to left, starting in the upper-right corner.

Unlike English, which is read from left to right, Japanese is read from right to left, meaning that action, sound effects and word-balloon order are completely reversed... something which can make readers unfamiliar with Japanese feel pretty backwards themselves. For this reason, manga or Japanese comics published in the U.S. in English have sometimes been published "flopped"–that is, printed in exact reverse order, as though seen from the other side of a mirror.

By flopping pages, U.S. publishers can avoid confusing readers, but the compromise is not without its downside. For one thing, a character in a flopped manga series who once wore in the original Japanese version a T-shirt emblazoned with "M A Y" (as in "the merry month of") now wears one which reads "Y A M"! Additionally, many manga creators in Japan are themselves unhappy with the process, as some feel the mirror-imaging of their art alters their original intentions.

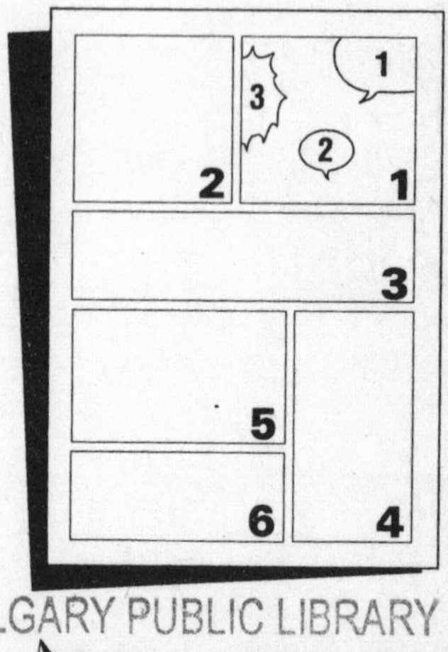
1
3
2
1
2
3
4
5
6

We are proud to bring you Masashi Kishimoto's **Naruto** in the original unflopped format. For now, though, turn to the other side of the book and let the ninjutsu begin...!

–Editor